SECOND EDITION

Data Visualization with Python and JavaScript

Scrape, Clean, Explore, and Transform Your Data

Kyran Dale

Beijing · Boston · Farnham · Sebastopol · Tokyo    **O'REILLY®**

Data Visualization with Python and JavaScript

by Kyran Dale

Copyright © 2023 Kyran Dale Limited. All rights reserved.

Published by O'Reilly Media, Inc., 1005 Gravenstein Highway North, Sebastopol, CA 95472.

O'Reilly books may be purchased for educational, business, or sales promotional use. Online editions are also available for most titles (*http://oreilly.com*). For more information, contact our corporate/institutional sales department: 800-998-9938 or *corporate@oreilly.com*.

Acquisitions Editor: Michelle Smith
Development Editor: Shira Evans
Production Editor: Kristen Brown
Copyeditor: Liz Wheeler
Proofreader: Piper Editorial Consulting, LLC

Indexer: Ellen Troutman-Zaig
Interior Designer: David Futato
Cover Designer: Karen Montgomery
Illustrator: Kate Dullea

July 2016:   First Edition
December 2022:   Second Edition

Revision History for the Second Edition
2022-12-07:   First Release

See *http://oreilly.com/catalog/errata.csp?isbn=9781098111878* for release details.

978-1-098-11187-8

[LSI]

Table of Contents

Part I.　Basic Toolkit

Part II. Getting Your Data

Part III.   Cleaning and Exploring Data with pandas

Part IV. Delivering the Data

Part V. Visualizing Your Data with D3 and Plotly

Preface

The chief ambition of this book is to describe a data visualization (dataviz) toolchain that, in the era of the internet, is starting to predominate. The guiding principle of this toolchain is that whatever insightful nuggets you have managed to mine from your data deserve a home on the web browser. Being on the web means you can easily choose to distribute your dataviz to a select few (using authentication or restricting to a local network) or the whole world. This is the big idea of the internet and one that dataviz is embracing at a rapid pace. And that means that the future of dataviz involves JavaScript, the only first-class language of the web browser. But JavaScript does not yet have the data-processing stack needed to refine raw data, which means data visualization is inevitably a multilanguage affair. I hope this book provides support for my belief that Python is the natural complementary language to JavaScript's monopoly of browser visualizations.

Although this book is a big one (that fact is felt most keenly by the author right now), it has had to be very selective, leaving out a lot of really cool Python and JavaScript dataviz tools and focusing on the ones that provide the best building blocks. The number of helpful libraries I couldn't cover reflects the enormous vitality of the Python and JavaScript data science ecosystems. Even while the book was being written, brilliant new Python and JavaScript libraries were being introduced, and the pace continues.

All data visualization is essentially transformative, and showing the journey from one reflection of a dataset (HTML tables and lists) to a more modern, engaging, interactive, and, fundamentally, browser-based one provides a good way to introduce key data visualization tools in a working context. The challenge is to transform a basic Wikipedia list of Nobel Prize winners into a modern, interactive, browser-based visualization. Thus, the same dataset is presented in a more accessible, engaging form.

The journey from unprocessed data to a fairly rich, user-driven visualization informs the choice of best-of-breed tools. First, we need to get our dataset. Often this is provided by a colleague or client, but to increase the challenge and learn some pretty vital dataviz skills along the way, we learn how to *scrape* the dataset from the web (Wikipedia's Nobel Prize pages) using Python's powerful Scrapy library. This unprocessed dataset then needs to be refined and explored, and there isn't a much better ecosystem for this than Python's pandas. Along with Matplotlib in support and driven by a Jupyter notebook, pandas is becoming the gold standard for this kind of forensic data work. With clean data stored (to SQL with SQLAlchemy and SQLLite) and explored, the cherry-picked data stories can be visualized. I cover the use of Matplotlib and Plotly to embed static and dynamic charts from Python to a web page. But for something more ambitious, the supreme dataviz library for the web is the JavaScript-based D3. We cover the essentials of D3 while using them to produce our showpiece Nobel data visualization.

This book is a collection of tools forming a chain, with the creation of the Nobel visualization providing a guiding narrative. You should be able to dip into relevant chapters when and if the need arises; the different parts of the book are self-contained so you can quickly review what you've learned when required.

This book is divided into five parts. The first part introduces a basic Python and JavaScript dataviz toolkit, while the next four show how to retrieve raw data, clean it, explore it, and finally transform it into a modern web visualization. Let's summarize the key lessons of each part now.

Part I: Basic Toolkit

Our basic toolkit consists of:

- A language-learning bridge between Python and JavaScript. This is designed to smooth the transition between the two languages, highlighting their many similarities and setting the scene for the bilingual process of modern dataviz. With the advent of the latest JavaScript,[1] Python and JavaScript have even more in common, making switching between them that much less stressful.

- Being able to read from and write to the key data formats (e.g., JSON and CSV) and databases (both SQL and NoSQL) with ease is one of Python's great strengths. We see how easy it is to pass data around in Python, translating formats and changing databases as we go. This fluid movement of data is the main lubricant of any dataviz toolchain.

- We cover the basic web development (webdev) skills needed to start producing modern, interactive, browser-based dataviz. By focusing on the concept of the single-page application (*https://oreil.ly/yqv6C*) rather than building whole websites, we minimize conventional webdev and place the emphasis on

---

[1] There are many versions of JavaScript based on ECMAScript (*https://oreil.ly/0uwuN*), but the most significant version, which provides the bulk of new functionality, is ECMAScript 6 (*https://oreil.ly/owrsZ*).

programming your visual creations in JavaScript. An introduction to Scalable Vector Graphics (SVG), the chief building block of D3 visualizations, sets the scene for the creation of our Nobel Prize visualization in Part V.

Part II: Getting Your Data

In this part of the book, we look at how to get data from the web using Python, assuming a nice, clean data file hasn't been provided to the data visualizer:

- If you're lucky, a clean file in an easily usable data format (i.e., JSON or CSV) is at an open URL, a simple HTTP request away. Alternatively, there may be a dedicated web API for your dataset, with any luck a RESTful one. As an example, we look at using the Twitter API (via Python's Tweepy library). We also see how to use Google spreadsheets, a widely used data-sharing resource in dataviz.

- Things get more involved when the data of interest is present on the web in human-readable form, often in HTML tables, lists, or hierarchical content blocks. In this case, you have to resort to *scraping*, getting the raw HTML content and then using a parser to make its embedded content available. We see how to use Python's lightweight Beautiful Soup scraping library and the much more feature-ful and heavyweight Scrapy, the biggest star in the Python scraping firmament.

Part III: Cleaning and Exploring Data with pandas

In this part, we turn the big guns of pandas, Python's powerful programmatic spreadsheet, onto the problem of cleaning and then exploring datasets. We first see how pandas is part of Python's NumPy ecosystem, which leverages the power of very fast, powerful low-level array processing libraries, while making them accessible. The focus is on using pandas to clean and then explore our Nobel Prize dataset:

- Most data, even that which comes from official web APIs, is dirty. And making it clean and usable will occupy far more of your time as a data visualizer than you probably anticipated. Taking the Nobel dataset as an example, we progressively clean it, searching for dodgy dates, anomalous datatypes, missing fields, and all the common grime that needs cleaning before you can start to explore and then transform your data into a visualization.

- With our clean (as we can make it) Nobel Prize dataset in hand, we see how easy it is to use pandas and Matplotlib to interactively explore data, easily creating inline charts, slicing the data every which way, and generally getting a feel for it, while looking for those interesting nuggets you want to deliver with visualization.

Part IV: Delivering the Data

In this part, we see how easy it is to create a minimal data API using Flask, to deliver data both statically and dynamically to the web browser:

First, we see how to use Flask to serve static files and then how to roll your own basic data API, serving data from a local database. Flask's minimalism allows you to create a very thin data-serving layer between the fruits of your Python data processing and their eventual visualization on the browser.

The glory of open source software is that you can often find robust, easy-to-use libraries that solve your problem better than you could. In the second chapter of this part, we see how easy it is to use best-of-breed Python (Flask) libraries to craft a robust, flexible RESTful API, ready to serve your data online. We also cover the easy online deployment of this data server using Heroku, a favorite of Pythonistas.

Part V: Visualizing Your Data with D3 and Plotly

In the first chapter of this part, we see how to take the fruits of your pandas-driven exploration, in the form of charts or maps, and put them on the web, where they belong. Matplotlib can produce publication-standard static charts while Plotly brings user controls and dynamic charts to the table. We see how to take a Plotly chart directly from a Jupyter notebook and put it in a web page.

The part of the book that covers D3 is some of the most challenging, but you may well end up being employed to construct the kind of multielement visualizations it produces. One of the joys of D3 is the huge number of examples (*https://oreil.ly/ AIWkI*) that can easily be found online, but most of them demonstrate a single technique and there are few showing how to orchestrate multiple visual elements. In these D3 chapters, we see how to synchronize the update of a timeline (featuring all the Nobel Prizes), a map, a bar chart, and a list as the user filters the Nobel Prize dataset or changes the prize-winning metric (absolute or per capita).

Mastery of the core themes demonstrated in these chapters should allow you to let loose your imagination and learn by doing. I'd recommend choosing some data close to your heart and designing a D3 creation around it.

The Second Edition

I was a little reluctant when O'Reilly offered me the opportunity of writing a second edition of this book. The first edition ended up larger than anticipated, and updating and augmenting it was potentially a lot of work. However, after reviewing the status of the libraries covered and changes to the Python and JavaScript dataviz ecosystem, it was clear that most of the libraries used (e.g., Scrapy, NumPy, pandas) were still solid choices and needed fairly small updates.

D3 was the library that had changed the most, but these changes had made D3 both easier to use and easier to teach. JavaScript modules were also solidly in place, making the code cleaner and more familiar to a Pythonista.

A few Python libraries no longer seemed like solid choices and a couple had been deprecated. The first edition dealt fairly extensively with MongoDB, a NoSQL database. I now think that good old-fashioned SQL is a better fit for dataviz work and that the minimal file-based, serverless SQLite represents a dataviz sweet spot if a database is required.

Rather than replace the deprecated RESTful data server with another Python library, I thought it would be particularly instructive to build a simple one from scratch, demonstrating the use of some brilliant Python libraries, such as marshmallow, which are useful in many dataviz scenarios.

With the time available for updating the book, I made the decision to use the first book's dataset for demonstrating exploration and analysis with Matplotlib and pandas, focusing on updating all the libraries to their current (as of mid-2022) versions. This allowed time to be spent on new material, chief of which is a chapter dedicated to Python's Plotly library, which allows you to easily transfer exploratory work from a Jupyter notebook to a web presentation with user interactions. A particular strength of this approach is the availability of Mapbox maps, a rich mapping ecosystem.

The main thrust of the second edition was:

- To bring all the libraries up to date.
- To remove and/or replace libraries that hadn't stood the test of time.
- To add some new material suggested by changes in the fast-developing world of Python and JavaScript dataviz.

The metaphor of the dataviz toolchain still holds good, I think, and the transformative pipeline, from raw, unprocessed web data through exploratory dataviz-driven analysis to polished web visualization, remains a good way to learn the key tools of the job.

Conventions Used in This Book

The following typographical conventions are used in this book:

Italic
    Indicates new terms, URLs, email addresses, filenames, and file extensions.

Constant width

> Used for program listings, as well as within paragraphs to refer to program elements such as variable or function names, databases, datatypes, environment variables, statements, and keywords.

Constant width bold

> Shows commands or other text that should be typed literally by the user.

Constant width italic

> Shows text that should be replaced with user-supplied values or by values determined by context.

 This element signifies a tip or suggestion.

 This element signifies a general note.

 This element indicates a warning or caution.

Using Code Examples

Supplemental material (code examples, exercises, etc.) is available for download at *https://github.com/Kyrand/dataviz-with-python-and-js-ed-2*.

This book is here to help you get your job done. In general, if example code is offered with this book, you may use it in your programs and documentation. You do not need to contact us for permission unless you're reproducing a significant portion of the code. For example, writing a program that uses several chunks of code from this book does not require permission. Selling or distributing a CD-ROM of examples from O'Reilly books does require permission. Answering a question by citing this book and quoting example code does not require permission. Incorporating a significant amount of example code from this book into your product's documentation does require permission.

We appreciate, but do not require, attribution. An attribution usually includes the title, author, publisher, and ISBN. For example: "*Data Visualization with Python and JavaScript*, second edition, by Kyran Dale (O'Reilly). Copyright 2023 Kyran Dale Limited, 978-1-098-11187-8."

If you feel your use of code examples falls outside fair use or the permission given above, feel free to contact us at *permissions@oreilly.com*.

O'Reilly Online Learning

O'REILLY® For more than 40 years, *O'Reilly Media* has provided technology and business training, knowledge, and insight to help companies succeed.

Our unique network of experts and innovators share their knowledge and expertise through books, articles, and our online learning platform. O'Reilly's online learning platform gives you on-demand access to live training courses, in-depth learning paths, interactive coding environments, and a vast collection of text and video from O'Reilly and 200+ other publishers. For more information, visit *https://oreilly.com*.

How to Contact Us

Please address comments and questions concerning this book to the publisher:

O'Reilly Media, Inc.
1005 Gravenstein Highway North
Sebastopol, CA 95472
800-998-9938 (in the United States or Canada)
707-829-0515 (international or local)
707-829-0104 (fax)

We have a web page for this book, where we list errata, examples, and any additional information. You can access this page at *https://oreil.ly/dvpj_2e*.

Email *bookquestions@oreilly.com* to comment or ask technical questions about this book.

For news and information about our books and courses, visit *https://oreilly.com*.

Find us on LinkedIn: *https://linkedin.com/company/oreilly-media*

Follow us on Twitter: *https://twitter.com/oreillymedia*

Watch us on YouTube: *https://www.youtube.com/oreillymedia*

Acknowledgments

Thanks first to Meghan Blanchette, who set the ball rolling and steered that ball through its first very rough chapters. Dawn Schanafelt then took the helm and did the bulk of the very necessary editing. Kristen Brown did a brilliant job taking the book through production, aided by Gillian McGarvey's impressively tenacious copyediting. Working with such talented, dedicated professionals has been an honor and a privilege—and an education: the book would have been so much easier to write if I'd known then what I know now. Isn't that always the way?

Many thanks to Amy Zielinski for making the author look better than he deserves.

The book benefited from some very helpful feedback. So many thanks to Christophe Viau, Tom Parslow, Peter Cook, Ian Macinnes, and Ian Ozsvald.

I'd also like to thank the valiant bug hunters who answered my appeal during this book's early release. At time of writing, these are Douglas Kelley, Pavel Suk, Brigham Hausman, Marco Hemken, Noble Kennamer, Manfredi Biasutti, Matthew Maldonado, and Geert Bauwens.

Second Edition

Primary thanks must go to Shira Evans for shepherding the book from conception to realization. Gregory Hyman did a great job keeping me abreast of early releases and providing feedback. Once again, I was lucky to have Kristen Brown bring the book through production.

I'd also like to thank my tech reviewers Jordan Goldmeier, Drew Winstel, and Jess Males for great advice.

Introduction

This book aims to get you up to speed with what is, in my opinion, the most powerful data visualization stack going: Python and JavaScript. You'll learn enough about big libraries like pandas and D3 to start crafting your own web data visualizations and refining your own toolchain. Expertise will come with practice, but this book presents a shallow learning curve to basic competence.

 If you're reading this, I'd love to hear any feedback you have. Please post it to *pyjsdataviz@kyrandale.com*. Thanks a lot.

You'll also find a working copy of the Nobel visualization the book literally and figuratively builds toward at my website (*https://www.kyrandale.com/viz/nobel_viz_v2*).

The bulk of this book tells one of the innumerable tales of data visualization, one carefully selected to showcase some powerful Python and JavaScript libraries and tools which together form a toolchain. This toolchain gathers raw, unrefined data at its start and delivers a rich, engaging web visualization at its end. Like all tales of data visualization, it is a tale of transformation—in this case, transforming a basic Wikipedia list of Nobel Prize winners into an interactive visualization, bringing the data to life and making exploration of the prize's history easy and fun.

Whatever data you have and whatever story you want to tell with it, the natural home for the visualizations you transform it into is the web. As a delivery platform, it is orders of magnitude more powerful than what came before, and this book aims to smooth the passage from desktop- or server-based data analysis and processing to the web.

Working with these two powerful languages doesn't only deliver powerful web visualizations—it's also fun and engaging.

Many potential dataviz programmers assume there is a big divide between *web development* and doing what they would like to do, which is program in Python and JavaScript. Web development involves loads of arcane knowledge about markup languages, style scripts, and administration, and can't be done without tools with strange names like *Webpack* or *Gulp*. These days, that big divide can be collapsed to a thin and very permeable membrane, allowing you to focus on what you do well: programming stuff (see Figure I-1) with minimal effort, relegating the web servers to data delivery.

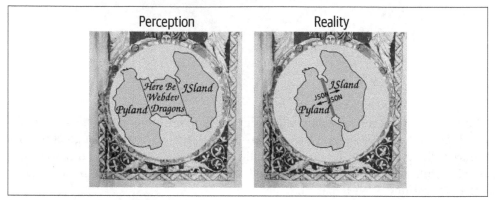

Figure I-1. Here be webdev dragons

Who This Book Is For

First off, this book is for anyone with a reasonable grasp of Python or JavaScript who wants to explore one of the most exciting areas in the data-processing ecosystem right now: the exploding field of data visualization for the web. It's also about addressing some specific challenges that, in my experience, are quite common.

When you get commissioned to write a technical book, chances are your editor will sensibly caution you to think in terms of *pain points* that your book could address. The two key pain points of this book are best illustrated by way of a couple of stories, including one of my own and one that has been told to me in various guises by JavaScripters I know.

Many years ago, as an academic researcher, I came across Python and fell in love. I had been writing some fairly complex simulations in C++, and Python's simplicity and power was a breath of fresh air from all the boilerplate Makefiles, declarations, definitions, and the like. Programming became fun. Python was the perfect glue, playing nicely with my C++ libraries (Python wasn't then and still isn't a speed demon) and doing, with consummate ease, all the stuff that is such a pain in low-level languages (e.g., file I/O, database access, and serialization). I started to write all my graphical user interfaces (GUIs) and visualizations in Python, using wxPython, PyQt, and a whole load of other refreshingly easy toolsets. Unfortunately, although some of these tools are pretty cool and I would love to share them with the world, the effort required to package them, distribute them, and make sure they still work with modern libraries represents a hurdle I'm unlikely to overcome.

At the time, there existed what in theory was the perfect universal distribution system for the software I'd so lovingly crafted—namely, the web browser. Web browsers were (and are) available on pretty much every computer on Earth, with their own built-in, interpreted programming language: write once, run everywhere. But Python didn't play in the web browsers' sandpit, and browsers were incapable of ambitious graphics and visualizations, being pretty much limited to static images and the odd jQuery transformation (*https://jquery.com*). JavaScript was a "toy" language tied to a very slow interpreter that was good for little DOM (*https://oreil.ly/QnE0a*) tricks but certainly nothing approaching what I could do on the desktop with Python. So that route was discounted, out of hand. My visualizations wanted to be on the web, but there was no route to it.

Fast forward a decade or so and, thanks to an arms race initiated by Google and their V8 engine, JavaScript is now orders of magnitude faster; in fact, it's now an awful lot faster than Python.[1] HTML has also tidied up its act a bit, in the guise of HTML5. It's a lot nicer to work with, with much less boilerplate code. What were loosely followed and distinctly shaky protocols like Scalable Vector Graphics (SVG) have firmed up nicely, thanks to powerful visualization libraries, D3 in particular. Modern browsers are obliged to work nicely with SVG and, increasingly, 3D in the form of WebGL and its children such as THREE.js. The visualizations I was doing in Python are now possible on your local web browser, and the payoff is that, with very little effort, they can be made accessible to every desktop, laptop, smartphone, and tablet in the world.

So why aren't Pythonistas flocking to get their data out there in a form they dictate? After all, the alternative to crafting it yourself is leaving it to somebody else, something most data scientists I know would find far from ideal. Well, first there's that term *web development*, connoting complicated markup, opaque stylesheets, a whole slew of new tools to learn, IDEs to master. And then there's JavaScript itself, a strange language, thought of as little more than a toy until recently and having something of the neither fish nor fowl to it. I aim to take those pain points head-on and show that you can craft modern web visualizations (often single-page apps) with a very minimal amount of HTML and CSS boilerplate, allowing you to focus on the programming, and that JavaScript is an easy leap for the Pythonista. But you don't have to leap; Chapter 2 is a language bridge that aims to help Pythonistas and JavaScripters bridge the divide between the languages by highlighting common elements and providing simple translations.

The second story is a common one among JavaScript data visualizers I know. Processing data in JavaScript is far from ideal. There are few heavyweight libraries, and

---

1 See the Benchmarks Game website (*https://oreil.ly/z6T6R*) for a fairly jaw-dropping comparison.

although recent functional enhancements to the language make data munging much more pleasant, there's still no real data-processing ecosystem to speak of. So, there's a distinct asymmetry between the hugely powerful visualization libraries available (D3, as ever, is the paramount library), and the ability to clean and process any data delivered to the browser. All of this mandates doing your data cleaning, processing, and exploring in another language or with a toolkit like Tableau, and this often devolves into piecemeal forays into vaguely remembered Matlab, the steepish learning curve that is R, or a Java library or two.

Toolkits like Tableau (*https://www.tableau.com*), although very impressive, are often ultimately frustrating for programmers. There's no way to replicate in a GUI the expressive power of a good, general-purpose programming language. Plus, what if you want to create a little web server to deliver your processed data? That means learning at least one new web development-capable language.

In other words, JavaScripters starting to stretch their data visualization are looking for a complementary data-processing stack that requires the least investment of time and has the shallowest learning curve.

Minimal Requirements to Use This Book

I always feel reluctant to place restrictions on people's explorations, particularly in the context of programming and the web, which is chock-full of autodidacts (how else would one learn with the halls of academia being light years behind the trends?), learning fast and furiously, gloriously uninhibited by the formal constraints that used to apply to learning. Python and JavaScript are pretty much as simple as it gets, programming-language-wise, and are both top candidates for best first language. There isn't a huge cognitive load in interpreting the code.

In that spirit, there are expert programmers who, without any experience of Python and JavaScript, could consume this book and be writing custom libraries within a week.

For beginner programmers, fresh to Python or JavaScript, this book is probably too advanced for you, and I recommend taking advantage of the plethora of books, web resources, screencasts, and the like that make learning so easy these days. Focus on a personal itch, a problem you want to solve, and learn to program by doing—it's the only way.

For people who have programmed a bit in either Python or JavaScript, my advised threshold to entry is that you have used a few libraries together, understand the basic idioms of your language, and can look at a piece of novel code and generally get a hook on what's going on—in other words, Pythonistas who can use a few modules of the standard library, and JavaScripters who have used the odd library and would understand a few lines of its source code.

Why Python and JavaScript?

Why JavaScript is an easy question to answer. For now and the foreseeable future, there is only one first-class, browser-based programming language. There have been various attempts to extend, augment, and usurp, but good old, plain-vanilla JS is still preeminent. If you want to craft modern, dynamic, interactive visualizations and, at the touch of a button, deliver them to the world, at some point you are going to run into JavaScript. You might not need to achieve mastery, but basic competence is a fundamental price of entry into one of the most exciting areas of modern data science. This book will get you into the ballpark.

Why Not Python in the Browser?

There have been recent initiatives to run a limited version of Python in the browser. For example, Pyodide (*https://github.com/pyodide/pyodide*) is a port of CPython to WebAssembly. These are impressive and interesting, but right now the main way to make web charts in Python is to have them automatically converted by an intermediate library.

There are currently some very impressive initiatives aimed at enabling Python-produced visualizations, often built on Matplotlib (*https://matplotlib.org*), to run in the browser. They achieve this by converting the Python code into JavaScript based on the canvas or svg drawing contexts. The most popular and mature of these are Plotly (*https://plot.ly*) and Bokeh (*https://bokeh.pydata.org/en/latest*). In Chapter 14, you'll see how to use Plotly to generate charts in a Jupyter notebook and transfer them to a web page. For many use cases this is a great dataviz tool to have in your toolbox.

While there is some brilliant coding behind these JavaScript converters and many solid use cases, they do have big limitations:

- Automated code conversion may well do the job, but the code produced is usually pretty impenetrable for a human being.
- Adapting and customizing the resulting plots using the powerful browser-based JavaScript development environment can be painful. We'll see how this pain can be mitigated in Chapter 14 by using Plotly's JS API.
- You are limited to the subset of plot types currently available in the libraries.
- Interactivity is very basic at the moment. Customizing user controls is best done in JavaScript, using the browser's developer tools.

Bear in mind that the people building these libraries have to be JavaScript experts, so if you want to understand anything of what they're doing and eventually express yourself, then you'll have to get up to scratch with some JavaScript.

Why Python for Data Processing

Why you should choose Python for your data-processing needs is a little more involved. For a start, there are good alternatives as far as data processing is concerned. Let's deal with a few candidates for the job, starting with the enterprise behemoth Java.

Java

Among the other main, general-purpose programming languages, only Java offers anything like the rich ecosystem of libraries that Python does, with considerably more native speed too. But while Java is a lot easier to program in than languages like C++, it isn't, in my opinion, a particularly nice language to program in, having rather too much in the way of tedious boilerplate code and excessive verbiage. This sort of thing starts to weigh heavily after a while and makes for a hard slog at the code face. As for speed, Python's default interpreter is slow, but Python is a great *glue* language that plays nicely with other languages. This ability is demonstrated by the big Python data-processing libraries like NumPy (and its dependent, pandas), SciPy, and the like, which use C++ and Fortran libraries to do the heavy lifting while providing the ease of use of a simple scripting language.

R

The venerable R has, until recently, been the tool of choice for many data scientists and is probably Python's main competitor in the space. Like Python, R benefits from a very active community, some great tools like the plotting library ggplot2, and a syntax specially crafted for data science and statistics. But this specialism is a double-edged sword. Because R was developed for a specific purpose, it means that if, for example, you wish to write a web server to serve your R-processed data, you have to skip out to another language with all the attendant learning overheads, or try to hack something together in a round-hole/square-peg sort of way. Python's general-purpose nature and its rich ecosystem mean one can do pretty much everything required of a data-processing pipeline (JS visuals aside) without having to leave its comfort zone. Personally, it is a small sacrifice to pay for a little syntactic clunkiness.

Others

There are other alternatives to doing your data processing with Python, but none of them come close to the flexibility and power afforded by a general-purpose, easy-to-use programming language with a rich ecosystem of libraries. For example, mathematical programming environments such as Matlab and Mathematica have active communities and a plethora of great libraries, but they hardly count as general purpose, because they are designed to be used within a closed garden. They are also proprietary, which means a significant initial investment and a different vibe to Python's resoundingly open source environment.

GUI-driven dataviz tools like Tableau (*https://www.tableau.com*) are great creations but will quickly frustrate someone used to freedom in programming. They tend to work great as long as you are singing from their songsheet, as it were. Deviations from the designated path get painful very quickly.

Python's Getting Better All the Time

As things stand, I think a very good case can be made for Python being the budding data scientist's language of choice. But things are not standing still; in fact, Python's capabilities in this area are growing at an astonishing rate. To put it in perspective, I have been programming in Python for over 20 years and have grown used to being surprised if I can't find a Python module to help solve a problem at hand, but I find myself surprised at the growth of Python's data-processing abilities, with a new, powerful library appearing weekly. To give an example, Python has traditionally been weak on statistical analysis libraries, with R being far ahead. Recently a number of powerful modules, such as statsmodels, have started to close this gap fast.

Python is a thriving data-processing ecosystem with a pretty much unmatched general purpose, and it's getting better week by week. It's understandable why so many in the community are in a state of such excitement—it's pretty exhilarating.

As far as visualization in the browser, the good news is that there's more to JavaScript than its privileged, nay, exclusive place in the web ecosystem. Thanks to an interpreter arms race that has seen performance increase in staggering leaps and bounds and some powerful visualization libraries such as D3, which would complement any language out there, JavaScript now has serious chops.

In short, Python and JavaScript are wonderful complements for data visualization on the web, each needing the other to provide a vital missing component.

What You'll Learn

There are some big Python and JavaScript libraries in our dataviz toolchain, and comprehensive coverage of them all would require a number of books. Nevertheless, I think that the fundamentals of most libraries, and certainly the ones covered here, can be grasped fairly quickly. Expertise takes time and practice but the basic knowledge needed to be productive is, so to speak, low-hanging fruit.

In that sense, this book aims to give you a solid backbone of practical knowledge, strong enough to take the weight of future development. I aim to make the learning curve as shallow as possible and get you over the initial climb with the practical skills needed to start refining your art.

This book emphasizes pragmatism and best practice. It's going to cover a fair amount of ground, and there isn't enough space for many theoretical diversions. I cover those aspects of the libraries in the toolchain that are most commonly used, and point you to resources for the other issues. Most libraries have a hard core of functions, methods, classes, and the like that are the chief, functional subset. With these at your disposal, you can actually do stuff. Eventually, you'll find an itch you can't scratch with those, at which time good books, documentation, and online forums will be your friend.

The Choice of Libraries

I had three things in mind while choosing the libraries used in the book:

- Open source and free as in beer (*https://oreil.ly/WwriM*)—you shouldn't have to invest any extra money to learn with this book.
- Longevity—generally well-established, community-driven, and popular.
- Best of breed (assuming good support and an active community), at the sweet spot between popularity and utility.

The skills you learn here should be relevant for a long time. Generally, the obvious candidates have been chosen—libraries that write their own ticket, as it were. Where appropriate, I will highlight the alternative choices and give a rationale for my selection.

Preliminaries

A few preliminary chapters are needed before beginning the transformative journey of our Nobel dataset through the toolchain. These cover the basic skills necessary to make the rest of the toolchain chapters run more fluidly. The first few chapters cover the following:

Chapter 2, "A Language-Learning Bridge Between Python and JavaScript"
Building a language bridge between Python and JavaScript

Chapter 3, "Reading and Writing Data with Python"
How to pass around data with Python, through various file formats and databases

Chapter 4, "Webdev 101"
Covering the basic web development needed by the book

These chapters are part tutorial, part reference, and it's fine to skip straight to the beginning of the toolchain, dipping back where needed.

The Dataviz Toolchain

The main part of the book demonstrates the data visualization toolchain, following the journey of a dataset of Nobel Prize winners from raw, freshly scraped data to engaging, interactive JavaScript visualization. During the collection process, the refinement and transformation of a number of big libraries are demonstrated, summarized in Figure I-2. These libraries are the industrial lathes of our toolchain: rich, mature tools that demonstrate the power of the Python+JavaScript dataviz stack. The following sections contain a brief introduction to the five stages of our toolchain and their major libraries.

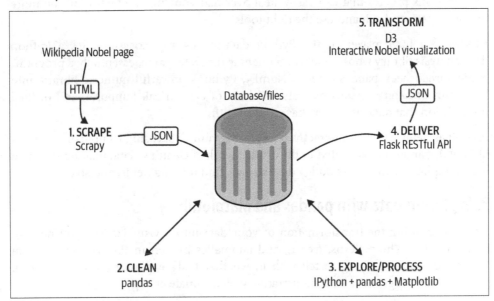

Figure I-2. The dataviz toolchain

1. Scraping Data with Scrapy

The first challenge for any data visualizer is getting hold of the data they need, whether inspired by a request or to scratch a personal itch. If you're very lucky, this will be delivered to you in pristine form, but more often than not you have to go find it. I'll cover the various ways you can use Python to get data off the web (e.g., web APIs or Google spreadsheets). The Nobel Prize dataset for the toolchain demonstration is scraped from its Wikipedia pages using Scrapy.[2]

---

2 Web scraping (*https://oreil.ly/g3LPa*) is a computer software technique to extract information from websites, usually involving getting and parsing web pages.

Python's Scrapy is an industrial-strength scraper that does all the data throttling and media pipelining, which are indispensable if you plan on scraping significant amounts of data. Scraping is often the only way to get the data you are interested in, and once you've mastered Scrapy's workflow, all those previously off-limits datasets are only a spider away.[3]

2. Cleaning Data with pandas

The dirty secret of dataviz is that pretty much all data is dirty, and turning it into something you can use may well occupy a lot more time than anticipated. This is an unglamorous process that can easily steal over half your time, which is all the more reason to get good at it and use the right tools.

pandas is a huge player in the Python data-processing ecosystem. It's a Python data-analysis library whose chief component is the DataFrame, essentially a programmatic spreadsheet. pandas extends NumPy, Python's powerful numeric library, into the realm of heterogeneous datasets, the kind of categorical, temporal, and ordinal information that data visualizers have to deal with.

As well as being great for interactively exploring your data (using its built-in Matplotlib plots), pandas is well suited to the drudge work of cleaning data, making it easy to locate duplicate records, fix dodgy date-strings, find missing fields, and so on.

3. Exploring Data with pandas and Matplotlib

Before beginning the transformation of your data into a visualization, you need to understand it. The patterns, trends, and anomalies hidden in the data will inform the stories you are trying to tell with it, whether that's explaining a recent rise in year-by-year widget sales or demonstrating global climate change.

In conjunction with *IPython*, the Python interpreter on steroids, pandas and Matplotlib (with additions such as seaborn) provide a great way to explore your data interactively, generating rich, inline plots from the command line, slicing and dicing your data to reveal interesting patterns. The results of these explorations can then be easily saved to file or database to be passed on to your JavaScript visualization.

4. Delivering Your Data with Flask

Once you've explored and refined your data, you'll need to serve it to the web browser, where a JavaScript library like D3 can transform it. One of the great strengths of using a general-purpose language like Python is that it's as comfortable rolling a web server in a few lines of code as it is crunching through large datasets

---

3 Scrapy's controllers are called spiders.

with special-purpose libraries like NumPy and SciPy.[4] *Flask* is Python's most popular lightweight server and is perfect for creating small, RESTful[5] APIs that can be used by JavaScript to get data from the server, in files or databases, to the browser. As I'll demonstrate, you can roll a RESTful API in a few lines of code, capable of delivering data from SQL or NoSQL databases.

5. Transforming Data into Interactive Visualizations with Plotly and D3

Once the data is cleaned and refined, we have the visualization phase, where selected reflections of the dataset are presented, perhaps allowing the user to explore them interactively. Depending on the data, this might involve conventional charts, maps, or novel visualizations.

Plotly is a brilliant charting library that allows you to develop your charts in Python and transfer them to the web. As we'll see in Chapter 14, it also has a JavaScript API that mimics the Python one, giving you a native JS charting library for free.

D3 is JavaScript's powerhouse visualization library, arguably one of the most powerful visualization tools irrespective of language. We'll use D3 to create a novel Nobel Prize visualization with multiple elements and user interaction, allowing people to explore the dataset for items of interest. D3 can be challenging to learn, but I'll bring you quickly up to speed and get you ready to start honing your skills in the doing.

Smaller Libraries

In addition to the big libraries covered, there is a large supporting cast of smaller libraries. These are the indispensable smaller tools, the hammers and spanners of the toolchain. Python in particular has an incredibly rich ecosystem, with small, specialized libraries for almost every conceivable job. Among the strong supporting cast, some particularly deserving of mention are:

Requests
Python's go-to HTTP library, fully deserving its motto "HTTP for humans." Requests is far superior to urllib2, one of Python's included batteries.

SQLAlchemy
The best Python SQL toolkit and object-relational mapper (ORM) there is. It's feature-rich and makes working with the various SQL-based databases a relative breeze.

---

4 The scientific Python library, part of the NumPy ecosystem.

5 REST is short for Representational State Transfer, the dominant style for HTTP-based web APIs and much recommended.

seaborn

A great addition to Python's plotting powerhouse Matplotlib, it adds some very useful plot types including some statistical ones of particular use to data visualizers. It also adds arguably superior aesthetics, overriding the Matplotlib defaults.

Crossfilter

Even though JavaScript's data-processing libraries are a work in progress, a few really useful ones have emerged recently, with Crossfilter being a standout. It enables very fast filtering of row-columnar datasets and is ideally suited to dataviz work, which is unsurprising because one of its creators is Mike Bostock, the father of D3.

marshmallow

A brilliant and very handy library that converts complex datatypes like objects to and from native Python datatypes.

Using the Book

Although the book's different parts follow a process of data transformation, this book doesn't need to be read cover to cover. The first part provides a basic toolkit for Python- and JavaScript-based web dataviz and will inevitably have content that is familiar to many readers. Cherry-pick for the stuff you don't know and dip back as required (there will be link-backs further on, as required). The language-learning bridge between Python and JavaScript will be unnecessary for those seasoned in both languages, although there may still be some useful nuggets.

The remaining parts of the book, following our toolchain as it transforms a fairly uninspiring web list into a fully fledged, interactive D3 visualization, are essentially self-contained. If you want to dive immediately into Part III and some data cleaning and exploration with pandas, go right ahead, but be aware that it assumes the existence of a dirty Nobel Prize dataset. You can see how that was produced by Scrapy later if that fits your schedule. Equally, if you want to dive straight into creating the Nobel-viz app in parts Part IV and Part V, be aware that they assume a clean Nobel Prize dataset.

Whatever route you take, I suggest eventually aiming to acquire all the basic skills covered in the book if you intend to make dataviz your profession.

A Little Bit of Context

This is a practical book and assumes that the reader has a pretty good idea of what he or she wants to visualize and how that visualization should look and feel, as well as a desire to get cracking on it, unencumbered by too much theory. Nevertheless, drawing on the history of data visualization can both clarify the central themes of the book and add valuable context. It can also help explain why now is such an exciting time to be entering the field, as technological innovation is driving novel dataviz forms, and people are grappling with the problem of presenting the increasing amount of multidimensional data generated by the internet.

Data visualization has an impressive body of theory behind it, and there are some great books out there that I recommend you read (see "Recommended Books" on page 36 for a little selection). The practical benefit of understanding the way humans visually harvest information cannot be overstated. It can be easily demonstrated, for example, that a pie chart is almost always a bad way of presenting comparative data and a simple bar chart is far preferable. By conducting psychometric experiments, we now have a pretty good idea of how to trick the human visual system and make relationships in the data harder to grasp. Conversely, we can show that some visual forms are close to optimal for amplifying contrast. The literature, at its very least, provides some useful rules of thumb that suggest good candidates for any particular data narrative.

In essence, good dataviz tries to present data, collected from measurements in the world (empirical) or as the product of abstract mathematical explorations (e.g., the beautiful fractal patterns of the Mandelbrot set (*https://oreil.ly/w5BIV*)), in such a way as to draw out or emphasize any patterns or trends that might exist. These patterns can be simple (e.g., average weight by country), or the product of sophisticated statistical analysis (e.g., data clustering in a higher dimensional space).

In its untransformed state, we can imagine this data floating as a nebulous cloud of numbers or categories. Any patterns or correlations are entirely obscure. It's easy to forget, but the humble spreadsheet (Figure I-3 a) is a data visualization—the ordering of data into row-columnar form is an attempt to tame it, make its manipulation easier, and highlight discrepancies (e.g., actuarial bookkeeping). Of course, most people are not adept at spotting patterns in rows of numbers, so more accessible, visual forms were developed to engage with our visual cortex, the prime human conduit for information about the world. Enter the bar chart, pie chart,[6] and line chart. More imaginative ways were employed to distill statistical data in a more accessible form, one of the most famous being Charles Joseph Minard's visualization of Napoleon's disastrous Russian campaign of 1812 (Figure I-3 b).

The lighter tan-colored stream in Figure I-3 b shows the advance of Napoleon's army on Moscow; the black line shows the retreat. The thickness of the stream represents the size of Napoleon's army, thinning as casualties mounted. A temperature chart below is used to indicate the temperature at locations along the way. Note the elegant way in which Minard has combined multidimensional data (casualty statistics, geographical location, and temperature) to give an impression of the carnage, which

---

6 William Playfair's *Statistical Breviary* of 1801 having the dubious distinction of originating the pie chart.

would be hard to grasp in any other way (imagine trying to jump from a chart of casualties to a list of locations and making the necessary connections). I would argue that the chief problem of modern interactive dataviz is exactly the same as that faced by Minard: how to move beyond conventional one-dimensional bar charts (perfectly good for many things) and develop new ways to communicate cross-dimensional patterns effectively.

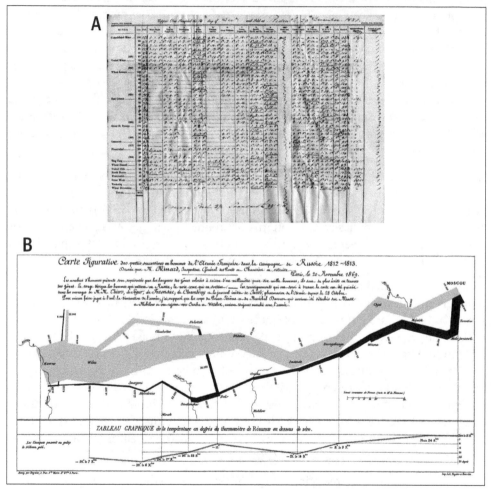

Figure I-3. (a) An early spreadsheet and (b) Charles Joseph Minard's visualization of Napoleon's Russian campaign of 1812

Until quite recently, most of our experience of charts was not much different from those of Charles Joseph Minard's audience. They were pre-rendered and inert, and showed one reflection of the data, hopefully an important and insightful one but nevertheless under total control of the author. In this sense, the replacement of real ink points with computer screen pixels was only a change in the scale of distribution.

The leap to the internet just replaced newsprint with pixels, the visualization still being unclickable and static. Recently, the combination of some powerful visualization libraries (D3 being preeminent among them) and a massive improvement in JavaScript's performance have opened the way to a new type of visualization, one that is easily accessible and dynamic, and actually encourages exploration and discovery. The clear distinction between data exploration and presentation is blurred. This new type of data visualization is the focus of this book and the reason why dataviz for the web is such an exciting area right now. People are trying to create new ways to visualize data and make it more accessible/useful to the end user. This is nothing short of a revolution.

Summary

Dataviz on the web is an exciting place to be right now, with innovations in interactive visualizations coming thick and fast, and many (if not most) of them being developed with D3. JavaScript is the only browser-based language, so the cool visuals are by necessity being coded in it (or converted into it). But JavaScript lacks the tools or environment necessary for the less dramatic but just as vital element of modern dataviz: the aggregation, curation, and processing of the data. This is where Python rules the roost, providing a general-purpose, concise, and eminently readable programming language with access to an increasing stable of first-class data-processing tools. Many of these tools leverage the power of very fast, low-level libraries, making Python data processing fast as well as easy.

This book introduces some of those heavyweight tools, as well as a host of other smaller but equally vital tools. It also shows how Python and JavaScript in concert represent the best dataviz stack out there for anyone wishing to deliver their visualizations to the internet.

Up next is the first part of the book, covering the preliminary skills needed for the toolchain. You can work through it now or skip ahead to Part II and the start of the toolchain, referring back when needed.

Recommended Books

Here are a few key data visualization books to whet your appetite, covering the gamut from interactive dashboards to beautiful and insightful infographics.

- Bertin, Jacques. *Semiology of Graphics: Diagrams, Networks, Maps.* Esri Press, 2010.

- Cairo, Alberto. *The Functional Art.* New Riders, 2012.

- Few, Stephen. *Information Dashboard Design: Displaying Data for At-a-Glance Monitoring,* 2nd Ed. Analytics Press, 2013.

- Rosenberg, Daniel and Anthony Grafton. *Cartographies of Time: A History of the Timeline.* Princeton Architectural Press, 2012.

- Tufte, Edward. *The Visual Display of Quantitative Information,* 2nd Ed. Graphics Press, 2001.

- Wexler, Steve. *The Big Book of Dashboards.* Wiley, 2017.

- Wilke, Claus. *Fundamentals of Data Visualization.* O'Reilly, 2019. (Free online version (*https://clauswilke.com/dataviz*).)

Basic Toolkit

This first part of the book provides a basic toolkit for the toolchain to come and is part tutorial, part reference. Given the fairly wide range of knowledge in the target audience, there will probably be things covered that you already know. My advice is just to cherry-pick the material to fill any gaps in your knowledge and maybe skim what you already know as a refresher.

If you're confident you already have the basic toolkit at hand, feel free to skip to the start of our journey along the toolchain in Part II.

You can find the code for this part of the book at the book's GitHub repo (*https://github.com/Kyrand/dataviz-with-python-and-js-ed-2*).

## CHAPTER 1

Development Setup

This chapter covers the downloads and software installations needed to use this book, and sketches out a recommended development environment. As you'll see, this isn't as onerous as it might once have been. I'll cover Python and JavaScript dependencies separately and give a brief overview of cross-language IDEs.

The Accompanying Code

There's a GitHub repository for the bulk of the code covered in this book, including the full Nobel Prize visualization. To get hold of it, just perform a git clone (*https://git-scm.com/docs/git-clone*) to a suitable local directory:

```
$ git clone https://github.com/Kyrand/dataviz-with-python-and-js-ed-2.git
```

This should create a local *dataviz-with-python-and-js-v2* directory with the key source code covered by the book.

Python

The bulk of the libraries covered in the book are Python-based, but what might have been a challenging attempt to provide comprehensive installation instructions for the various operating systems and their quirks is made much easier by the existence of Anaconda (*https://www.anaconda.com*), a Python platform that bundles together most of the popular analytics libraries in a convenient package. The book assumes you are using Python 3, which was released in 2008 and is now firmly established.

Anaconda

Installing some of the bigger Python libraries used to be a challenge all in itself, particularly those such as NumPy that depend on complex low-level C and Fortran packages. That's a great deal easier now and most will happily install using Python's `easy_install` with a `pip` command:

```
$ pip install NumPy
```

But some big number-crunching libraries are still tricky to install. Dependency management and versioning (you might need to use different versions of Python on the same machine) can make things trickier still, and this is where Anaconda comes into its own. It does all the dependency checking and binary installs so you don't have to. It's also a very convenient resource for a book like this.

To get your free Anaconda install, just navigate your browser to the Anaconda site (*https://oreil.ly/4FkCT*), choose the version for your operating system (ideally at least Python 3.5), and follow the instructions. Windows and OS X get a graphical installer (just download and double-click), whereas Linux requires you to run a little bash script:

```
$ bash Anaconda3-2021.11-Linux-x86_64.sh
```

Here's the latest installing instructions:

- For Windows (*https://oreil.ly/KErTO*)
- For macOS (*https://oreil.ly/5cVfC*)
- For Linux (*https://oreil.ly/tIQT5*)

I recommend sticking to defaults when installing Anaconda.

The official check guide can be found at the Anaconda site (*https://oreil.ly/tL7c9*). Windows and macOS users can use the Anaconda's Navigator GUI or, along with Linux users, use the Conda command-line interface.

Installing Extra Libraries

Anaconda contains almost all the Python libraries covered in this book (see the Anaconda documentation (*https://oreil.ly/c2vRS*) for the full list of Anaconda library packages). Where we need a non-Anaconda library, we can use `pip` (*https://oreil.ly/b0Eni*) (short for Pip Installs Python), the de facto standard for installing Python libraries. Using `pip` to install is as easy as can be. Just call `pip install` followed by the name of the package from the command line and it should be installed or, with any luck, give a sensible error:

```
$ pip install dataset
```

Virtual Environments

Virtual environments (*https://oreil.ly/x7Uq5*) provide a way of creating a sandboxed development environment with a particular Python version and/or set of third-party libraries. Using these virtual environments avoids polluting your global Python with these installs and gives you a lot more flexibility (you can play with different package versions or change your Python version if need be). The use of virtual environments is becoming a best practice in Python development, and I strongly suggest that you follow it.

Anaconda comes with a conda system command that makes creating and using virtual environments easy. Let's create a special one for this book, based on the full Anaconda package:

```
$ conda create --name pyjsviz anaconda
...
#
# To activate this environment, use:
# $ source activate pyjsviz
#
# To deactivate this environment, use:
# $ source deactivate
#
```

As the final message says, to use this virtual environment you need only source activate it (for Windows machines, you can leave out the source):

```
$ source activate pyjsviz
discarding /home/kyran/anaconda/bin from PATH
prepending /home/kyran/.conda/envs/pyjsviz/bin to PATH
(pyjsviz) $
```

Note that you get a helpful cue at the command line to let you know which virtual environment you're using.

The conda command can do a lot more than just facilitate virtual environments, combining the functionality of Python's pip installer and virtualenv command, among other things. You can get a full rundown in the Anaconda documentation (*https://oreil.ly/KN0ZL*).

If you're confident with standard Python virtual environments, these have been made a lot easier to work with by their incorporation in Python's Standard Library. To create a virtual environment from the command line:

```
$ python -m venv python-js-viz
```

This creates a python-js-viz directory containing the various elements of the virtual environment. This includes some activation scripts. To activate the virtual environment with macOS or Linux, run the activate script:

```
$ source python-js-viz/bin/activate
```

On Windows machines, run the *.bat* file:

```
$ python-js-viz/Scripts/activate.bat
```

You can then use `pip` to install Python libraries to the virtual environment, avoiding polluting your global Python distribution:

```
$ (python-js-viz) pip install NumPy
```

To install all the libraries required by this book, you can use the *requirements.txt* file in the book's GitHub repo (*https://github.com/Kyrand/dataviz-with-python-and-js-ed-2*):

```
$ (python-js-viz) pip install -r requirements.txt
```

You can find information on the virtual environment in the Python documentation (*https://oreil.ly/dhCvZ*).

JavaScript

The good news is that you don't need much JavaScript software at all. The only must-have is the Chrome/Chromium web browser, which is used in this book. It offers the most powerful set of developer tools of any current browser and is cross-platform.

To download Chrome, just go to the home page (*https://oreil.ly/jNTUl*) and download the version for your operating system. This should be automatically detected.

All the JavaScript libraries used in this book can be found in the accompanying GitHub repo (*https://github.com/Kyrand/dataviz-with-python-and-js-ed-2*), but there are generally two ways to deliver them to the browser. You can use a content delivery network (CDN), which efficiently caches a copy of the library retrieved from the delivery network. Alternatively, you can use a local copy of the library served to the browser. Both of these methods use the `script` tag in an HTML document.

Content Delivery Networks

With CDNs, rather than having the libraries installed on your local machine, the JavaScript is retrieved by the browser over the web, from the closest available server. This should make things very fast—faster than if you served the content yourself.

To include a library via CDN, you use the usual `<script>` tag, typically placed at the bottom of your HTML page. For example, the following call adds a current version of D3:

```
<script
 src="https://cdnjs.cloudflare.com/ajax/libs/d3/7.1.1/d3.min.js"
 charset="utf-8">
</script>
```

Installing Libraries Locally

If you need to install JavaScript libraries locally, because, for example, you anticipate doing some offline development work or can't guarantee an internet connection, there are a number of fairly simple ways to do so.

You can just download the separate libraries and put them in your local server's static folder. This is a typical folder structure. Third-party libraries go in the *static/libs* directory off root, like so:

```
nobel_viz/
  └── static
        ├── css
        ├── data
        ├── libs
        │     └── d3.min.js
        └── js
```

If you organize things this way, to use D3 in your scripts now requires a local file reference with the <script> tag:

```
<script src="/static/libs/d3.min.js"></script>
```

Databases

The recommended database for small to medium-sized dataviz projects is the brilliant, serverless, file-based, SQL-based SQLite (*https://www.sqlite.org*). This database is used throughout the dataviz toolchain demonstrated in the book and is the only database you really need.

The book also covers basic Python interactions with MongoDB (*https://www.mongodb.org*), the most popular nonrelational, or NoSQL database (*https://oreil.ly/uvX4e*):

SQLite
> SQLite should come as standard with macOS and Linux machines. For Windows, follow this guide (*https://oreil.ly/Ck6qR*).

MongoDB
> You can find installation instructions for the various operating systems in the MongoDB documentation (*https://oreil.ly/JIt8R*).

Note that we'll be using Python's SQLAlchemy (*https://www.sqlalchemy.org*) SQL library either directly or through libraries that build on it. This means we can convert any SQLite examples to another SQL backend (e.g., MySQL (*https://www.mysql.com*) or PostgreSQL (*https://www.postgresql.org*)) by changing a configuration line or two.

Getting MongoDB Up and Running

MongoDB can be a little trickier to install than some databases. As mentioned, you can follow this book perfectly well without going through the hassle of installing the server-based MongoDB, but if you want to try it out or find yourself needing to use it at work, here are some installation notes:

For OS X users, check out the official docs (*https://oreil.ly/zTEH5*) for MongoDB installation instructions.

This Windows-specific guide (*https://oreil.ly/OI5gB*) from the official docs should get your MongoDB server up and running. You will probably need to use administrator privileges to create the necessary data directories and so on.

More often than not these days, you'll be installing MongoDB to a Linux-based server, most commonly an Ubuntu variant, which uses the deb (*https://oreil.ly/rRQrG*) file format to deliver its packages. The official MongoDB docs (*https://oreil.ly/SrRzJ*) do a good job covering an Ubuntu install.

MongoDB uses a *data* directory to store to and, depending how you install it, you may need to create this yourself. On OS X and Linux boxes, the default is a *data* directory off the root directory, which you can create using `mkdir` as a superuser (`sudo`):

```
$ sudo mkdir /data
$ sudo mkdir /data/db
```

You'll then want to set ownership to yourself:

```
$ sudo chown 'whoami' /data/db
```

With Windows, installing the MongoDB Community Edition (*https://oreil.ly/3Vtft*), you can create the necessary *data* directory with the following command:

```
$ cd C:\
$ md "\data\db"
```

The MongoDB server will often be started by default on Linux boxes; otherwise, on Linux and OS X the following command will start a server instance:

```
$ mongod
```

On Windows Community Edition, the following, run from a command prompt, will start a server instance:

```
C:\mongodb\bin\mongod.exe
```

Easy MongoDB with Docker

MongoDB can be tricky to install. For example, current Ubuntu variants (> version 22.04) have incompatible SSL libs (*https://oreil.ly/ShOjF*). If you have Docker installed (*https://oreil.ly/ZF5Uf*), a working development DB on the default port 27017 is only a single command away:

```
$ sudo docker run -dp 27017:27017 -v local-mongo:/data/db
              --name local-mongo --restart=always mongo
```

This nicely side-steps local library incompatibilities and the like.

Integrated Development Environments

As I explain in "The Myth of IDEs, Frameworks, and Tools" on page 82, you don't need an IDE to program in Python or JavaScript. The development tools provided by modern browsers, Chrome in particular, mean you only really need a good code editor to have pretty much the optimal setup.

One caveat here is that these days intermediate to advanced JavaScript tends to involve frameworks like React, Vue, and Svelte that do benefit from the bells and whistles provided by a decent IDE, particularly handling multiformat files (where HTML, CSS, and JS are all embedded together). The good news is that the freely available Visual Studio Code (*https://code.visualstudio.com*) (VSCode) has become the de facto standard for modern web development. It's got plug-ins for pretty much everything and a very large and active community, so questions tend to be answered and bugs hunted down fast.

For Python, I have tried a few dedicated IDEs but they've never stuck. The main itch I was trying to scratch was finding a decent debugging system. Setting breakpoints in Python with a text editor isn't particularly elegant, and using the command-line debugger pdb feels a little too old school sometimes. Nevertheless, Python does have a pretty good logging system included, which takes the edge off its rather clunky default debugging. VSCode is pretty good for Python programming, but there are some Python-specific IDEs that are arguably a little smoother.

In no particular order, here are a few that I've tried and not disliked:

PyCharm (https://www.jetbrains.com/pycharm)
This option offers solid code assistance and good debugging and would probably top a favorite IDE poll of seasoned Pythonistas.

PyDev (https://pydev.org)
If you like Eclipse and can tolerate its rather large footprint, this might well be for you.

Wing Python IDE (https://www.wingware.com)
This is a solid bet, with a great debugger and incremental improvements over a decade-and-a-half's worth of development.

Summary

With free, packaged Python distributions such as Anaconda, and the inclusion of sophisticated JavaScript development tools in freely available web browsers, the necessary Python and JavaScript elements of your development environment are a couple of clicks away. Add a favorite editor and a database of choice,[1] and you are pretty much good to go. There are additional libraries, such as *node.js*, that can be useful but don't count as essential. Now that we've established our programming environment, the next chapters will teach the preliminaries needed to start our journey of data transformation along the toolchain, starting with a language bridge between Python and JavaScript.

---

1 SQLite is great for development purposes and doesn't need a server running on your machine.

## CHAPTER 2

A Language-Learning Bridge Between Python and JavaScript

Probably the most ambitious aspect of this book is that it deals with two programming languages. Moreover, it only requires that you are competent in one of these languages. This is only possible because Python and JavaScript (JS) are fairly simple languages with much in common. The aim of this chapter is to draw out those commonalities and use them to make a learning bridge between the two languages such that core skills acquired in one can easily be applied to the other.

After showing the key similarities and differences between the two languages, I'll show how to set up a learning environment for Python and JS. The bulk of the chapter will then deal with core syntactical and conceptual differences, followed by a selection of patterns and idioms that I use often while doing data visualization work.

Similarities and Differences

Syntax differences aside, Python and JavaScript actually have a lot in common. After a short while, switching between them can be almost seamless.[1] Let's compare the two from a data visualizer's perspective:

These are the chief similarities:

- They both work without needing a compilation step (i.e., they are interpreted).
- You can use both with an interactive interpreter, which means you can type in lines of code and see the results right away.

---

1 One particularly annoying little gotcha is that while Python uses pop to remove a list item, it uses append—not push—to add an item. JavaScript uses push to add an item, whereas append is used to concatenate arrays.

- Both have garbage collection (*https://oreil.ly/3QDQA*), which means they manage program memory automatically.

- Neither language has header files, package boilerplate, and so on, as compared to languages like C++, Java, etc.

- Both can happily be developed with a text editor or lightweight IDE.

- In both, functions are first-class citizens, which can be passed as arguments.

These are the key differences:

- Possibly the biggest difference is that JavaScript is single-threaded and non-blocking (*https://oreil.ly/Ja0FW*), using asynchronous I/O. This means that simple things like file access involve the use of a callback function (*https://oreil.ly/L9DA5*), passed to another function and called on completion of some code, usually asynchronously.

- JS is used essentially in web development and until relatively recently was browser-bound,[2] but Python is used almost everywhere.

- JS is the only first-class language in web browsers, Python being excluded.

- Python has a comprehensive standard library, whereas JS has a limited set of utility objects (e.g., JSON, Math).

- Python has fairly classical object-oriented classes, whereas JS uses prototype objects.

- JS lacks heavyweight general-purpose data-processing libs.[3]

The differences here emphasize the need for this book to be bilingual. The JavaScript monopoly on browser dataviz needs the complement of a conventional data-processing stack. And Python has the best there is.

Interacting with the Code

One of the great advantages of Python and JavaScript is that because they are interpreted on the fly, you can interact with them. Python's interpreter can be run from the command line, whereas JavaScript's is generally accessed from the web browser through a console, usually available from the built-in development tools. In this section, we'll see how to fire up a session with the interpreter and start trying out your code.

---

2 The ascent of node.js (*https://nodejs.org/en*) has extended JavaScript to the server.

3 This is changing with libraries like TensorFlow.js (*https://oreil.ly/kDw6M*) and Danfo.js (*https://oreil.ly/dJnOl*) (a JavaScript pandas-alike based on TensorFlow), but JS is still well behind Python, R, and others.

Python

By far, the best command-line Python interpreter is IPython (*https://ipython.org*), which comes in three shades: the basic terminal version, an enhanced graphical version, and a browser-based notebook. Since IPython version 4.0, the latter two have been spun out into project Jupyter (*https://jupyter.org*). The Jupyter notebook is a rather brilliant and fairly recent innovation, providing a browser-based interactive computational environment. The great boon of the notebook is session persistence and the possibility of web access.[4] The ease with which one can share programming sessions, complete with embedded data visualizations, makes the notebook a fantastic teaching tool as well as a great way to recover programming context. That's why the Python chapters of this book have accompanying Jupyter notebooks.

To start a Jupyter notebook just run `jupyter` at the command line:

```
$ jupyter notebook
[I 15:27:44.553 NotebookApp] Serving notebooks from local
directory:
...
[I 15:27:44.553 NotebookApp] http://localhost:8888/?token=5e09...
```

Then open a browser tab at the URL specified (*http://localhost:8888* in this case) and start reading or writing Python notebooks.

JavaScript

There are lots of options for trying out JavaScript code without starting a server, though the latter isn't that difficult. Because the JavaScript interpreter comes embedded in all modern web browsers, there are a number of sites that let you try out bits of JavaScript along with HTML and CSS and see the results. CodePen (*https://oreil.ly/ZtROX*) is a good option. These sites are great for sharing code and trying out snippets, and usually allow you to add libraries such as *D3.js* with a few mouse-clicks.

If you want to try out code one-liners or quiz the state of live code, browser-based consoles are your best bet. With Chrome, you can access the console with the key combo Ctrl-Shift-J (Command + Option + J on a Mac). As well as trying little JS snippets, the console allows you to drill down into any objects in scope, revealing their methods and properties. This is a great way to quiz the state of a live object and search for bugs.

One disadvantage of using online JavaScript editors is losing the power of your favorite editing environment, with linting, familiar keyboard shortcuts, and the like (see Chapter 4). Online editors tend to be rudimentary, to say the least. If you anticipate

---

4 At the cost of running a Python interpreter on the server.

an extensive JavaScript session and want to use your favorite editor, the best bet is to run a local server.

First, create a project directory—called *sandpit*, for example—and add a minimal HTML file that includes a JS script:

```
sandpit
├── index.html
└── script.js
```

The *index.html* file need only be a few lines long, with an optional `div` placeholder on which to start building your visualization or just trying out a little DOM manipulation:

```
<!-- index.html -->
<!DOCTYPE html>
<meta charset="utf-8">

<div id='viz'></div>

<script type="text/javascript" src="script.js" async></script>
```

You can then add a little JavaScript to your *script.js* file:

```
// script.js
let data = [3, 7, 2, 9, 1, 11];
let sum = 0;
data.forEach(function(d){
    sum += d;
});

console.log('Sum = ' + sum);
// outputs 'Sum = 33'
```

Start your development server in the project directory using Python's `http` module:

```
$ python -m http.server 8000
Serving HTTP on 0.0.0.0 port 8000 ...
```

Then open your browser at *http://localhost:8000*, press Ctrl-Shift-J (Cmd-Opt-J on OS X) to access the console and you should see Figure 2-1, showing the logged output of the script (see Chapter 4 for further details).

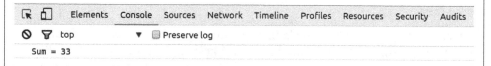

Figure 2-1. Outputting to the Chrome console

Now that we've established how to run the demo code, let's start building a bridge between Python and JavaScript. First, we'll cover the basic differences in syntax. As you'll see, they're fairly minor and easily absorbed.

Basic Bridge Work

In this section, I'll contrast the basic nuts and bolts of programming in the two languages.

Style Guidelines, PEP 8, and use strict

Where JavaScript style guidelines are a bit of a free-for-all (with people often defaulting to those used by a big library like React), Python has a Python Enhancement Proposal (PEP) dedicated to it. I'd recommend getting acquainted with PEP-8 but not submitting totally to its leadership. It's right about most things, but there's room for some personal choice here. There's a handy online checker called PEP8 Online (*http://pep8online.com*), which will pick up any infractions of PEP-8. Many Pythonistas are turning to the Black Python code formatter (*https://oreil.ly/C9xWO*), which takes over formatting duties in accordance with PEP-8.

In Python, you should use four spaces to indent a code block. JavaScript is less strict, but two spaces is the most common indent.

One recent addition to JavaScript (ECMAScript 5) is the `'use strict'` directive, which imposes strict mode. This mode enforces some good JavaScript practice, which includes catching accidental global declarations, and I thoroughly recommend its use. To use it, just place the string at the top of your function or module:

```
(function(foo){
  'use strict';
  // ...
}(window.foo = window.foo || {}));
```

CamelCase Versus Underscore

JS conventionally uses CamelCase (e.g., `processStudentData`) for its variables, whereas Python, in accordance with PEP-8, uses underscores (e.g., `process_stu dent_data`) in its variable names (see Section B in Examples 2-3 and 2-4). By convention (and convention is more important in the Python ecosystem than it is in JS), Python uses capitalized CamelCase for class declarations (see the following example), uppercase for constants, and underscores for everything else:

```
FOO_CONST = 10
class FooBar(object): # ...
def foo_bar():
    baz_bar = 'some string'
```

Importing Modules, Including Scripts

Using other libraries in your code, either your own or third-party, is fundamental to modern programming, which makes it all the more surprising that until relatively recently JavaScript didn't have a dedicated way of doing it.[5] Python has a simple import system that, on the whole, works pretty well.

The good news on the JavaScript front is that since ECMAScript 6, JavaScript has addressed this issue, with the addition of `import` and `export` statements for encapsulated modules. We now have JavaScript modules (typically with the `.mjs` suffix) that can import and export encapsulated functions and objects, a huge step forward. In Part V, we'll see how easy these are to work with.

While getting comfortable with JS you'll probably want to import third-party libraries using the `script` tag, which will typically see them added to the global namespace as an object. For example, in order to use D3 you add the following `script` tag to your HTML entry file (typically *index.html*):

```
<!DOCTYPE html>
<meta charset="utf-8">
  <script src="http://d3js.org/d3.v7.min.js"></script>
```

You can now use the D3 library like this:

```
let r = d3.range(0, 10, 2)
console.log(r)
// out: [0, 2, 4, 6, 8]
```

Python comes with "batteries included," a comprehensive set of libraries covering everything from extended data containers (collections) to working with the family of CSV files (csv). If you want to use one of these, just import it using the `import` keyword:

```
In [1]: import sys

In [2]: sys.platform
Out[2]: 'linux'
```

If you don't want to import the whole library or want to use an alias, you can use the `as` and `from` keywords instead:

```
import pandas as pd
from csv import DictWriter, DictReader
from numpy import * ❶

df = pd.read_json('data.json')
reader = DictReader('data.csv')
md = median([12, 56, 44, 33])
```

---

5 The constraint of having to deliver JS scripts over the web via HTTP is largely responsible for this.

❶ This imports all the variables from the module into the current namespace and is almost always a bad idea. One of the variables could mask an existing one, and it goes against the Python best practice of explicit being better than implicit. One exception to this rule is if you are using the Python interpreter interactively. In this limited context, it may make sense to import all functions from a library to cut down on key presses; for example, importing all the math functions (`from math import *`) if doing some Python math hacking.

If you import a nonstandard library, Python uses `sys.path` to try to find it. `sys.path` consists of:

- The directory containing the importing module (current directory)
- The `PYTHONPATH` variable, containing a list of directories
- The installation-dependent default, where libraries installed using `pip` or `easy_install` will usually be placed

Big libraries are often packaged, divided into submodules. These submodules are accessed by dot notation:

```
import matplotlib.pyplot as plt
```

Packages are constructed from the filesystem via *__init__.py* files, usually empty, as shown in Example 2-1. The presence of an init file makes the directory visible to Python's import system.

Example 2-1. Building a Python package

```
mypackage
├── __init__.py
...
├── core
│   └── __init__.py
│   ...
...
└── io
    ├── __init__.py
    └── api.py
    ...
    └── tests
        └── __init__.py
        └── test_data.py
        └── test_excel.py ❶
        ...
...
```

You would import this module using `from mypackage.io.tests import test_excel`.

You can access packages on `sys.path` from the root directory (that's `mypackage` in Example 2-1) using dot notation. A special case of `import` is intrapackage references. The `test_excel.py` submodule in Example 2-1 can import submodules from the `mypackage` package both absolutely and relatively:

```
from mypackage.io.tests import test_data ❶
from . import test_data ❷
import test_data ❷
from ..io import api ❸
```

❶ Imports the `test_data.py` module absolutely, from the package's head directory.

❷ An explicit (`.import`) and implicit relative import.

❸ A relative import from a sibling package of `tests`.

JavaScript Modules

JavaScript now has modules with import and export of encapsulated variables. JS cherry-picked its import syntax, using a lot of stuff that will be familiar to Pythonistas but, in my opinion, improving on it. Here's a brief run-down:

Let's say we have a JS entry-point module `index.js`, which wants to use some functions or objects from a library module `libFoo.js` in a `lib` directory. The file structure looks like this:

```
.
├── index.mjs
└── lib
    └── libFoo.mjs
```

In `libFoo.mjs` we export a dummy function and can use `export default` to export a single object for the module, typically an API with, for example, utility methods:

```
// lib/libFoo.mjs
export let findOdds = (a) => {
  return a.filter(x => x%2)
}

let api = {findOdds} ❶

export default api
```

❶ An example of object creation with shorthand property name, equivalent to `{findOdds: findOdds}`

To import the exported functions and objects from our index module we use the `import` statement, which allows us to import the default API or select exported variables by name using curly brackets:

```
// index.mjs
import api from './lib/libFoo.mjs'
import { findOdds } from './lib/libFoo.mjs'

let odds = findOdds([2, 4, 24, 33, 5, 66, 24])
console.log('Odd numbers: ', odds)

odds = api.findOdds([12, 43, 22, 39, 52, 21])
console.log('Odd numbers: ', odds)
```

JS imports also support aliasing, which can be a great code sanitizer:

```
// index.mjs
import api as foo from './lib/libFoo.mjs'
import { findOdds as odds } from './lib/libFoo.mjs'
// ...
```

As you can see, JavaScript imports and exports are very similar to Python's, though a little more user-friendly in my experience. You can see more details in Mozilla's documentation for exports (*https://oreil.ly/J0aDV*) and imports (*https://oreil.ly/slsT5*).

Keeping Your Namespaces Clean

The variables defined in Python modules are encapsulated, which means that unless you import them explicitly (e.g., `from foo import baa`), you will be accessing them from the imported module's namespace using dot notation (e.g., `foo.baa`). This modularization of the global namespace is quite rightly seen as a very good thing and plays to one of Python's key tenets: the importance of explicit statements over implicit. When analyzing someone's Python code you should be able to see exactly where a class, function, or variable has come from. Just as importantly, preserving the namespace limits the chance of conflicting or masking variables—a big potential problem as codebases get larger.

In the past one of the main criticisms of JavaScript, and a fair one, was that it played fast and loose with namespace conventions. The most egregious example of this is that variables declared outside of functions or missing the `var` keyword[6] are global rather than confined to the script in which they are declared. With modern, modular JavaScript you get Python-like encapsulation with imported and exported variables.

JS modules are a relatively recent game changer—a common pattern used in the past and one that you may well run into is the creation of a self-calling function in order

---

6 You can eliminate the possibility of a missing `var` by using the ECMAScript 5 `'use strict'` directive.

to isolate local variables from the global namespace. This makes all variables declared via var local to the script/function, preventing them from polluting the global namespace. The JavaScript let (*https://oreil.ly/cTxOy*) keyword, which is block-scoped, is pretty much always preferable to var. Any objects, functions, and variables you want to make available to other scripts can be attached to an object that is part of the global namespace.

Example 2-2 demonstrates a module pattern. The boilerplate head and tail (labeled ❶ and ❸) effectively create an encapsulated module. This pattern is far from a perfect solution to modular JavaScript but was the best compromise I knew of until ECMAScript 6's dedicated import system was adopted by all major browsers.

Example 2-2. A module pattern for JavaScript

```
(function(nbviz) { ❶
    'use strict';
    // ...
    nbviz.updateTimeChart = function(data) {..} ❷
    // ...
}(window.nbviz = window.nbviz || {})); ❸
```

❶   Receives the global nbviz object.

❷   Attaches the updateTimeChart method to the global nbviz object, effectively *exporting* it.

❸   If an nbviz object exists in the global (window) namespace, pass it into the module function; otherwise, add it to the global namespace.

Outputting "Hello World!"

By far the most popular initial demonstration of any programming language is getting it to print or communicate "Hello World!" in some form, so let's start with getting output from Python and JavaScript.

Python's output couldn't be much simpler:

```
print('Hello World!')
```

JavaScript has no print function, but you can log output to the browser console:

```
console.log('Hello World!')
```

Simple Data Processing

A good way to get an overview of the language differences is to see the same function written in both. Examples 2-3 and 2-4 show a small, contrived example of data munging in Python and JavaScript, respectively. We'll use these to compare Python and JS syntax and label them with capital letters (A, B...) to allow comparison of the code blocks.

Example 2-3. Simple data transformation with Python

```python
# A
student_data = [
    {'name': 'Bob', 'id':0, 'scores':[68, 75, 56, 81]},
    {'name': 'Alice', 'id':1,  'scores':[75, 90, 64, 88]},
    {'name': 'Carol', 'id':2, 'scores':[59, 74, 71, 68]},
    {'name': 'Dan', 'id':3, 'scores':[64, 58, 53, 62]},
]

# B
def process_student_data(data, pass_threshold=60,
                         merit_threshold=75):
    """ Perform some basic stats on some student data. """

    # C
    for sdata in data:
        av = sum(sdata['scores'])/float(len(sdata['scores']))

        if av > merit_threshold:
            sdata['assessment'] = 'passed with merit'
        elif av >= pass_threshold:
            sdata['assessment'] = 'passed'
        else:
            sdata['assessment'] = 'failed'
        # D
        print(f"{sdata['name']}'s (id: {sdata['id']}) final assessment is:\
{sdata['assessment'].upper()}")
        # For Python versions before 3.7, the old-style string formatting is equivalent
        # print("%s's (id: %d) final assessment is: %s"%(sdata['name'],\
        # sdata['id'], sdata['assessment'].upper()))      sdata['name'], sdata['id'],\
        # sdata['assessment'].upper()))
        print(f"{sdata['name']}'s (id: {sdata['id']}) final assessment is:\
          {sdata['assessment'].upper()}")

        sdata['average'] = av

# E
if __name__ == '__main__':
    process_student_data(student_data)
```

Example 2-4. Simple data munging with JavaScript

```javascript
let studentData = [ ●
    {name: 'Bob', id:0, 'scores':[68, 75, 76, 81]},
    {name: 'Alice', id:1, 'scores':[75, 90, 64, 88]},
    {'name': 'Carol', id:2, 'scores':[59, 74, 71, 68]},
    {'name': 'Dan', id:3, 'scores':[64, 58, 53, 62]},
];

// B
function processStudentData(data, passThreshold, meritThreshold){
    passThreshold = typeof passThreshold !== 'undefined'?\
    passThreshold: 60;
    meritThreshold = typeof meritThreshold !== 'undefined'?\
    meritThreshold: 75;

    // C
    data.forEach(function(sdata){
        let av = sdata.scores.reduce(function(prev, current){
            return prev+current;
        },0) / sdata.scores.length;

        if(av > meritThreshold){
            sdata.assessment = 'passed with merit';
        }
        else if(av >= passThreshold){
            sdata.assessment = 'passed';
        }
        else{
            sdata.assessment = 'failed';
        }
        // D
        console.log(sdata.name + "'s (id: " + sdata.id +
          ") final assessment is: " +
            sdata.assessment.toUpperCase());
        sdata.average = av;
    });

}

// E
processStudentData(studentData);
```

 Note the deliberate and valid inconsistency in the object keys with some quoted and some unquoted.

String Construction

The D sections in Examples 2-3 and 2-4 show the standard way to print output to the console or terminal. JavaScript has no print statement but will log to the browser's console through the console object:

```
console.log(sdata.name + "'s (id: " + sdata.id +
    ") final assessment is: " + sdata.assessment.toUpperCase());
```

Note that the integer variable `id` is coerced to a string, allowing concatenation. Python doesn't perform this implicit coercion, so attempting to add a string to an integer in this way gives an error. Instead, explicit conversion to string form is achieved through one of the `str` or `repr` functions.

In section A of Example 2-3, the output string is constructed with C type formatting. String (`%s`) and integer (`%d`) placeholders are provided by a final tuple (`%(…)`):

```
print("%s's (id: %d) final assessment is: %s"
    %(sdata['name'], sdata['id'], sdata['assessment'].upper()))
```

These days, I rarely use Python's `print` statement, opting for the much more powerful and flexible `logging` module, which is demonstrated in the following code block. It takes a little more effort to use, but it is worth it. Logging gives you the flexibility to direct output to a file and/or the screen, adjusting the logging level to prioritize certain information, and a whole load of other useful things. Check out the details in the Python documentation (*https://oreil.ly/aJzyx*).

```
import logging
logger = logging.getLogger(__name__)  ❶
//...
logger.debug('Some useful debugging output')
logger.info('Some general information')

// IN INITIAL MODULE
logging.basicConfig(level=logging.DEBUG)  ❷
```

❶ Creates a logger with the name of this module.

❷ Setting the logging level to "debug" provides the most detailed information available (see the Python documentation (*https://oreil.ly/xAiP1*) for further details).

Significant Whitespace Versus Curly Brackets

The syntactic feature most associated with Python is significant whitespace. Whereas languages like C and JavaScript use whitespace for readability and could easily be condensed into one line,[7] in Python leading spaces are used to indicate code blocks and removing them changes the meaning of the code. The extra effort required to maintain correct code alignment is more than compensated for by increased readability—you spend far longer reading than writing code, and the easy reading of Python is probably the main reason why the Python library ecosystem is so healthy. Four spaces is pretty much mandatory (see PEP-8) and my personal preference is for

---

7 This is actually done by JavaScript compressors to reduce the file size of downloaded web pages.

what are known as *soft tabs*, where your editor inserts (and deletes) multiple spaces instead of a tab character.[8]

In the following code, the indentation of the return statement must be four spaces by convention:[9]

```
def doubler(x):
    return x * 2
#   |<-this spacing is important
```

JavaScript doesn't care about the number of spaces between statements and variables, using curly brackets to demark code blocks; the two doubler functions in this code are equivalent:

```
let doubler = function(x){
    return x * 2;
}
```

```
let doubler=function(x){return x*2;}
```

Much is made of Python's whitespace, but most good coders I know set up their editors to enforce indented code blocks and a consistent look and feel. Python merely enforces this good practice. And, to reiterate, I believe the extreme readability of Python code contributes as much to Python's supremely healthy ecosystem as its simple syntax.

Comments and Doc-Strings

To add comments to code, Python uses hashes, #:

```
# ex.py, a single informative comment
```

```
data = {} # Our main data-ball
```

By contrast, JavaScript uses the C language convention of double backslashes (//) or /* … */ for multiline comments:

```
// script.js, a single informative comment
/* A multiline comment block for
function descriptions, library script
headers, and the like */
let data = {}; // Our main data-ball
```

---

8 The soft versus hard tab debate generates controversy, with much heat and little light. PEP-8 stipulates spaces, which is good enough for me.

9 It could be two or even three spaces, but this number must be consistent throughout the module.

In addition to comments, and in keeping with its philosophy of readability and transparency, Python has documentation strings (doc-strings) by convention. The `process_student_data` function in Example 2-3 has a triple-quoted line of text at its top that will automatically be assigned to the function's `__doc__` attribute. You can also use multiline doc-strings:

```
def doubler(x):
    """This function returns double its input."""
    return 2 * x

def sanitize_string(s):
    """This function replaces any string spaces
    with '-' after stripping any whitespace
    """
    return s.strip().replace(' ', '-')
```

Doc-strings are a great habit to get into, particularly if you are working collaboratively. They are understood by most decent Python editing toolsets and are also used by such automated documentation libraries as Sphinx (*http://sphinx-doc.org*). The string-literal doc-string is accessible as the doc property of a function or class.

Declaring Variables Using let or var

JavaScript uses `let` or `var` to declare variables. Generally speaking, `let` is almost always the right choice.

Strictly speaking, JS statements should be terminated with a semicolon as opposed to Python's newline. You will see examples where the semicolon is dispensed with, and modern browsers will usually do the right thing here. There are a few edge cases that could necessitate the use of a semicolon (e.g., it can trip up code minifiers and compressors that remove whitespace), but generally I find that the loss of clutter and improvement in readability are a worthwhile compromise to coding without the semicolons.

JavaScript has *variable hoisting*, which means variables declared with `var` are processed before any other code. This means declaring them anywhere in the function is equivalent to declaring them at the top. This can result in weird errors and confusion. Explicitly placing `var`s at the top avoids this, but it's better to use the modern `let` and have scoped declarations.

Strings and Numbers

The *name* strings used in the student data (see Section A of Examples 2-3 and 2-4) will be interpreted as UCS-2 (the parent of unicode UTF-16) in JavaScript,[10] and Unicode (UTF-8 by default) in Python 3.[11]

Both languages allow single and double quotes for strings. If you want to include a single or double quote in the string, then enclose with the alternative, like so:

```
pub_name = "The Brewer's Tap"
```

The `scores` in Section A of Example 2-4 are stored as JavaScript's one numeric type, double-precision 64-bit (IEEE 754) floating-point numbers. Although JavaScript has a `parseInt` conversion function, when used with floats,[12] it is really just a rounding operator, similar to `floor`. The type of the parsed `number` is still `number`:

```
let x = parseInt(3.45); // 'cast' x to 3
typeof(x); // "number"
```

Python has two numeric types: the 32-bit `int`, to which the student scores are cast, and a `float` equivalent (IEE 754) to JS's `number`. This means that Python can represent any integer, whereas JavaScript is more limited.[13] Python's casting changes type:

```
foo = 3.4 # type(foo) -> float
bar = int(3.4) # type(bar) -> int
```

The nice thing about Python and JavaScript numbers is that they are easy to work with and usually do what you want. If you need something more efficient, Python has the NumPy library, which allows fine-grained control of your numeric types (you'll learn more about NumPy in Chapter 7). In JavaScript, aside from some cutting-edge projects, you're pretty much stuck with 64-bit floats.

---

10 The quite fair assumption that JavaScript uses UTF-16 has been the cause of much bug-driven misery. See this blog post by Mathias Bynens (*https://oreil.ly/9otVB*) for an interesting analysis.

11 The change to Unicode strings in Python 3 is a big one. Given the confusion that often attends Unicode de/encoding, it's worth reading a little bit about it (*https://oreil.ly/5FNwi*). Python 2 used strings of bytes.

12 `parseInt` can do quite a bit more than round. For example, `parseInt(12.5px)` gives 12, first removing the *px* and then casting the string to a number. It also has a second `radix` argument to specify the base of the cast. See the Mozilla documentation (*https://oreil.ly/ZtA4n*) for the specifics.

13 Because all numbers in JavaScript are floating point, it can only support 53-bit integers. Using larger integers (such as the commonly used 64-bit) can result in discontinuous integers. See this 2ality blog post (*https://oreil.ly/hBxvS*) for further information.

Booleans

Python differs from the JavaScript and the C class languages in using named Boolean operators. Other than that, they work pretty much as expected. This table gives a comparison:

Python	bool	True	False	not	and	or
JavaScript	boolean	true	false	!	&&	||

Python's capitalized `True` and `False` is an obvious trip-up for any JavaScripter and vice versa, but any decent syntax highlighting should catch that, as should your code linter.

Rather than always returning Boolean true or false, both Python and JavaScript and/or expressions return the result of one of the arguments, which may of course be a Boolean value. Table 2-1 shows how this works, using Python to demonstrate.

Table 2-1. Python's Boolean operators

Operation	Result
x or y	if x is false, then y, else x
x and y	if x is false, then x, else y
not x	if x is false, then `True`, else `False`

This fact allows for some occasionally useful variable assignments:

```
rocket_launch = True
(rocket_launch == True and 'All OK') or 'We have a problem!'
Out:
'All OK'
```

```
rocket_launch = False
(rocket_launch == True and 'All OK') or 'We have a problem!'
Out:
'We have a problem!'
```

Data Containers: dicts, objects, lists, Arrays

Roughly speaking, JavaScript `objects` can be used like Python `dicts`, and Python `lists` like JavaScript arrays. Python also has a tuple container, which functions like an immutable list. Here are some examples:

```
# Python
d = {'name': 'Groucho', 'occupation': 'Ruler of Freedonia'}
l = ['Harpo', 'Groucho', 99]
t = ('an', 'immutable', 'container')

// JavaScript
d = {'name': 'Groucho', 'occupation': 'Ruler of Freedonia'}
l = ['Harpo', 'Groucho', 99]
```

As shown in Section A of Examples 2-3 and 2-4, while Python's dict keys must be quote-marked strings (or hashable types), JavaScript allows you to omit the quotes if the property is a valid identifier (i.e., not containing special characters such as spaces and dashes). So in our studentData objects, JS implicitly converts the property 'name' to string form.

The student data declarations look pretty much the same and, in practice, are used pretty much the same too. The key difference to note is that while the curly-bracketed containers in the JS studentData look like Python dicts, they are actually a short-hand declaration of JS objects (*https://oreil.ly/QTlNc*), a somewhat different data container.

In JS data visualization, we tend to use arrays of objects as the chief data container and here, JS objects function much as a Pythonista would expect. In fact, as demonstrated in the following code, we get the advantage of both dot notation and key-string access, the former being preferred where applicable (keys with spaces or dashes needing quoted strings):

```
let foo = {bar:3, baz:5};
foo.bar; // 3
foo['baz']; // 5, same as Python
```

It's good to be aware that although they can be used like Python dictionaries, Java-Script objects are much more than just containers (aside from primitives like strings and numbers, pretty much everything in JavaScript is an object).[14] But in most dataviz examples you see, they are used very much like Python dicts.

Table 2-2 converts basic list operations.

---

14 This makes iterating over their properties a little trickier than it might be. See this Stack Overflow thread (*https://oreil.ly/3kJW3*) for more details.

Table 2-2. Lists and arrays

JavaScript array (a)	Python list (l)
a.length	len(l)
a.push(item)	l.append(item)
a.pop()	l.pop()
a.shift()	l.pop(0)
a.unshift(item)	l.insert(0, item)
a.slice(start, end)	l[start:end]
a.splice(start, howMany, i1, …)	l[start:end] = [i1, …]

Functions

The B sections of Examples 2-3 and 2-4 show a function declaration. Python uses def to indicate a function:

```
def process_student_data(data, pass_threshold=60,
                         merit_threshold=75):
    """ Perform some basic stats on some student data. """
    ...
```

whereas JavaScript uses function:

```
function processStudentData(data, passThreshold=60, meritThreshold=75){
    ...
}
```

Both have a list of parameters. With JS, the function code block is indicated by the curly brackets { … }; with Python, the code block is defined by a colon and indentation.

JS has an alternative way of defining a function called the *function expression*, which you may see in this example:

```
let processStudentData = function( ...){...}
```

There is now a shortened form, which is becoming more popular:

```
let processStudentData = ( ...) => {...}
```

The differences are subtle enough not to worry about for now.[15]

Function parameters is an area where Python's handling is more sophisticated than JavaScript's. As you can see in process_student_data (Section B in Example 2-3),

---

15 For the curious, there's a nice summation in a blog post by Angus Croll (*https://oreil.ly/YyUyx*).

Python allows default arguments for the parameters. In JavaScript, all parameters not used in the function call are declared as *undefined*.

Iterating: for Loops and Functional Alternatives

The C sections in Examples 2-3 and 2-4 shows our first key difference between Python and JavaScript—their handling of for loops.

Python's for loops are simple, intuitive, and effective on any iterator, such as arrays and dicts. One gotcha with dicts is that standard iteration is by key, not items. For example:

```
foo = {'a':3, 'b':2}
for x in foo:
    print(x)
# outputs 'a' 'b'
```

To iterate over the key-value pairs, use the dict's items method like so:

```
for x in foo.items():
    print(x)
# outputs key-value tuples ('a', 3) ('b' 2)
```

You can assign the key-values in the for statement for convenience. For example:

```
for key, value in foo.items():
```

Because Python's for loop works on anything with the correct iterator plumbing, you can do cool things like loop over file lines:

```
for line in open('data.txt'):
    print(line)
```

Coming from Python, JS's for loop is a pretty horrible, unintuitive thing. Here's an example:

```
for(let i in ['a', 'b', 'c']){
  console.log(i)
}
// outputs 1, 2, 3
```

JS's for .. in returns the index of the array's items, not the items themselves. To compound matters, for the Pythonista, the order of iteration is not guaranteed, so the indices could be returned in nonconsecutive order.

Shifting between Python and JS for loops is hardly seamless, demanding you keep on the ball. The good news is that you hardly need to use JS for loops these days. In fact, I almost never find the need. That's because JS has recently acquired some very powerful first-class functional abilities, which have more expressive power and less scope for confusion with Python and, once you get used to them, quickly become indispensable.[16]

Section C in Example 2-4 demonstrates forEach(), one of the *functional* methods available to modern JavaScript arrays.[17] forEach() iterates over the array's items, sending them in turn to an anonymous callback function defined in the first argument, where they can be processed. The true expressive power of these functional methods comes from chaining them (maps, filters, etc.), but already we have a cleaner, more elegant iteration with none of the awkward bookkeeping of old.

The callback function receives the index and the original array as an optional second argument:

```
data.forEach(function(currentValue, index){...})
```

Until recently even iterating over an object's key-value pairs was fairly tricky. Unlike Python's dicts, objects could have inherited properties from the prototyping chain, so you had to use a hasOwnProperty guard to filter these out. You may well come across code like this:

```
let obj = {a:3, b:2, c:4};
for (let prop in obj) {
  if( obj.hasOwnProperty( prop ) ) {
    console.log("o." + prop + " = " + obj[prop]);
  }
}
// out: o.a = 3, o.b = 2, o.c = 4
```

Whereas JS arrays have a set of native functional iterator methods (map, reduce, filter, every, sum, reduceRight), objects—in their guise as pseudodictionaries—don't. The good news is that the object class has recently acquired some useful additional methods that fill this gap. So you can iterate through the key-value pairs using the entries method:

```
let obj = {a:3, b:2, c:4};
for (const [key, value] of Object.entries(object1)) {
  console.log(`${key}: ${value}`); ❶
}
// out: a: 3
//      b: 2 ...
```

 Note the string template form ${foo} for printing variables.

---

16 This is one area where JS beats Python hands-down and which finds many of us wishing for similar functionality in Python.

17 Added with ECMAScript 5 and available on all modern browsers.

Conditionals: if, else, elif, switch

Section C in Examples 2-3 and 2-4 shows Python and JavaScript conditionals in action. Aside from JavaScript's use of brackets, the statements are very similar; the only real difference being Python's extra `elif` keyword, a convenient conjunction of `else if`.

Though much requested, Python does not have the `switch` statement found in most high-level languages. JS does, allowing you to do this:

```
switch(expression){
  case value1:
    // execute if expression === value1
    break; // optional end expression
  case value2:
    //...
  default:
    // if other matches fail
}
```

The good news for Pythonistas is that with 3.10 Python gets a very powerful pattern-matching conditional that can function as a `switch` statement but do a whole lot more (*https://oreil.ly/5x76a*). So we can do this to switch between cases:

```
for value in [value1, value2, value3]:
    match value:
        case value1:
            # do foo
        case value2:
            # do baa
        case value3:
            # do baz
```

File Input and Output

Browser-based JavaScript has no real equivalent of file input and output (I/O), but Python's is as simple as could be:

```
# READING A FILE
f = open("data.txt") # open file for reading

for line in f: # iterate over file lines
    print(line)

lines = f.readlines() # grab all lines in file into array
data = f.read() # read all of file as single string

# WRITING TO A FILE
f = open("data.txt", 'w')
# use 'w' to write, 'a' to append to file
```

```
f.write("this will be written as a line to the file")
f.close() # explicitly close the file
```

One much recommended best practice is to use Python's with, as context manager when opening files. This ensures they are closed automatically when leaving the block, essentially providing syntactic sugar (*https://oreil.ly/DPxaM*) for a try, except, finally block. Here's how to open a file using with, as:

```
with open("data.txt") as f:
    lines = f.readlines()
    ...
```

JavaScript does, however, have the roughly analogous fetch method for fetching a resource from the network, based on its URL. So to fetch a dataset from the website's server, in the *static/data* directory you do this:

```
fetch('/static/data/nobel_winners.json')
  .then(function(response) {
  console.log(response.json())
})
Out:
[{name: 'Albert Einstein', category: 'Physics'...},]
```

The Fetch API (*https://oreil.ly/OFjns*) is thoroughly documented at Mozilla.

Classes and Prototypes

Possibly the cause of more confusion that any other topic is JavaScript's choice of prototypes rather than classical classes as its chief object-oriented programming (OOP) element. This does require some adaption for a Pythonista, where classes are ubiquitous, but in practice this learning curve is, in my experience, short and fairly shallow.

I remember, when I first started my forays into more advanced languages like C++, falling for the promise of OOP, particularly class-based inheritance. Polymorphism was all the rage and shape classes were being subclassed to rectangles and ellipses, which were in turn subclassed to more specialized squares and circles.

It didn't take long to realize that the clean class divisions found in the textbooks were rarely found in real programming and that trying to balance generic and specific APIs quickly became fraught. In this sense, I find composition and mix-ins much more useful as programming concepts than attempts at extended subclassing, and often avoid all these by using functional programming techniques, particularly in JavaScript. Nevertheless, the class/prototype distinction is an obvious difference between the two languages, and the more you understand its nuances, the better you'll code.[18]

Python's classes are fairly simple affairs and, as with most of the language, easy to use. I tend to think of them these days as a handy way to encapsulate data with a convenient API, and rarely extend subclassing beyond one generation. Here's a simple example:

```python
class Citizen(object):

    def __init__(self, name, country): ❶
        self.name = name
        self.country = country

    def __str__(self): ❷
        return f'Citizen {self.name} from {self.country}'

    def print_details(self):
        print(f'Citizen {self.name} from {self.country}')

groucho = Citizen('Groucho M.', 'Freedonia') ❸
print(groucho) # or groucho.print_details()
# Out:
# Citizen Groucho M. from Freedonia
```

❶ Python classes have a number of double-underscored special methods, __init__ being the most common, called when the class instance is created. All instance methods have a first, explicit self argument (you could name it something else, but it's a very bad idea), which refers to the instance. In this case, we use it to set name and country properties.

❷ You can override the class's string method, which is used when the print function is called on an instance.

❸ Creates a new Citizen instance, initialized with name and country.

Python follows a fairly classical pattern of class inheritance. It's easy to do, which is probably why Pythonistas make a lot of use of it. Let's customize the Citizen class to create a (Nobel Prize) Winner class with a couple of extra properties:

---

18 I mentioned to a talented programmer friend that I was faced with the challenge of explaining prototypes to Python programmers, and he pointed out that most JavaScripters could probably do with some pointers too. There's a lot of truth in this and many JSers do manage to be productive by using prototypes in a *classy* way, hacking their way around the edge cases.

```
class Winner(Citizen):

    def __init__(self, name, country, category, year):
        super().__init__(name, country) ❶
        self.category = category
        self.year = year

    def __str__(self):
        return 'Nobel winner %s from %s, category %s, year %s'\
        %(self.name, self.country, self.category,\
        str(self.year))

w = Winner('Albert E.', 'Switzerland', 'Physics', 1921)
w.print_details()
# Out:
# Nobel prizewinner Albert E. from Switzerland, category Physics,
# year 1921
```

❶ We want to reuse the superclass `Citizen`'s `__init__` method, using this `Winner`
    instance as `self`. The `super` method scales the inheritance tree one branch from
    its first argument, supplying the second as instance to the class-instance method.

I think the best article I have read on the key difference between JavaScript's prototypes and classical classes is Reginald Braithwaite's "OOP, JavaScript, and so-called
Classes" (*https://oreil.ly/92Kxk*). This quote sums up the difference between classes
and prototypes as nicely as any I've found:

> The difference between a prototype and a class is similar to the difference between a
> model home and a blueprint for a home.

When you instantiate a C++ or Python class, a blueprint is followed, creating an
object and calling its various constructors in the inheritance tree. In other words, you
start from scratch and build a nice, pristine new class instance.

With JavaScript prototypes, you start with a model home (object) that has rooms
(methods). If you want a new living room, you can just replace the old one with
something in better colors. If you want a new conservatory, then just make an
extension. But rather than building from scratch with a blueprint, you're adapting
and extending an existing object.

With that necessary theory out of the way and the reminder that object inheritance is
useful to know but hardly ubiquitous in dataviz, let's see a simple JavaScript prototype
object in Example 2-5.

Example 2-5. A simple JavaScript object

```javascript
let Citizen = function(name, country){ ❶
  this.name = name; ❷
  this.country = country;
};

Citizen.prototype = { ❸
  logDetails: function(){
    console.log(`Citizen ${this.name} from ${this.country}`);
  }
};

let c = new Citizen('Groucho M.', 'Freedonia'); ❹

c.logDetails();
Out:
Citizen Groucho M. from Freedonia

typeof(c) # object
```

❶ This function is essentially an initializer, invoked by the new operator.

❷ this is an implicit reference to the *calling context* of the function. For now, it behaves as you would expect and even though it looks a little like Python's self, the two are quite different, as we'll see.

❸ The methods specified here will both override any prototypical methods up the inheritance chain and be inherited by any objects derived from Citizen.

❹ new is used to create a new object, set its prototype to that of the Citizen constructor function, and then call the Citizen constructor function on the new object.

JavaScript has recently acquired some syntactic sugar (*https://oreil.ly/43NXG*) allowing classes to be declared. This essentially wraps the object-based form (see Example 2-5) in something more familiar to programmers coming from **class**-based languages like Java and C#. I think it's fair to say that classes haven't really taken off in frontend, browser-based JavaScript, having been usurped somewhat by new frameworks with an emphasis on reusable components (e.g., React, Vue, Svelte). Here's how we would implement the Citizen Object shown in Example 2-5:

```javascript
class Citizen {
  constructor(name, country) {
    this.name = name
    this.country = country
```

```
  }

  logDetails() {
    console.log(`Citizen ${this.name} from ${this.country}`)
  }
}

const c = new Citizen('Groucho M.', 'Freedonia')
```

---

self Versus this

At first glance, it would be easy enough to assume that Python's `self` and JavaScript's `this` are essentially the same, the latter being an implicit version of the former, which is supplied to all class instance methods. Actually, `this` and `self` are significantly different. Let's use our bilingual `Citizen` class to demonstrate.

Python's `self` is a variable supplied to each class method (you can call it anything you like, but it's not advisable), representing the class instance. But `this` is a keyword that refers to the object calling the method. This calling object can be different from the method's object instance, and JavaScript provides the `call`, `bind`, and `apply` function methods (*https://oreil.ly/ONAkj*) to allow you to exploit this fact.

Let's use the `call` method to change the calling object of a `print_details` method and therefore the reference for `this`, used in the method to get the citizen's name:

```
let groucho = new Citizen('Groucho M.', 'Freedonia');
let harpo = new Citizen('Harpo M.', 'Freedonia');

groucho.logDetails.call(harpo);
// Out:
// "Citizen Harpo M. from Freedonia"
```

So JavaScript's `this` is a much more malleable proxy than Python's `self`, offering more freedom but also the responsibility of tracking calling context and, should you use it, making sure new is always used in creating objects.[19]

I included Example 2-5, which shows new in JavaScript object instantiation, because you will run into its use a fair deal. But the syntax is already a little awkward and gets quite a bit worse when you try to do inheritance. ECMAScript 5 introduced the `Object.create` method, a better way to create objects and to implement inheritance. I'd recommend using it in your own code, but new will probably crop up in some third-party libraries.

---

19 This is another reason to use ECMAScript 5's `'use strict;'` injunction, which calls attention to such mistakes.

Let's use `Object.create` to create a `Citizen` and its `Winner` inheritor. To emphasize, JavaScript has many ways to do this, but Example 2-6 shows the cleanest I have found and my personal pattern.

Example 2-6. Prototypical inheritance with `Object.create`

```
let Citizen = { ❶
    setCitizen: function(name, country){
        this.name = name;
        this.country = country;
        return this;
    },
    printDetails: function(){
        console.log('Citizen ' + this.name + ' from ',\
        + this.country);
    }
};

let Winner = Object.create(Citizen);

Winner.setWinner = function(name, country, category, year){
    this.setCitizen(name, country);
    this.category = category;
    this.year = year;
    return this;
};

Winner.logDetails = function(){
    console.log('Nobel winner ' + this.name + ' from ' +
    this.country + ', category ' + this.category + ', year ' +
    this.year);
};

let albert = Object.create(Winner)
    .setWinner('Albert Einstein', 'Switzerland', 'Physics', 1921);

albert.logDetails();
// Out:
// Nobel winner Albert Einstein from Switzerland, category
// Physics, year 1921
```

 `Citizen` is now an object rather than a constructor function. Think of this as the base house for any new buildings such as `Winner`.

To reiterate, prototypical inheritance is not seen that often in JavaScript dataviz, particularly the 800-pound gorilla D3 with its emphasis on declarative and functional patterns, with *raw* unencapsulated data being used to stamp its impression on the web page.

The tricky class/prototype comparison concludes this section on basic syntactic differences. Now let's look at some common patterns seen in dataviz work with Python and JS.

Differences in Practice

The syntactic differences between JS and Python are important to know and are thankfully outweighed by their syntactic similarities. The meat and potatoes of imperative programming, loops, conditionals, data declaration, and manipulation is much the same. This is all the more so in the specialized domain of data processing and data visualization where the languages' first-class functions allow common idioms.

What follows is a less-than-comprehensive list of some important patterns and idioms seen in Python and JavaScript, from the perspective of a data visualizer. Where possible, a translation between the two languages is given.

Method Chaining

A common JavaScript idiom is *method chaining*, popularized by its most-used library, jQuery, and much used in D3. Method chaining involves returning an object from its own method in order to call another method on the result, using dot notation:

```
let sel = d3.select('#viz')
    .attr('width', '600px') ❶
    .attr('height', '400px')
    .style('background', 'lightgray');
```

  The `attr` method returns the D3 selection that called it, which is then used to call another `attr` method.

Method chaining is not much seen in Python, which generally advocates one statement per line in keeping with simplicity and readability.

Enumerating a List

Often it's useful to iterate through a list while keeping track of the item's index. Python has the very handy built-in `enumerate` function for just this reason:

```
names = ['Alice', 'Bob', 'Carol']

for i, n in enumerate(names):
    print(f'{i}: {n}')
Out:
0: Alice
1: Bob
2: Carol
```

JavaScript's list methods, such as forEach and the functional map, reduce, and fil
ter, supply the iterated item and its index to the callback function:

```
let names = ['Alice', 'Bob', 'Carol'];

names.forEach(function(n, i){
    console.log(i + ': ' + n);
});
Out:
0: Alice
1: Bob
2: Carol
```

Tuple Unpacking

One of the first cool tricks Python initiates uses tuple unpacking to switch variables:

```
(a, b) = (b, a)
```

Note that the brackets are optional. This can be put to more practical purpose as
a way of reducing the temporary variables, such as in a Fibonacci function (*https://
oreil.ly/OAT8Q*):

```
def fibonacci(n):
    x, y = 0, 1
    for i in range(n):
        print(x)
        x, y = y, x + y
# fibonacci(6) -> 0, 1, 1, 2, 3, 5
```

If you want to ignore one of the unpacked variables, use an underscore:

```
winner = 'Albert Einstein', 'Physics', 1921, 'Swiss'

name, _, _, nationality = winner ❶
print(f'{name}, {nationality}')
# Albert Einstein, Swiss
```

❶ Python 3 has an * operator (*https://oreil.ly/MFjiR*) that means, in this case, we
could unpack our variables with this: name, *_, nationality = winner

The JavaScript language is adapting rapidly and has recently acquired some very
powerful destructuring abilities (*https://oreil.ly/97rbT*). With the addition of the
spread operator (. . .), this enables some very succinct data manipulation:

```
let a, b, rem ❶

[a, b] = [1, 2]
// swap variables
[a, b] = [b, a]
// using the spread operator
[a, b, ...rem] = [1, 2, 3, 4, 5, 6,] // rem = [3, 4, 5, 6]
```

❶ Unlike in Python, you still need to declare any variables you are going to use.

Collections

One of the most useful Python "batteries" is the `collections` module. This provides some specialized container datatypes to augment Python's standard set. It has a `deque`, which provides a list-like container with fast appends and pops at either end; an `OrderedDict`, which remembers the order entries were added; a `defaultdict`, which provides a factory function to set the dictionary's default; and a `Counter` container for counting hashable objects, among others. I find myself using the last three a lot. Here are a few examples:

```
from collections import Counter, defaultdict, OrderedDict

items = ['F', 'C', 'C', 'A', 'B', 'A', 'C', 'E', 'F']

cntr = Counter(items)
print(cntr)
cntr['C'] -=1
print(cntr)
Out:
Counter({'C': 3, 'A': 2, 'F': 2, 'B': 1, 'E': 1})
Counter({'A': 2, 'C': 2, 'F': 2, 'B': 1, 'E': 1})


d = defaultdict(int) ❶

for item in items:
    d[item] += 1 ❷

d
Out:
defaultdict(<type 'int'>, {'A': 2, 'C': 3, 'B': 1, 'E': 1, 'F': 2})


OrderedDict(sorted(d.items(), key=lambda i: i[1])) ❸
Out:
OrderedDict([('B', 1), ('E', 1), ('A', 2), ('F', 2), ('C', 3)]) ❹
```

❶ Sets the dictionary default to an integer, with value 0 by default.

❷ If the item-key doesn't exist, its value is set to the default of 0 and 1 added to that.

❸ Gets the list of items in the dictionary d as key-value tuple pairs, sorts using the integer value, and then creates an `OrderedDict` with the sorted list.

❹ The `OrderedDict` remembers the (sorted) order of the items as they were added to it.

You can get more details on the collections module in the Python documentation (*https://oreil.ly/IOK7c*).

If you want to replicate some of Python's collections function using more conventional JavaScript libraries, Underscore (or its functionally identical replacement Lodash[20]) is a good place to start. These libraries offer some enhanced functional programming utilities. Let's take a quick look at this very handy tool.

Underscore

Underscore is probably the most popular JavaScript library after the ubiquitous jQuery and offers a bevy of functional programming utilities for the JavaScript dataviz programmer. The easiest way to use Underscore is to use a content delivery network (CDN) to load it remotely (these loads will be cached by your browser, making things very efficient for common libraries), like so:

```
<script src="https://cdnjs.cloudflare.com/ajax/libs/
             underscore.js/1.13.1/underscore-min.js"></script>
```

Underscore has loads of useful functions. There is, for example, a countBy method, which serves the same purpose as the Python's collections counter just discussed:

```
let items = ['F', 'C', 'C', 'A', 'B', 'A', 'C', 'E', 'F'];

_.countBy(items) ❶
Out:
Object {F: 2, C: 3, A: 2, B: 1, E: 1}
```

❶ Now you see why the library is called Underscore.

As we'll now see, the inclusion in modern JavaScript of native functional methods (map, reduce, filter) and a forEach iterator for arrays has made Underscore slightly less indispensable, but it still has some great utilities to augment vanilla JS. With a little chaining, you can produce extremely terse but very powerful code. Underscore was my introduction to functional programming in JavaScript, and the idioms are just as appealing today. Check out Underscore's repertoire of utilities on their website (*https://underscorejs.org*).

Let's have a look at Underscore in action, tackling a more involved task:

```
journeys = [
  {period:'morning', times:[44, 34, 56, 31]},
  {period:'evening', times:[35, 33],},
  {period:'morning', times:[33, 29, 35, 41]},
  {period:'evening', times:[24, 45, 27]},
  {period:'morning', times:[18, 23, 28]}
```

---

20 My personal choice for performance reasons.

```
];
let groups = _.groupBy(journeys, 'period');
let mTimes = _.pluck(groups['morning'], 'times');
mTimes = _.flatten(mTimes); ❶
let average = function(l){
  let sum = _.reduce(l, function(a,b){return a+b},0);
  return sum/l.length;
};
console.log('Average morning time is ' + average(mTimes));
Out:
Average morning time is 33.81818181818182
```

❶ Our array of morning times arrays ([[44, 34, 56, 31], [33...]]) needs to be *flattened* into a single array of numbers.

Functional Array Methods and List Comprehensions

I find myself using Underscore a lot less since the addition, with ECMAScript 5, of functional methods to JavaScript arrays. I don't think I've used a conventional for loop since then, which, given the ugliness of JS for loops, is a very good thing.

Once you get used to processing arrays functionally, it's hard to consider going back. Combined with JS's anonymous functions, it makes for very fluid, expressive programming. It's also an area where method chaining seems very natural. Let's look at a highly contrived example:

```
let nums = [1, 2, 3, 4, 5, 6, 7, 8, 9, 10];

let sum = nums.filter(x => x%2) ❶
  .map(x => x * x) ❷
  .reduce((total, current) => total + current, 0); ❸

console.log('Sum of the odd squares is ' + sum);
```

❶ Filters the list for odd numbers (i.e., returning 1 for the modulus (%) 2 operation).

❷ map produces a new list by applying a function to each member (i.e., [1, 3, 5...] → [1, 9, 25...]).

❸ reduce processes the resultant mapped list in sequence, providing the current (in this case, summed) value (total) and the item value (current). By default, the initial value of the first argument (total) is 0 but we provide it explicitly here, as the second argument.

Python's powerful list comprehensions can emulate the previous example easily enough:

```
nums = range(10) ❶

odd_squares = [x * x for x in nums if x%2] ❷
sum(odd_squares) ❸
Out:
165
```

❶ Python has a handy built-in range function, which can also take a start, end, and step (e.g., range(2, 8, 2) → (2, 4, 6)).

❷ The if condition tests for oddness of x, and any numbers passing this filter are squared and inserted into the list.

❸ Python also has a built-in and often used sum statement.

 Python's list comprehensions can use recursive control structures, such as applying a second for/if expression to the iterated items. Although this can create terse and powerful lines of code, it goes against the grain of Python's readability and I discourage its use. Even simple list comprehensions are less than intuitive and, as much as it appeals to the leet hacker in all of us, you risk creating incomprehensible code.

Python's list comprehensions work well for basic filtering and mapping. They do lack the convenience of JavaScript's anonymous functions (which are fully fledged, with their own scope, control blocks, exception handling, etc.), but there are arguments against the use of anonymous functions. For example, they are not reusable and, being unnamed, they make it hard to follow exceptions and debug. See Ultimate Courses (*https://oreil.ly/7u1j6*) for some persuasive arguments. Having said that, for libraries like D3, replacing the small, throwaway anonymous functions used to set DOM attributes (*https://oreil.ly/hYN27*) and properties with named ones would be far too onerous and would just add to the boilerplate.

Python does have functional lambda expressions, which we'll look at in the next section, but for full functional processing in Python by necessity and JavaScript for best practice, we can use named functions to increase our control scope. For our simple odd-squares example, named functions are a contrivance—but note that they increase the first-glance readability of the list comprehension, which becomes much more important as your functions get more complex:

```
items = [1, 2, 3, 4, 5]

def is_odd(x):
    return x%2

def sq(x):
    return x * x

sum([sq(x) for x in items if is_odd(x)])
```

With JavaScript, a similar contrivance can also increase readability and facilitate DRY code:[21]

```
let isOdd = function(x){ return x%2; };

sum = l.filter(isOdd)
...
```

Map, Reduce, and Filter with Python's Lambdas

Although Python lacks anonymous functions, it does have *lambdas*, which are nameless expressions that take arguments. Though lacking the bells and whistles of JavaScript's anonymous functions, these are a powerful addition to Python's functional programming repertoire, especially when combined with its functional methods.

 Python's functional built-ins (map, reduce, filter methods, and lambda expressions) have a checkered past. It's no secret that the creator of Python wanted to remove them from the language. The clamor of disapproval led to their reluctant preservation. With the recent trend toward functional programming, this looks like a very good thing. They're not perfect but are far better than nothing. And given JavaScript's strong functional emphasis, they're a good way to leverage skills acquired in that language.

Python's lambdas take a number of parameters and return an operation on them, using a colon separator to define the function block, in much the same way that standard Python functions, only pared to the bare essentials and with an implicit return. The following example shows a few lambdas employed in functional programming:

```
from functools import reduce # if using Python 3+

nums = [0, 1, 2, 3, 4, 5, 6, 7, 8, 9]

odds = filter(lambda x: x % 2, nums)
```

---

21 Don't Repeat Yourself (DRY) is a solid coding convention.

```
odds_sq = map(lambda x: x * x, odds)
reduce(lambda x, y: x + y, odds_sq) ❶
Out:
165
```

❶ Here, the reduce method provides two arguments to the lambda, which uses them to return the expression after the colon.

JavaScript Closures and the Module Pattern

One of the key concepts in JavaScript is that of the *closure*, which is essentially a nested function declaration that uses variables declared in an outer (but not global) scope that are *kept alive* after the function is returned. Closures allow for a number of very useful programming patterns and are a common feature of the language.

Let's look at possibly the most common usage of closures and one we've already seen exploited in our module pattern (Example 2-2): exposing a limited API while having access to essentially private member variables.

A simple example of a closure is this little counter:

```
function Counter(inc) {
  let count = 0;
  let add = function() { ❶
    count += inc;
    console.log('Current count: ' + count);
  }
  return add;
}

let inc2 = Counter(2); ❷
inc2(); ❸
Out:
Current count: 2
inc2();
Out:
Current count: 4
```

❶ The add function gets access to the essentially private, outer-scope count and inc variables.

❷ This returns an add function with the closure variables, count (0) and inc (2).

❸ Calling inc2 calls add, updating the *closed* count variable.

We can extend the Counter to add a little API. This technique is the basis of JavaScript modules and many simple libraries, particularly when using script-based

JavaScript.[22] In essence, it selectively exposes public methods while hiding private methods and variables, which is generally seen as good practice in the programming world:

```javascript
function Counter(inc) {
  let count = 0
  let api = {}
  api.add = function() {
    count += inc
    console.log('Current count: ' + count);
  }
  api.sub = function() {
    count -= inc
    console.log('Current count: ' + count)
  }
  api.reset = function() {
    count = 0;
    console.log('Count reset to 0')
  }

  return api
}

cntr = Counter(3);
cntr.add() // Current count: 3
cntr.add() // Current count: 6
cntr.sub() // Current count: 3
cntr.reset() // Count reset to 0
```

Closures have all sorts of uses in JavaScript and I'd recommend getting your head around them—you'll see them a lot as you start investigating other people's code. These are three particularly good web articles that provide a lot of good use cases for closures:

- Mozilla's introduction (*https://oreil.ly/T6itS*)
- "JavaScript Module Pattern: In-Depth" (*https://oreil.ly/0P2EI*) by Ben Cherry
- "Use Cases for JavaScript Closures" (*https://oreil.ly/xz4G5*) by Juriy Zaytsev

Python has closures, but they are not used nearly as much as JavaScript's, perhaps because of a few quirks that, though surmountable, make for some slightly awkward code. To demonstrate, Example 2-7 tries to replicate the previous JavaScript counter.

---

22 Modern JavaScript has proper modules that can import and export encapsulated variables. There is an overhead to using these as they currently require a build phase to make ready for the browser.

Example 2-7. A first-pass attempt at a Python counter closure

```python
def get_counter(inc):
    count = 0
    def add():
        count += inc
        print('Current count: ' + str(count))
    return add
```

If you create a counter with `get_counter` (Example 2-7) and try to run it, you'll get an `UnboundLocalError`:

```python
cntr = get_counter(2)
cntr()
Out:
...
UnboundLocalError: local variable 'count' referenced before
assignment
```

Interestingly, although we can read the value of `count` within the `add` function (comment out the `count += inc` line to try it), attempts to change it throw an error. This is because attempts to assign a value to something in Python assume it is local in scope. There is no `count` local to the `add` function and so an error is thrown.

In Python 3, we can get around the error in Example 2-7 by using the `nonlocal` keyword to tell Python that `count` is in a nonlocal scope:

```python
...
def add():
    nonlocal count
    count += inc
...
```

If you are obliged to use Python 2+ (please try and upgrade), we can use a little dictionary hack to allow mutation of our closed variables:

```python
def get_counter(inc):
    vars = {'count': 0}
    def add():
        vars['count'] += inc
        print('Current count: ' + str(vars['count']))
    return add
```

This hack works because we are not assigning a new value to `vars` but are instead mutating an existing container, which is perfectly valid even if it is out of local scope.

As you can see, with a bit of effort, JavaScripters can transfer their closure skills to Python. The use cases are similar, but Python, being a richer language with lots of useful batteries included, has more options to apply to the same problem. Probably the most common use of closures is in Python's decorators.

Decorators are essentially function wrappers that extend the function's utility without having to alter the function itself. They're a relatively advanced concept, but you can find a user-friendly introduction on The Code Ship website (*https://oreil.ly/Skz8b*).

This concludes my cherry-picked selection of patterns and hacks that I find myself using a lot in dataviz work. You'll doubtless acquire your own, but I hope these give you a leg up.

A Cheat Sheet

As a handy reference guide, Figures 2-2 to 2-7 include a set of cheat sheets to translate basic operations between Python and JavaScript.

```
            JavaScript                              Python

<script src='lib/vizUtils.js" >          import visutils as viz
</script>                                from visutils import gblur

((function(foolib){
...//module pattern
} (window.foolib = window.foolib || {})):
\
var foo; // undefined variables
var  bar=20;                             bar = 20

var foo = function(a, b){                def  foo(a, b=10):
  // clunky defaults, fixed in ES6!        var x = a%b;
  b = typeof b !== 'undefined' ? b : 10;
  var x = a%b;                             ...
...
  return results;                          return result
}
```

Significant whitespace!

Figure 2-2. Some basic syntax

```
            JavaScript                              Python

var x = false;                           x = False
var y = true;                            y = True
var l = []                               l = []

if(!x &&  y == x) {...                   if not x and y == x:

if(l.length === 0){...                   if l: ...
```

Figure 2-3. Booleans

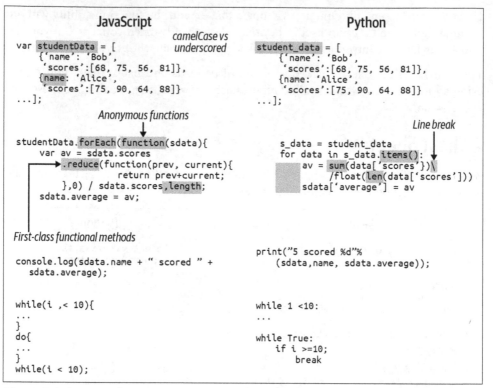

JavaScript — Python

```
                      camelCase vs
                      underscored
var studentData = [                    student_data = [
    {'name': 'Bob',                        {'name': 'Bob',
     'scores':[68, 75, 56, 81]},            'scores':[68, 75, 56, 81]},
    {name: 'Alice',                        {name: 'Alice',
     'scores':[75, 90, 64, 88]}             'scores':[75, 90, 64, 88]}
...];                                   ...];

            Anonymous functions                          Line break

studentData.forEach(function(sdata){   s_data = student_data
    var av = sdata.scores              for data in s_data.items():
      .reduce(function(prev, current){     av = sum(data['scores'})\
            return prev+current;                 /float(len(data['scores']))
      },0) / sdata.scores.length;          sdata['average'] = av
    sdata.average = av;

First-class functional methods

console.log(sdata.name + " scored " +  print("5 scored %d"%
    sdata.average);                         (sdata,name, sdata.average));


while(i ,< 10){                         while 1 <10:
...                                     ...
}
do{                                     while True:
...                                         if i >=10;
}                                               break
while(i < 10);
```

Figure 2-4. Loops and iterations

JavaScript — Python

```
if(x === 'foo'){                        if x === 'foo':
    ...}                                    ...
else if(x === 'bar'){                   elif x === 'bar':
    ...}                                    ...
else{                                   else:
    ...}                                    ...

if(x === foo && y !== bar){...          if x === foo and y !== bar:
                                            ...
if(['foo', 'bar', 'baz']               if s in ['foo', 'bar', 'baz']:
    .indexOf(s) != -1){...                  ...

switch(foo){
  case bar:
    ...
    break;
  case baz: ...
  default:
    return false;
}
```

Figure 2-5. Conditionals

```
                    JavaScript                              Python

va1 l = [1, 2, 3, 4]:                      l = [1, 2, 3, 4]
l.push('foo'): // [...4, 'foo']            l.append('foo') # [...4, 'foo']
l.pop(); // 'foo', l=[..., 4]             l.pop() # 'foo', l=[..., 4]
l.slice(1,3) // [2,3]                       l[1,3] # [2,3]
l.slice(-3, -1) // [2, 3]                   l[-3, -1] # [2, 3]
                                           l[0:4:2] # [1, 3] (stride of 2)
l.map(function(o)[ return o*o;})
// [1, 4, 9, 16]                           [o*o for o in l]
                                           // [1, 4, 9, 16]
d = {1:1, b:2, c:3};
d.a === d[1'] // 1                          d = {'a':1, 'b':2, 'c':3};
d.z // undefined                           d['a'] # 1
                                           d.get['z'] # NoneType
// OLD BROWSERS                            d['z'] # KeyError!
for(key in d){
  if(d.hasOwnProperty(key){
    var item = d[key]:                     for key, value in d.items(): ...
                                           for key in d:
                                           for value in d.values(): ...
// NEW AND BETTER
Object.keys(d).forEach(key, i){
  var item - d[key];
```

Figure 2-6. Containers

```
                    JavaScript                              Python

var Foo = {                                class Foo(object):
  initFoo: function(bar){                    def __init__(self, bar):
    this.bar = bar;                            self.bar = bar
    return this:
  }                                        class Baz(Foo):
};                                           def __init__(self, bar, qux):
                                               self.qux = qux
var Baz = Object.create(Foo);
                                           baz = Baz('answer', 42)
Baz.initBaz = function(bar, qux){          baz.bar # 'answer'
  this.initFoo(bar);
  this.qux - qux;
  return this;
};

var baz = Object.create(Baz)
            .initBaz('answer'. 42);
```

Figure 2-7. Classes and prototypes

Summary

I hope this chapter has shown that JavaScript and Python have a lot of common syntax and that most common idioms and patterns from one of the languages can be expressed in the other without too much fuss. The meat and potatoes of programming—iteration, conditionals, and basic data manipulation—is simple in both languages, and the translation of functions is straightforward. If you can program in one to any degree of competency, the threshold to entry for the other is low. That's the huge appeal of these simple scripting languages, which have a lot of common heritage.

I provided a list of patterns, hacks, and idioms I find myself using frequently in dataviz work. I'm sure this list has its idiosyncrasies, but I've tried to tick the obvious boxes.

Treat this as part tutorial, part reference for the chapters to come. Anything not covered here will be dealt with when introduced.

## CHAPTER 3

Reading and Writing Data with Python

One of the fundamental skills of any data visualizer is the ability to move data around. Whether your data is in an SQL database, a comma-separated value (CSV) file, or in some more esoteric form, you should be comfortable reading the data, converting it, and writing it into a more convenient form if need be. One of Python's great strengths is how easy it makes manipulating data in this way. The focus of this chapter is to bring you up to speed with this essential aspect of our dataviz toolchain.

This chapter is part tutorial, part reference, and sections of it will be referred to in later chapters. If you know the fundamentals of reading and writing Python data, you can cherry-pick parts of the chapter as a refresher.

Easy Does It

I remember when I started programming back in the day (using low-level languages like C) how awkward data manipulation was. Reading from and writing to files was an annoying mixture of boilerplate code, hand-rolled improvisations, and the like. Reading from databases was equally difficult, and as for serializing data, the memories are still painful. Discovering Python was a breath of fresh air. It wasn't a speed demon, but opening a file was pretty much as simple as it could be:

```
file = open('data.txt')
```

Back then, Python made reading from and writing to files refreshingly easy, and its sophisticated string processing made parsing the data in those files just as easy. It even had an amazing module called Pickle that could serialize pretty much any Python object.

In the years since, Python has added robust, mature modules to its standard library that make dealing with CSV and JSON files, the standard for web dataviz work, just as easy. There are also some great libraries for interacting with SQL databases such as SQLAlchemy, my thoroughly recommended go-to. The newer NoSQL databases are also well served. MongoDB is the most popular of these newer document-based databases, and Python's PyMongo library, which is demonstrated later in the chapter, makes interacting with it a relative breeze.

Passing Data Around

A good way to demonstrate how to use the key data-storage libraries is to pass a single data packet among them, reading and writing it as we go. This will give us an opportunity to see in action the key data formats and databases employed by data visualizers.

The data we'll be passing around is probably the most commonly used in web visualizations, a list of dictionary-like objects (see Example 3-1). This dataset is transferred to the browser in JSON form (*https://oreil.ly/JgjAp*), which is, as we'll see, easily converted from a Python dictionary.

Example 3-1. Our target list of data objects

```
nobel_winners = [
 {'category': 'Physics',
  'name': 'Albert Einstein',
  'nationality': 'Swiss',
  'gender': 'male',
  'year': 1921},
 {'category': 'Physics',
  'name': 'Paul Dirac',
  'nationality': 'British',
  'gender': 'male',
  'year': 1933},
 {'category': 'Chemistry',
  'name': 'Marie Curie',
  'nationality': 'Polish',
  'gender': 'female',
  'year': 1911}
]
```

We'll start by creating a CSV file from the Python list shown in Example 3-1 as a demonstration of reading (opening) and writing system files.

The following sections assume you're in a working (root) directory with a *data* subdirectory at hand. You can run the code from a Python interpreter or file.

Working with System Files

In this section, we'll create a CSV file from a Python list of dictionaries (Example 3-1). Typically, you would do this using the csv module, which we'll demonstrate after this section, so this is just a way of demonstrating basic Python file manipulation.

First, let's open a new file, using w as a second argument to indicate we'll be writing data to it.

```
f = open('data/nobel_winners.csv', 'w')
```

Now we'll create our CSV file from the nobel_winners dictionary (Example 3-1):

```
cols = nobel_winners[0].keys() ❶
cols = sorted(cols) ❷

with open('data/nobel_winners.csv', 'w') as f: ❸
    f.write(','.join(cols) + '\n') ❹

    for o in nobel_winners:
        row = [str(o[col]) for col in cols] ❺
        f.write(','.join(row) + '\n')
```

❶ Gets our data columns from the keys of the first object (i.e., ['category', 'name', ...]).

❷ Sorts the columns in alphabetical order.

❸ Uses Python's with statement to guarantee the file is closed on leaving the block or if any exceptions occur.

❹ join creates a concatenated string from a list of strings (cols here), joined by the initial string (i.e., "category,name,..").

❺ Creates a list using the column keys to the objects in nobel_winners.

Now that we've created our CSV file, let's use Python to read it and make sure everything is correct:

```
with open('data/nobel_winners.csv') as f:
    for line in f.readlines():
        print(line)

Out:
category,name,nationality,gender,year
Physics,Albert Einstein,Swiss,male,1921
Physics,Paul Dirac,British,male,1933
Chemistry,Marie Curie,Polish,female,1911
```

As the previous output shows, our CSV file is well formed. Let's use Python's built-in csv module to first read it and then create a CSV file the right way.

CSV, TSV, and Row-Column Data Formats

Comma-separated values (CSV) or their tab-separated cousins (TSV) are probably the most ubiquitous file-based data formats and, as a data visualizer, these will often be the forms you'll receive to work your magic with. Being able to read and write CSV files and their various quirky variants, such as pipe- or semicolon-separated or those using ` in place of the standard double quotes, is a fundamental skill; Python's csv module is capable of doing pretty much all your heavy lifting here. Let's put it through its paces reading and writing our nobel_winners data:

```
nobel_winners = [
 {'category': 'Physics',
  'name': 'Albert Einstein',
  'nationality': 'Swiss',
  'gender': 'male',
  'year': 1921},
  ...
]
```

Writing our nobel_winners data (see Example 3-1) to a CSV file is a pretty simple affair. csv has a dedicated DictWriter class that will turn our dictionaries into CSV rows. The only piece of explicit bookkeeping we have to do is write a header to our CSV file, using the keys of our dictionaries as fields (i.e., "category, name, nationality, gender"):

```
import csv

with open('data/nobel_winners.csv', 'w') as f:
    fieldnames = nobel_winners[0].keys() ❶
    fieldnames = sorted(fieldnames) ❷
    writer = csv.DictWriter(f, fieldnames=fieldnames)
    writer.writeheader() ❸
    for w in nobel_winners:
        writer.writerow(w)
```

❶ You need to explicitly tell the writer which fieldnames to use (in this case, the 'category', 'name', etc., keys).

❷ We'll sort the CSV header fields alphabetically for readability.

❸ Writes the CSV-file header ("category, name,...").

You'll probably be reading CSV files more often than writing them.[1] Let's read back the *nobel_winners.csv* file we just wrote.

---

1 I recommend using JSON over CSV as your preferred data format.

If you just want to use csv as a superior and eminently adaptable file line reader, a couple of lines will produce a handy iterator, which can deliver your CSV rows as lists of strings:

```python
with open('data/nobel_winners.csv') as f:
    reader = csv.reader(f)
    for row in reader: ❶
        print(row)

Out:
['category', 'name', 'nationality', 'gender', 'year']
['Physics', 'Albert Einstein', 'Swiss', 'male', '1921']
['Physics', 'Paul Dirac', 'British', 'male', '1933']
['Chemistry', 'Marie Curie', 'Polish', 'female', '1911']
```

❶ Iterates over the reader object, consuming the lines in the file.

Note that the numbers are read in string form. If you want to manipulate them numerically, you'll need to convert any numeric columns to their respective type, which is integer years in this case.

A more convenient way to consume CSV data is to convert the rows into Python dictionaries. This *record* form is also the one we are using as our conversion target (a list of dicts). csv has a handy DictReader for just this purpose:

```python
import csv

with open('data/nobel_winners.csv') as f:
    reader = csv.DictReader(f)
    nobel_winners = list(reader) ❶

nobel_winners

Out:
[OrderedDict([('category', 'Physics'),
              ('name', 'Albert Einstein'),
              ('nationality', 'Swiss'),
              ('gender', 'male'),
              ('year', '1921')]),
 OrderedDict([('category', 'Physics'),
              ('name', 'Paul Dirac'),
              ('nationality', 'British'),
              ... ])]
```

❶ Inserts all of the reader items into a list.

As the output shows, we just need to cast the dicts year attributes to integers to make nobel_winners conform to the chapter's target data (Example 3-1), thus:

```python
for w in nobel_winners:
    w['year'] = int(w['year'])
```

For more flexibility we can easily create a Python `datetime` from the year column:

```
from datetime import datetime

dt = datetime.strptime('1947', '%Y')
dt
# datetime.datetime(1947, 1, 1, 0, 0)
```

The `csv` readers don't infer datatypes from your file, and instead interpret everything as a string. pandas, Python's preeminent data-hacking library, will try to guess the correct type of the data columns, usually successfully. We'll see this in action in the later dedicated pandas chapters.

`csv` has a few useful arguments to help parse members of the CSV family:

dialect

By default, `'excel'`; specifies a set of dialect-specific parameters. `excel-tab` is a sometimes-used alternative.

delimiter

Files are usually comma-separated, but they could use |, : or ' ' instead.

quotechar

By default, double quotes are used, but you occasionally find | or ` instead.

You can find the full set of `csv` parameters in the online Python docs (*https://oreil.ly/ 9zZvt*).

Now that we've successfully written and read our target data using the `csv` module, let's pass on our CSV-derived `nobel_winners` dict to the `json` module.

JSON

In this section, we'll write and read our `nobel_winners` data using Python's `json` module. Let's remind ourselves of the data we're using:

```
nobel_winners = [
 {'category': 'Physics',
  'name': 'Albert Einstein',
  'nationality': 'Swiss',
  'gender': 'male',
  'year': 1921},
  ...
 ]
```

For data primitives such as strings, integers, and floats, Python dictionaries are easily saved (or *dumped*, in the JSON vernacular) into JSON files, using the `json` module. The dump method takes a Python container and a file pointer, saving the former to the latter:

```
import json

with open('data/nobel_winners.json', 'w') as f:
    json.dump(nobel_winners, f)

open('data/nobel_winners.json').read()

Out: '[{"category": "Physics", "name": "Albert Einstein",
"gender": "male", "year": 1921,
"nationality": "Swiss"}, {"category": "Physics",
"nationality": "British", "year": 1933, "name": "Paul Dirac",
"gender": "male"}, {"category": "Chemistry", "nationality":
"Polish", "year": 1911, "name": "Marie Curie", "gender":
"female"}]'
```

Reading (or loading) a JSON file is just as easy. We just pass the opened JSON file to the json module's load method:

```
import json

with open('data/nobel_winners.json') as f:
    nobel_winners = json.load(f)

nobel_winners
Out:
[{'category': 'Physics',
  'name': 'Albert Einstein',
  'nationality': 'Swiss',
  'gender': 'male',
  'year': 1921}, ❶
... }]
```

❶ Note that, unlike in our CSV file conversion, the integer type of the year column is preserved.

json has the methods loads and dumps, which are counterparts to the file access methods, loading JSON strings to Python containers and dumping Python containers to JSON strings.

Dealing with Dates and Times

Trying to dump a datetime object to json produces a TypeError:

```
from datetime import datetime

json.dumps(datetime.now())
Out:
...
TypeError: datetime.datetime(2021, 9, 13, 10, 25, 52, 586792)
is not JSON serializable
```

When serializing simple datatypes such as strings or numbers, the default `json` encoders and decoders are fine. But for more specialized data such as dates, you will need to do your own encoding and decoding. This isn't as hard as it sounds and quickly becomes routine. Let's first look at encoding your Python `datetimes` (*https://oreil.ly/aHI4h*) into sensible JSON strings.

The easiest way to encode Python data containing `datetimes` is to create a custom encoder like the one shown in Example 3-2, which is provided to the `json.dumps` method as a `cls` argument. This encoder is applied to each object in your data in turn and converts dates or datetimes to their ISO-format string (see "Dealing with Dates, Times, and Complex Data" on page 75).

Example 3-2. Encoding a Python datetime to JSON

```
import datetime
import json


class JSONDateTimeEncoder(json.JSONEncoder):     ❶
    def default(self, obj):
        if isinstance(obj, (datetime.date, datetime.datetime)):     ❷
            return obj.isoformat()
        else:
            return json.JSONEncoder.default(self, obj)

def dumps(obj):
    return json.dumps(obj, cls=JSONDateTimeEncoder)     ❸
```

❶ Subclasses a `JSONEncoder` in order to create a customized date-handling one.

❷ Tests for a `datetime` object and if true, returns the `isoformat` of any dates or datetimes (e.g., 2021-11-16T16:41:14.650802).

❸ Uses the `cls` argument to set a custom date encoder.

Let's see how our new `dumps` method copes with some `datetime` data:

```
now_str = dumps({'time': datetime.datetime.now()})
now_str
Out:
'{"time": "2021-11-16T16:41:14.650802"}'
```

The `time` field is correctly converted into an ISO-format string, ready to be decoded into a JavaScript `Date` object (see "Dealing with Dates, Times, and Complex Data" on page 75 for a demonstration).

While you could write a generic decoder to cope with date strings in arbitrary JSON files,[2] it's probably not advisable. Date strings come in so many weird and wonderful varieties that this is a job best done by hand on what is pretty much always a known dataset.

The venerable `strptime` method, part of the `datetime.datetime` package, is good for the job of turning a time string in a known format into a Python `datetime` instance:

```
In [0]: from datetime import datetime

In [1]: time_str = '2021/01/01 12:32:11'

In [2]: dt = datetime.strptime(time_str, '%Y/%m/%d %H:%M:%S') ❶

In [3]: dt
Out[2]: datetime.datetime(2021, 1, 1, 12, 32, 11)
```

❶ `strptime` tries to match the time string to a format string using various directives such as `%Y` (year with century) and `%H` (hour as a zero-padded decimal number). If successful, it creates a Python `datetime` instance. See the Python docs (*https://oreil.ly/Fi40k*) for a full list of the directives available.

If `strptime` is fed a time string that does not match its format, it throws a handy `ValueError`:

```
dt = datetime.strptime('1/2/2021 12:32:11', '%Y/%m/%d %H:%M:%S')
----------------------------------------------------------------
ValueError                    Traceback (most recent call last)
<ipython-input-111-af657749a9fe> in <module>()
----> 1 dt = datetime.strptime('1/2/2021 12:32:11',\
      '%Y/%m/%d %H:%M:%S')
...
ValueError: time data '1/2/2021 12:32:11' does not match
            format '%Y/%m/%d %H:%M:%S'
```

So to convert date fields of a known format into `datetimes` for a `data` list of dictionaries, you could do something like this:

```
data = [
    {'id': 0, 'date': '2020/02/23 12:59:05'},
    {'id': 1, 'date': '2021/11/02 02:32:00'},
    {'id': 2, 'date': '2021/23/12 09:22:30'},
]

for d in data:
    try:
        d['date'] = datetime.strptime(d['date'],\
```

---

2 The Python module `dateutil` has a parser that will parse most dates and times sensibly, and might be a good basis for this.

```
            '%Y/%m/%d %H:%M:%S')
    except ValueError:
        print('Oops! - invalid date for ' + repr(d))
# Out:
# Oops! - invalid date for {'id': 2, 'date': '2021/23/12 09:22:30'}
```

Now that we've dealt with the two most popular data file formats, let's shift to the big guns and see how to read our data from and write our data to SQL and NoSQL databases.

SQL

For interacting with an SQL database, SQLAlchemy is the most popular and, in my opinion, best Python library. It allows you to use raw SQL instructions if speed and efficiency is an issue, but also provides a powerful object-relational mapping (ORM) that allows you to operate on SQL tables using a high-level, Pythonic API, treating them essentially as Python classes.

Reading and writing data using SQL while allowing the user to treat that data as a Python container is a complicated process, and though SQLAlchemy is considerably more user-friendly than a low-level SQL engine, it is still a fairly complex library. I'll cover the basics here, using our data as a target, but encourage you to spend a little time reading some of the rather excellent documentation on SQLAlchemy (*https://oreil.ly/mCHr8*). Let's remind ourselves of the nobel_winners dataset we're aiming to write and read:

```
nobel_winners = [
  {'category': 'Physics',
   'name': 'Albert Einstein',
   'nationality': 'Swiss',
   'gender': 'male',
   'year': 1921},
   ...
]
```

Let's first write our target data to an SQLite file using SQLAlchemy, starting by creating the database engine.

Creating the Database Engine

The first thing you need to do when starting an SQLAlchemy session is to create a database engine. This engine will establish a connection with the database in question and perform any conversions needed to the generic SQL instructions generated by SQLAlchemy and the data being returned.

There are engines for pretty much every popular database, as well as a *memory* option, which holds the database in RAM, allowing fast access for testing.[3] The great thing about these engines is that they are interchangeable, which means you could develop your code using the convenient file-based SQLite database and then switch during production to something a little more industrial, such as PostgreSQL, by changing a single config string. Check SQLAlchemy (*https://oreil.ly/QmIj6*) for the full list of engines available.

The form for specifying a database URL is:

```
dialect+driver://username:password@host:port/database
```

So, to connect to a 'nobel_winners' MySQL database running on localhost requires something like the following. Note that create_engine does not actually make any SQL requests at this point, but merely sets up the framework for doing so:[4]

```
engine = create_engine(
        'mysql://kyran:mypsswd@localhost/nobel_winners')
```

We'll use a file-based SQLite database, setting the echo argument to True, which will output any SQL instructions generated by SQLAlchemy. Note the use of three backslashes after the colon:

```
from sqlalchemy import create_engine

engine = create_engine(
        'sqlite:///data/nobel_winners.db', echo=True)
```

SQLAlchemy offers various ways to engage with databases, but I recommend using the more recent declarative style unless there are good reasons to go with something more low-level and fine-grained. In essence, with declarative mapping, you subclass your Python SQL-table classes from a base, and SQLAlchemy introspects their structure and relationships. See SQLAlchemy (*https://oreil.ly/q3IZf*) for more details.

Defining the Database Tables

We first create a Base class using declarative_base. This base will be used to create table classes, from which SQLAlchemy will create the database's table schemas. You can use these table classes to interact with the database in a fairly Pythonic fashion:

```
from sqlalchemy.ext.declarative import declarative_base

Base = declarative_base()
```

---

3 On a cautionary note, it is probably a bad idea to use different database configurations for testing and production.

4 See details on SQLAlchemy (*https://oreil.ly/winYu*) of this *lazy initialization*.

Note that most SQL libraries require you to formally define table schemas. This is in contrast to such schema-less NoSQL variants as MongoDB. We'll take a look at the Dataset library later in this chapter, which enables schemaless SQL.

Using this `Base`, we define our various tables—in our case, a single `Winner` table. Example 3-3 shows how to subclass `Base` and use SQLAlchemy's datatypes to define a table schema. Note the `__tablename__` member, which will be used to name the SQL table and as a keyword to retrieve it, and the optional custom `__repr__` method, which will be used when printing a table row.

Example 3-3. Defining an SQL database table

```
from sqlalchemy import Column, Integer, String, Enum
// ...

class Winner(Base):
    __tablename__ = 'winners'
    id = Column(Integer, primary_key=True)
    category = Column(String)
    name = Column(String)
    nationality = Column(String)
    year = Column(Integer)
    gender = Column(Enum('male', 'female'))
    def __repr__(self):
        return "<Winner(name='%s', category='%s', year='%s')>"\
%(self.name, self.category, self.year)
```

Having declared our `Base` subclass in Example 3-3, we supply its `metadata create_all` method with our database engine to create our database.[5] Because we set the echo argument to `True` when creating the engine, we can see the SQL instructions generated by SQLAlchemy from the command line:

```
Base.metadata.create_all(engine)

2021-11-16 17:58:34,700 INFO sqlalchemy.engine.Engine BEGIN (implicit)
...
CREATE TABLE winners (
        id INTEGER NOT NULL,
        category VARCHAR,
        name VARCHAR,
        nationality VARCHAR,
        year INTEGER,
        gender VARCHAR(6),
        PRIMARY KEY (id)
```

---

5 This assumes the database doesn't already exist. If it does, `Base` will be used to create new insertions and to interpret retrievals.

```
)...
2021-11-16 17:58:34,742 INFO sqlalchemy.engine.Engine COMMIT
```

With our new winners table declared, we can start adding winner instances to it.

Adding Instances with a Session

Now that we have created our database, we need a session to interact with:

```
from sqlalchemy.orm import sessionmaker

Session = sessionmaker(bind=engine)
session = Session()
```

We can now use our Winner class to create instances and table rows and add them to the session:

```
albert = Winner(**nobel_winners[0]) ❶
session.add(albert)
session.new ❷
Out:
IdentitySet([<Winner(name='Albert Einstein', category='Physics',
            year='1921')>])
```

❶ Python's handy ** operator unpacks our first nobel_winners member into key-value pairs: (name='Albert Einstein', category='Physics'...).

❷ new is the set of any items that have been added to this session.

Note that all database insertions and deletions take place in Python. It's only when we use the commit method that the database is altered.

 Use as few commits as possible, allowing SQLAlchemy to work its magic behind the scenes. When you commit, your various database manipulations should be summarized by SQLAlchemy and communicated in an efficient fashion. Commits involve establishing a database handshake and negotiating transactions, which is often a slow process and one you want to limit as much as possible, leveraging SQLAlchemy's bookkeeping abilities to full advantage.

As the new method shows, we have added a Winner to the session. We can remove the object using expunge, leaving an empty IdentitySet:

```
session.expunge(albert) ❶
session.new
Out:
IdentitySet([])
```

❶ Removes the instance from the session (there is an expunge_all method that removes all new objects added to the session).

At this point, no database insertions or deletions have taken place. Let's add all the members of our nobel_winners list to the session and commit them to the database:

```
winner_rows = [Winner(**w) for w in nobel_winners]
session.add_all(winner_rows)
session.commit()
Out:
INFO:sqlalchemy.engine.base.Engine:BEGIN (implicit)
...
INFO:sqlalchemy.engine.base.Engine:INSERT INTO winners (name,
category, year, nationality, gender) VALUES (?, ?, ?, ?, ?)
INFO:sqlalchemy.engine.base.Engine:('Albert Einstein',
'Physics', 1921, 'Swiss', 'male')
...
INFO:sqlalchemy.engine.base.Engine:COMMIT
```

Now that we've committed our nobel_winners data to the database, let's see what we can do with it and how to re-create the target list in Example 3-1.

Querying the Database

To access data, you use the session's query method, the result of which can be filtered, grouped, and intersected, allowing the full range of standard SQL data retrieval. You can check out available querying methods in the SQLAlchemy docs (*https://oreil.ly/2rEB4*). For now, I'll quickly run through some of the most common queries on our Nobel dataset.

Let's first count the number of rows in our winners table:

```
session.query(Winner).count()
Out:
3
```

Next, let's retrieve all Swiss winners:

```
result = session.query(Winner).filter_by(nationality='Swiss')  ❶
list(result)
Out:
[<Winner(name='Albert Einstein', category='Physics',\
  year='1921')>]
```

❶ filter_by uses keyword expressions; its SQL expressions counterpart is filter —for example, filter(Winner.nationality == *Swiss*). Note the Boolean equivalence == used in filter.

Now let's get all non-Swiss physics winners:

```
result = session.query(Winner).filter(\
            Winner.category == 'Physics', \
            Winner.nationality != 'Swiss')
list(result)
Out:
[<Winner(name='Paul Dirac', category='Physics', year='1933')>]
```

Here's how to get a row based on ID number:

```
session.query(Winner).get(3)
Out:
<Winner(name='Marie Curie', category='Chemistry', year='1911')>
```

Now let's retrieve winners ordered by year:

```
res = session.query(Winner).order_by('year')
list(res)
Out:
[<Winner(name='Marie Curie', category='Chemistry',\
year='1911')>,
 <Winner(name='Albert Einstein', category='Physics',\
year='1921')>,
 <Winner(name='Paul Dirac', category='Physics', year='1933')>]
```

To reconstruct our target list requires a little effort when converting the Winner objects returned by our session query into Python dicts. Let's write a little function to create a dict from an SQLAlchemy class. We'll use a little table introspection to get the column labels (see Example 3-4).

Example 3-4. Converts an SQLAlchemy instance to a dict

```
def inst_to_dict(inst, delete_id=True):
    dat = {}
    for column in inst.__table__.columns: ❶
        dat[column.name] = getattr(inst, column.name)
    if delete_id:
        dat.pop('id') ❷
    return dat
```

❶ Accesses the instance's table class to get a list of column objects.

❷ If delete_id is true, remove the SQL primary ID field.

We can use Example 3-4 to reconstruct our nobel_winners target list:

```
winner_rows = session.query(Winner)
nobel_winners = [inst_to_dict(w) for w in winner_rows]
nobel_winners
Out:
[{'category': 'Physics',
```

```
        'name': 'Albert Einstein',
        'nationality': 'Swiss',
        'gender': 'male',
        'year': 1921},
    ...
    ]
```

You can update database rows easily by changing the property of their reflected objects:

```
marie = session.query(Winner).get(3) ❶
marie.nationality = 'French'
session.dirty ❷
Out:
IdentitySet([<Winner(name='Marie Curie', category='Chemistry',
year='1911')>])
```

❶   Fetches Marie Curie, nationality Polish.

❷   dirty shows any changed instances not yet committed to the database.

Let's commit Marie's changes and check that her nationality has changed from Polish to French:

```
session.commit()
Out:
INFO:sqlalchemy.engine.base.Engine:UPDATE winners SET
nationality=? WHERE winners.id = ?
INFO:sqlalchemy.engine.base.Engine:('French', 3)
...

session.dirty
Out:
IdentitySet([])

session.query(Winner).get(3).nationality
Out:
'French'
```

In addition to updating database rows, you can delete the results of a query:

```
session.query(Winner).filter_by(name='Albert Einstein').delete()
Out:
INFO:sqlalchemy.engine.base.Engine:DELETE FROM winners WHERE
winners.name = ?
INFO:sqlalchemy.engine.base.Engine:('Albert Einstein',)
1

list(session.query(Winner))
Out:
[<Winner(name='Paul Dirac', category='Physics', year='1933')>,
 <Winner(name='Marie Curie', category='Chemistry',\
 year='1911')>]
```

You can also drop the whole table if required, using the declarative class's __table__ attribute:

```
Winner.__table__.drop(engine)
```

In this section, we've dealt with a single winners table, without any foreign keys or relationship to any other tables, akin to a CSV or JSON file. SQLAlchemy adds the same level of convenience in dealing with many-to-one, one-to-many, and other database table relationships as it does to basic querying using implicit joins, by supplying the query method with more than one table class or explicitly using the query's join method. Check out the examples in the SQLAlchemy docs (*https://oreil.ly/6KFCf*) for more details.

Easier SQL with Dataset

One library I've found myself using a fair deal recently is Dataset (*https://oreil.ly/aGqTL*), a module designed to make working with SQL databases a little easier and more Pythonic than existing powerhouses like SQLAlchemy.[6] Dataset tries to provide the same degree of convenience you get when working with schema-less NoSQL databases such as MongoDB by removing a lot of the formal boilerplate, such as schema definitions, which are demanded by the more conventional libraries. Dataset is built on top of SQLAlchemy, which means it works with pretty much all major databases and can exploit the power, robustness, and maturity of that best-of-breed library. Let's see how it deals with reading and writing our target dataset (from Example 3-1).

Let's use the SQLite *nobel_winners.db* database we've just created to put Dataset through its paces. First, we connect to our SQL database, using the same URL/file format as SQLAlchemy:

```
import dataset

db = dataset.connect('sqlite:///data/nobel_winners.db')
```

To get our list of winners, we grab a table from our db database, using its name as a key, and then use the find method without arguments to return all winners:

```
wtable = db['winners']
winners = wtable.find()
winners = list(winners)
winners
#Out:
#[OrderedDict([(u'id', 1), ('name', 'Albert Einstein'),
# ('category', 'Physics'), ('year', 1921), ('nationality',
```

---

6 Dataset's official motto is "Databases for lazy people." It is not part of the standard Anaconda package, so you'll want to install it using pip from the command line: $ pip install dataset.

```
# 'Swiss'), ('gender', 'male')]), OrderedDict([('id', 2),
# ('name', 'Paul Dirac'), ('category', 'Physics'),
# ('year', 1933), ('nationality', 'British'), ('gender',
# 'male')]), OrderedDict([('id', 3), ('name', 'Marie
# Curie'), ('category', 'Chemistry'), ('year', 1911),
# ('nationality', 'Polish'), ('gender', 'female')])]
```

Note that the instances returned by Dataset's find method are OrderedDicts. These useful containers are an extension of Python's dict class and behave just like dictionaries except that they remember the order in which items were inserted, meaning you can guarantee the result of iteration, pop the last item inserted, and more. This is a very handy additional functionality.

 One of the most useful Python "batteries" for data manipulators is collections, which is where Dataset's OrderedDicts come from. The defaultdict and Counter classes are particularly useful. Check out what's available in the Python docs (*https://oreil.ly/Vh4EF*).

Let's re-create our winners table with Dataset, first dropping the existing one:

```
wtable = db['winners']
wtable.drop()

wtable = db['winners']
wtable.find()
#Out:
#[]
```

To re-create our dropped winners table, we don't need to define a schema as with SQLAlchemy (see "Defining the Database Tables" on page 63). Dataset will infer that from the data we add, doing all the SQL creation implicitly. This is the kind of convenience one is used to when working with collection-based NoSQL databases. Let's use our nobel_winners dataset (Example 3-1) to insert some winner dictionaries. We use a database transaction and the with statement to efficiently insert our objects and then commit them:[7]

```
with db as tx:  ❶
    tx['winners'].insert_many(nobel_winners)
```

❶ Use the with statement to guarantee the transaction tx is committed to the database.

Let's check that everything has gone well:

---

7 See this documentation (*https://oreil.ly/vqvbv*) for further details of how to use transactions to group updates.

```
list(db['winners'].find())
Out:
[OrderedDict([('id', 1), ('name', 'Albert Einstein'),
('category', 'Physics'), ('year', 1921), ('nationality',
'Swiss'), ('gender', 'male')]),
...
]
```

The winners have been correctly inserted and their order of insertion preserved by the OrderedDict.

Dataset is great for basic SQL-based work, particularly retrieving data you might wish to process or visualize. For more advanced manipulation, it allows you to drop down into SQLAlchemy's core API using the query method.

Now that we've covered the basics of working with SQL databases, let's see how Python makes working with the most popular NoSQL database just as painless.

MongoDB

Document-centric datastores like MongoDB offer a lot of convenience to data wranglers. As with all tools, there are good and bad use cases for NoSQL databases. If you have data that has already been refined and processed and don't anticipate needing SQL's powerful query language based on optimized table joins, MongoDB will probably prove easier to work with initially. MongoDB is a particularly good fit for web dataviz because it uses binary JSON (BSON) as its data format. An extension of JSON, BSON can deal with binary data and datetime objects, and plays very nicely with JavaScript.

Let's remind ourselves of the target dataset we're aiming to write and read:

```
nobel_winners = [
 {'category': 'Physics',
  'name': 'Albert Einstein',
  'nationality': 'Swiss',
  'gender': 'male',
  'year': 1921},
  ...
 ]
```

Creating a MongoDB collection with Python is the work of a few lines:

```
from pymongo import MongoClient

client = MongoClient() ❶
db = client.nobel_prize ❷
coll = db.winners ❸
```

❶ Creates a Mongo client, using the default host and ports.

---

❷ Creates or accesses the nobel_prize database.

❸ If a winners collection exists, this will retrieve it; otherwise (as in our case), it creates it.

Using Constants for MongoDB Access

Accessing and creating a MongoDB database with Python involves the same operation, using dot notation and square-bracket key access:

```
db = client.nobel_prize
db = client['nobel_prize']
```

This is all very convenient, but it means a single spelling mistake, such as noble_prize, could both create an unwanted database and cause future operations to fail to update the correct one. For this reason, I advise using constant strings to access your MongoDB databases and collections:

```
DB_NOBEL_PRIZE = 'nobel_prize'
COLL_WINNERS = 'winners'

db = client[DB_NOBEL_PRIZE]
coll = db[COLL_WINNERS]
```

MongoDB databases run on localhost port 27017 by default but could be anywhere on the web. They also take an optional username and password. Example 3-5 shows how to create a simple utility function to access our database, with standard defaults.

Example 3-5. Accessing a MongoDB database

```
from pymongo import MongoClient

def get_mongo_database(db_name, host='localhost',\
                       port=27017, username=None, password=None):
    """ Get named database from MongoDB with/out authentication """
    # make Mongo connection with/out authentication
    if username and password:
        mongo_uri = 'mongodb://%s:%s@%s/%s'\    ❶
        (username, password, host, db_name)
        conn = MongoClient(mongo_uri)
    else:
        conn = MongoClient(host, port)

    return conn[db_name]
```

❶ We specify the database name in the MongoDB URI (Uniform Resource Identifier) as the user may not have general privileges for the database.

We can now create a Nobel Prize database and add our target dataset (Example 3-1). Let's first get a winners collection, using the string constants for access:

```
db = get_mongo_database(DB_NOBEL_PRIZE)
coll = db[COLL_WINNERS]
```

Inserting our Nobel Prize dataset is then as easy as can be:

```
coll.insert_many(nobel_winners)
coll.find()
Out:
[{'_id': ObjectId('61940b7dc454e79ffb14cd25'),
  'category': 'Physics',
  'name': 'Albert Einstein',
  'nationality': 'Swiss',
  'year': 1921,
  'gender': 'male'},
 {'_id': ObjectId('61940b7dc454e79ffb14cd26'), ... }
 ...]
```

The resulting array of ObjectIds can be used for future retrieval, but MongoDB has already left its stamp on our nobel_winners list, adding a hidden id property.[8]

 MongoDB's ObjectIds have quite a bit of hidden functionality, being a lot more than a simple random identifier. You can, for example, get the generation time of the ObjectId, which gives you access to a handy timestamp:

```
import bson
oid = bson.ObjectId()
oid.generation_time
Out: datetime.datetime(2015, 11, 4, 15, 43, 23...
```

Find the full details in the MongoDB BSON documentation (*https://oreil.ly/NBwsk*).

Now that we've got some items in our winners collection, MongoDB makes finding them very easy, with its find method taking a dictionary query:

```
res = coll.find({'category':'Chemistry'})
list(res)
Out:
[{'_id': ObjectId('55f8326f26a7112e547879d6'),
  'category': 'Chemistry',
  'name': 'Marie Curie',
  'nationality': 'Polish',
  'gender': 'female',
  'year': 1911}]
```

---

8 One of the cool things about MongoDB is that the ObjectIds are generated on the client side, removing the need to quiz the database for them.

There are a number of special dollar-prefixed operators that allow for sophisticated querying. Let's find all the winners after 1930 using the $gt (greater-than) operator:

```
res = coll.find({'year': {'$gt': 1930}})
list(res)
Out:
[{'_id': ObjectId('55f8326f26a7112e547879d5'),
  'category': 'Physics',
  'name': 'Paul Dirac',
  'nationality': 'British',
  'gender': 'male',
  'year': 1933}]
```

You can also use a Boolean expression, for instance, to find all winners after 1930 or all female winners:

```
res = coll.find({'$or':[{'year': {'$gt': 1930}},\
{'gender':'female'}]})
list(res)
Out:
[{'_id': ObjectId('55f8326f26a7112e547879d5'),
  'category': 'Physics',
  'name': 'Paul Dirac',
  'nationality': 'British',
  'gender': 'male',
  'year': 1933},
 {'_id': ObjectId('55f8326f26a7112e547879d6'),
  'category': 'Chemistry',
  'name': 'Marie Curie',
  'nationality': 'Polish',
  'gender': 'female',
  'year': 1911}]
```

You can find the full list of available query expressions in the MongoDB documentation (*https://oreil.ly/1D2Sr*).

As a final test, let's turn our new winners collection back into a Python list of dictionaries. We'll create a utility function for the task:

```
def mongo_coll_to_dicts(dbname='test', collname='test',\
                        query={}, del_id=True, **kw):  ❶

    db = get_mongo_database(dbname, **kw)
    res = list(db[collname].find(query))

    if del_id:
        for r in res:
            r.pop('_id')

    return res
```

❶ An empty `query dict {}` will find all documents in the collection. `del_id` is a flag to remove MongoDB's `ObjectIds` from the items by default.

We can now create our target dataset:

```
mongo_coll_to_dicts(DB_NOBEL_PRIZE, COLL_WINNERS)
Out:
[{'category': 'Physics',
  'name': 'Albert Einstein',
  'nationality': 'Swiss',
  'gender': 'male',
  'year': 1921},
  ...
]
```

MongoDB's schema-less databases are great for fast prototyping in solo work or small teams. There will probably come a point, particularly with large codebases, when a formal schema becomes a useful reference and sanity check; when you are choosing a data model, the ease with which document forms can be adapted is a bonus. Being able to pass Python dictionaries as queries to PyMongo and having access to client-side generated `ObjectIds` are a couple of other conveniences.

We've now passed the `nobel_winners` data in Example 3-1 through all our required file formats and databases. Let's consider the special case of dealing with dates and times before summing up.

Dealing with Dates, Times, and Complex Data

The ability to deal comfortably with dates and times is fundamental to dataviz work but can be quite tricky. There are many ways to represent a date or datetime as a string, each one requiring a separate encoding or decoding. For this reason it's good to settle on one format in your own work and encourage others to do the same. I recommend using the International Standard Organization (ISO) 8601 time format (*https://oreil.ly/HePpN*) as your string representation for dates and times, and using the Coordinated Universal Time (UTC) form (*https://oreil.ly/neP2I*).[9] Here are a few examples of ISO 8601 date and datetime strings:

2021-09-23	A date (Python/C format code `'%Y-%m-%d'`)
2021-09-23T16:32:35Z	A UTC (*Z* after time) date and time (`'T%H:%M:%S'`)
2021-09-23T16:32+02:00	A positive two-hour (+02:00) offset from UTC (e.g., Central European Time)

---

9 To get the actual local time from UTC, you can store a time zone offset or, better still, derive it from a geocoordinate; this is because time zones do not follow lines of longitude very exactly.

Note the importance of being prepared to deal with different time zones. These are not always on lines of longitude (see Wikipedia's Time Zone entry (*https://oreil.ly/ NZyE4*)), and often the best way to derive an accurate time is by using UTC time plus a geographic location.

ISO 8601 is the standard used by JavaScript and is easy to work with in Python. As web data visualizers, our key concern is in creating a string representation that can be passed between Python and JavaScript using JSON and encoded and decoded easily at both ends.

Let's take a date and time in the shape of a Python `datetime`, convert it into a string, and then see how that string can be consumed by JavaScript.

First, we produce our Python `datetime`:

```
from datetime import datetime

d = datetime.now()
d.isoformat()
Out:
'2021-11-16T22:55:48.738105'
```

This string can then be saved to JSON or CSV, read by JavaScript, and used to create a Date object:

```
// JavaScript
d = new Date('2021-11-16T22:55:48.738105')
> Tue Nov 16 2021 22:55:48 GMT+0000 (Greenwich Mean Time)
```

We can return the datetime to ISO 8601 string form with the `toISOString` method:

```
// JavaScript
d.toISOString()
> '2021-11-16T22:55:48.738Z'
```

Finally, we can read the string back into Python.

If you know that you're dealing with an ISO-format time string, Python's `dateutil` module should do the job.[10] But you'll probably want to sanity check the result:

```
from dateutil import parser

d = parser.parse('2021-11-16T22:55:48.738Z')
d
Out:
datetime.datetime(2021, 11, 16, 22, 55, 48, 738000,\
tzinfo=tzutc())
```

---

10 To install, just run `pip install python-dateutil`. `dateutil` is a pretty powerful extension of Python's datetime; check it out on Read the Docs (*https://oreil.ly/y6YWS*).

Note that we've lost some resolution in the trip from Python to JavaScript and back again, the latter dealing in milliseconds, not microseconds. This is unlikely to be an issue in any dataviz work but is good to bear in mind just in case some strange temporal errors occur.

Summary

This chapter aimed to make you comfortable using Python to move data around the various file formats and databases that a data visualizer might expect to bump into. Using databases effectively and efficiently is a skill that takes a while to learn, but you should now be comfortable with basic reading and writing for the large majority of dataviz use cases.

Now that we have the vital lubrication for our dataviz toolchain, let's get up to scratch on the basic web development skills you'll need for the chapters ahead.

## CHAPTER 4

Webdev 101

This chapter introduces the core web-development knowledge you will need to understand the web pages you scrape for data and to structure those you want to deliver as the skeleton of your JavaScripted visualizations. As you'll see, a little knowledge goes a long way in modern webdev, particularly when your focus is building self-contained visualizations and not entire websites (see "Single-Page Apps" on page 80 for more details).

The usual caveats apply: this chapter is part reference, part tutorial. There will probably be stuff here you know already, so feel free to skip over it and get to the new material.

The Big Picture

The humble web page, the basic building block of the World Wide Web (WWW)—that fraction of the internet consumed by humans—is constructed from files of various types. Apart from the multimedia files (images, videos, sound, etc.), the key elements are textual, consisting of Hypertext Markup Language (HTML), Cascading Style Sheets (CSS), and JavaScript. These three, along with any necessary data files, are delivered using the Hypertext Transfer Protocol (HTTP) and used to build the page you see and interact with in your browser window, which is described by the Document Object Model (DOM), a hierarchical tree off which your content hangs. A basic understanding of how these elements interact is vital to building modern web visualizations, and the aim of this chapter is to get you quickly up to speed.

Web development is a big field, and the aim here is not to turn you into a full-fledged web developer. I assume you want to limit the amount of webdev you have to do as much as possible, focusing only on that fraction necessary to build a modern visualization. In order to build the sort of visualizations showcased at *d3js.org*, published in the *New York Times*, or incorporated in basic interactive data dashboards, you actually need surprisingly little webdev fu. The result of your labors should be easy to add to a larger website by someone dedicated to that job. In the case of small, personal websites, it's easy enough to incorporate the visualization yourself.

Single-Page Apps

Single-page applications (SPAs) are web applications (or whole sites) that are dynamically assembled using JavaScript, often building upon a lightweight HTML backbone and CSS styles that can be applied dynamically using class and ID attributes. Many modern data visualizations fit this description, including the Nobel Prize visualization this book builds toward.

Often self-contained, the SPA's root folder can be easily incorporated in an existing website or stand alone, requiring only an HTTP server such as Apache or NGINX.

Thinking of our data visualizations in terms of SPAs removes a lot of the cognitive overhead from the webdev aspect of JavaScript visualizations, allowing us to focus on programming challenges. The skills required to put the visualization on the web are still fairly basic and quickly amortized. Often it will be someone else's job.

Tooling Up

As you'll see, the webdev needed to make modern data visualizations requires no more than a decent text editor, modern browser, and a terminal (Figure 4-1). I'll cover what I see as the minimal requirements for a webdev-ready editor and nonessential but nice-to-have features.

My browser development tools of choice are Chrome's web-developer kit (*https:// oreil.ly/52Z3e*), freely available on all platforms. It has a lot of tab-delineated functionality, the following of which I'll cover in this chapter:

- The *Elements* tab, which allows you to explore the structure of a web page, its HTML content, CSS styles, and DOM presentation
- The *Sources* tab, where most of your JavaScript debugging will take place

You'll need a terminal for output, starting your local web server, and maybe sketching ideas with the IPython interpreter. These days I tend to use browser-based Jupyter notebooks (*https://jupyter.org*) as my Python dataviz *sketchpad*—one of the key advantages being that the session persists in the form of a notebook (*.ipynb*) file, which you can use to restart the session at later dates. You also get to iteratively explore your data with embedded charts. We'll be putting this to good use in Part III.

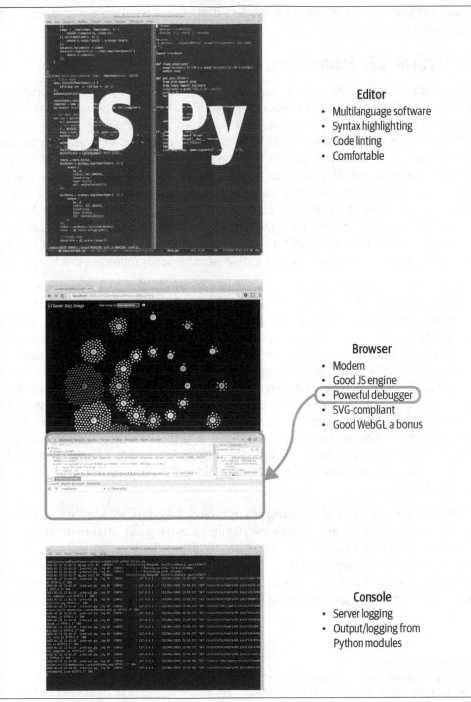

Editor

- Multilanguage software
- Syntax highlighting
- Code linting
- Comfortable

Browser

- Modern
- Good JS engine
- Powerful debugger
- SVG-compliant
- Good WebGL a bonus

Console

- Server logging
- Output/logging from Python modules

Figure 4-1. Primary webdev tools

Before dealing with what you do need, let's deal with a few things you don't need when setting out, laying a couple of myths to rest on the way.

The Myth of IDEs, Frameworks, and Tools

There is a common assumption among the prospective JavaScripter that to program for the web requires a complex toolset, primarily an Intelligent Development Environment (IDE), as used by enterprise—and other—coders everywhere. This is potentially expensive and presents another learning curve. The good news is that you can create professional-level web dataviz with nothing more than a decent text editor. In fact, until you start dealing with modern JavaScript frameworks (and I would hold off on that while you get your webdev legs) an IDE doesn't provide much advantage, while usually being less performant. More good news is that the free as in beer lightweight Visual Studio Code IDE (VSCode) (*https://code.visualstudio.com*) has become the de facto standard for web development. If you already use VSCode or want a few more bells and whistles, it's a good workhorse for following this book.

There is also a common myth that one cannot be productive in JavaScript without using a framework of some kind.[1] At the moment, a number of these frameworks are vying for control of the JS ecosystem, most sponsored by the various huge companies that created them. These frameworks come and go at a dizzying rate, and my advice for anyone starting out in JavaScript is to ignore them entirely while you develop your core skills. Use small, targeted libraries, such as those in the jQuery ecosystem or Underscore's functional programming extensions, and see how far you can get before needing a *my way or the highway* framework. Only lock yourself into a framework to meet a clear and present need, not because the current JS groupthink is raving about how great it is.[2] Another important consideration is that D3, the prime web dataviz library, doesn't really play well with any of the bigger frameworks I know, particularly the ones that want control over the DOM. Making D3 framework-compliant is an advanced skill.

Another thing you'll find if you hang around webdev forums, Reddit lists, and Stack Overflow is a huge range of tools constantly clamoring for attention. There are JS+CSS minifiers and watchers to automatically detect file changes and reload web pages during development, among others. While a few of these have their place, in my experience there are a lot of flaky tools that probably cost more time in hair-tearing than they gain in productivity. To reiterate, you can be very productive

---

1 There are some interesting alternatives to full-blown frameworks currently generating a buzz, such as Alpine.js and htmx (*https://oreil.ly/daXEB*), which play well with Python web servers like Django and Flask (*https://oreil.ly/3zlEU*).

2 I bear the scars so you don't have to.

without these things and should only reach for one to scratch an urgent itch. Some are keepers, but very few are even remotely essential for data visualization work.

A Text-Editing Workhorse

First and foremost among your webdev tools is a text editor that you are comfortable with and which can, at the very least, do syntax highlighting for multiple languages—in our case, HTML, CSS, JavaScript, and Python. You can get away with a plain, nonhighlighting editor, but in the long run it will prove to be a pain. Things like syntax highlighting, code linting, intelligent indentation, and the like remove a huge cognitive load from the process of programming, so much so that I see their absence as a limiting factor. These are my minimal requirements for a text editor:

- Syntax highlighting for all languages you use
- Configurable indentation levels and types for languages (e.g., Python 4 soft tabs, JavaScript 2 soft tabs)
- Multiple windows/panes/tabs to allow easy navigation around your codebase
- A decent code linter (*https://oreil.ly/6BOEU*) (see Figure 4-2)

If you are using a relatively advanced text editor, all the above should come as standard with the exception of code linting, which may require a bit of configuration.

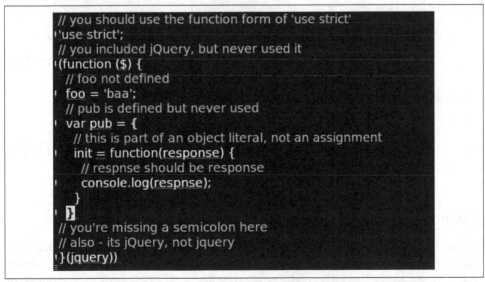

```
 // you should use the function form of 'use strict'
! 'use strict';
 // you included jQuery, but never used it
!(function ($) {
   // foo not defined
!  foo = 'baa';
   // pub is defined but never used
!  var pub = {
     // this is part of an object literal, not an assignment
!    init = function(response) {
       // respnse should be response
!      console.log(respnse);
     }
!  }
   // you're missing a semicolon here
   // also - its jQuery, not jquery
!}(jquery))
```

Figure 4-2. A running code linter analyzes the JavaScript continuously, highlighting syntax errors in red and adding an ! to the left of the offending line

Browser with Development Tools

One of the reasons a full-fledged IDE is less vital in modern webdev is that the best place to do debugging is in the web browser itself, and such is the pace of change there that any IDE attempting to emulate that context will have its work cut out for it. On top of this, modern web browsers have evolved a powerful set of debugging and development tools. The best among these is Chrome DevTools (*https://oreil.ly/ jBLc9*), which offers a huge amount of functionality, from sophisticated (certainly to a Pythonista) debugging (parametric breakpoints, variable watches, etc.) to memory and processor optimization profiling, device emulation (want to know what your web page looks like on a smartphone or tablet?), and a whole lot more. Chrome DevTools is my debugger of choice and will be used in this book. Like everything covered, it's free to use.

Terminal or Command Prompt

The terminal or command line is where you initiate the various servers and probably output useful logging information. It's also where you'll try out Python modules or run a Python interpreter (IPython being in many ways the best).

Building a Web Page

There are four elements to a typical web visualization:

- An HTML skeleton, with placeholders for our programmatic visualization
- Cascading Style Sheets (CSS), which define the look and feel (e.g., border widths, colors, font sizes, placement of content blocks)
- JavaScript to build the visualization
- Data to be transformed

The first three of these are just text files, created using our favorite editor and delivered to the browser by the web server (see Chapter 12). Let's examine each in turn.

Serving Pages with HTTP

The delivery of the HTML, CSS, and JS files that are used to make a particular web page (and any related data files, multimedia, etc.) is negotiated between a server and browser using the Hypertext Transfer Protocol. HTTP provides a number of methods, the most commonly used being GET, which requests a web resource, retrieving data from the server if all goes well or throwing an error if it doesn't. We'll be using GET, along with Python's requests module, to scrape some web page content in Chapter 6.

To negotiate the browser-generated HTTP requests, you'll need a server. In development, you can run a little server locally using Python's built-in web server (one of the batteries included), part of the http module. You start the server at the command line, with an optional port number (default 8000), like this:

```
$ python -m http.server 8080
Serving HTTP on 0.0.0.0 port 8080 (http://0.0.0.0:8080/) ...
```

This server is now serving content locally on port 8080. You can access the site it is serving by going to the URL *http://localhost:8080* in your browser.

The http.server module is a nice thing to have and OK for demos and the like, but it lacks a lot of basic functionality. For this reason, as we'll see in Part IV, it's better to master the use of a proper development (and production) server like Flask (this book's server of choice).

The DOM

The HTML files you send through HTTP are converted at the browser end into a Document Object Model, or DOM, which can in turn be adapted by JavaScript because this programmatic DOM is the basis of dataviz libraries like D3. The DOM is a tree structure, represented by hierarchical nodes, the top node being the main web page or document.

Essentially, the HTML you write or generate with a template is converted by the browser into a tree hierarchy of nodes, each one representing an HTML element. The top node is called the *Document Object*, and all other nodes descend in a parent-child fashion. Programmatically manipulating the DOM is at the heart of such libraries as jQuery and the mighty D3, so it's vital to have a good mental model of what's going on. A great way to get the feel for the DOM is to use a web tool such as *Chrome DevTools* (my recommended toolset) to inspect branches of the tree.

Whatever you see rendered on the web page, the bookkeeping of the object's state (displayed or hidden, matrix transform, etc.) is being done with the DOM. D3's powerful innovation was to attach data directly to the DOM and use it to drive visual changes (Data-Driven Documents).

The HTML Skeleton

A typical web visualization uses an HTML skeleton, and builds the visualization on top of it using JavaScript.

HTML is the language used to describe the content of a web page. It was first proposed by physicist Tim Berners-Lee in 1980 while he was working at the CERN particle accelerator complex in Switzerland. It uses tags such as <div>, <img>, and <h>

to structure the content of the page, while CSS is used to define the look and feel.[3] The advent of HTML5 has reduced the boilerplate considerably, but the essence has remained essentially unchanged over those thirty years.

Fully specced HTML used to involve a lot of rather confusing header tags, but with HTML5 some thought was put into a more user-friendly minimalism. This is pretty much the minimal requirement for a starting template:[4]

```
<!DOCTYPE html>
<meta charset="utf-8">
<body>
    <!-- page content -->
</body>
```

So we need only declare the document HTML, our character set 8-bit Unicode, and a <body> tag below which to add our page content. This is a big improvement on the bookkeeping required before and provides a very low threshold to entry as far as creating the documents that will be turned into web pages goes. Note the comment tag form: <!-- comment -->.

More realistically, we would probably want to add some CSS and JavaScript. You can add both directly to an HTML document by using the <style> and <script> tags like this:

```
<!DOCTYPE html>
<meta charset="utf-8">
<style>
/* CSS */
</style>
<body>
    <!-- page content -->
    <script>
    // JavaScript...
    </script>
</body>
```

This single-page HTML form is often used in examples such as the visualizations at *d3js.org*. It's convenient to have a single page to deal with when demonstrating code or keeping track of files, but generally I'd suggest separating the HTML, CSS, and JavaScript elements into separate files. The big win here, apart from easier navigation as the codebase gets larger, is that you can take full advantage of your editor's specific language enhancements such as solid syntax highlighting and code linting (essentially syntax checking on the fly). While some editors and libraries claim to deal with embedded CSS and JavaScript, I haven't found an adequate one.

---

3 You can code style in HTML tags using the style attribute, but it's generally bad practice. It's better to use classes and ids defined in CSS.

4 As demonstrated by Mike Bostock (*https://oreil.ly/MgWtS*), with a hat-tip to Paul Irish.

To use CSS and JavaScript files, we just include them in the HTML using `<link>` and `<script>` tags like this:

```
<!DOCTYPE html>
<meta charset="utf-8">
<link rel="stylesheet" href="style.css" />
<body>
    <!-- page content -->
    <script type="text/javascript" src="script.js"></script>
</body>
```

Marking Up Content

Visualizations often use a small subset of the available HTML tags, usually building the page programmatically by attaching elements to the DOM tree.

The most common tag is the `<div>`, marking a block of content. `<div>`s can contain other `<div>`s, allowing for a tree hierarchy, the branches of which are used during element selection and to propagate user interface (UI) events such as mouse clicks. Here's a simple `<div>` hierarchy:

```
<div id="my-chart-wrapper" class="chart-holder dev">
    <div id="my-chart" class="bar chart">
        this is a placeholder, with parent #my-chart-wrapper
    </div>
</div>
```

Note the use of `id` and `class` attributes. These are used when you're selecting DOM elements and to apply CSS styles. IDs are unique identifiers; each element should have only one and there should be only one occurrence of any particular ID per page. The class can be applied to multiple elements, allowing bulk selection, and each element can have multiple classes.

For textual content, the main tags are `<p>`, `<h*>`, and `<br>`. You'll be using these a lot. This code produces Figure 4-3:

```
<h2>A Level-2 Header</h2>
<p>A paragraph of body text with a line break here..</br>
and a second paragraph...</p>
```

A Level-2 Header

A paragraph of body-text with a line-break here..
and a second paragraph...

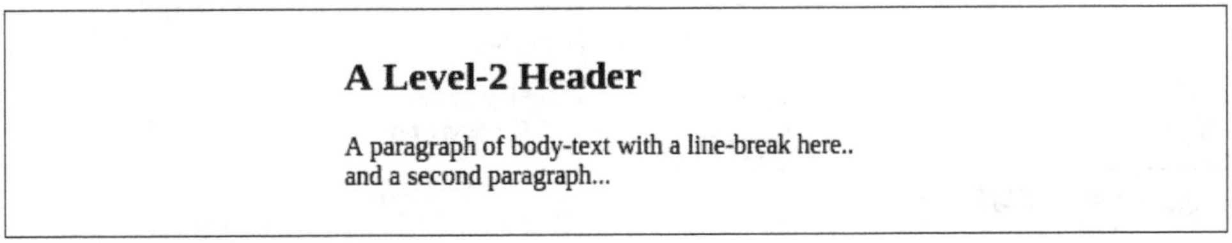

Figure 4-3. An h2 header and text

Header tags are reverse-ordered by size from the largest `<h1>`.

`<div>`, `<h*>`, and `<p>` are what is known as *block elements*. They normally begin and end with a new line. The other class of tag is *inline elements*, which display without line breaks. Images `<img>`, hyperlinks `<a>`, and table cells `<td>` are among these, which include the `<span>` tag for inline text:

```
<div id="inline-examples">
    <img src="path/to/image.png" id="prettypic"> ❶
    <p>This is a <a href="link-url">link</a> to
        <span class="url">link-url</span></p> ❷
</div>
```

❶ Note that we don't need a closing tag for images.

❷ The span and link are continuous in the text.

Other useful tags include lists, ordered `<ol>` and unordered `<ul>`:

```
<div style="display: flex; gap: 50px"> ❶
  <div>
    <h3>Ordered (ol) list</h3>
    <ol>
      <li>First Item</li>
      <li>Second Item</li>
    </ol>
  </div>
  <div>
    <h3>Unordered (ul) list</h3>
    <ul>
      <li>First Item</li>
      <li>Second Item</li>
    </ul>
  </div>
</div>
```

❶ Here we apply a CSS style directly (inline) on the div tag. See "Positioning and Sizing Containers with Flex" on page 98 for an introduction to the flex display property.

Figure 4-4 shows the rendered lists.

Ordered (ol) list	Unordered (ul) list
1. First item 2. Second item	• First item • Second item

Figure 4-4. HTML lists

HTML also has a dedicated `<table>` tag, useful if you want to present raw data in your visualization. This HTML produces the header and row in Figure 4-5:

```
<table id="chart-data">
  <tr> ❶
    <th>Name</th>
    <th>Category</th>
    <th>Country</th>
  </tr>
  <tr> ❷
    <td>Albert Einstein</td>
    <td>Physics</td>
    <td>Switzerland</td>
  </tr>
</table>
```

❶ The header row

❷ The first row of data

Name	Category	Country
Albert Einstein	Physics	Switzerland

Figure 4-5. An HTML table

When you are making web visualizations, the most often used of the previous tags are the textual tags, which provide instructions, information boxes, and so on. But the meat of our JavaScript efforts will probably be devoted to building DOM branches rooted on the Scalable Vector Graphics (SVG) <svg> and <canvas> tags. On most modern browsers, the <canvas> tag also supports a 3D *WebGL* context, allowing *OpenGL* visualizations to be embedded in the page.[5]

We'll deal with SVG, the focus of this book and the format used by the mighty D3 library, in "Scalable Vector Graphics" on page 105. Now let's look at how we add style to our content blocks.

CSS

CSS, short for Cascading Style Sheets, is a language for describing the look and feel of a web page. Though you can hardcode style attributes into your HTML, it's generally considered bad practice.[6] It's much better to label your tag with an id or class and use that to apply styles in the stylesheet.

---

[5] OpenGL (Open Graphics Language) and its web counterpart WebGL are cross-platform APIs for rendering 2D and 3D vector graphics (see the Wikipedia page (*https://oreil.ly/eytfV*) for details).

[6] This is not the same as programmatically setting styles, which is a hugely powerful technique that allows styles to adapt to user interaction.

The key word in CSS is *cascading*. CSS follows a precedence rule so that in the case of a clash, the latest style overrides earlier ones. This means the order of inclusion for sheets is important. Usually, you want your stylesheet to be loaded last so that you can override both the browser defaults and styles defined by any libraries you are using.

Figure 4-6 shows how CSS is used to apply styles to the HTML elements. First, you select the element using hashes (#) to indicate a unique ID and dots (.) to select members of a class. You then define one or more property/value pairs. Note that the font-family property can be a list of fallbacks, in order of preference. Here we want the browser default font-family of serif (capped strokes) to be replaced with the more modern sans-serif, with Helvetica Neue as our first choice.

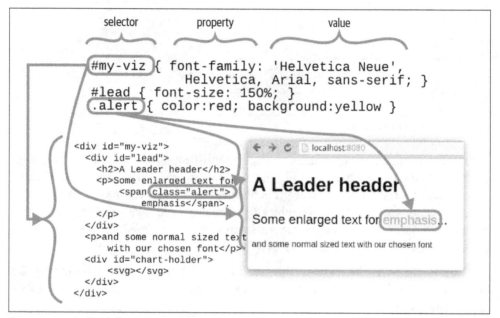

Figure 4-6. Styling the page with CSS

Understanding CSS precedence rules is key to successfully applying styles. In a nutshell, the order is:

1. !important after CSS property trumps all.

2. The more specific the better (i.e., IDs override classes).

3. The order of declaration: last declaration wins, subject to *1* and *2*.

So, for example, say we have a <span> of class alert:

```
<span class="alert" id="special-alert">
something to be alerted to</span>
```

Putting the following in our *style.css* file will make the alert text red and bold:

```
.alert { font-weight:bold; color:red }
```

If we then add this to the *style.css*, the ID color black will override the class color red, while the class `font-weight` remains bold:

```
#special-alert {background: yellow; color:black}
```

To enforce the color red for alerts, we can use the `!important` directive:[7]

```
.alert { font-weight:bold; color:red !important }
```

If we then add another stylesheet, *style2.css*, after *style.css*:

```
<link rel="stylesheet" href="style.css" type="text/css" />
<link rel="stylesheet" href="style2.css" type="text/css" />
```

with *style2.css* containing the following:

```
.alert { font-weight:normal }
```

then the `font-weight` of the alert will be reverted to `normal` because the new class style was declared last.

JavaScript

JavaScript is the only browser-based programming language, with an interpreter included in all modern browsers. In order to do anything remotely advanced (and that includes all modern web visualizations), you should have a JavaScript grounding. TypeScript (*https://www.typescriptlang.org*) is a superset of JavaScript that provides strong typing and is currently gaining a lot of traction. TypeScript compiles to and presupposes competence in JavaScript.

99% of all coded web visualization examples, the ones you should aim to be learning from, are in JavaScript, and voguish alternatives have a way of fading with time. In essence, good competence in (if not mastery of) JavaScript is a prerequisite for interesting web visualizations.

The good news for Pythonistas is that JavaScript is actually quite a nice language once you've tamed a few of its more awkward quirks.[8] As I showed in Chapter 2, JavaScript and Python have a lot in common and it's usually easy to translate from one to the other.

---

7 This is generally considered bad practice and is usually an indication of poorly structured CSS. Use with extreme caution, as it can make life very difficult for code developers.

8 These are succinctly discussed in Douglas Crockford's famously short *JavaScript: The Good Parts* (O'Reilly).

Data

The data needed to fuel your web visualization will be provided by the web server as static files (e.g., JSON or CSV files) or dynamically through some kind of web API (e.g., RESTful APIs (*https://oreil.ly/RwvhM*)), usually retrieving the data server-side from a database. We'll be covering all these forms in Part IV.

Although a lot of data used to be delivered in XML form (*https://oreil.ly/2IvEi*), modern web visualization is predominantly about JSON and, to a lesser extent, CSV or TSV files.

JSON (*https://oreil.ly/kCBDk*) (short for JavaScript Object Notation) is the de facto web visualization data standard and I recommend you learn to love it. It obviously plays very nicely with JavaScript, but its structure will also be familiar to Pythonistas. As we saw in "JSON" on page 58, reading and writing JSON data with Python is a snap. Here's a little example of some JSON data:

```
{
  "firstName": "Groucho",
  "lastName": "Marx",
  "siblings": ["Harpo", "Chico", "Gummo", "Zeppo"],
  "nationality": "American",
  "yearOfBirth": 1890
}
```

Chrome DevTools

The arms race in JavaScript engines in recent years, which has produced huge increases in performance, has been matched by an increasingly sophisticated range of development tools built into the various browsers. Firefox's Firebug led the pack for a while but Chrome DevTools (*https://oreil.ly/djHBp*) have surpassed it, and are adding functionality all the time. There's now a huge amount you can do with Chrome's tabbed tools, but here I'll introduce the two most useful tabs, the HTML+CSS-focused *Elements* and the JavaScript-focused *Sources*. Both of these work in complement to Chrome's developer console, demonstrated in "JavaScript" on page 13.

The Elements Tab

To access the Elements tab, select More Tools→Developer Tools from the righthand options menu or use the Ctrl-Shift-I keyboard shortcut (Cmd-Option-I in Mac).

Figure 4-7 shows the Elements tab at work. You can select DOM elements on the page by using the lefthand magnifying glass and see their HTML branch in the left panel. The right panel allows you to see CSS styles applied to the element and look at any event listeners that are attached or DOM properties.

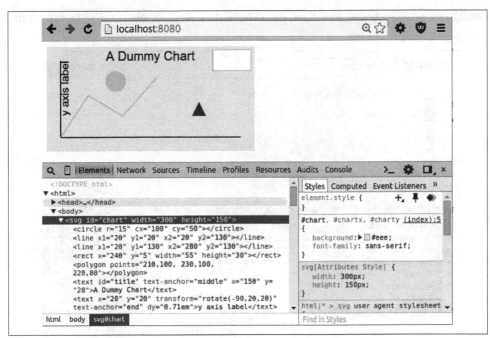

Figure 4-7. Chrome DevTools Elements tab

One really cool feature of the Elements tab is that you can interactively change element styling for both CSS styles and attributes.[9] This is a great way to refine the look and feel of your data visualizations.

Chrome's Elements tab provides a great way to explore the structure of a page, finding out how the different elements are positioned. This is good way to get your head around positioning content blocks with the `position` and `float` properties. Seeing how the pros apply CSS styles is a really good way to up your game and learn some useful tricks.

The Sources Tab

The Sources tab allows you to see any JavaScript included in the page. Figure 4-8 shows the tab at work. In the lefthand panel, you can select a script or an HTML file with embedded `<script>` tagged JavaScript. As shown, you can place a breakpoint in the code, load the page, and, on break, see the call stack and any scoped or global variables. These breakpoints are parametric, so you can set conditions for them to trigger, which is handy if you want to catch and step through a particular

---

9 Being able to play with attributes is particularly useful when trying to get Scalable Vector Graphics (SVG) to work.

configuration. On break, you have the standard to step in, out, and over functions, and so on.

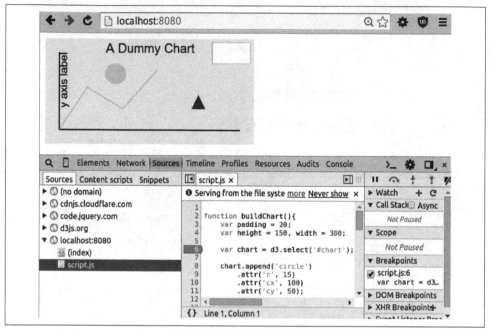

Figure 4-8. Chrome DevTools Sources tab

The Sources tab is a fantastic resource and greatly reduces the need for console logging[10] when trying to debug JavaScript. In fact, where JS debugging was once a major pain point, it is now almost a pleasure.

Other Tools

There's a huge amount of functionality in those Chrome DevTools tabs, and they are being updated almost daily. You can do memory and CPU timelines and profiling, monitor your network downloads, and test out your pages for different form factors. But you'll spend the large majority of your time as a data visualizer in the Elements and Sources tabs.

---

10 Logging is a great way of tracking data flow through your app. I recommend you adopt a consistent approach here.

A Basic Page with Placeholders

Now that we have covered the major elements of a web page, let's put them together. Most web visualizations start off as HTML and CSS skeletons, with placeholder elements ready to be fleshed out with a little JavaScript plus data (see "Single-Page Apps" on page 80).

We'll first need our HTML skeleton, using the code in Example 4-1. This consists of a tree of `<div>` content blocks defining three chart elements: a header, main, and sidebar section. We'll save this file as *index.html*.

Example 4-1. The file index.html, our HTML skeleton

```
<!DOCTYPE html>
<meta charset="utf-8">

<link rel="stylesheet" href="style.css" type="text/css" />

<body>

  <div id="chart-holder" class="dev">
    <div id="header">
      <h2>A Catchy Title Coming Soon...</h2>
      <p>Some body text describing what this visualization is all
      about and why you should care.</p>
    </div>
    <div id="chart-components">
      <div id="main">
        A placeholder for the main chart.
      </div><div id="sidebar">
        <p>Some useful information about the chart,
          probably changing with user interaction.</p>
      </div>
    </div>
  </div>

  <script src="script.js"></script>
</body>
```

Now that we have our HTML skeleton, we want to style it using some CSS. This will use the classes and IDs of our content blocks to adjust size, position, background color, etc. To apply our CSS, in Example 4-1 we import a *style.css* file, shown in Example 4-2.

Example 4-2. The style.css file, providing our CSS styling

```
body {
    background: #ccc;
```

```
    font-family: Sans-serif;
}

div.dev { ❶
    border: solid 1px red;
}

div.dev div {
    border: dashed 1px green;
}

div#chart-holder {
    width: 600px;
    background :white;
    margin: auto;
    font-size :16px;
}

div#chart-components {
    height :400px;
    position :relative; ❷
}

div#main, div#sidebar {
    position: absolute; ❸
}

div#main {
    width: 75%;
    height: 100%;
    background: #eee;
}

div#sidebar {
    right: 0; ❹
    width: 25%;
    height: 100%;
}
```

❶ This dev class is a handy way to see the border of any visual blocks, which is useful for visualization work.

❷ Makes chart-components the relative parent.

❸ Makes the main and sidebar positions relative to chart-components.

❹ Positions this block flush with the right wall of chart-components.

We use absolute positioning of the main and sidebar chart elements (Example 4-2). There are various ways to position the content blocks with CSS, but absolute positioning gives you explicit control over their placement, which is a must if you want to get the look just right.

After specifying the size of the `chart-components` container, the `main` and `sidebar` child elements are sized and positioned using percentages of their parent. This means any changes to the size of `chart-components` will be reflected in its children.

With our HTML and CSS defined, we can examine the skeleton by firing up Python's single-line HTTP server in the project directory containing the *index.html* and *style.css* files defined in Examples 4-1 and 4-2, like so:

```
$ python -m http.server 8000
Serving HTTP on 0.0.0.0 port 8000 ...
```

Figure 4-9 shows the resulting page with the Elements tab open, displaying the page's DOM tree.

The chart's content blocks are now positioned and sized correctly, ready for JavaScript to add some engaging content.

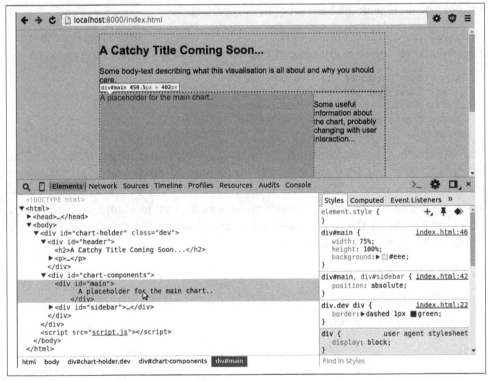

Figure 4-9. Building a basic web page

Positioning and Sizing Containers with Flex

Historically positioning and sizing content (usually <div> containers) with CSS was somewhat of a dark art. It didn't help that there were a lot of cross-browser incompatibilities and disagreements about what constituted padding or margins. But even allowing for that, the CSS properties used seemed pretty ad-hoc. Often achieving what seems to be a perfectly reasonable positioning or sizing ambition turned out to involve arcane CSS knowledge, hidden in the deep recesses of a Stack Overflow thread. One example being centering a div in the horizontal and vertical.[11] This has all changed with the advent of the CSS flex-box, which uses some powerful new CSS properties to provide almost all the sizing and positioning you'll ever need.

Flex-boxes aren't quite one CSS property to rule them all—the absolute positioning demonstrated in the previous section still has its place, particularly with data visualizations—but they are a collection of very powerful properties which, more often than not, represent the simplest, and sometimes the only, way to achieve a particular placing/sizing mission. Effects that used to require CSS expertise are now well within the grasp of a relative newbie and the icing on the cake is that flex-boxes play really well with variable screen ratios—the power of the flex. With that in mind, let's see what can be done with the basic set of flex properties.

First, we'll use a little HTML to create a container div with three child divs (boxes). The child boxes will be of class box with an ID to enable specific CSS to be applied:

```
<div class="container" id="top-container">
  <div class="box" id="box1">box 1</div>
  <div class="box" id="box2">box 2</div>
  <div class="box" id="box3">box 3</div>
</div>
```

The initial CSS gives the container a red border, width, and height (600x400). The boxes are 100 pixels wide and high (80 pixels plus 10 pixels padding) and have a green border. A novel CSS property is the container's display: flex, which establishes a flex display context. The result of this can be seen in Figure 4-10 (display: flex), which shows the boxes presented in a row rather than the default column, where each box occupies its own row:

```
.container {
  display: flex;
  width: 600px;
  height: 400px;
  border: 2px solid red;
}
```

---

11 Here's a thread showing the many and varied solutions to the problem (*https://oreil.ly/casbD*), none of which could be called elegant.

```
.box {
  border: 2px solid green;
  font-size: 28px;
  padding: 10px;
  width: 80px;
  height: 80px;
}
```

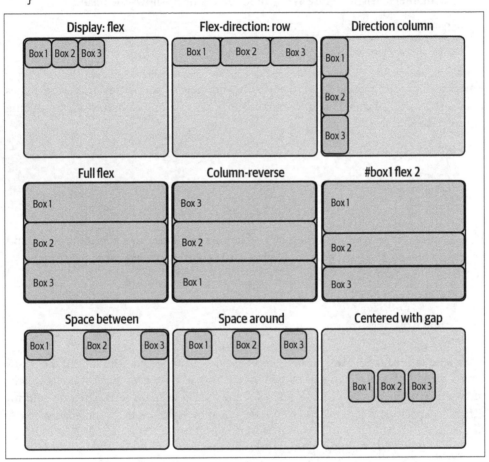

Figure 4-10. Positioning and sizing with flex-boxes

Flex displays respond to children with the `flex` property by expanding their size to fit the available space. If we make the boxes flexible, they respond by expanding to fill the container row. Figure 4-10 (flex-direction: row) shows the result. Note that the `flex` property overrides the boxes' width property, allowing them to expand:

```
.box {
    /* ... */
    flex: 1;
}
```

The `flex-direction` property is row by default. By setting it to `column`, the boxes are placed in a column and the height property is overridden to allow them to expand to fit the container's height. Figure 4-10 (direction column) shows the result:

```
.container {
    /* ... */
    flex-direction: column;
}
```

Removing or commenting out the width and height properties from the boxes makes them fully flexible, able to expand in the horizontal and vertical, producing Figure 4-10 (full flex):

```
.box {
    /* ... */
    /* width: 80px;
    height: 80px; */
    flex: 1;
}
```

If you want to reverse the order of the flex-boxes, there are a `row-reverse` and `column-reverse` `flex-direction`. Figure 4-10 (column reverse) shows the result of reversing the columns:

```
.container {
    /* ... */
    flex-direction: column-reverse;
}
```

The value of the boxes' `flex` property represents a sizing weight. Initially all the boxes have a weight of one, which makes them of equal size. If we give the first box a weight of two, it will occupy half (2 / (1 + 1 + 2)) the available space in the row or column direction specified. Figure 4-10 (#box1 flex 2) shows the result of increasing box1's flex value:

```
#box1 {
    flex: 2;
}
```

If we return the 100-pixel height and width (including padding) constraints to the boxes and remove their `flex` property, we can demonstrate the power of flex display positioning. We'll also need to remove the flex directive from box1:

```
.box {
    width: 80px;
    height: 80px;
    /* flex: 1; */
```

```
}
#box1 {
    /* flex: 2; */
}
```

With fixed-size content, flex displays have a number of properties that allow precise placement of the content. This sort of manipulation used to involve all manner of tricky CSS hacks. First, let's distribute the boxes evenly in their container, using row-based spacing. The magic property is `justify-content` with the value `space-between`; Figure 4-10 (space between) shows the result:

```
.container {
    /* ... */
    flex-direction: row;
    justify-content: space-between;
}
```

There is a `space-around` complement to `space-between`, which spaces the content by adding equal padding to left and right. Figure 4-10 (space around) shows the result:

```
.container {
    /* ... */
    justify-content: space-around;
}
```

By combining the `justify-content` and `align-items` properties, we can achieve the holy grail of CSS positioning, centering the content in the vertical and the horizontal. We'll add a gap of 20 pixels between the boxes using the flex display's `gap` property:

```
.container {
    /* ... */
    gap: 20px;
    justify-content: center;
    align-items: center;
}
```

Figure 4-10 (centered with `gap`) shows our content sitting squarely in the middle of its container.

Another great thing about the flex display is that it is fully recursive. `div`s can both *have* a display flex property and *be* flex content. This makes achieving complex content layouts a breeze. Let's see a little demonstration of nested flex-boxes, to make the point clear.

We'll first use some HTML to build a nested tree of boxes (including the main container box). We'll give each box and container an ID and class:

```
<div class="main-container">

    <div class="container" id="top-container">
        <div class="box" id="box1">box 1</div>
```

```
    <div class="box" id="box2">box 2</div>
  </div>

  <div class="container" id="middle-container">
    <div class="box" id="box3">box 3</div>
  </div>

  <div class="container" id="bottom-container">
    <div class="box" id="box4">box 4</div>
    <div class="box" id="box5">
      <div class="box" id="box6">box 6</div>
      <div class="box" id="box7">box 7</div>
    </div>
  </div>

</div>
```

The following CSS gives the main container a height of 800 pixels (it will fill the available width by default), a flex display, and a flex-direction of column, making it stack its flex content.

There are three containers to be stacked, which are both flexible and provide a flex display for their content. The boxes have a red border and are fully flexible (no width or height specified). By default all boxes have a flex weight of one.

The middle container has a fixed width box (width 66%) and uses `justify-content: center` to center it.

The bottom container has a flex value of 2, making it twice the height of its siblings. It has two boxes of equal weight, one of which (box 5) contains two boxes that are stacked (`flex-direction: column`). The fairly complex layout (see Figure 4-11) is achieved with impressively little CSS and is easily adapted by changing a few flex display properties:

```
.main-container {
  height: 800px;
  padding: 10px;
  border: 2px solid green;
  display: flex;
  flex-direction: column;
}

.container {
  flex: 1;
  display: flex;
}

.box {
  flex: 1;
  border: 2px solid red;
  padding: 10px;
```

```
    font-size: 30px;
}

#middle-container {
    justify-content: center;
}

#box3 {
    width: 66%;
    flex: initial;
}

#bottom-container {
    flex: 2;
}

#box5 {
    display: flex;
    flex-direction: column;
}
```

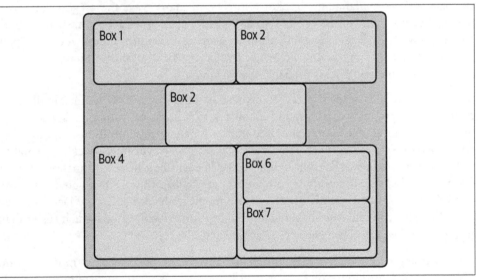

Figure 4-11. Nested flex-boxes

Flex-boxes provide a very powerful sizing and positioning context for your HTML content that responds to container size and can be easily adapted. If you want your content in a column rather than a row, then a single property change makes it so. For more precise positioning and sizing control there is the CSS grid layout (*https://oreil.ly/lVilF*), but I would recommend focusing your initial energies on the flex display—it represents the best return on your learning investment in CSS right now.

For further examples, see the CSS-Tricks article (*https://oreil.ly/JJgbG*) on flex-boxes and this handy cheat sheet (*https://flexboxsheet.com*).

Filling the Placeholders with Content

With our content blocks defined in HTML and positioned with CSS, a modern data visualization uses JavaScript to construct its interactive charts, menus, tables, and the like. There are many ways to create visual content (aside from image or multimedia tags) in your modern browser, the main ones being:

- Scalable Vector Graphics (SVG) using special HTML tags
- Drawing to a 2D `canvas` context
- Drawing to a 3D `canvas` WebGL context, allowing a subset of OpenGL commands
- Using modern CSS to create animations, graphic primitives, and more

Because SVG is the language of choice for D3, in many ways the biggest JavaScript dataviz library, many of the cool web data visualizations you have seen, such as those by the *New York Times*, are built using it. Broadly speaking, unless you anticipate having lots (>1,000) of moving elements in your visualization or need to use a specific `canvas`-based library, SVG is probably the way to go.

By using vectors instead of pixels to express its primitives, SVG will generally produce cleaner graphics that respond smoothly to scaling operations. It's also much better at handling text, a crucial consideration for many visualizations. Another key advantage of SVG is that user interaction (e.g., mouse hovering or clicking) is native to the browser, being part of the standard DOM event handling.[12] A final point in its favor is that because the graphic components are built on the DOM, you can inspect and adapt them using your browser's development tools (see "Chrome DevTools" on page 92). This can make debugging and refining your visualizations much easier than trying to find errors in the `canvas`'s relatively black box.

`canvas` graphics contexts come into their own when you need to move beyond simple graphic primitives like circles and lines, such as when incorporating images like PNGs and JPGs. `canvas` is usually considerably more performant than SVG, so anything with lots of moving elements[13] is better off rendered to a canvas. If you want to be really ambitious or move beyond 2D graphics, you can even unleash the awesome power of modern graphics cards by using a special form of `canvas` context,

---

[12] With a `canvas` graphic context, you generally have to contrive your own event handling.

[13] This number changes with time and the browser in question, but as a rough rule of thumb, SVG often starts to strain in the low thousands.

the OpenGL-based WebGL context. Just bear in mind that what would be simple user interaction with SVG (e.g., clicking on a visual element) often has to be derived from mouse coordinates manually, which adds a tricky layer of complexity.

The Nobel Prize data visualization realized at the end of this book's toolchain is built primarily with D3, so SVG graphics are the focus of this book. Being comfortable with SVG is fundamental to modern web-based dataviz, so let's explore a little primer.

Scalable Vector Graphics

All SVG creations start with an `<svg>` root tag. All graphical elements, such as circles and lines, and groups thereof, are defined on this branch of the DOM tree. Example 4-3 shows a little SVG context we'll use in upcoming demonstrations, a light-gray rectangle with ID `chart`. We also include the D3 library, loaded from *d3js.org* and a *script.js* JavaScript file in the project folder.

Example 4-3. A basic SVG context

```
<!DOCTYPE html>
<meta charset="utf-8">
<!-- A few CSS style rules -->
<style>
  svg#chart {
  background: lightgray;
  }
</style>

<svg id="chart" width="300" height="225">
</svg>

<!-- Third-party libraries and our JS script. -->
<script src="http://d3js.org/d3.v7.min.js"></script>
<script src="script.js"></script>
```

Now that we've got our little SVG canvas in place, let's start doing some drawing.

The <g> Element

We can group shapes within our `<svg>` element by using the group `<g>` element. As we'll see in "Working with Groups" on page 113, shapes contained in a group can be manipulated together, including changing their position, scale, or opacity.

Circles

Creating SVG visualizations, from the humblest little static bar chart to full-fledged interactive, geographic masterpieces, involves putting together elements from a fairly small set of graphical primitives such as lines, circles, and the very powerful paths.

Each of these elements will have its own DOM tag, which will update as it changes.[14] For example, its *x* and *y* attributes will change to reflect any translations within its <svg> or group (<g>) context.

Let's add a circle to our <svg> context to demonstrate:

```
<svg id="chart" width="300" height="225">
  <circle r="15" cx="100" cy="50"></circle>
</svg>
```

With a little CSS to provide the circle's fill color:

```
#chart circle{ fill: lightblue }
```

This produces Figure 4-12. Note that the *y* coordinate is measured from the top of the <svg> '#chart' container, a common graphic convention.

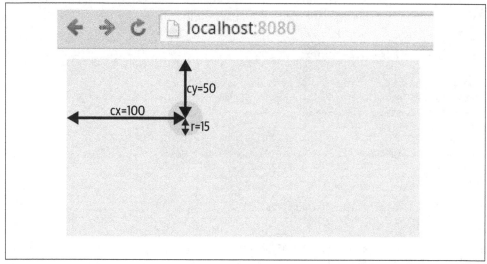

Figure 4-12. An SVG circle

Now let's see how we go about applying styles to SVG elements.

---

14 You should be able to use your browser's development tools to see the tag attributes updating in real time.

Applying CSS Styles

The circle in Figure 4-12 is fill-colored light blue using CSS styling rules:

```
#chart circle{ fill: lightblue }
```

In modern browsers, you can set most visual SVG styles using CSS, including `fill`, `stroke`, `stroke-width`, and `opacity`. So if we wanted a thick, semitransparent green line (with ID `total`) we could use the following CSS:

```
#chart line#total {
    stroke: green;
    stroke-width: 3px;
    opacity: 0.5;
}
```

You can also set the styles as attributes of the tags, though CSS is generally preferable:

```
<svg>
  <circle r="15" cx="100" cy="50" fill="lightblue"></circle>
</svg>
```

> Which SVG features can be set by CSS and which can't is a source of some confusion and plenty of gotchas. The SVG spec distinguishes between element properties (*https://oreil.ly/K0enr*) and attributes, the former being more likely to be found among the valid CSS styles. You can investigate the valid CSS properties using Chrome's Elements tab and its autocomplete. Also, be prepared for some surprises. For example, SVG text is colored by the `fill`, not `color`, property.

For `fill` and `stroke`, there are various color conventions you can use:

- Named HTML colors, such as lightblue
- Using HTML hex codes (#RRGGBB); for example, white is #FFFFFF
- RGB values; for example, red = rgb(255, 0, 0)
- RGBA values, where A is an alpha channel (0–1); for example, half-transparent blue is rgba(0, 0, 255, 0.5)

In addition to adjusting the color's alpha channel with RGBA, you can fade the SVG elements using their `opacity` property. Opacity is used a lot in D3 animations.

Stroke width is measured in pixels by default but can use points.

Lines, Rectangles, and Polygons

We'll add a few more elements to our chart to produce Figure 4-13.

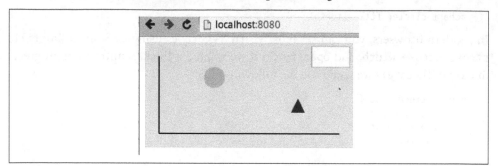

Figure 4-13. Adding a few elements to our dummy chart

First, we'll add a couple of simple axis lines to our chart, using the `<line>` tag. Line positions are defined by a start coordinate (x1, y1) and an end one (x2, y2):

```
<svg>
  <line x1="20" y1="20" x2="20" y2="130"></line>
  <line x1="20" y1="130" x2="280" y2="130"></line>
</svg>
```

We'll also add a dummy legend box in the top-right corner using an SVG rectangle. Rectangles are defined by *x* and *y* coordinates relative to their parent container, and a width and height:

```
<svg>
  <rect x="240" y="5" width="55" height="30"></rect>
</svg>
```

You can create irregular polygons using the `<polygon>` tag, which takes a list of coordinate pairs. Let's make a triangle marker in the bottom right of our chart:

```
<svg>
  <polygon points="210,100, 230,100, 220,80"></polygon>
</svg>
```

We'll style the elements with a little CSS:

```
#chart circle {fill: lightblue}
#chart line {stroke: #555555; stroke-width: 2}
#chart rect {stroke: red; fill: white}
#chart polygon {fill: green}
```

Now that we've got a few graphical primitives in place, let's see how we add some text to our dummy chart.

Text

One of the key strengths of SVG over the rasterized `canvas` context is how it handles text. Vector-based text tends to look a lot clearer than its pixelated counterparts and benefits from smooth scaling too. You can also adjust stroke and fill properties, just like any SVG element.

Let's add a bit of text to our dummy chart: a title and labeled y-axis (see Figure 4-14).

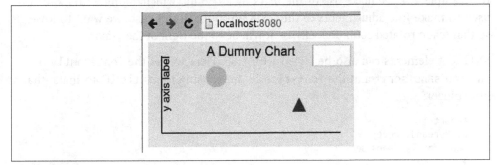

Figure 4-14. Some SVG text

We place text using *x* and *y* coordinates. One important property is the `text-anchor`, which stipulates where the text is placed relative to its x position. The options are `start`, `middle`, and `end`; `start` is the default.

We can use the `text-anchor` property to center our chart title. We set the *x* coordinates at half the chart width and then set the `text-anchor` to `middle`:

```
<svg>
  <text id="title" text-anchor="middle" x="150" y="20">
    A Dummy Chart
  </text>
</svg>
```

As with all SVG primitives, we can apply scaling and rotation transforms to our text. To label our y-axis, we'll need to rotate the text to the vertical (Example 4-4). By convention, rotations are clockwise by degree, so we'll want a counterclockwise, –90 degree rotation. By default rotations are around the (0,0) point of the element's container (`<svg>` or group `<g>`). We want to rotate our text around its own position, so first translate the rotation point using the extra arguments to the `rotate` function. We also want to first set the `text-anchor` to the end of the y axis label string to rotate about its endpoint.

Example 4-4. Rotating text

```
<svg>
  <text x="20" y="20" transform="rotate(-90,20,20)"
      text-anchor="end" dy="0.71em">y axis label</text>
</svg>
```

In Example 4-4, we make use of the text's dy attribute, which, along with dx, can be used to make fine adjustments to the text's position. In this case, we want to lower it so that when rotated counterclockwise it will be to the right of the y-axis.

SVG text elements can also be styled with CSS. Here we set the font-family of the chart to sans-serif and the font-size to 16px, using the title ID to make that a little bigger:

```
#chart {
background: #eee;
font-family: sans-serif;
}
#chart text{ font-size: 16px }
#chart text#title{ font-size: 18px }
```

Note that the text elements inherit font-family and font-size from the chart's CSS; you don't have to specify a text element.

Paths

Paths are the most complicated and powerful SVG element, enabling the creation of multiline, multicurve component paths that can be closed and filled, creating pretty much any shape you want. A simple example is adding a little chart line to our dummy chart to produce Figure 4-15.

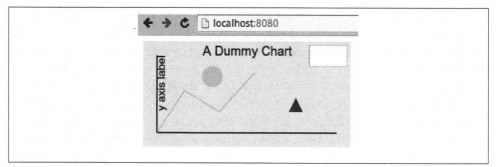

Figure 4-15. A red line path from the chart axis

The red path in Figure 4-15 is produced by the following SVG:

```
<svg>
  <path d="M20 130L60 70L110 100L160 45"></path>
</svg>
```

The path's d attribute specifies the series of operations needed to make the red line. Let's break it down:

- "M20 130": move to coordinate (20, 130)
- "L60 70": draw a line to (60, 70)
- "L110 100": draw a line to (110, 100)
- "L160 45": draw a line to (160, 45)

You can imagine d as a set of instructions to a pen to move to a point, with M raising the pen from the canvas.

A little CSS styling is needed. Note that the fill is set to none; otherwise, to create a fill area, the path would be closed, drawing a line from its end to beginning points, and any enclosed areas filled in with the default color black:

```
#chart path {stroke: red; fill: none}
```

As well as the moveto 'M' and lineto 'L', the path has a number of other commands to draw arcs, Bézier curves, and the like. SVG arcs and curves are commonly used in dataviz work, with many of D3's libraries making use of them.[15] Figure 4-16 shows some SVG elliptical arcs created by the following code:

```
<svg id="chart" width="300" height="150">
  <path d="M40 40
           A30 40    ❶
           0 0 1     ❷
           80 80
           A50 50    0 0 1   160   80
           A30 30    0 0 1   190   80
  ">
</svg>
```

❶ Having moved to position (40, 40), draw an elliptical arc with x-radius 30, y-radius 40, and endpoint (80, 80).

❷ The first flag (0) sets the x axis rotation, in this case the conventional zero. See the Mozilla developer site (*https://oreil.ly/KGCDZ*) for a visual demonstration. The last two flags (0, 1) are large-arc-flag, specifying which arc of the ellipse to use, and sweep-flag, which specifies which of the two possible ellipses defined by start and endpoints to use.

---

15 Mike Bostock's chord diagram (*https://oreil.ly/ujCxf*) is a nice example, and uses D3's chord function.

Figure 4-16. Some SVG elliptical arcs

The key flags used in the elliptical arc (`large-arc-flag` and `sweep-flag`) are, like most things geometric, better demonstrated than described. Figure 4-17 shows the effect of changing the flags for the same relative beginning and endpoints, like so:

```
<svg id="chart" width="300" height="150">
  <path d="M40 80
           A30 40  0 0 1  80 80
           A30 40  0 0 0  120  80
           A30 40  0 1 0  160  80
           A30 40  0 1 1  200  80
  ">
  </svg>
```

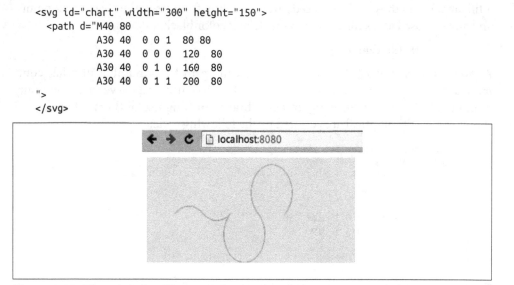

Figure 4-17. Changing the elliptic-arc flags

As well as lines and arcs, the `path` element offers a number of Bézier curves, including quadratic, cubic, and compounds of the two. With a little work, these can create any line path you want. There's a nice run-through on SitePoint (*https://oreil.ly/ PRdVF*) with good illustrations.

For the definitive list of `path` elements and their arguments, go to the World Wide Web Consortium (W3C) source (*https://oreil.ly/s7YSY*). And for a nice round-up, see Jakob Jenkov's introduction (*https://oreil.ly/fdERF*).

Scaling and Rotating

As befits their vector nature, all SVG elements can be transformed by geometric operations. The most commonly used are rotate, translate, and scale, but you can also apply skewing using skewX and skewY or use the powerful, multipurpose *matrix* transform.

Let's demonstrate the most popular transforms, using a set of identical rectangles. The transformed rectangles in Figure 4-18 are achieved like so:

```
<svg id="chart" width="300" height="150">
  <rect width="20" height="40" transform="translate(60, 55)"
        fill="blue"/>
  <rect width="20" height="40" transform="translate(120, 55),
        rotate(45)" fill="blue"/>
  <rect width="20" height="40" transform="translate(180, 55),
        scale(0.5)" fill="blue"/>
  <rect width="20" height="40" transform="translate(240, 55),
        rotate(45),scale(0.5)" fill="blue"/>
</svg>
```

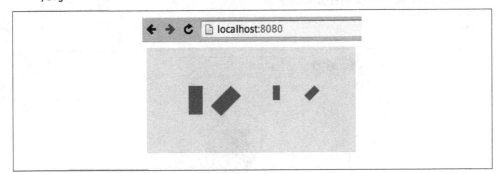

Figure 4-18. Some SVG transforms: rotate(45), scale(0.5), scale(0.5), then rotate(45)

The order in which transforms are applied is important. A rotation of 45 degrees clockwise followed by a translation along the x-axis will see the element moved southeasterly, whereas the reverse operation moves it to the left and then rotates it.

Working with Groups

Often when you are constructing a visualization, it's helpful to group the visual elements. A couple of particular uses are:

- When you require local coordinate schemes (e.g., if you have a text label for an icon and you want to specify its position relative to the icon, not the whole <svg> canvas).

- If you want to apply a scaling and/or rotation transformation to a subset of the visual elements.

SVG has a group <g> tag for this, which you can think of as a mini canvas within the <svg> canvas. Groups can contain groups, allowing for very flexible geometric mappings.[16]

Example 4-5 groups shapes in the center of the canvas, producing Figure 4-19. Note that the position of circle, rect, and path elements is relative to the translated group.

Example 4-5. Grouping SVG shapes

```
<svg id="chart" width="300" height="150">
  <g id="shapes" transform="translate(150,75)">
    <circle cx="50" cy="0" r="25" fill="red" />
    <rect x="30" y="10" width="40" height="20" fill="blue" />
    <path d="M-20 -10L50 -10L10 60Z" fill="green" />
    <circle r="10" fill="yellow">
  </g>
</svg>
```

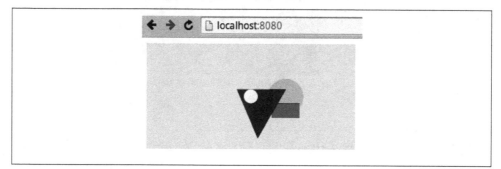

Figure 4-19. Grouping shapes with SVG <g>` tag

If we now apply a transform to the group, all shapes within it will be affected. Figure 4-20 shows the result of scaling Figure 4-19 by a factor of 0.75 and then rotating it 90 degrees, which we achieve by adapting the transform attribute, like so:

```
<svg id="chart" width="300" height="150">
  <g id="shapes",
     transform = "translate(150,75),scale(0.5),rotate(90)">
     ...
</svg>
```

---

16 For example, a body group can contain an arm group, which can contain a hand group, which can contain finger elements.

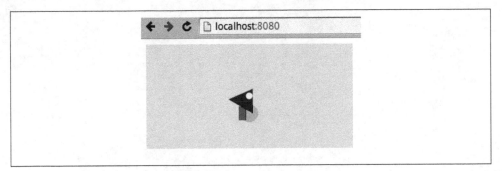

Figure 4-20. Transforming an SVG group

Layering and Transparency

The order in which the SVG elements are added to the DOM tree is important, with later elements taking precedence, layering over others. In Figure 4-19, for example, the triangle path obscures the red circle and blue rectangle and is in turn obscured by the yellow circle.

Manipulating the DOM ordering is an important part of JavaScripted dataviz (e.g., D3's `insert` method allows you to place an SVG element before an existing one).

Element transparency can be manipulated using the alpha channel of `rgba(R,G,B,A)` colors or the more convenient `opacity` property. Both can be set using CSS. For overlaid elements, opacity is cumulative, as demonstrated by the color triangle in Figure 4-21, produced by the following SVG:

```
<style>
  #chart circle { opacity: 0.33 }
</style>

<svg id="chart" width="300" height="150">
  <g transform="translate(150, 75)">
    <circle cx="0" cy="-20" r="30" fill="red"/>
    <circle cx="17.3" cy="10" r="30" fill="green"/>
    <circle cx="-17.3" cy="10" r="30" fill="blue"/>
  </g>
</svg>
```

The SVG elements demonstrated here were handcoded in HTML, but in data visualization work they are almost always added programmatically. Thus the basic D3 workflow is to add SVG elements to a visualization, using data files to specify their attributes and properties.

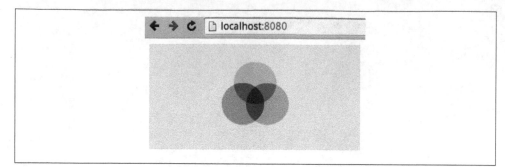

Figure 4-21. Manipulating opacity with SVG

JavaScripted SVG

The fact that SVG graphics are described by DOM tags has a number of advantages over a black box such as the `<canvas>` context. For example, it allows nonprogrammers to create or adapt graphics and is a boon for debugging.

In web dataviz, pretty much all your SVG elements will be created with JavaScript, through a library such as D3. You can inspect the results of this scripting using the browser's Elements tab (see "Chrome DevTools" on page 92), which is a great way to refine and debug your work (e.g., nailing an annoying visual glitch).

As a little taster for things to come, let's use D3 to scatter a few red circles on an SVG canvas. The dimensions of the canvas and circles are contained in a `data` object sent to a `chartCircles` function.

We use a little HTML placeholder for the `<svg>` element:

```
<!DOCTYPE html>
<meta charset="utf-8">

<style>
  #chart { background: lightgray; }
  #chart circle {fill: red}
</style>

<body>
  <svg id="chart"></svg>

  <script src="http://d3js.org/d3.v7.min.js"></script>
  <script src="script.js"></script>
</body>
```

With our placeholder SVG `chart` element in place, a little D3 in the *script.js* file is used to turn some data into the scattered circles (see Figure 4-22):

```
// script.js

var chartCircles = function(data) {

    var chart = d3.select('#chart');
    // Set the chart height and width from data
    chart.attr('height', data.height).attr('width', data.width);
    // Create some circles using the data
    chart.selectAll('circle').data(data.circles)
        .enter()
        .append('circle')
        .attr('cx', function(d) { return d.x })
        .attr('cy', d => d.y) ❶
        .attr('r', d => d.r);
};

var data = {
    width: 300, height: 150,
    circles: [
        {'x': 50, 'y': 30, 'r': 20},
        {'x': 70, 'y': 80, 'r': 10},
        {'x': 160, 'y': 60, 'r': 10},
        {'x': 200, 'y': 100, 'r': 5},
    ]
};

chartCircles(data);
```

❶ This is the modern shorthand arrow-based anonymous function, equivalent to the long form on the previous line. D3 makes use of a lot of these for accessing the properties of bound data objects, so this new syntax is a big win.

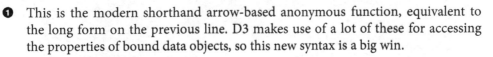

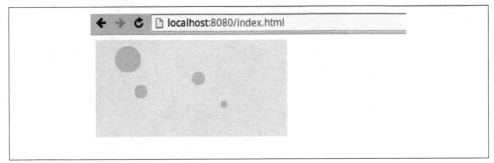

Figure 4-22. D3-generated circles

We'll see exactly how D3 works its magic in Chapter 17. For now, let's summarize what we've learned in this chapter.

Summary

This chapter provided a basic set of modern web-development skills for the budding data visualizer. It showed how the various elements of a web page (HTML, CSS stylesheets, JavaScript, and media files) are delivered by HTTP and, on being received by the browser, combined to become the web page the user sees. We saw how content blocks are described, using HTML tags such as div and p, and then styled and positioned using CSS. We also covered Chrome's Elements and Sources tabs, which are the key browser development tools. Finally we had a little primer in SVG, the language in which most modern web data visualizations are expressed. These skills will be extended when our toolchain reaches its D3 visualization and new ones will be introduced in context.

## PART II

Getting Your Data

In this part of the book, we start our journey along the dataviz toolchain (see Figure II-1), beginning with a couple of chapters on how to get your data if it hasn't been provided for you.

In Chapter 5 we see how to get data off the web, using Python's Requests library to grab web-based files and consume RESTful APIs. We also see how to use a couple of Python libraries that wrap more complex web APIs, namely Twitter (with Python's Tweepy) and Google Docs. The chapter ends with an example of lightweight web scraping (*https://oreil.ly/ffBEA*) with the Beautiful Soup library.

In Chapter 6 we use Scrapy, Python's industrial-strength web scraper, to get the Nobel Prize dataset we'll be using for our web visualization. With this *dirty* dataset to hand, we're ready for the next part of the book, Part III.

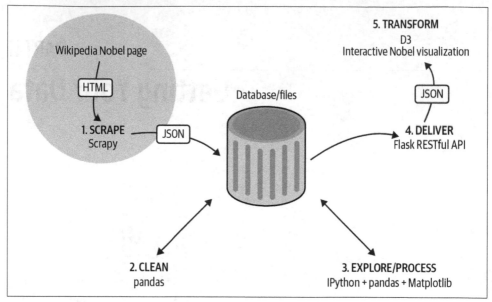

Figure II-1. Our dataviz toolchain: getting the data

You can find the code for this part of the book at the book's GitHub repo (*https://github.com/Kyrand/dataviz-with-python-and-js-ed-2*).

## CHAPTER 5

Getting Data Off the Web with Python

A fundamental part of the data visualizer's skill set is getting the right dataset in as clean a form as possible. Sometimes you will be given a nice, clean dataset to analyze but often you will be tasked with either finding the data and/or cleaning the data supplied.

And more often than not these days, getting data involves getting it off the web. There are various ways you can do this, and Python provides some great libraries that make sucking up the data easy.

The main ways to get data off the web are:

- Get a raw data file in a recognized data format (e.g., JSON or CSV) over HTTP.
- Use a dedicated API to get the data.
- Scrape the data by getting web pages via HTTP and parsing them locally for the required data.

This chapter will deal with these ways in turn, but first let's get acquainted with the best Python HTTP library out there: Requests.

Getting Web Data with the Requests Library

As we saw in Chapter 4, the files that are used by web browsers to construct web pages are communicated via the Hypertext Transfer Protocol (HTTP), first developed by Tim Berners-Lee (*https://oreil.ly/uKF5f*). Getting web content in order to parse it for data involves making HTTP requests.

Negotiating HTTP requests is a vital part of any general-purpose language, but getting web pages with Python used to be a rather irksome affair. The venerable urllib2 library was hardly user-friendly, with a very clunky API. *Requests (https://*

oreil.ly/6VkKZ), courtesy of Kenneth Reitz, changed that, making HTTP a relative breeze and fast establishing itself as the go-to Python HTTP library.

Requests is not part of the Python standard library[1] but is part of the Anaconda package (*https://oreil.ly/LD0ee*) (see Chapter 1). If you're not using Anaconda, the following `pip` command should do the job:

```
$ pip install requests
Downloading/unpacking requests
...
Cleaning up...
```

If you're using a Python version prior to 2.7.9 (I strongly recommend using Python 3+ wherever possible), then using Requests may generate some Secure Sockets Layer (SSL) warnings (*https://oreil.ly/8D08s*). Upgrading to newer SSL libraries should fix this:[2]

```
$ pip install --upgrade ndg-httpsclient
```

Now that you have Requests installed, you're ready to perform the first task mentioned at the beginning of this chapter and grab some raw data files off the web.

Getting Data Files with Requests

A Python interpreter session is a good way to put Requests through its paces, so find a friendly local command line, fire up IPython, and import `requests`:

```
$ ipython
Python 3.8.9 (default, Apr  3 2021, 01:02:10)
...

In [1]: import requests
```

To demonstrate, let's use the library to download a Wikipedia page. We use the Requests library's `get` method to get the page and, by convention, assign the result to a `response` object:

```
response = requests.get(\
"https://en.wikipedia.org/wiki/Nobel_Prize")
```

Let's use Python's `dir` (*https://oreil.ly/CrJ8h*) method to get a list of the `response` object's attributes:

---

1 This is actually a deliberate policy (*https://oreil.ly/WOjdB*) of the developers.

2 There are some platform dependencies that might still generate errors. This Stack Overflow thread (*https://oreil.ly/Zm082*) is a good starting point if you still have problems.

```
dir(response)
Out:
...
 ['content',
 'cookies',
 'elapsed',
 'encoding',
 'headers',
 ...
 'iter_content',
 'iter_lines',
 'json',
 'links',
 ...
 'status_code',
 'text',
 'url']
```

Most of these attributes are self-explanatory and together provide a lot of information about the HTTP response generated. You'll use a small subset of these attributes generally. Firstly, let's check the status of the response:

```
response.status_code
Out: 200
```

As all good minimal web developers know, 200 is the HTTP status code (*https://oreil.ly/ucEoo*) for OK, indicating a successful transaction. Other than 200, the most common codes are:

401 (Unauthorized)
Attempting unauthorized access

400 (Bad Request)
Trying to access the web server incorrectly

403 (Forbidden)
Similar to 401 but no login opportunity was available

404 (Not Found)
Trying to access a web page that doesn't exist

500 (Internal Server Error)
A general-purpose, catchall error

So, for example, if we made a spelling mistake with our request, asking to see the SNoble_Prize page, we'd get a 404 (Not Found) error:

```
not_found_response = requests.get(\
"http://en.wikipedia.org/wiki/SNobel_Prize")
not_found_response.status_code
Out: 404
```

With our 200 OK response, from the correctly spelled request, let's look at some of the info returned. A quick overview can be had with the headers property:

```
response.headers

Out: {
  'date': 'Sat, 23 Oct 2021 23:58:49 GMT',
  'server': 'mw1435.eqiad.wmnet',
  'content-encoding': 'gzip', ...
  'last-modified': 'Sat, 23 Oct 2021 17:14:09 GMT', ...
  'content-type': 'text/html; charset=UTF-8'...
  'content-length': '88959'
  }
```

This shows, among other things, that the page returned was gzip-encoded and 87 KB in size with content-type of text/html, encoded with Unicode UTF-8.

Since we know text has been returned, we can use the text property of the response to see what it is:

```
response.text
#Out: u'<!DOCTYPE html>\n<html lang="en"
#dir="ltr" class="client-nojs">\n<head>\n<meta charset="UTF-8"
#/>\n<title>Nobel Prize - Wikipedia, the free
#encyclopedia</title>\n<script>document.documentElement... =
```

This shows that we do indeed have our Wikipedia HTML page, with some inline JavaScript. As we'll see in "Scraping Data" on page 134, in order to make sense of this content, we'll need a parser to read the HTML and provide the content blocks.

Now that we've grabbed a raw page off the web, let's see how to use Requests to consume a web data API.

Using Python to Consume Data from a Web API

If the data file you need isn't on the web, there may well be an Application Programming Interface (API) serving the data you need. Using this will involve making a request to the appropriate server to retrieve your data in a fixed format or one you get to specify in the request.

The most popular data formats for web APIs are JSON and XML, though a number of esoteric formats exist. For the purposes of the JavaScripting data visualizer, JavaScript Object Notation (JSON) is obviously preferred (see "Data" on page 92). Lucky for us, it is also starting to predominate.

There are different approaches to creating a web API, and for a few years there was a little war of the architectures among the three main types of APIs inhabiting the web:

REST (https://oreil.ly/ujgdJ)
> Short for REpresentational State Transfer, using a combination of HTTP verbs (GET, POST, etc.) and Uniform Resource Identifiers (URIs; e.g., */user/kyran*) to access, create, and adapt data.

XML-RPC (https://oreil.ly/ZMQvW)
> A remote procedure call (RPC) protocol using XML encoding and HTTP transport.

SOAP (https://oreil.ly/l5LVL)
> Short for Simple Object Access Protocol, using XML and HTTP.

This battle seems to be resolving in a victory for RESTful APIs (*https://oreil.ly/apc1l*), and this is a very good thing. Quite apart from RESTful APIs being more elegant, and easier to use and implement (see Chapter 13), some standardization here makes it much more likely that you will recognize and quickly adapt to a new API that comes your way. Ideally, you will be able to reuse existing code. There is a new player on the scene in the form of GraphQL (*https://oreil.ly/JUGVS*), which bills itself as a better REST, but as a datavizzer you're far more likely to be consuming conventional RESTful APIs.

Most access and manipulation of remote data can be summed up by the acronym CRUD (create, retrieve, update, delete), originally coined to describe all the major functions implemented in relational databases. HTTP provides CRUD counterparts with the POST, GET, PUT, and DELETE verbs and the REST abstraction builds on this use of these verbs, acting on a Universal Resource Identifier (URI) (*https://oreil.ly/xmX1k*).

Discussions about what is and isn't a proper RESTful interface can get quite involved, but essentially the URI (e.g., *https://example.com/api/items/2*) should contain all the information required in order to perform a CRUD operation. The particular operation (e.g., GET or DELETE) is specified by the HTTP verb. This excludes architectures such as SOAP, which place stateful information in metadata on the requests header. Imagine the URI as the virtual address of the data and CRUD as all the operations you can perform on it.

As data visualizers keen to lay our hands on some interesting datasets, we are avid consumers here, so our HTTP verb of choice is GET, and the examples that follow will focus on the fetching of data with various well-known web APIs. Hopefully, some patterns will emerge.

Although the two constraints of stateless URIs and the use of the CRUD verbs is a nice constraint on the shape of RESTful APIs, there still manage to be many variants on the theme.

Consuming a RESTful Web API with Requests

Requests has a fair number of bells and whistles based around the main HTTP request verbs. For a good overview, see the Requests quickstart (*https://oreil.ly/Bp8VG*). For the purposes of getting data, you'll use GET and POST pretty much exclusively, with GET being by a long way the most used verb. POST allows you to emulate web forms, including login details, field values, etc. in the request. For those occasions where you find yourself driving a web form with, for example, lots of options selectors, Requests makes automation with POST easy. GET covers pretty much everything else, including the ubiquitous RESTful APIs, which provide an increasing amount of the well-formed data available on the web.

Let's look at a more complicated use of Requests, getting a URL with arguments. The Organisation for Economic Cooperation and Development (OECD) (*https://oreil.ly/QAj3A*) provides some useful datasets on its site (*https://data.oecd.org*). These datasets provide mainly economic measures and statistics for the member countries of the OECD, and such data can form the basis of many interesting visualizations. The OECD provides a few of its own, such as one allowing you to compare your country (*https://oreil.ly/aFmUv*) with others in the OECD.

The OECD web API is described in this documentation (*https://oreil.ly/f5VDc*), and queries are constructed with the dataset name (dsname) and some dot-separated dimensions, each of which can be a number of + separated values. The URL can also take standard HTTP parameters initiated by a ? and separated by &:

```
<root_url>/<dsname>/<dim 1>.<dim 2>...<dim n>
/all?param1=foo&param2=baa..
<dim 1> = 'AUS'+'AUT'+'BEL'...
```

So the following is a valid URL:

```
http://stats.oecd.org/sdmx-json/data/QNA    ❶
    /AUS+AUT.GDP+B1_GE.CUR+VOBARSA.Q          ❷
    /all?startTime=2009-Q2&endTime=2011-Q4   ❸
```

❶ Specifies the QNA (Quarterly National Accounts) dataset.

❷ Four dimensions, by location, subject, measure, and frequency.

❸ Data from the second quarter of 2009 to the fourth quarter of 2011.

Let's construct a little Python function to query the OECD's API (Example 5-1).

Example 5-1. Making a URL for the OECD API

```
OECD_ROOT_URL = 'http://stats.oecd.org/sdmx-json/data'

def make_OECD_request(dsname, dimensions, params=None, \
root_dir=OECD_ROOT_URL):
    """ Make a URL for the OECD API and return a response """

    if not params:    ❶
        params = {}

    dim_args = ['+'.join(d) for d in dimensions]    ❷
    dim_str = '.'.join(dim_args)

    url = root_dir + '/' + dsname + '/' + dim_str + '/all'
    print('Requesting URL: ' + url)
    return requests.get(url, params=params)    ❸
```

❶ You shouldn't use mutable values, such as {}, for Python function defaults. See this Python guide (*https://oreil.ly/Yv6bX*) for an explanation of this gotcha.

❷ We first use a Python list comprehension and the `join` method to create a list of dimensions, with members concatenated with plus signs (e.g., [*USA+AUS, ...*]). `join` is then used again to concatenate the members of `dim_str` with periods.

❸ Note that `requests`' `get` can take a parameter dictionary as its second argument, using it to make the URL query string.

We can use this function like so, to grab economic data for the USA and Australia from 2009 to 2010:

```
response = make_OECD_request('QNA',
    (('USA', 'AUS'),('GDP', 'B1_GE'),('CUR', 'VOBARSA'), ('Q')),
    {'startTime':'2009-Q1', 'endTime':'2010-Q1'})

Requesting URL: http://stats.oecd.org/sdmx-json/data/QNA/
    USA+AUS.GDP+B1_GE.CUR+VOBARSA.Q/all
```

Now, to look at the data, we just check that the response is OK and have a look at the dictionary keys:

```
if response.status_code == 200:
    json = response.json()
    json.keys()
Out: [u'header', u'dataSets', u'structure']
```

The resulting JSON data is in the SDMX format (*https://oreil.ly/HeE7G*), designed to facilitate the communication of statistical data. It's not the most intuitive format around, but it's often the case that datasets have a less than ideal structure. The good news is that Python is a great language for knocking data into shape. For Python's pandas library (*https://pandas.pydata.org*) (see Chapter 8), there is pandaSDMX (*https://oreil.ly/2PKxZ*), which currently handles the XML-based format.

The OECD API is essentially RESTful with all of the query being contained in the URL and the HTTP verb GET specifying a fetch operation. If a specialized Python library isn't available to use the API (e.g., Tweepy for Twitter), then you'll probably end up writing something like Example 5-1. Requests is a very friendly, well-designed library and can cope with pretty much all the manipulations required to use a web API.

Getting Country Data for the Nobel Dataviz

There are some national statistics that will come in handy for the Nobel Prize visualization we're using our toolchain to build. Population sizes, three-letter international codes (e.g., GDR, USA), and geographic centers are potentially useful when you are visualizing an international prize and its distribution. REST countries (*https://restcountries.com*) is a handy RESTful web resource with various international stats. Let's use it to grab some data.

Requests to REST countries take the following form:

```
https://restcountries.com/v3.1/<field>/<name>?<params>
```

As with the OECD API (see Example 5-1), we can make a simple calling function to allow easy access to the API's data, like so:

```python
REST_EU_ROOT_URL = "https://restcountries.com/v3.1"

def REST_country_request(field='all', name=None, params=None):

    headers={'User-Agent': 'Mozilla/5.0'} ❶

    if not params:
        params = {}

    if field == 'all':
        response = requests.get(REST_EU_ROOT_URL + '/all')
        return response.json()

    url = '%s/%s/%s'%(REST_EU_ROOT_URL, field, name)
    print('Requesting URL: ' + url)
    response = requests.get(url, params=params, headers=headers)

    if not response.status_code == 200: ❷
        raise Exception('Request failed with status code ' \
        + str(response.status_code))

    return response.json() # JSON encoded data
```

❶ It's usually a good idea to specify a valid `User-Agent` in the header of your request. Some sites will reject the request otherwise.

❷ Before returning the response, make sure it has an OK (200) HTTP code; otherwise, raise an exception with a helpful message.

With the REST_country_request function in hand, let's get a list of all the countries using the US dollar as currency:

```
response = REST_country_request('currency', 'usd')
response
Out:
[{u'alpha2Code': u'AS',
  u'alpha3Code': u'ASM',
  u'altSpellings': [u'AS',
  ...
  u'capital': u'Pago Pago',
  u'currencies': [u'USD'],
  u'demonym': u'American Samoan',
  ...
  u'latlng': [12.15, -68.266667],
  u'name': u'Bonaire',
  ...
  u'name': u'British Indian Ocean Territory',
  ...
  u'name': u'United States Minor Outlying Islands',
  ... ]}]
```

The full dataset at REST countries is pretty small, so for convenience we'll store a copy as a JSON file. We'll be using this in later chapters in both exploratory and presentational dataviz:

```
import json

country_data = REST_country_request() # all world data

with open('data/world_country_data.json', 'w') as json_file:
    json.dump(country_data, json_file)
```

Now that we've rolled a couple of our own API consumers, let's take a look at some dedicated libraries that wrap some of the larger web APIs in an easy-to-use form.

Using Libraries to Access Web APIs

Requests is capable of negotiating with pretty much all web APIs, but as the APIs start adding authentication and the data structures become more complicated, a good wrapper library can save a lot of hassle and reduce the tedious bookkeeping. In this section, I'll cover a couple of the more popular wrapper libraries (*https://oreil.ly/DBrZ8*) to give you a feel for the workflow and some useful starting points.

Using Google Spreadsheets

It's becoming more common these days to have live datasets *in the cloud*. So, for example, you might find yourself required to visualize aspects of a Google spreadsheet that is the shared data pool for a group. My preference is to get this data out of the Google-plex and into pandas to start exploring it (see Chapter 11), but a good library will let you access and adapt the data *in place*, negotiating the web traffic as required.

gspread (*https://oreil.ly/DNKYT*) is the best known Python library for accessing Google spreadsheets and makes doing so a relative breeze.

You'll need OAuth 2.0 (*https://oreil.ly/z3u6y*) credentials to use the API.[3] The most up-to-date guide can be found on the Google Developers site (*https://oreil.ly/tnO3b*). Following those instructions should provide a JSON file containing your private key.

You'll need to install *gspread* and the latest *google-auth* client library. Here's how to do it with `pip`:

```
$ pip install gspread
$ pip install --upgrade google-auth
```

Depending on your system, you may also need pyOpenSSL:

```
$ pip install PyOpenSSL
```

Read the docs (*https://oreil.ly/1xAPm*) for more details and troubleshooting.

 Google's API assumes that the spreadsheets you are trying to access are owned or shared by your API account, not your personal one. The email address to share the spreadsheet with is available at your Google developers console (*https://oreil.ly/z5KyM*) and in the JSON credentials key needed to use the API. It should look something like *account-1@My Project…iam.gserviceaccount.com*.

With those libraries installed, you should be able to access any of your spreadsheets with just a few lines. I'm using the Microbe-scope spreadsheet (*https://oreil.ly/AAj9X*). Example 5-2 shows how to load the spreadsheet.

---

3 OAuth1 access has been deprecated recently.

Example 5-2. Opening a Google spreadsheet

```
import gspread

gc = gspread.service_account(\
                    filename='data/google_credentials.json') ❶

ss = gc.open("Microbe-scope") ❷
```

❶ The JSON credentials file is the one provided by Google services, usually of the form *My Project-b8ab5e38fd68.json*.

❷ Here we're opening the spreadsheet by name. Alternatives are open_by_url or open_by_id. See the gspread documentation (*https://oreil.ly/sa4sa*) for details.

Now that we've got our spreadsheet, we can see the worksheets it contains:

```
ss.worksheets()
Out:
[<Worksheet 'bugs' id:0>,
 <Worksheet 'outrageous facts' id:430583748>,
 <Worksheet 'physicians per 1,000' id:1268911119>,
 <Worksheet 'amends' id:1001992659>]

ws = ss.worksheet('bugs')
```

With the worksheet bugs selected from the spreadsheet, gspread allows you to access and change column, row, and cell values (assuming the sheet isn't read-only). So we can get the values in the second column with the col_values command:

```
ws.col_values(1)
Out: [None,
 'grey = not plotted',
 'Anthrax (untreated)',
 'Bird Flu (H5N1)',
 'Bubonic Plague (untreated)',
 'C.Difficile',
 'Campylobacter',
 'Chicken Pox',
 'Cholera',...]
```

 If you get a BadStatusLine error while accessing a Google spreadsheet with gspread, it is probably because the session has expired. Reopening the spreadsheet should get things working again. This outstanding gspread issue (*https://oreil.ly/xTGg9*) provides more information.

Although you can use *gspread*'s API to plot directly, using a plot library like Matplotlib, I prefer to send the whole sheet to pandas, Python's powerhouse programmatic spreadsheet. This is easily achieved with gspread's `get_all_records`, which returns a list of item dictionaries. This list can be used directly to initialize a pandas DataFrame (see "The DataFrame" on page 195):

```
df = pd.DataFrame(ws.get_all_records(expected_headers=[]))
df.info()
Out:
<class 'pandas.core.frame.DataFrame'>
Int64Index: 41 entries, 0 to 40
Data columns (total 23 columns):
                                      41 non-null object
average basic reproductive rate       41 non-null object
case fatality rate                    41 non-null object
infectious dose                       41 non-null object
...
upper R0                              41 non-null object
viral load in acute stage             41 non-null object
yearly fatalities                     41 non-null object
dtypes: object(23)
memory usage: 7.5+ KB
```

In Chapter 11, we'll see how to interactively explore a DataFrame's data.

Using the Twitter API with Tweepy

The advent of social media has generated a lot of data and an interest in visualizing the social networks, trending hashtags, and media storms contained in them. Twitter's broadcast network is probably the richest source of cool data visualizations, and its API provides tweets[4] filtered by user, hashtag, date, and the like.

Python's Tweepy is an easy-to-use Twitter library that provides a number of useful features, such as a `StreamListener` class for streaming live Twitter updates. To start using it, you'll need a Twitter access token, which you can acquire by following the instructions at the Twitter docs (*https://oreil.ly/ZkWNf*) to create your Twitter application. Once this application is created, you can get the keys and access tokens for your app by clicking on the link at your Twitter app page (*https://apps.twitter.com*).

Tweepy typically requires the four authorization elements shown here:

```
# The user credential variables to access Twitter API
access_token = "2677230157-Ze3bWuBAw4kwoj4via2dEntU86...TD7z"
access_token_secret = "DxwKAvVzMFLq7WnQGnty49jgJ39Acu...paR8ZH"
consumer_key = "pIorGFGQHShuYQtIxzYWk1jMD"
consumer_secret = "yLc4Hw82G0Zn4vTi4q8pSBcNyHkn35BfIe...oVa4P7R"
```

---

4 The free API is currently limited to around 350 requests per hour (*https://oreil.ly/LKzJX*).

With those defined, accessing tweets could hardly be easier. Here we create an OAuth auth object using our tokens and keys and use it to start an API session. We can then grab the latest tweets from our timeline:

```
In [0]: import tweepy

        auth = tweepy.OAuthHandler(consumer_key,\
                                    consumer_secret)
        auth.set_access_token(access_token, access_token_secret)

        api = tweepy.API(auth)

        public_tweets = api.home_timeline()
        for tweet in public_tweets:
            print(tweet.text)

RT @Glinner: Read these tweets https://t.co/QqzJPsDxUD
Volodymyr Bilyachat https://t.co/VIyOHlje6b +1 bmeyer
#javascript
RT @bbcworldservice: If scientists edit genes to
make people healthier does it change what it means to be
human? https://t.co/Vciuyu6BCx h…
RT @ForrestTheWoods:
Launching something pretty cool tomorrow. I'm excited. Keep
...
```

Tweepy's `API` class offers a lot of convenience methods, which you can check out in the Tweepy docs (*https://oreil.ly/2FTRw*). A common visualization is using a network graph to show patterns of friends and followers among Twitter subpopulations. The Tweepy method `followers_ids` (get all users following) and `friends_ids` (get all users being followed) can be used to construct such a network:

```
my_follower_ids = api.get_follower_ids() ❶

followers_tree = {'followers': []}
for id in my_follower_ids:
    # get the followers of your followers
    try:
        follower_ids = api.get_follower_ids(user_id=id) ❷
    except tweepy.errors.Unauthorized:
        print("Unauthorized to access user %d's followers"\
            %(id))

    followers_tree['followers'].append(\
        {'id': id, 'follower_ids': follower_ids})
```

❶ Gets a list of your followers' IDs (e.g., [1191701545, 1554134420, …]).

❷ The first argument to `follower_ids` can be a user ID or screen name.

Note that you will probably run into rate-limit errors if you try and construct a network for anyone with more than a hundred followers (see this Stack Overflow thread (*https://oreil.ly/1KDH2*) for an explanation). To overcome this you will need to implement some basic rate limiting to reduce your request count to 180 per 15 minutes. Alternatively, you can pay Twitter for a premium account.

By mapping followers of followers, you can create a network of connections that might just reveal something interesting about groups and subgroups clustered about a particular individual or subject. There's a nice example of just such a Twitter analysis on Gabe Sawhney's blog (*https://oreil.ly/sWH99*).

One of the coolest features of Tweepy is its `StreamListener` class, which makes it easy to collect and process filtered tweets in real time. Live updates of Twitter streams have been used by many memorable visualizations (see these examples from FlowingData (*https://oreil.ly/mNOYX*) and DensityDesign (*https://oreil.ly/ZpmLq*) for some inspiration). Let's set up a little stream to record tweets mentioning Python, JavaScript, and dataviz. We'll just print the results to the screen (in `on_data`) here, but you would normally cache them in a file or database (or do both with SQLite):

```python
import json


class MyStream(tweepy.Stream):
    """ Customized tweet stream """

    def on_data(self, tweet):
        """Do something with the tweet data..."""
        print(tweet)

    def on_error(self, status):
        return True # keep stream open

stream = MyStream(consumer_key, consumer_secret,\
                    access_token, access_token_secret)
# Start the stream with track list of keywords
stream.filter(track=['python', 'javascript', 'dataviz'])
```

Now that we've had a taste of the kind of APIs you might run into during your search for interesting data, let's look at the primary technique you'll use if, as is often the case, no one is providing the data you want in a neat, user-friendly form: scraping data with Python.

Scraping Data

Scraping is the chief metaphor used for the practice of getting data that wasn't designed to be programmatically consumed off the web. It is a pretty good metaphor because scraping is often about getting the balance right between removing too much and too little. Creating procedures that extract just the right data, as cleanly as possible, from web pages is a craft skill and often a fairly messy one at that. But the payoff is access to visualizable data that often cannot be acquired in any other way. Approached in the right way, scraping can even have an intrinsic satisfaction.

Why We Need to Scrape

In an ideal virtual world, online data would be organized in a library, with everything cataloged through a sophisticated Dewey decimal system for the web page. Unfortunately for the keen data hunter, the web has grown organically, often unconstrained by considerations of easy data access for the budding data visualizer. So, in reality, the web resembles a big mound of data, some of it clean and usable (and thankfully this percentage is increasing) but much of it poorly formed and designed for human consumption. And humans are able to parse the kind of messy, poorly formed data that our relatively dumb computers have problems with.[5]

Scraping is about fashioning selection patterns that grab the data we want and leave the rest behind. If we're lucky, the web pages containing the data will have helpful pointers, like named tables, specific identities in preference to generic classes, and so on. If we're unlucky, then these pointers will be missing and we will have to resort to using other patterns or, in the worst case, ordinal specifiers such as *third table in the main div*. These are obviously pretty fragile, and will break if somebody adds a table above the third.

In this section, we'll tackle a little scraping task, to get the same Nobel Prize winners data. We'll use Python's best-of-breed Beautiful Soup for this lightweight scraping foray, saving the heavy guns of Scrapy for the next chapter.

The fact that data and images are on the web does not mean that they are necessarily free to use. For our scraping examples we'll be using Wikipedia, which allows full reuse under the Creative Commons license (*https://oreil.ly/jBTaC*). It's a good idea to make sure anything you scrape is available and, if in doubt, contact the site maintainer. You may be required to at least cite the original author.

---

5 Much of modern machine learning and artificial intelligence (AI) research is dedicated to creating computer software that can cope with messy, noisy, fuzzy, informal data but, as of this book's publication, there's no off-the-shelf solution I know of.

Beautiful Soup and lxml

Python's key lightweight scraping tools are Beautiful Soup and lxml. Their primary selection syntax is different but, confusingly, each can use the other's parsers. The consensus seems to be that lxml's parser is considerably faster, but Beautiful Soup's might be more robust when dealing with poorly formed HTML. Personally, I've found lxml to be robust enough and its syntax, based on xpaths (*https://oreil.ly/A43cY*), more powerful and often more intuitive. I think for someone coming from web development, familiar with CSS and jQuery, selection based on CSS selectors is much more natural. Depending on your system, lxml is usually the default parser for Beautiful Soup. We'll be using it in the following sections.

Beautiful Soup is part of the Anaconda packages (see Chapter 1) and easily installed with pip:

```
$ pip install beautifulsoup4
$ pip install lxml
```

A First Scraping Foray

Armed with Requests and Beautiful Soup, let's give ourselves a little task to get the names, years, categories, and nationalities of all the Nobel Prize winners. We'll start at the main Wikipedia Nobel Prize page (*https://oreil.ly/cSFFW*). Scrolling down shows a table with all the laureates by year and category, which is a good start to our minimal data requirements.

Some kind of HTML explorer is pretty much a must for web scraping, and the best I know is Chrome's web developer's Elements tab (see "The Elements Tab" on page 92). Figure 5-1 shows the key elements involved in quizzing a web page's structure. We need to know how to select the data of interest, in this case a Wikipedia table, while avoiding other elements on the page. Crafting good selector patterns is the key to effective scraping, and highlighting the DOM element using the element inspector gives us both the CSS pattern and, with a right-click, the xpath. The latter is a particularly powerful syntax for DOM element selection and the basis of our industrial-strength scraping solution, Scrapy.

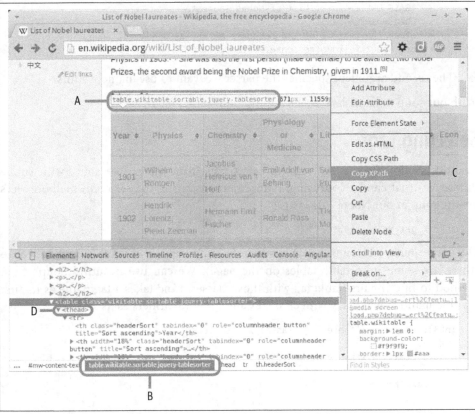

Figure 5-1. Wikipedia's main Nobel Prize page: A and B show the wikitable's CSS selector. Right-clicking and selecting C (Copy XPath) gives the table's xpath (//*[@id="mw-content-text"]/table[1]). D shows a thead tag generated by jQuery.

Getting the Soup

The first thing you need to do before scraping the web page of interest is to parse it with Beautiful Soup, converting the HTML into a tag tree hierarchy or soup:

```python
from bs4 import BeautifulSoup
import requests

BASE_URL = 'http://en.wikipedia.org'
# Wikipedia will reject our request unless we add
# a 'User-Agent' attribute to our http header.
HEADERS = {'User-Agent': 'Mozilla/5.0'}

def get_Nobel_soup():
    """ Return a parsed tag tree of our Nobel prize page """
    # Make a request to the Nobel page, setting valid headers
    response = requests.get(
```

```
      BASE_URL + '/wiki/List_of_Nobel_laureates',
      headers=HEADERS)
# Return the content of the response parsed by Beautiful Soup
return BeautifulSoup(response.content, "lxml")  ❶
```

❶ The second argument specifies the parser we want to use, namely lxml's.

With our soup in hand, let's see how to find our target tags.

Selecting Tags

Beautiful Soup offers a few ways to select tags from the parsed soup, with subtle differences that can be confusing. Before demonstrating the selection methods, let's get the soup of our Nobel Prize page:

```
soup = get_Nobel_soup()
```

Our target table (see Figure 5-1) has two defining classes, wikitable and sortable (there are some unsortable tables on the page). We can use Beautiful Soup's find method to find the first table tag with those classes. find takes a tag name as its first argument and a dictionary with class, ID, and other identifiers as its second:

```
In[3]: soup.find('table', {'class':'wikitable sortable'})
Out[3]:
<table class="wikitable sortable">
<tr>
<th>Year</th>
...
```

Although we have successfully found our table by its classes, this method is not very robust. Let's see what happens when we change the order of our CSS classes:

```
In[4]: soup.find('table', {'class':'sortable wikitable'})
# nothing returned
```

So find cares about the order of the classes, using the class string to find the tag. If the classes were specified in a different order—something that might well happen during an HTML edit, then the find fails. This fragility makes it difficult to recommend the Beautiful Soup selectors, such as find and find_all. When doing quick hacking, I find lxml's CSS selectors (*https://lxml.de/cssselect.html*) easier and more intuitive.

Using the soup's select method (available if you specified the lxml parser when creating it), you can specify an HTML element using its CSS class, ID, and so on. This CSS selector is converted into the xpath syntax lxml uses internally.[6]

---

6 This CSS selection syntax should be familiar to anyone who's used JavaScript's jQuery library (*https:// jquery.com*) and is also similar to that used by D3 (*https://d3js.org*).

To get our wikitable, we just select a table in the soup, using the dot notation to indicate its classes:

```
In[5]: soup.select('table.sortable.wikitable')
Out[5]:
[<table class="wikitable sortable">
 <tr>
 <th>Year</th>
 ...
 ]
```

Note that `select` returns an array of results, finding all the matching tags in the soup. lxml provides the `select_one` convenience method if you are selecting just one HTML element. Let's grab our Nobel table and see what headers it has:

```
In[8]: table = soup.select_one('table.sortable.wikitable')

In[9]: table.select('th')
Out[9]:
[<th>Year</th>,
 <th width="18%"><a href="/wiki/..._in_Physics..</a></th>,
 <th width="16%"><a href="/wiki/..._in_Chemis..</a></th>,
 ...
 ]
```

As a shorthand for `select`, you can call the tag directly on the soup; so these two are equivalent:

```
table.select('th')
table('th')
```

With lxml's parser, Beautiful Soup provides a number of different filters for finding tags, including the simple string name we've just used, searching by regular expression (*https://oreil.ly/GeU8Q*), using a list of tag names, and more. See this comprehensive list (*https://oreil.ly/iBQwc*) for more details.

As well as lxml's `select` and `select_one`, there are 10 BeautfulSoup convenience methods for searching the parsed tree. These are essentially variants on `find` and `find_all` that specify which parts of the tree they search. For example, `find_parent` and `find_parents`, rather than looking for descendants down the tree, look for parent tags of the tag being searched. All 10 methods are available in the Beautiful Soup official docs (*https://oreil.ly/oPrQl*).

Now that we know how to select our Wikipedia table and are armed with lxml's selection methods, let's see how to craft some selection patterns to get the data we want.

Crafting Selection Patterns

Having successfully selected our data table, we now want to craft some selection patterns to scrape the required data. Using the HTML explorer, you can see that the individual winners are contained in <td> cells, with an href <a> link to Wikipedia's bio pages (in the case of individuals). Here's a typical target row with CSS classes that we can use as targets to get the data in the <td> cells:

```
<tr>
 <td align="center">
  1901
 </td>
 <td>
  <span class="sortkey">
  Röntgen, Wilhelm
  </span>
  <span class="vcard">
   <span class="fn">
    <a href="/wiki/Wilhelm_R%C3%B6ntgen" \
       title="Wilhelm Röntgen">
     Wilhelm Röntgen
    </a>
   </span>
  </span>
 </td>
 <td>
 ...
</tr>
```

If we loop through these data cells, keeping track of their row (year) and column (category), then we should be able to create a list of winners with all the data we specified except nationality.

The following `get_column_titles` function scrapes our table for the Nobel category column headers, ignoring the first Year column. Often the header cell in a Wikipedia table contains a web-linked 'a' tag; all the Nobel categories fit this model, pointing to their respective Wikipedia pages. If the header is not clickable, we store its text and a null href:

```
def get_column_titles(table):
    """ Get the Nobel categories from the table header """
    cols = []
    for th in table.select_one('tr').select('th')[1:]: ❶
        link = th.select_one('a')
        # Store the category name and any Wikipedia link it has
        if link:
            cols.append({'name':link.text,\
                        'href':link.attrs['href']})
        else:
            cols.append({'name':th.text, 'href':None})
    return cols
```

❶ We loop through the table head, ignoring the first Year column ([1:]). This selects the column headers shown in Figure 5-2.

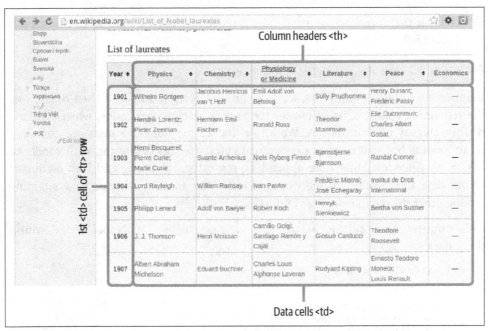

Figure 5-2. Wikipedia's table of Nobel Prize winners

Let's make sure `get_column_titles` is giving us what we want:

```
get_column_titles(table)
Out:
[{'name': 'Physics', \
  'href': '/wiki/List_of_Nobel_laureates_in_Physics'},
 {'name': 'Chemistry',\
  'href': '/wiki/List_of_Nobel_laureates_in_Chemistry'},...
]

def get_Nobel_winners(table):
    cols = get_column_titles(table)
    winners = []
    for row in table.select('tr')[1:-1]:  ❶
        year = int(row.select_one('td').text) # Gets 1st <td>
        for i, td in enumerate(row.select('td')[1:]):  ❷
            for winner in td.select('a'):
                href = winner.attrs['href']
                if not href.startswith('#endnote'):
                    winners.append({
                        'year':year,
                        'category':cols[i]['name'],
                        'name':winner.text,
```

```
            'link':winner.attrs['href']
        })
    return winners
```

❶ Gets all the Year rows, starting from the second, corresponding to the rows in Figure 5-2.

❷ Finds the <td> data cells shown in Figure 5-2.

Iterating through the Year rows, we take the first Year column and then iterate over the remaining columns, using enumerate to keep track of our index, which will map to the category column names. We know that all the winner names are contained in an <a> tag but that there are occasional extra <a> tags beginning with #endnote, which we filter for. Finally we append a year, category, name, and link dictionary to our data array. Note that the winner selector has an attrs dictionary containing, among other things, the <a> tag's href.

Let's confirm that get_Nobel_winners delivers a list of Nobel Prize winner dictionaries:

```
get_Nobel_winners(table)

[{'year': 1901,
  'category': 'Physics',
  'name': 'Wilhelm Röntgen',
  'link': '/wiki/Wilhelm_R%C3%B6ntgen'},
 {'year': 1901,
  'category': 'Chemistry',
  'name': "Jacobus Henricus van 't Hoff",
  'link': '/wiki/Jacobus_Henricus_van_%27t_Hoff'},
 {'year': 1901,
  'category': 'Physiologyor Medicine',
  'name': 'Emil Adolf von Behring',
  'link': '/wiki/Emil_Adolf_von_Behring'},
 {'year': 1901,
 ...}]
```

Now that we have the full list of Nobel Prize winners and links to their Wikipedia pages, we can use these links to scrape data from the individuals' biographies. This will involve making a largish number of requests, and it's not something we really want to do more than once. The sensible and respectful[7] thing is to cache the data we scrape, allowing us to try out various scraping experiments without returning to Wikipedia.

---

7 When scraping, you're using other people's web bandwidth, which ultimately costs them money. It's just good manners to try to limit your number of requests.

Caching the Web Pages

It's easy enough to rustle up a quick cacher in Python, but as often as not it's easier still to find a better solution written by someone else and kindly donated to the open source community. Requests has a nice plug-in called requests-cache that, with a few lines of configuration, will take care of all your basic caching needs.

First, we install the plug-in using pip:

```
$ pip install --upgrade requests-cache
```

requests-cache uses monkey patching (*https://oreil.ly/8IklZ*) to dynamically replace parts of the requests API at runtime. This means it can work transparently. You just have to install its cache and then use requests as usual, with all the caching being taken care of. Here's the simplest way to use requests-cache:

```
import requests
import requests_cache

requests_cache.install_cache()
# use requests as usual...
```

The install_cache method has a number of useful options, including allowing you to specify the cache backend (sqlite, memory, mongodb, or redis) or set an expiry time (expiry_after) in seconds on the caching. So the following creates a cache named nobel_pages with an sqlite backend and pages that expire in two hours (7,200 s):

```
requests_cache.install_cache('nobel_pages',\
                    backend='sqlite', expire_after=7200)
```

requests-cache will serve most of your caching needs and couldn't be much easier to use. For more details, see the official docs (*https://oreil.ly/d67bK*) where you'll also find a little example of request throttling, which is a useful technique when doing bulk scraping.

Scraping the Winners' Nationalities

With caching in place, let's try getting the winners' nationalities, using the first 50 for our experiment. A little get_winner_nationality() function will use the winner links we stored earlier to scrape their page and then use the info-box shown in Figure 5-3 to get the Nationality attribute.

Figure 5-3. *Scraping a winner's nationality*

> When scraping, you are looking for reliable patterns and repeating elements with useful data. As we'll see, the Wikipedia info-boxes for individuals are not such a reliable source, but clicking on a few random links certainly gives that impression. Depending on the size of the dataset, it's good to perform a few experimental sanity checks. You can do this manually but, as mentioned at the start of the chapter, this won't scale or improve your craft skills.

Example 5-3 takes one of the winner dictionaries we scraped earlier and returns a name-labeled dictionary with a `Nationality` key if one is found. Let's run it on the first 50 winners and see how often a `Nationality` attribute is missing.

Example 5-3. *Scraping the winner's country from their biography page*

```python
HEADERS = {'User-Agent': 'Mozilla/5.0'}

def get_winner_nationality(w):
    """ scrape biographic data from the winner's wikipedia page """
    response = requests.get('http://en.wikipedia.org' \
                            + w['link'], headers=HEADERS)
    content = response.content.decode('utf-8')
    soup = BeautifulSoup(content)
    person_data = {'name': w['name']}
    attr_rows = soup.select('table.infobox tr')    ❶
    for tr in attr_rows:                            ❷
```

```
        try:
            attribute = tr.select_one('th').text
            if attribute == 'Nationality':
                person_data[attribute] = tr.select_one('td').text
        except AttributeError:
            pass

    return person_data
```

❶ We use a CSS selector to find all the `<tr>` rows of the table with class `infobox`.

❷ Cycles through the rows looking for a Nationality field.

Example 5-4 shows that 14 of the 50 first winners failed our attempt to scrape their nationality. In the case of the Institut de Droit International, national affiliation may well be moot, but Theodore Roosevelt is about as American as they come. Clicking on a few of the names shows the problem (see Figure 5-4). The lack of a standardized biography format means synonyms for *Nationality* are often employed, as in Marie Curie's *Citizenship*; sometimes no reference is made, as with Niels Finsen; and Randall Cremer has nothing but a photograph in his info-box. We can discard the info-boxes as a reliable source of winners' nationalities but, as they appeared to be the only regular source of potted data, this sends us back to the drawing board. In the next chapter, we'll see a successful approach using Scrapy and a different start page.

Example 5-4. Testing for scraped nationalities

```
wdata = []
# test first 50 winners
for w in winners[:50]:
    wdata.append(get_winner_nationality(w))
missing_nationality = []
for w in wdata:
    # if missing 'Nationality' add to list
    if not w.get('Nationality'):
        missing_nationality.append(w)
# output list
missing_nationality

[{'name': 'Theodor Mommsen'},
 {'name': 'Élie Ducommun'},
 {'name': 'Charles Albert Gobat'},
 {'name': 'Pierre Curie'},
 {'name': 'Marie Curie'},
 {'name': 'Niels Ryberg Finsen'},
 ...
 {'name': 'Theodore Roosevelt'}, ... ]
```

Figure 5-4. Winners without a recorded nationality

Although Wikipedia is a relative free-for-all, production-wise, where data is designed for human consumption, you can expect a lack of rigor. Many sites have similar gotchas and as the datasets get bigger, more tests may be needed to find the flaws in a collection pattern.

Although our first scraping exercise was a little artificial in order to introduce the tools, I hope it captured something of the slightly messy spirit of web scraping. The ultimately abortive pursuit of a reliable Nationality field for our Nobel dataset could have been forestalled by a bit of web browsing and manual HTML-source trawling. However, if the dataset were significantly larger and the failure rate a bit smaller, then programmatic detection, which gets easier and easier as you become acquainted with the scraping modules, really starts to deliver.

This little scraping test was designed to introduce Beautiful Soup, and shows that collecting the data we seek requires a little more thought, which is often the case with scraping. In the next chapter, we'll wheel out the big gun, Scrapy, and, with what we've learned in this section, harvest the data we need for our Nobel Prize visualization.

Summary

In this chapter, we've seen examples of the most common ways in which data can be sucked out of the web and into Python containers, databases, or pandas datasets. Python's Requests library is the true workhorse of HTTP negotiation and a fundamental tool in our dataviz toolchain. For simpler, RESTful APIs, consuming data with Requests is a few lines of Python away. For the more awkward APIs, such as those with potentially complicated authorization, a wrapper library like Tweepy (for Twitter) can save a lot of hassle. Decent wrappers can also keep track of access rates and, where necessary, throttle your requests. This is a key consideration, particularly when there is the possibility of blacklisting unfriendly consumers.

We also started our first forays into data scraping, which is often a necessary fallback where no API exists and the data is for human consumption. In the next chapter, we'll get all the Nobel Prize data needed for the book's visualization using Python's Scrapy, an industrial-strength scraping library.

Heavyweight Scraping with Scrapy

As your scraping goals get more ambitious, hacking solutions with Beautiful Soup and requests can get very messy very fast. Managing the scraped data as requests spawn more requests gets tricky, and if your requests are being made synchronously, things start to slow down rapidly. A whole load of problems you probably hadn't anticipated start to make themselves known. It's at this point that you want to turn to a powerful, robust library that solves all these problems and more. And that's where Scrapy comes in.

Where Beautiful Soup is a very handy little penknife for fast and dirty scraping, Scrapy is a Python library that can do large-scale data scrapes with ease. It has all the things you'd expect, like built-in caching (with expiration times), asynchronous requests via Python's Twisted web framework, user-agent randomization, and a whole lot more. The price for all this power is a fairly steep learning curve, which this chapter is intended to smooth, using a simple example. I think Scrapy is a powerful addition to any dataviz toolkit and really opens up possibilities for web data collection.

In "Scraping Data" on page 134, we managed to scrape a dataset containing all the Nobel Prize winners by name, year, and category. We did a speculative scrape of the winners' linked biography pages, which showed that extracting the country of nationality was going to be difficult. In this chapter, we'll set the bar on our Nobel Prize data a bit higher and aim to scrape objects of the form shown in Example 6-1.

Example 6-1. Our targeted Nobel JSON object

```
{
  "category": "Physiology or Medicine",
  "country": "Argentina",
  "date_of_birth': "8 October 1927",
  "date_of_death': "24 March 2002",
  "gender": "male",
  "link": "http:\/\/en.wikipedia.org\/wiki\/C%C3%A9sar_Milstein",
  "name": "C\u00e9sar Milstein",
  "place_of_birth": "Bah\u00eda Blanca , Argentina",
  "place_of_death": "Cambridge , England",
  "text": "C\u00e9sar Milstein , Physiology or Medicine, 1984",
  "year": 1984
}
```

In addition to this data, we'll aim to scrape prizewinners' photos (where applicable) and some potted biographical data (see Figure 6-1). We'll be using the photos and body text to add a little character to our Nobel Prize visualization.

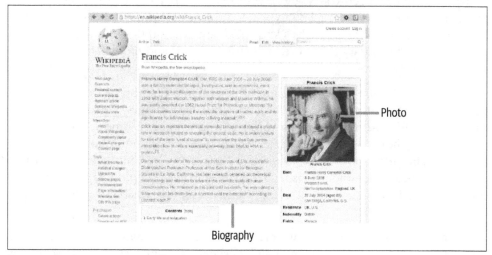

Figure 6-1. Scraping targets for the prizewinners' pages

Setting Up Scrapy

Scrapy should be one of the Anaconda packages (see Chapter 1), so you should already have it on hand. If that's not the case, then you can install it with the following conda command line:

```
$ conda install -c https://conda.anaconda.org/anaconda scrapy
```

If you're not using Anaconda, a quick `pip` install will do the job:[1]

```
$ pip install scrapy
```

With Scrapy installed, you should have access to the `scrapy` command. Unlike the vast majority of Python libraries, Scrapy is designed to be driven from the command line within the context of a scraping project, defined by configuration files, scraping spiders, pipelines, and so on. Let's generate a fresh project for our Nobel Prize scraping, using the `startproject` option. This is going to generate a project folder, so make sure you run it from a suitable work directory:

```
$ scrapy startproject nobel_winners
New Scrapy project 'nobel_winners' created in:
    /home/kyran/workspace/.../scrapy/nobel_winners

You can start your first spider with:
    cd nobel_winners
    scrapy genspider example example.com
```

As the output of `startproject` says, you'll want to switch to the *nobel_winners* directory in order to start driving Scrapy.

Let's take a look at the project's directory tree:

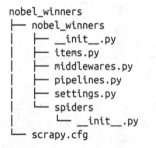

```
nobel_winners
├── nobel_winners
│   ├── __init__.py
│   ├── items.py
│   ├── middlewares.py
│   ├── pipelines.py
│   ├── settings.py
│   └── spiders
│       └── __init__.py
└── scrapy.cfg
```

As shown, the project directory has a subdirectory with the same name and a config file *scrapy.cfg*. The *nobel_winners* subdirectory is a Python module (containing an *__init__.py* file) with a few skeleton files and a *spiders* directory, which will contain your scrapers.

Establishing the Targets

In "Scraping Data" on page 134, we tried to scrape the Nobel winners' nationalities from their biography pages but found they were missing or inconsistently labeled in many cases (see Chapter 5). Rather than get the country data indirectly, a little Wikipedia searching shows a way through. There is a page (*https://oreil.ly/p6pXm*)

---

1 See the Scrapy install docs (*https://oreil.ly/LamAt*) for platform-specific details.

that lists winners by country. The winners are presented in titled, ordered lists (see Figure 6-2), not in tabular form, which makes recovering our basic name, category, and year data a little harder. Also the data organization is not ideal (e.g., the country header titles and winner lists aren't in useful, separate blocks). As we'll see, a few well-structured Scrapy queries will easily net us the data we need.

Figure 6-2 shows the starting page for our first spider along with the key elements it will be targeting. A list of country name titles (A) is followed by an ordered list (B) of their Nobel Prize–winning citizens.

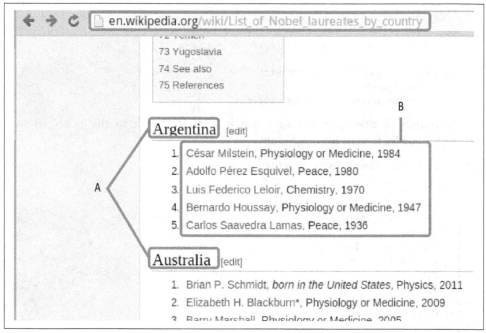

Figure 6-2. Scraping Wikipedia's Nobel Prizes by nationality

In order to scrape the list data, we need to fire up our Chrome browser's DevTools (see "The Elements Tab" on page 92) and inspect the target elements using the Elements tab and its inspector (magnifying glass). Figure 6-3 shows the key HTML targets for our first spider: header titles (h2) containing a country name and followed by an ordered list (ol) of winners (li).

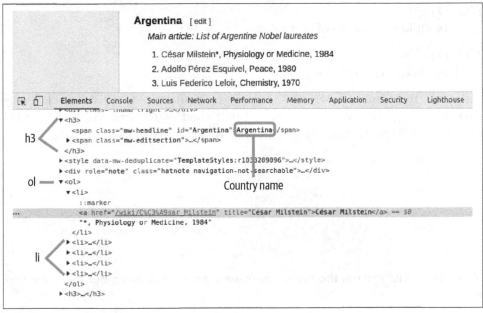

Figure 6-3. Finding the HTML targets for the wikilist

Targeting HTML with Xpaths

Scrapy uses xpaths (*https://oreil.ly/Y67BF*) to define its HTML targets. Xpath is a syntax for describing parts of an X(HT)ML document, and while it can get rather complicated, the basics are straightforward and will often solve the job at hand.

You can get the xpath of an HTML element by using Chrome's Elements tab to hover over the source and then right-clicking and selecting Copy XPath. For example, in the case of our Nobel Prize wikilist's country names (h3 in Figure 6-3), selecting the xpath of Argentina (the first country) gives the following:

```
//*[@id="mw-content-text"]/div[1]/h3[1]
```

We can use the following xpath rules to decode it:

//E
Element <E> anywhere in the document (e.g., //img gets all images on the page)

//E[@id="foo"]
Select element <E> with ID foo

//*[@id="foo"]
Select any element with ID foo

```
//E/F[1]
```
First child element <F> of element <E>

```
//E/*[1]
```
First child of element <E>

Following these rules shows that our Argentinian title `//*[@id="mw-content-text"]/div[1]/h3[1]` is the first header (h2) child of the first `div` of the DOM element with ID `mw-content-text`. This is equivalent to the following HTML:

```
<div id="mw-content-text">
  <div>
    <h2>
      ...
    </h2>
  </div>
  ...
</div>
```

Note that unlike Python, the xpaths don't use a zero-based index but make the first member *1*.

Testing Xpaths with the Scrapy Shell

Getting your xpath targeting right is crucial to good scraping and can involve a degree of iteration. Scrapy makes this process much easier by providing a command-line shell, which takes a URL and creates a response context in which you can try out your xpaths, like so:

```
$ scrapy shell
  https://en.wikipedia.org/wiki/List_of_Nobel_laureates_by_country


2021-12-09 14:31:06 [scrapy.utils.log] INFO: Scrapy 2.5.1 started
(bot: nobel_winners)
...

2021-12-09 14:31:07 [scrapy.core.engine] INFO: Spider opened
2021-12-09 14:31:07 [scrapy.core.engine] DEBUG: Crawled (200)
<GET https://en.wikip...List_of_Nobel_laureates_by_country>
(referer: None)
[s] Available Scrapy objects:

[s]   crawler  <scrapy.crawler.Crawler object at 0x3a8f510>
[s]   item {}
[s]   request  <GET https://...Nobel_laureates_by_country>
[s]   response  <200 https://...Nobel_laureates_by_country>
[s]   settings  <scrapy.settings.Settings object at 0x34a98d0>
[s]   spider  <DefaultSpider 'default' at 0x3f59190>

[s] Useful shortcuts:
```

```
[s]   shelp()   Shell help (print this help)
[s]   fetch(url[, redirect=True]) Fetch URL and update local objects
(by default, redirects are followed)
[s]   fetch(req)                  Fetch a scrapy.Request and update
[s]   view(response)    View response in a browser

In [1]:
```

Now we have an IPython-based shell with code-complete and syntax highlighting in which to try out our xpath targeting. Let's grab all the <h3> headers on the wiki page:

```
In [1]: h3s = response.xpath('//h3')
```

The resulting h3s is a SelectorList (*https://oreil.ly/zpbqa*), a specialized Python list object. Let's see how many headers we have:

```
In [2]: len(h3s)
Out[2]: 91
```

We can grab the first Selector object (*https://oreil.ly/uBhdU*) and query its methods and properties in the Scrapy shell by pressing Tab after appending a dot:

```
In [3] h3 = h3s[0]
In [4] h3.
attrib          get           re                 remove            ...
css             getall        re_first           remove_namespaces ...
extract         namespaces    register_namespace response          ...
```

You'll often use the extract method to get the raw result of the xpath selector:

```
In [5]: h3.extract()
Out[6]:
u'<h3>
  <span class="mw-headline" id="Argentina">Argentina</span>
  <span class="mw-editsection">
  <span class="mw-editsection-bracket">
  ...
  </h3>'
```

This shows that our country headers start on the first <h3> and contain a span with class mw-headline. We can use the presence of the mw-headline class as a filter for our country headers and the contents as our country label. Let's try out an xpath, using the selector's text method to extract the text from the mw-headline span. Note that we use the xpath method of the <h3> selector, which makes the xpath query relative to that element:

```
In [7]: h3_arg = h3
In [8]: country = h3_arg.xpath(\
                        'span[@class="mw-headline"]/text()')\
.extract()
In [9]: country
Out[9]: ['Argentina']
```

The extract method returns a list of possible matches, in our case the single 'Argen tina' string. By iterating through the h3s list, we can now get our country names.

Assuming we have a country's <h3> header, we now need to get the <ol> ordered list of Nobel winners following it (Figure 6-2 B). Handily, the xpath following-sibling selector can do just that. Let's grab the first ordered list after the Argentina header:

```
In [10]: ol_arg = h3_arg.xpath('following-sibling::ol[1]')\
Out[10]: ol_arg
[<Selector xpath='following-sibling::ol[1]' data=u'<ol><li>
<a href="/wiki/C%C3%A9sar_Milst'>]
```

Looking at the truncated data for ol_arg shows that we have selected an ordered list. Note that even though there's only one Selector, xpath still returns a SelectorList. For convenience, you'll generally just select the first member directly:

```
In [11]: ol_arg = h2_arg.xpath('following-sibling::ol[1]')[0]
```

Now that we've got the ordered list, let's get a list of its member <li> elements (as of mid 2022):

```
In [12]: lis_arg = ol_arg.xpath('li')
In [13]: len(lis_arg)
Out[13]: 5
```

Let's examine one of those list elements using extract. As a first test, we're looking to scrape the name of the winner and capture the list element's text:

```
In [14]: li = lis_arg[0] # select the first list element
In [15]: li.extract()
Out[15]:
'<li><a href="/wiki/C%C3%A9sar_Milstein"
        title="C\xe9sar Milstein">C\xe9sar Milstein</a>,
        Physiology or Medicine, 1984</li>'
```

Extracting the list element shows a standard pattern: a hyperlinked name to the winner's Wikipedia page followed by a comma-separated winning category and year. A robust way to get the winning name is just to select the text of the list element's first <a> tag:

```
In [16]: name = li.xpath('a//text()')[0].extract()
In [17]: name
Out[17]: 'César Milstein'
```

It's often useful to get all the text in, for example, a list element, stripping the various HTML <a>, <span>, and other tags. descendant-or-self gives us a handy way of doing this, producing a list of the descendants' text:

```
In [18]: list_text = li.xpath('descendant-or-self::text()')\
.extract()
In [19]: list_text
Out[19]: ['César Milstein', '*', Physiology or Medicine, 1984']
```

We can get the full text by joining the list elements together:

```
In [20]: ' '.join(list_text)
Out[20]: 'César Milstein *, Physiology or Medicine, 1984'
```

Note that the first item of `list_text` is the winner's name, giving us another way to access it if, for example, it were missing a hyperlink.

Now that we've established the xpaths to our scraping targets (the name and link text of the Nobel Prize winners), let's incorporate them into our first Scrapy spider.

Selecting with Relative Xpaths

As just shown, Scrapy `xpath` selections return lists of selectors which, in turn, have their own `xpath` methods. When using the `xpath` method, it's important to be clear about relative and absolute selections. Let's make the distinction clear using the Nobel page's table of contents as an example.

The table of contents has the following structure:

```
<div id='toc'... >
  ...
  <ul ... >
    <li ... >
      <a href='Argentina'> ... </a>
    </li>
    ...
  </ul>
  ...
</div>
```

We can select the table of contents of the Nobel wiki page using a standard `xpath` query on the response, and getting the `div` with ID toc:

```
In [21]: toc = response.xpath('//div[@id="toc"]')[0]
```

If we want to get all the country `<li>` list tags, we can use a relative `xpath` on the selected `toc` div. Looking at the HTML in Figure 6-3 shows that the unordered list ul of countries is the first list member of the second list item of the table of content's top list. This list can be selected by the following equivalent xpaths, both selecting children of the current `toc` selection relatively:

```
In [22]: lis = toc.xpath('.//ul/li[2]/ul/li')
In [23]: lis = toc.xpath('ul/li[2]/ul/li')
In [24]: len(lis)
Out[24]: 81 # the number of countries in the table of contents (July 2022)
```

A common mistake is to use a nonrelative `xpath` selector on the current selection, which selects from the whole document, in this case getting all unordered (`<ul>`) `<li>` tags:

```
In [25]: lis = toc.xpath('//ul/li')
In [26]: len(lis)
OUt[26]: 271
```

Errors made from mistaking relative and nonrelative queries crop up a lot in the forums, so it's good to be very aware of the distinction and watch those dots.

 Getting the right xpath expression for your target element(s) can be a little tricky, and those difficult edge cases can demand a complex nest of clauses. The use of a well-written cheat sheet can be a great help here, and thankfully there are many good xpath ones. A very nice selection can be found at devhints.io (*https://devhints.io/xpath*).

A First Scrapy Spider

Armed with a little xpath knowledge, let's produce our first scraper aiming to get the country and link text for the winners (Figure 6-2 A and B).

Scrapy calls its scrapers *spiders*, each of which is a Python module placed in the *spiders* directory of your project. We'll call our first scraper *nwinner_list_spider.py*:

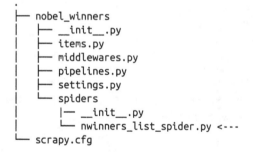
```
.
├── nobel_winners
│   ├── __init__.py
│   ├── items.py
│   ├── middlewares.py
│   ├── pipelines.py
│   ├── settings.py
│   └── spiders
│       ├── __init__.py
│       └── nwinners_list_spider.py <---
└── scrapy.cfg
```

Spiders are subclassed `scrapy.Spider` classes, and any placed in the *spiders* directory will be automatically detected by Scrapy and made accessible by name to the `scrapy` command.

The basic Scrapy spider shown in Example 6-2 follows a pattern you'll be using with most of your spiders. First, you subclass a Scrapy `item` to create fields for your scraped data (section A in Example 6-2). You then create a named spider by subclassing `scrapy.Spider` (section B in Example 6-2). You will use the spider's name when calling `scrapy` from the command line. Each spider has a `parse` method, which deals with the HTTP requests to a list of start URLs contained in a `start_url` class attribute. In our case, the start URL is the Wikipedia page for Nobel laureates by country.

Example 6-2. A first Scrapy spider

```python
# nwinners_list_spider.py

import scrapy
import re
# A. Define the data to be scraped
class NWinnerItem(scrapy.Item):
    country = scrapy.Field()
    name = scrapy.Field()
    link_text = scrapy.Field()

# B Create a named spider
class NWinnerSpider(scrapy.Spider):
    """ Scrapes the country and link text of the Nobel-winners. """

    name = 'nwinners_list'
    allowed_domains = ['en.wikipedia.org']
    start_urls = [
        "http://en.wikipedia.org ... of_Nobel_laureates_by_country"
    ]
    # C A parse method to deal with the HTTP response
    def parse(self, response):

        h3s = response.xpath('//h3')   ❶

        for h3 in h3s:
            country = h3.xpath('span[@class="mw-headline"]'\
            'text()').extract()   ❷
            if country:
                winners = h2.xpath('following-sibling::ol[1]')   ❸
                for w in winners.xpath('li'):
                    text = w.xpath('descendant-or-self::text()')\
                    .extract()
                    yield NWinnerItem(
                        country=country[0], name=text[0],
                        link_text = ' '.join(text)
                    )
```

❶   Gets all the <h3> headers on the page, most of which will be our target country titles.

❷   Where possible, gets the text of the <h3> element's child <span> with class mw-headline.

❸   Gets the list of country winners.

The parse method in Example 6-2 receives the response from an HTTP request to the Wikipedia Nobel Prize page and yields Scrapy items, which are then converted to JSON objects and appended to the output file, a JSON array of objects.

Let's run our first spider to make sure we're correctly parsing and scraping our Nobel data. First, navigate to the *nobel_winners* root directory (containing the *scrapy.cfg* file) of the scraping project. Let's see what scraping spiders are available:

```
$ scrapy list
nwinners_list
```

As expected, we have one `nwinners_list` spider sitting in the *spiders* directory. To start it scraping, we use the `crawl` command and direct the output to a *nwinners.json* file. By default, we get a lot of Python logging information accompanying the crawl:

```
$ scrapy crawl nwinners_list -o nobel_winners.json
2021- ... [scrapy] INFO: Scrapy started (bot: nobel_winners)
...
2021- ... [nwinners_list] INFO: Closing spider (finished)
2021- ... [nwinners_list] INFO: Dumping Scrapy stats:
        {'downloader/request_bytes': 1147,
         'downloader/request_count': 4,
         'downloader/request_method_count/GET': 4,
         'downloader/response_bytes': 66459,

         ...
         'item_scraped_count': 1169,  ❶
2021- ...  [scrapy.core.engine] INFO: Spider closed (finished)
```

❶   We scraped 1,169 Nobel winners from the page.

The output of the scrapy `crawl` shows 1,169 items successfully scraped. Let's look at our JSON output file to make sure things have gone according to plan:

```
$ head nobel_winners.json
[{"country": "Argentina",
  "link_text": "C\u00e9sar Milstein , Physiology or Medicine,"\
  " 1984",
  "name": "C\u00e9sar Milstein"},
 {"country": "Argentina",
  "link_text": "Adolfo P\u00e9rez Esquivel , Peace, 1980",
  "name": "Adolfo P\u00e9rez Esquivel"},
  ...
```

As you can see, we have an array of JSON objects with the four key fields present and correct.

Now that we have a spider that successfully scrapes the list data for all the Nobel winners on the page, let's start refining it to grab all the data we are targeting for our Nobel Prize visualization (see Example 6-1 and Figure 6-1).

First, let's add all the data we plan to scrape as fields to our `scrapy.Item`:

```
...
class NWinnerItem(scrapy.Item):
    name = scrapy.Field()
    link = scrapy.Field()
    year = scrapy.Field()
    category = scrapy.Field()
    country = scrapy.Field()
    gender = scrapy.Field()
    born_in = scrapy.Field()
    date_of_birth = scrapy.Field()
    date_of_death = scrapy.Field()
    place_of_birth = scrapy.Field()
    place_of_death = scrapy.Field()
    text = scrapy.Field()
...
```

It's also sensible to simplify the code a bit and use a dedicated function, `process_win ner_li`, to process the winners' link text. We'll pass a link selector and country name to it and return a dictionary containing the scraped data:

```
...

def parse(self, response):

    h3s = response.xpath('//h3')

    for h3 in h3s:
        country = h3.xpath('span[@class="mw-headline"]/text()')\
        .extract()
        if country:
            winners = h3.xpath('following-sibling::ol[1]')
            for w in winners.xpath('li'):
                wdata = process_winner_li(w, country[0])
                ...
```

Embracing Regexes

> Some people, when confronted with a problem, think "I know, I'll use regular expressions." Now they have two problems.
>
> —Jamie Zawinskie

The preceding quote is a hoary old classic but does sum up how many people feel about regular expressions (regexes) (*https://oreil.ly/OfQls*). Regexes use a sequence of characters to define a search expression used for string matching. Both Python and JavaScript have built-in handling of them.

In Python, the `re` module provides a number of regex methods. A common task might be to find all the email addresses in a document, recognizing email strings by the form *foo@bar.com*. Let's create a regex to find them, breaking down the process:[2]

```
In [12]: txt = 'Feel free to contact me at '\
' pyjdataviz@kyrandale.com with any feedback.'

In [13]: re.findall(r'[\w\.-]+@[\w\.-]+', txt)
Out[13]: ['pyjdataviz@kyrandale.com']
```

The `findall` method takes a regex string (with an *r* prepended) as its first argument and the text to search as its second. The email search pattern uses the following rules:

\w   Matches an alphanumeric string containing numbers and upper and lowercase letters (regex shorthand is [0-9a-zA-Z_])

\   Escapes a special character

\.   Matches a dot

\-   Matches a hyphen

\+   Matches one or more of the square-bracketed strings

Taken together, these rules match any two strings connected by @ and containing alphanumeric characters or dots or hyphens. This is obviously a pretty broad pattern (e.g., .@. would provide a match) that you might want to refine. For example, you could use `r'[\w\.-]@gmail.com` if you were searching for only Gmail addresses.

Although the syntax of regexes can be challenging at first, the fact is that web scraping is often about pattern-matching messy and underspecified data, and a regex is pretty much tailor-made for many of the jobs that crop up. You can probably hack your way around them, but embracing them a little will make your life that much easier, and the good news is that a little goes a long way. See Example 6-3 for some examples.

---

2 There are some handy online tools for testing regexes, some of them programming-language-specific. Pyregex (*http://www.pyregex.com*) is a good Python one, with a handy cheat sheet included.

The `process_winner_li` method is shown in Example 6-3. A `wdata` dictionary is filled with information extracted from the winner's `li` tag, using a couple of regexes to find the prize year and category.

Example 6-3. Processing a winner's list item

```
# ...
import re
BASE_URL = 'http://en.wikipedia.org'
# ...

def process_winner_li(w, country=None):
    """
    Process a winner's <li> tag, adding country of birth or
    nationality, as applicable.
    """
    wdata = {}
    # get the href link-address from the <a> tag
    wdata['link'] = BASE_URL + w.xpath('a/@href').extract()[0] ❶

    text = ' '.join(w.xpath('descendant-or-self::text()')\
        .extract())
    # get comma-delineated name and strip trailing whitespace
    wdata['name'] = text.split(',')[0].strip()

    year = re.findall('\d{4}', text) ❷
    if year:
        wdata['year'] = int(year[0])
    else:
        wdata['year'] = 0
        print('Oops, no year in ', text)

    category = re.findall(
            'Physics|Chemistry|Physiology or Medicine|Literature|'\
            'Peace|Economics',
                text) ❸
    if category:
        wdata['category'] = category[0]
    else:
        wdata['category'] = ''
        print('Oops, no category in ', text)

    if country:
        if text.find('*') != -1: ❹
            wdata['country'] = ''
            wdata['born_in'] = country
        else:
            wdata['country'] = country
            wdata['born_in'] = ''
```

```
# store a copy of the link's text-string for any manual corrections
wdata['text'] = text
return wdata
```

 To grab the `href` attribute from the list item's `<a>` tag (`<li><a href=/wiki…`
`>[winner name]</a>…`), we use the xpath attribute referent @.

 Here, we use `re`, Python's built-in regex library, to find the four-digit year strings
in the list item's text.

❸ Another use of the regex library to find the Nobel Prize category in the text.

❹ An asterisk following the winner's name is used to indicate that the country is
the winner's by birth—not nationality—at the time of the prize (e.g., `"William
Lawrence Bragg*, Physics, 1915"` in the list for Australia).

Example 6-3 returns all the winners' data available on the main Wikipedia Nobels by
Country page—that is, the name, year, category, country (country of birth or country
of nationality when awarded the prize), and a link to the individual winners' pages.
We'll need to use this last information to get those biographical pages and use them to
scrape our remaining target data (see Example 6-1 and Figure 6-1).

Scraping the Individual Biography Pages

The main Wikipedia Nobels by Country page gave us a lot of our target data, but
the winner's date of birth, date of death (where applicable), and gender are still to be
scraped. It is hoped that this information is available, either implicitly or explicitly,
on their biography pages (for nonorganization winners). Now's a good time to fire up
Chrome's Elements tab and take a look at those pages to work out how we're going to
extract the desired data.

We saw in the last chapter (Chapter 5) that the visible information boxes on individual's pages are not a reliable source of information and are often missing entirely. Until
recently,[3] a hidden `persondata` table (see Figure 6-4) gave fairly reliable access to such
information as place of birth, date of death, and the like. Unfortunately, this handy
resource has been deprecated.[4] The good news is that this is part of an attempt to
improve the categorization of biographical information by giving it a dedicated space
in Wikidata (*https://oreil.ly/ICbBi*), Wikipedia's central storage for its structured data.

---

3 The author got stung by this removal.

4 See Wikipedia (*https://oreil.ly/pLVcE*) for an explanation.

```
</table>
<table id="persondata" class="persondata noprint" style="border:1px solid #a
<tr>
<th colspan="2"><a href="/wiki/Wikipedia:Persondata" title="Wikipedia:Person
</tr>
<tr>
<td class="persondata-label" style="color:#aaa;">Name</td>
<td>Röntgen, Wilhelm</td>
</tr>
<tr>
<td class="persondata-label" style="color:#aaa;">Alternative names</td>
<td>Conrad</td>
</tr>
```

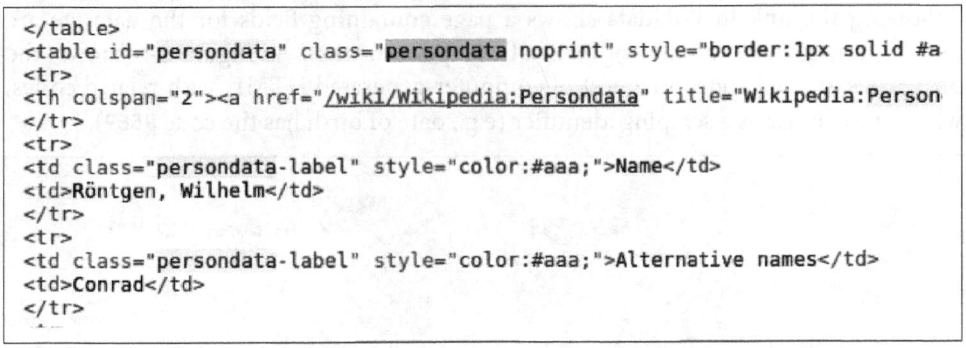

Figure 6-4. A Nobel Prize winner's hidden persondata table

Examining Wikipedia's biography pages with Chrome's Elements tab shows a link to
the relevant Wikidata item (see Figure 6-5), which takes you to the biographical data
held at *https://www.wikidata.org*. By following this link, we can scrape whatever we
find there, which we hope will be the bulk of our target data—significant dates and
places (see Example 6-1). 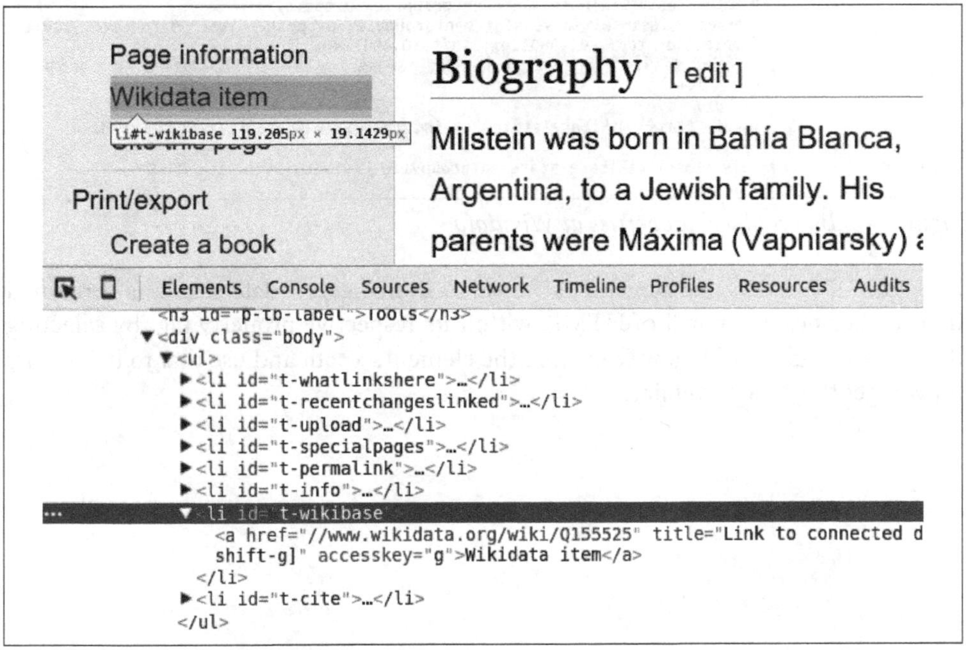

Figure 6-5. Hyperlink to the winner's Wikidata

Following the link to Wikidata shows a page containing fields for the data we are looking for, such as the date of birth of our prize winner. As Figure 6-6 shows, the properties are embedded in a nest of computer-generated HTML, with related codes, which we can use as a scraping identifier (e.g., date of birth has the code P569).

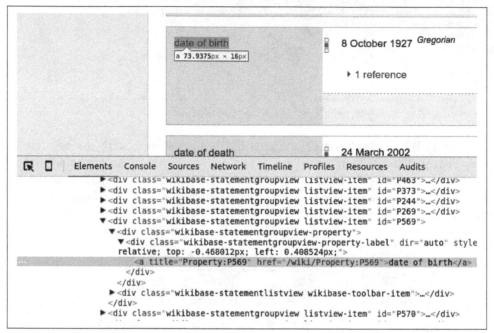

Figure 6-6. Biographical properties at Wikidata

As Figure 6-7 shows, the actual data we want, in this case a date string, is contained in a further nested branch of HTML, within its respective property tag. By selecting the div and right-clicking, we can store the element's xpath and use that to tell Scrapy how to get the data it contains.

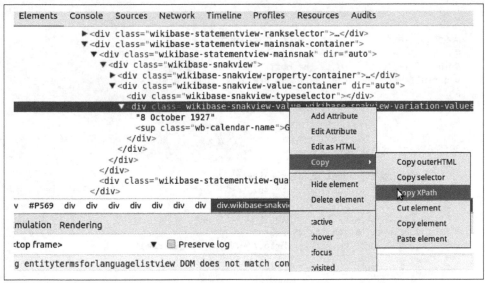

Figure 6-7. Getting the xpath for a Wikidata property

Now that we have the xpaths necessary to find our scraping targets, let's put it all together and see how Scrapy chains requests, allowing for complex, multipage scraping operations.

Chaining Requests and Yielding Data

In this section we'll see how to chain Scrapy requests, allowing us to follow hyperlinks, scraping data as we go. First, let's enable Scrapy's page caching. While experimenting with xpath targets, we want to limit the number of calls to Wikipedia, and it's good manners to store our fetched pages. Unlike some datasets out there, our Nobel Prize winners change but once a year.[5]

Caching Pages

As you might expect, Scrapy has a sophisticated caching system (*https://oreil.ly/ytYWP*) that gives you fine-grained control over your page caching (e.g., allowing you to choose between database or filesystem storage backends, how long before your pages are expired, etc.). It is implemented as middleware (*https://oreil.ly/w8v7c*) enabled in our project's `settings.py` module. There are various options available but for the purposes of our Nobel scraping, simply setting `HTTPCACHE_ENABLED` to `True` will suffice:

---

5 Strictly speaking, there are edits being made continually by the Wikipedia community, but the fundamental details should be stable until the next set of prizes.

```
# -*- coding: utf-8 -*-

# Scrapy settings for nobel_winners project
#
# This file contains only the most important settings by
# default. All the other settings are documented here:
#
#     http://doc.scrapy.org/en/latest/topics/settings.html
#

BOT_NAME = 'nobel_winners'

SPIDER_MODULES = ['nobel_winners.spiders']
NEWSPIDER_MODULE = 'nobel_winners.spiders'

# Crawl responsibly by identifying yourself
# (and your website) on the user-agent
#USER_AGENT = 'nobel_winners (+http://www.yourdomain.com)'

HTTPCACHE_ENABLED = True
```

Check out the full range of Scrapy middleware in Scrapy's documentation (*https:// oreil.ly/9CMc4*).

Having ticked the caching box, let's see how to chain Scrapy requests.

Yielding Requests

Our existing spider's `parse` method cycles through the Nobel winners, using the `pro cess_winner_li` method to scrape the country, name, year, category, and biography-hyperlink fields. We now want to use the biography hyperlinks to generate a Scrapy request that will fetch the bio pages and send them to a custom method for scraping.

Scrapy implements a Pythonic pattern for chaining requests, using Python's `yield` statement to create a generator,[6] allowing Scrapy to easily consume any extra page requests we make. Example 6-4 shows the pattern in action.

Example 6-4. Yielding a request with Scrapy

```
class NWinnerSpider(scrapy.Spider):
    name = 'nwinners_full'
    allowed_domains = ['en.wikipedia.org']
    start_urls = [
        "https://en.wikipedia.org/wiki/List_of_Nobel_laureates" \
        "_by_country"
    ]
```

---

6 See Jeff Knupp's blog, "Everything I Know About Python" (*https://oreil.ly/qgku4*), for a nice rundown of Python generators and the use of `yield`.

```
def parse(self, response):

    h3s = response.xpath('//h3')
    for h3 in h3s:
        country = h3.xpath('span[@class="mw-headline"]/text()')
                    .extract()
        if country:
            winners = h2.xpath('following-sibling::ol[1]')
            for w in winners.xpath('li'):
                wdata = process_winner_li(w, country[0])
                request = scrapy.Request( ❶
                    wdata['link'],
                    callback=self.parse_bio, ❷
                    dont_filter=True)
                request.meta['item'] = NWinnerItem(**wdata) ❸
                yield request ❹

def parse_bio(self, response):
    item = response.meta['item'] ❺
    ...
```

❶ Makes a request to the winner's biography page, using the link (wdata[*link*]) scraped from process_winner_li.

❷ Sets the callback function to handle the response.

❸ Creates a Scrapy Item to hold our Nobel data and initializes it with the data just scraped from process_winner_li. This Item data is attached to the metadata of the request to allow any response access to it.

❹ By yielding the request, we make the parse method a generator of consumable requests.

❺ This method handles the callback from our bio-link request. In order to add scraped data to our Scrapy Item, we first retrieve it from the response metadata.

Our investigation of the Wikipedia pages in "Scraping the Individual Biography Pages" on page 164 showed that we need to locate a winner's Wikidata link from their biography page and use it to generate a request. We will then scrape the date, place, and gender data from the response.

Example 6-5 shows parse_bio and parse_wikidata, the two methods used to scrape our winners' biographical data. parse_bio uses the scraped Wikidata link to request the Wikidata page, yielding the request as it in turn was yielded in the parse method. At the end of the request chain, parse_wikidata retrieves the item and fills in any of the fields available from Wikidata, eventually yielding the item to Scrapy.

Example 6-5. Parsing the winners' biography data

```
# ...

    def parse_bio(self, response):

        item = response.meta['item']
        href = response.xpath("//li[@id='t-wikibase']/a/@href")  ❶
                .extract()
        if href:
            url = href[0]  ❷
            wiki_code = url.split('/')[-1]
            request = scrapy.Request(href[0],\
                            callback=self.parse_wikidata,\  ❸
                            dont_filter=True)
            request.meta['item'] = item
            yield request


    def parse_wikidata(self, response):

        item = response.meta['item']
        property_codes = [  ❹
            {'name':'date_of_birth', 'code':'P569'},
            {'name':'date_of_death', 'code':'P570'},
            {'name':'place_of_birth', 'code':'P19', 'link':True},
            {'name':'place_of_death', 'code':'P20', 'link':True},
            {'name':'gender', 'code':'P21', 'link':True}
          ]

        for prop in property_codes:

            link_html = ''
            if prop.get('link'):
                link_html = '/a'
            # select the div with a property-code id
            code_block = response.xpath('//*[@id="%s"]'%(prop['code']))
            # continue if the code_block exists
            if code_block:
            # We can use the css selector, which has superior class
            # selection
                values = code_block.css('.wikibase-snakview-value')
            # the first value corresponds to the code property\
            # (e.g., '10 August 1879')
                value = values[0]
                prop_sel = value.xpath('.%s/text()'%link_html)
                if prop_sel:
                    item[prop['name']] = prop_sel[0].extract()

        yield item  ❺
```

❶ Extracts the link to Wikidata identified in Figure 6-5.

Extracts the `wiki_code` from the URL, e.g., *http://wikidata.org/wiki/Q155525* →
Q155525.

❸ Uses the Wikidata link to generate a request with our spider's `parse_wikidata` as
a callback to deal with the response.

❹ These are the property codes we found earlier (see Figure 6-6), with names
corresponding to fields in our Scrapy item, `NWinnerItem`. Those with a `True link`
attribute are contained in `<a>` tags.

❺ Finally we yield the item, which at this point should have all the target data
available from Wikipedia.

With our request chain in place, let's check that the spider is scraping our required
data:

```
$ scrapy crawl nwinners_full
2021-... [scrapy] ... started (bot: nobel_winners)
...
2021-... [nwinners_full] DEBUG: Scraped from
        <200 https://www.wikidata.org/wiki/Q155525>
  {'born_in': '',
   'category': u'Physiology or Medicine',
   'date_of_birth': u'8 October 1927',
   'date_of_death': u'24 March 2002',
   'gender': u'male',
   'link': u'http://en.wikipedia.org/wiki/C%C3%A9sar_Milstein',
   'name': u'C\xe9sar Milstein',
   'country': u'Argentina',
   'place_of_birth': u'Bah\xeda Blanca',
   'place_of_death': u'Cambridge',
   'text': u'C\xe9sar Milstein , Physiology or Medicine, 1984',
   'year': 1984}
2021-... [nwinners_full] DEBUG: Scraped from
        <200 https://www.wikidata.org/wiki/Q193672>
  {'born_in': '',
   'category': u'Peace',
   'date_of_birth': u'1 November 1878',
   'date_of_death': u'5 May 1959',
   'gender': u'male',
   'link': u'http://en.wikipedia.org/wiki/Carlos_Saavedra_Lamas',
   ...
```

Things are looking good. With the exception of the `born_in` field, which is dependent
on a name in the main Wikipedia Nobel Prize winners list having an asterisk, we're
getting all the data we were targeting. This dataset is now ready to be cleaned by
pandas in the coming chapter.

Now that we've scraped our basic biographical data for the Nobel Prize winners, let's go scrape our remaining targets, some biographical body text, and a picture of the great man or woman, where available.

Scrapy Pipelines

In order to add a little personality to our Nobel Prize visualization, it would be good to have a little biographical text and an image of the winner. Wikipedia's biographical pages generally provide these things, so let's go about scraping them.

Up to now, our scraped data has been text strings. In order to scrape images in their various formats, we need to use a Scrapy *pipeline*. Pipelines (*https://oreil.ly/maUyE*) provide a way of postprocessing the items we have scraped, and you can define any number of them. You can write your own or take advantage of those already provided by Scrapy, such as the ImagesPipeline we'll be using.

In its simplest form, a pipeline need only define a process_item method. This receives the scraped items and the spider object. Let's write a little pipeline to reject genderless Nobel Prize winners (so we can omit prizes given to organizations rather than individuals) using our existing nwinners_full spider to deliver the items. First, we add a DropNonPersons pipeline to the pipelines.py module of our project:

```
# nobel_winners/nobel_winners/pipelines.py

# Define your item pipelines here
#
# Don't forget to add your pipeline to the ITEM_PIPELINES setting
# See: http://doc.scrapy.org/en/latest/topics/item-pipeline.html

from scrapy.exceptions import DropItem


class DropNonPersons(object):
    """ Remove non-person winners """

    def process_item(self, item, spider):
        if not item['gender']:                              ❶
            raise DropItem("No gender for %s"%item['name'])
        return item ❷
```

❶ If our scraped item failed to find a gender property at Wikidata, it is probably an organization such as the Red Cross. Our visualization is focused on individual winners, so here we use DropItem to remove the item from our output stream.

❷ We need to return the item to further pipelines or for saving by Scrapy.

As mentioned in the `pipelines.py` header, in order to add this pipeline to the spiders of our project, we need to register it in the `settings.py` module by adding it to a `dict` of pipelines and setting it to active (1):

```
# nobel_winners/nobel_winners/settings.py

BOT_NAME = 'nobel_winners'
SPIDER_MODULES = ['nobel_winners.spiders']
NEWSPIDER_MODULE = 'nobel_winners.spiders'

HTTPCACHE_ENABLED = True
ITEM_PIPELINES = {'nobel_winners.pipelines.DropNonPersons':300}
```

Now that we've got the basic workflow for our pipelines, let's add a useful one to our project.

Scraping Text and Images with a Pipeline

We now want to scrape the winners' biographies and photos (see Figure 6-1), where available. We can scrape the biographical text using the same method as our last spider, but the photos are best dealt with by an image pipeline.

We could easily write our own pipeline to take a scraped image URL, request it from Wikipedia, and save to disk, but to do it properly requires a bit of care. For example, we would like to avoid reloading an image that was recently downloaded or hasn't changed in the meantime. Some flexibility in specifying where to store the images is a useful feature. It would also be good to have the option of converting the images into a common format (e.g., JPG or PNG) or of generating thumbnails. Luckily, Scrapy provides an `ImagesPipeline` object with all this functionality and more. This is one of its media pipelines (*https://oreil.ly/y9vAT*), which includes a `FilesPipeline` for dealing with general files.

We could add the image and biography-text scraping to our existing `nwinners_full` spider, but that's starting to get a little large, and segregating this character data from the more formal categories makes sense. So we'll create a new spider called `nwinners_minibio` that will reuse parts of the previous spider's `parse` method in order to loop through the Nobel winners.

As usual, when creating a Scrapy spider, our first job is to get the xpaths for our scraping targets—in this case, where available that's the first part of the winners' biographical text and a photograph of them. To do this, we fire up Chrome Elements and explore the HTML source of the biography pages looking for the targets shown in Figure 6-8.

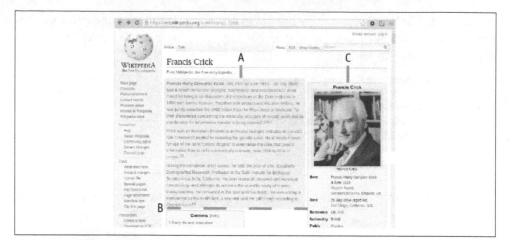

Figure 6-8. The target elements for our biography scraping: the first part of the biography (A) marked by a stop point (B), and the winner's photograph (C)

Example 6-6. Scraping the biographical text

```
<div id="mw-content-text">
  <div class="mw-parser-output">
    ...
    <table class="infobox biography vcard">...</table>
    /* target paragraphs: */
    <p>...</p>
    <p>...</p>
    <p>...</p>
    <div id="toc">...</div>
  ...
  </div>
</div>
```

Investigating with Chrome Elements (see Example 6-6) shows the biographical text (Figure 6-8 A) is contained in child paragraphs of the div with class mw-parser-output, which is a child of the div with ID mw-content-text. The paragraphs are sandwiched between a table with class infobox and a table-of-contents div with ID toc. We can use the xpath following-sibling and preceding-sibling operators to craft a selector that captures the target paragraphs:

```
ps = response.xpath(\
  '//*[@id="mw-content-text"]/div/table/following-sibling::p' ❶
  '[not(preceding-sibling::div[@id="toc"])]').extract() ❷
```

❶ All paragraphs following the first table in the child div of the div with ID mw-content-text.

❷ Exclude (not) all paragraphs that have a preceding sibling div with ID toc.

Testing this with the Scrapy shell shows it consistently captures the Nobel winners' mini-bios.

Further exploration of the winners' pages shows that their photos (Figure 6-8 C) are contained in a table of class infobox and are the only image tags (<img>) in that table:

```
<table class="infobox biography vcard">
    ...
        <img alt="Francis Crick crop.jpg" src="//upload..." />
    ...
</table>
```

The xpath '//table[contains(@class,"infobox")]//img/@src will get the source address of the image.

As with our first spider, we first need to declare a Scrapy Item to hold our scraped data. We'll scrape the bio link and name of the winner, which we can use as identifiers for the image and text. We also need somewhere to store our image-urls (though we will only scrape one bio image, I'll cover the multiple-image use case), the resultant images references (a file path), and a bio_image field to store the particular image we're interested in:

```
import scrapy
import re

BASE_URL = 'http://en.wikipedia.org'


class NWinnerItemBio(scrapy.Item):
    link = scrapy.Field()
    name = scrapy.Field()
    mini_bio = scrapy.Field()
    image_urls = scrapy.Field()
    bio_image = scrapy.Field()
    images = scrapy.Field()
...
```

Now we reuse the scraping loop over our Nobel Prize winners (see Example 6-4 for details), this time yielding a request to our new get_mini_bio method, which will scrape the image URLs and bio text:

```
class NWinnerSpiderBio(scrapy.Spider):

    name = 'nwinners_minibio'
    allowed_domains = ['en.wikipedia.org']
    start_urls = [
        "https://en.wikipedia.org/wiki/List_of_Nobel_" \
        "laureates_by_country"
    ]
```

```
def parse(self, response):

    filename = response.url.split('/')[-1]
    h3s = response.xpath('//h3')

    for h3 in h3s:
        country = h3.xpath('span[@class="mw-headline"]'\
        'text()').extract()
        if country:
            winners = h3.xpath('following-sibling::ol[1]')
            for w in winners.xpath('li'):
                wdata = {}
                wdata['link'] = BASE_URL + \
                w.xpath('a/@href').extract()[0]
                # Process the winner's bio page with
                # the get_mini_bio method
                request = scrapy.Request(wdata['link'],
                            callback=self.get_mini_bio)
                request.meta['item'] = NWinnerItemBio(**wdata)
                yield request
```

Our get_mini_bio method will add any available photo URLs to the image_urls list and add all paragraphs of the biography up to the <p></p> stop point to the item's mini_bio field:

```
...
def get_mini_bio(self, response):
    """ Get the winner's bio text and photo """

    BASE_URL_ESCAPED = 'http:\/\/en.wikipedia.org'
    item = response.meta['item']
    item['image_urls'] = []
    img_src = response.xpath(\
        '//table[contains(@class,"infobox")]//img/@src') ❶
    if img_src:
        item['image_urls'] = ['http:' +\
        img_src[0].extract()]

    ps = response.xpath(
        '//*[@id="mw-content-text"]/div/table/'
        'following-sibling::p[not(preceding-sibling::div[@id="toc"])]')\
        .extract() ❷
    # Concatenate the biography paragraphs for a mini_bio string
    mini_bio = ''
    for p in ps:
        mini_bio += p
    # correct for wiki-links
    mini_bio = mini_bio.replace('href="/wiki', 'href="'
                    + BASE_URL + '/wiki"') ❸
    mini_bio = mini_bio.replace('href="#',\
     'href="' + item['link'] + '#"')
```

```
        item['mini_bio'] = mini_bio
        yield item
```

❶ Targets the first (and only) image in the table of class infobox and gets its source (src) attribute (e.g., `<img src='//upload.wikimedia.org/.../ Max_Perutz.jpg'...`).

❷ Grab our mini-bio paragraphs in a sibling sandwich.

❸ Replaces Wikipedia's internal hrefs (e.g., */wiki/...*) with the full addresses our visualization will need.

With our bio-scraping spider defined, we need to create its complementary pipeline, which will take the image URLs scraped and convert them into saved images. We'll use Scrapy's images pipeline (*https://oreil.ly/MqUuX*) for this job.

The `ImagesPipeline` shown in Example 6-7 has two main methods, `get_media_requests`, which generates the requests for the image URLs, and `item_completed`, called after the requests have been consumed.

Example 6-7. Scraping images with the image pipeline

```
import scrapy
from itemadapter import ItemAdapter
from scrapy.pipelines.images import ImagesPipeline
from scrapy.exceptions import DropItem

class NobelImagesPipeline(ImagesPipeline):

    def get_media_requests(self, item, info): ❶

        for image_url in item['image_urls']:
            yield scrapy.Request(image_url)

    def item_completed(self, results, item, info): ❷

        image_paths = [img['path'] for ok, img in results if ok] ❸

        if not image_paths:
            raise DropItem("Item contains no images")
        adapter = ItemAdapter(item) ❹
        adapter['bio_image'] = image_paths[0]

        return item
```

❶ This takes any image URLs scraped by our *nwinners_minibio* spider and generates an HTTP request for their content.

❷ After the image URL requests have been made, the results are delivered to the `item_completed` method.

❸ This Python list comprehension filters the list of result tuples (of form `[(True, Image), (False, Image) …])` for those that were successful and stores their file paths relative to the directory specified by the `IMAGES_STORE` variable in `settings.py`.

❹ We use a Scrapy item adapter (*https://oreil.ly/8P6uq*), which provides a common interface for working with supported item types.

Now that we have the spider and pipeline defined, we just need to add the pipeline to our `settings.py` module and set the `IMAGES_STORE` variable to the directory we want to save the images in:

```
# nobel_winners/nobel_winners/settings.py

...

ITEM_PIPELINES = {'nobel_winners.pipelines'\
                  '.NobelImagesPipeline':300}
IMAGES_STORE = 'images'
```

Let's run our new spider from the *nobel_winners* root directory of our project, and check its output:

```
$ scrapy crawl nwinners_minibio -o minibios.json
...
2021-12-13 17:18:05 [scrapy.core.scraper] DEBUG: Scraped from
    <200 https://en.wikipedia.org/wiki/C%C3%A9sar_Milstein>

{'bio_image': 'full/65ac9541c305ab4728ed889385d422a2321a117d.jpg',
 'image_urls': ['http://upload.wikimedia...
          150px-Milstein_lnp_restauraci%C3%B3n.jpg'],
 'link': 'http://en.wikipedia.org/wiki/C%C3%A9sar_Milstein',
 'mini_bio': '<p><b>César Milstein</b>, <a ...'
            'href="http://en.wikipedia.org/wiki/Order_of_the_...'
            'title="Order of the Companions of Honour">CH</a>'
            'href="http://en.wikipedia.org/wiki/Royal_Society'
            'Society">FRS</a><sup id="cite_ref-frs_2-1" class'...>
            'href="http://en.wikipedia.org/wiki/C%C3%A9sar_Mi'
            '(8 October 1927 - 24 March 2002) was an <a ...>'
            'href="http://en.wikipedia.org/wiki/Argentine" '

...
```

The spider is correctly harvesting mini-bios and, using its image pipeline, photos of the Nobel winners. The image was stored in `image_urls` and successfully processed, loading the JPG file stored in the *images* directory we specified with `IMAGE_STORE` with a relative path (`full/a5f763b828006e704cb291411b8b643bfb1886c.jpg`). The filename is, conveniently enough, a SHA1 hash (*https://oreil.ly/SlSl2*) of the image's URL, which allows the image pipeline to check for existing images, enabling it to prevent redundant requests.

A quick listing of our images directory shows a nice array of Wikipedia Nobel Prize winner images, ready to be used in our web visualization:

```
$ (nobel_winners) tree images
images
└── full
    ├── 0512ae11141584da1262661992a1b05dfb20dd52.jpg
    ├── 092a92689118c16b15b1613751af422439df2850.jpg
    ├── 0b6a8ca56e6ff115b7d30087df9c21da09684db1.jpg
    ├── 1197aa95299a1fec983b3dbdeaeb97a1f7e545c9.jpg
    ├── 1f6fb8e9e2241733da47328291b25bd1a78fa588.jpg
    ├── 272cf1b089c7a28ea0109ad8655bc3ef1c03fb52.jpg
    ├── 28dcc7978d9d5710f0c29d6dfcf09caa7e13a1d0.jpg
    ...
```

As we'll see in Chapter 16, we will be placing these in the *static* folder of our web app, ready to be accessed via the winner's bio_image field.

With our images and biography text to hand, we've successfully scraped all the targets we set ourselves at the beginning of the chapter (see Example 6-1 and Figure 6-1). Now, it's time for a quick summary before moving on to clean this inevitably dirty data with help from pandas.

Specifying Pipelines with Multiple Spiders

The pipelines enabled in settings.py are applied to all spiders in our Scrapy project. Often, if you have a number of spiders, you'll want to be able to specify which pipelines are applied on a spider-by-spider basis. There are a number of ways (*https://oreil.ly/62Uzn*) to achieve this, but the best I've seen is to use the spiders' custom_set tings class property to set the ITEM_PIPELINES dictionary instead of setting it in settings.py. In the case of our nwinners_minibio spider, this means adapting the NWinnerSpiderBio class like so:

```python
class NWinnerSpiderBio(scrapy.Spider):
    name = 'nwinners_minibio'
    allowed_domains = ['en.wikipedia.org']
    start_urls = [
      "http://en.wikipedia.org/wiki"\
      "List_of_Nobel_laureates_by_country"
    ]

    custom_settings = {
        'ITEM_PIPELINES':\
        {'nobel_winners.pipelines.NobelImagesPipeline':1}
    }
```

```
    # ...
```

Now the `NobelImagesPipeline` pipeline will only be applied while scraping the Nobel Prize winners' biographies.

Summary

In this chapter, we produced two Scrapy spiders that managed to grab the simple statistical dataset of our Nobel Prize winners plus some biographical text (and, where available, a photograph, to add some color to the stats). Scrapy is a powerful library that takes care of everything you could need in a full-fledged scraper. Although the workflow requires more effort to implement than doing some hacking with Beautiful Soup, Scrapy has far more power and comes into its own as your scraping ambitions increase. All Scrapy spiders follow the standard recipe demonstrated here, and the workflow should become routine after you program a few.

I hope this chapter has conveyed the rather hacky, iterative nature of scraping, and some of the quiet satisfaction that can be had when producing relatively clean data from the unpromising mound of stuff so often found on the web. The fact is that now and for the foreseeable future, the large majority of interesting data (the fuel for the art and science of data visualization) is trapped in a form that is unusable for the web-based visualizations that this book focuses on. Scraping is, in this sense, an emancipating endeavor.

The data we scraped, much of it human-edited, will certainly have some errors—from badly formatted dates to categorical anomalies to missing fields. Making that data presentable is the focus of the next pandas-based chapters. But first, we need a little introduction to pandas and its building block, NumPy.

PART III

Cleaning and Exploring Data with pandas

In this part of the book, in the second phase of our toolchain (see Figure III-1), we take the Nobel Prize dataset we just scraped with Scrapy in Chapter 6 and first clean it up, then explore it for interesting nuggets. The principal tools we'll be using are the large Python libraries Matplotlib and pandas.

The second edition of this book is using the same Nobel dataset scraped in the first. It was felt that available time was better spent writing new material and updating all the libraries than changing the exploration and analysis. Dataviz usually involves working with older datasets, and the few additional Nobel winners don't change the substance of the material at all.

pandas will be introduced in the next couple of chapters, along with its building block, NumPy. In Chapter 9, we'll use pandas to clean the Nobel dataset. Then in Chapter 11, in conjunction with Python's plotting library Matplotlib, we'll use it to explore it.

In Part IV, we'll see how to deliver the freshly cleaned Nobel Prize dataset to the browser, using Python's Flask web server.

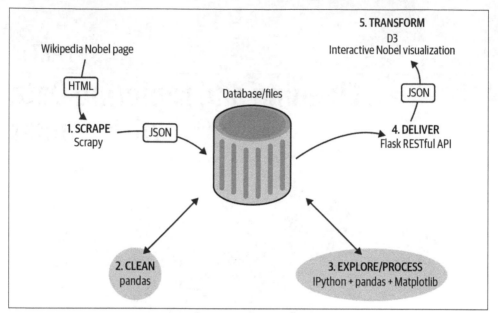

Figure III-1. Our dataviz toolchain: cleaning and exploring the data

 You can find the code for this part of the book at the book's GitHub repo (*https://github.com/Kyrand/dataviz-with-python-and-js-ed-2*).

## CHAPTER 7

Introduction to NumPy

This chapter aims to introduce the Numeric Python library (NumPy) to those unacquainted. NumPy is the key building block of pandas, the powerhouse data analysis library that we will be using in the upcoming chapters to clean and explore our recently scraped Nobel Prize dataset (see Chapter 6). A basic understanding of NumPy's core elements and principles is important if you are to get the most out of pandas. Therefore, the emphasis of the chapter is to provide a foundation for the upcoming introduction to pandas.

NumPy is a Python module that allows access to very fast, multidimensional array manipulation, implemented by low-level libraries written in C and Fortran.[1] Python's native performance with large quantities of data is relatively slow, but NumPy allows you to perform parallel operations on large arrays all at once, making it very fast. Given that NumPy is the chief building block of most of the heavyweight Python data-processing libraries, pandas included, it's hard to argue with its status as linchpin of the Python data-processing world.

In addition to pandas, NumPy's huge ecosystem includes Science Python (SciPy), which supplements NumPy with hardcore science and engineering modules; scikit-learn, which adds a host of modern machine-learning algorithms in such domains as classification and feature extraction; and many other specialized libraries that use NumPy's multidimensional arrays as their primary data objects. In this sense, basic NumPy mastery can massively extend your Python range in the data-processing realm.

---

1 Python's scripted ease of use comes at the cost of raw speed. By wrapping fast, low-level libraries, initiatives like NumPy aim for simple, cruft-free programming and blinding performance.

The key to understanding NumPy is its arrays. If you understand how these work and how to manipulate them, then a lot of other stuff should follow painlessly.[2] The next few sections will cover basic array manipulation with a few examples of NumPy in action, setting the scene for the introduction of pandas's datasets in Chapter 8.

The NumPy Array

Everything in NumPy is built around its homogeneous[3], multidimensional ndarray object. Operations on these arrays are performed using very fast, compiled libraries, allowing NumPy to massively outperform native Python. Among other things you can perform standard arithmetic on these arrays, much as you would a Python int or float.[4] In the following code, a whole array is added to itself as easily and as quickly as adding two integers:

```
import numpy as np ❶

a = np.array([1, 2, 3]) ❷
a + a
# output array([2, 4, 6])
```

❶ The standard way to use the NumPy library and much preferred to "from numpy import *".[5]

❷ Automatically converts a Python list of numbers.

Behind the scenes, NumPy can leverage the massively parallel computation available to modern CPUs allowing, for example, large matrices (2D arrays) to be crunched in acceptable times.

The key properties of the NumPy ndarray are its number of dimensions (ndim), shape (shape), and numeric type (dtype). The same array of numbers can be reshaped in place, which will sometimes involve changing the array's number of dimensions. Let's demonstrate some reshaping with a little eight-member array. We'll use a print_array_details method to output the key array properties:

```
def print_array_details(a):
    print('Dimensions: %d, shape: %s, dtype: %s'\
        %(a.ndim, a.shape, a.dtype))
```

---

2 NumPy is used to implement some very advanced math, so don't expect to understand everything you see online—just the building blocks.

3 This means NumPy deals with arrays of the same datatype (dtype) rather than Python lists, for example, which can have strings, numbers, dates, etc.

4 This assumes the arrays meet shape and type constraints.

5 Importing all module variables into your namespace using * is almost always a bad idea.

First, we'll create our one-dimensional array. As the printed details show, by default this has a 64-bit integer numeric type (int64):

```
In [1]: a = np.array([1, 2, 3, 4, 5, 6, 7, 8])

In [2]: a
Out[2]: array([1, 2, 3, 4, 5, 6, 7, 8])

In [3]: print_array_details(a)
Dimensions: 1, shape: (8,), dtype: int64
```

Using the reshape method, we can change the shape and number of dimensions of a. Let's reshape a into a two-dimensional array composed of two four-member arrays:

```
In [4]: a = a.reshape([2, 4])
In [5]: a
Out[5]:
array([[1, 2, 3, 4],
       [5, 6, 7, 8]])

In [6]: print_array_details(a)
Dimensions: 2, shape: (2, 4), dtype: int64
```

An eight-member array can also be reshaped into a three-dimensional array:

```
In [7]: a = a.reshape([2, 2, 2])

In [8]: a
Out[8]:
array([[[1, 2],
        [3, 4]],

       [[5, 6],
        [7, 8]]])

In [9]: print_array_details(a)
Dimensions: 3, shape: (2, 2, 2), dtype: int64
```

The shape and numeric type can be specified on creation of the array or later. The easiest way to change an array's numeric type is by using the astype method to make a resized copy of the original with the new type:[6]

```
In [0]: x = np.array([[1, 2, 3], [4, 5, 6]], np.int32) ❶
In [1]: x.shape
Out[1]: (2, 3)
In [2]: x.shape = (6,)
In [3]: x
Out[3]: array([1, 2, 3, 4, 5, 6], dtype=int32)
```

---

6 A more memory-efficient and performant way involves manipulating the array's view, but it does involve some extra steps. See this Stack Overflow article (https://oreil.ly/FOQWt) for some examples and a discussion of the pros and cons.

```
In [4]  x = x.astype('int64')
In [5]: x.dtype
Out[5]: dtype('int64')
```

 The array will convert a nested list of numbers into a suitably shaped multidimensional form.

Creating Arrays

As well as creating arrays with lists of numbers, NumPy provides some utility functions to create arrays with a specific shape. zeros and ones are the most common functions used, creating prefilled arrays. Here's a couple of examples. Note that the default dtype of these methods is a 64-bit float (float64):

```
In [32]: a = np.zeros([2,3])
In [33]: a
Out[33]:
array([[ 0.,  0.,  0.],
       [ 0.,  0.,  0.]])

In [34]: a.dtype
Out[34]: dtype('float64')

In [35]: np.ones([2, 3])
Out[35]:
array([[ 1.,  1.,  1.],
       [ 1.,  1.,  1.]])
```

The faster empty method just takes a memory block without the fill overhead, leaving the initialization up to you. This means you don't know and can't guarantee what values the array has, unlike np.zeros, so use with caution:

```
empty_array = np.empty((2,3)) # create an uninitialized array

empty_array
Out[3]:
array([[  6.93185732e-310,   2.52008024e-316,   4.71690401e-317],
       [  2.38085057e-316,   6.93185752e-310,   6.93185751e-310]])
```

Another useful utility function is random, found along with some useful siblings in NumPy's random module. This creates a shaped random array:

```
>>> np.random.random((2,3))
>>> Out:
array([[ 0.97519667,  0.94934859,  0.98379541],  ❶
       [ 0.10407003,  0.35752882,  0.62971186]])
```

❶ A 2×3 array of random numbers within the range 0 <= x < 1.

The handy linspace creates a specified number of evenly spaced samples over a set interval. arange is similar but uses a step-size argument:

```
np.linspace(2, 10, 5) # 5 numbers in range 2-10
Out: array([2., 4.,6., 8., 10.]) ❶

np.arange(2, 10, 2) # from 2 to 10 (exlusive) with step-size 2.
Out: array([2, 4, 6, 8])
```

Note that unlike arange, linspace is inclusive of the upper value and that the array's datatype is the default float64.

Array Indexing and Slicing

One-dimensional arrays are indexed and sliced much as Python lists:

```
a = np.array([1, 2, 3, 4, 5, 6])
a[2] # Out: 3
a[3:5] # Out: array([4, 5])
# every second item from 0-4 set to 0
a[:4:2] = 0 # Out: array([0, 2, 0, 4, 5, 6])
a[::-1] # Out: array([6, 5, 4, 0, 2, 0]), reversed
```

Indexing multidimensional arrays is similar to the *1-D* form. Each dimension has its own indexing/slicing operation and these are specified in a comma-separated tuple.[7] Figure 7-1 shows how this works.

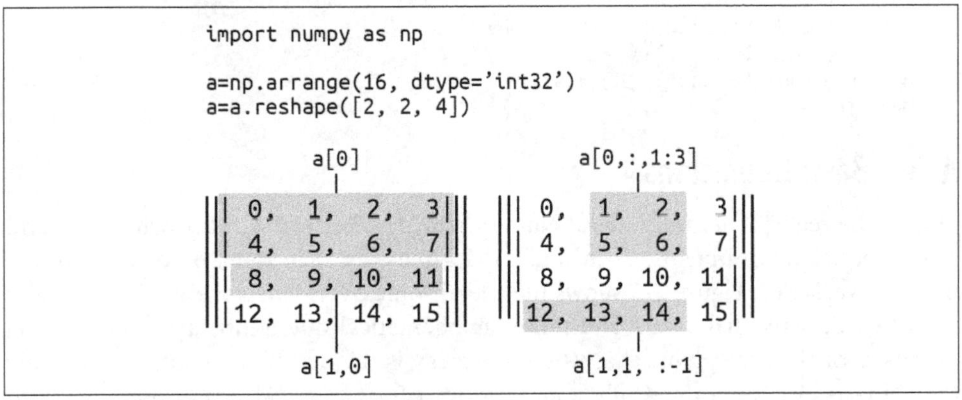

```
import numpy as np

a=np.arange(16, dtype='int32')
a=a.reshape([2, 2, 4])
```

Figure 7-1. Multidimensional indexing with NumPy

Note that if the number of objects in the selection tuple is less than the number of dimensions, the remaining dimensions are assumed to be fully selected (:). Ellipsis can also be used as a shorthand for full selection of all indices, expanding to the required number of : objects. We will use a three-dimensional array to demonstrate:

```
a = np.arange(8)
a.shape = (2, 2, 2)
```

---

7 There is a shorthand dot notation (e.g., [..1:3]) to select all indices.

```
a
Out:
array([[[0, 1],
        [2, 3]],

       [[4, 5],
        [6, 7]]])
```

NumPy has a handy `array_equal` method, which compares arrays by shape and elements. We can use it to show the equivalence of the following array selections, taking the second subarray of axis 0:

```
a1 = a[1]
a1
Out:
array([[4, 5],
       [6, 7]])
```

Testing for equivalence:

```
np.array_equal(a1, a[1,:])
Out: True

np.array_equal(a1, a[1,:,:])
Out: True
# Taking the first element of the subarrays
# array([[0, 2], [4, 6]])
np.array_equal(a[...,0], a[:,:,0])
Out: True
```

A Few Basic Operations

One of the really cool things about NumPy arrays is that you can perform basic (and not so basic) math operations in much the same way that you would with normal numeric variables. Figure 7-2 shows the use of some overloaded arithmetic operators on a two-dimensional array. The simple mathematical operations are applied to all members of the array. Note that where the array is divided by a floating-point value (2.0), the result is automatically converted to a float type (`float64`). Being able to manipulate arrays as easily as single numbers is a huge strength of NumPy and a large part of its expressive power.

```
a=np.arrange([1, 2, 3, 4, 5, 6])
a=a.reshape([2, 3])
```

$$
\begin{array}{cccc}
 & a+2 & a-2 & a\ /\ 2.0 \\
\begin{vmatrix} 1, & 2, & 3 \\ 4, & 5, & 6 \end{vmatrix} &
\begin{vmatrix} 2, & 4, & 6 \\ 8, & 8, & 20 \end{vmatrix} &
\begin{vmatrix} -1, & 0, & 1 \\ 2, & 3, & 4 \end{vmatrix} &
\begin{vmatrix} 0.5, & 1., & 1.5 \\ 2., & 2.5, & 3. \end{vmatrix}
\end{array}
$$

dtype= float64

Figure 7-2. A few basic math operations on a two-dimensional NumPy array

Boolean operators work in a similar way to the arithmetic ones. As we'll see in the next chapter, this is a very useful way to create the Boolean masks often used in pandas. Here's a little example:

```
a = np.array([45, 65, 76, 32, 99, 22])
a < 50
Out[69]: array([ True, False, False,  True, False,  True]
              , dtype=bool)
```

Arrays also have a number of useful methods, a selection of which is demonstrated in Example 7-1. You can get a comprehensive rundown in the official NumPy docs (*https://oreil.ly/qmnDX*).

Example 7-1. Some array methods

```
a = np.arange(8).reshape((2,4))
# array([[0, 1, 2, 3],
#        [4, 5, 6, 7]])
a.min(axis=1)
# array([0, 4])
a.sum(axis=0)
# array([4, 6, 8, 10])
a.mean(axis=1) ❶
# array([ 1.5, 5.5 ])
a.std(axis=1) ❷
# array([ 1.11803399,  1.11803399])
```

❶ Average along second axis.

❷ The standard deviation of [0, 1, 2, 3],…

There are also a large number of built-in array functions. Example 7-2 demonstrates a selection of these, and you will find a comprehensive list of NumPy's built-in mathematical routines at the official NumPy site (*https://oreil.ly/vvfzm*).

Example 7-2. Some NumPy array math functions

```
# Trigonometric functions
pi = np.pi
a = np.array([pi, pi/2, pi/4, pi/6])

np.degrees(a) # radians to degrees
# Out: array([ 180., 90., 45., 30.,])

sin_a = np.sin(a)
# Out: array([  1.22464680e-16,   1.00000000e+00, ❶
#              7.07106781e-01,   5.00000000e-01])
# Rounding
np.round(sin_a, 7) # round to 7 decimal places
```

```
# Out: array([ 0.,   1.,   0.7071068,   0.5 ])

# Sums, products, differences
a = np.arange(8).reshape((2,4))
# array([[0, 1, 2, 3],
#        [4, 5, 6, 7]])

np.cumsum(a, axis=1) # cumulative sum along second axis
# array([[ 0,  1,  3,  6],
#        [ 4,  9, 15, 22]])

np.cumsum(a) # without axis argument, array is flattened
# array([ 0,  1,  3,  6, 10, 15, 21, 28])
```

❶ Note the floating-point rounding error for sin(pi).

Creating Array Functions

Whether you're using pandas or one of the many Python data-processing libraries, such as SciPy, scikit-learn, or PyTorch, chances are the core data structure being used is the NumPy array. The ability to craft little array processing functions is therefore a great addition to your data-processing toolkit and the data visualization toolchain. Often a short internet search will turn up a community solution, but there's a lot of satisfaction to be gained from crafting your own, besides being a great way to learn. Let's see how we can harness the NumPy array to calculate a moving average (*https://oreil.ly/ajLZJ*). A moving average is a series of averages based on a moving window of the last *n* values, where *n* is variable, also known as a *moving mean* or *rolling mean*.

Calculating a Moving Average

Example 7-3 shows the few lines needed to calculate a moving average on a one-dimensional NumPy array.[8] As you can see, it's nice and concise, but there's a fair amount going on in those few lines. Let's break it down a bit.

Example 7-3. A moving average with NumPy

```
def moving_average(a, n=3):
    ret = np.cumsum(a, dtype=float)
    ret[n:] = ret[n:] - ret[:-n]
    return ret[n - 1:] / n
```

---

8 NumPy has a convolve method, which is the easiest way to calculate a simple moving average but less instructive. Also, pandas has a number of specialized methods for this.

The function receives an array *a* and number *n* specifying the size of the moving window.

We first calculate the cumulative sum of the array using NumPy's built-in method:

```
a = np.arange(6)
# array([0, 1, 2, 3, 4, 5])
csum = np.cumsum(a)
csum
# Out: array([0, 1, 3, 6, 10, 15])
```

Starting at the *n*th index of the cumulative sum array, we subtract the *i*–*n*th value for all *i*, which means *i* now has the sum of the last *n* values of *a*, inclusive. Here's an example with a window of size three:

```
# a = array([0, 1, 2, 3, 4, 5])
# csum = array([0, 1, 3, 6, 10, 15])
csum[3:] = csum[3:] - csum[:-3]
# csum = array([0, 1, 3, 6, 9, 12])
```

Comparing the array `a` with the final array `csum`, index 5 is now the sum of the window [3, 4, 5].

Because a moving average only makes sense for index $(n-1)$ onward, it only remains to return these values, divided by the window size *n* to give the average.

The `moving_average` function takes a bit of time to get but is a good example of the concision and expressiveness that can be achieved with NumPy arrays and array slicing. You could easily write the function in vanilla Python, but it would likely be a fair bit more involved and, crucially, be much slower for arrays of significant size.

Putting the function to work:

```
a = np.arange(10)
moving_average(a, 4)
# Out[98]: array([ 1.5,  2.5,  3.5,  4.5,  5.5,  6.5,  7.5])
```

Summary

This chapter laid the foundations of NumPy, focusing on its building block, the NumPy array or `ndarray`. Being proficient with NumPy is a core skill for any Pythonista working with data. It underpins most of Python's hardcore data-processing stack, so for this reason alone, you should be comfortable with its array manipulations.

Being comfortable with NumPy will make pandas work that much easier and open up the rich NumPy ecosystem of scientific, engineering, machine learning, and statistical algorithmics to your pandas workflow. Although pandas hides its NumPy arrays behind data containers such as its DataFrame and Series, which are adapted to deal with heterogeneous data, these containers behave for the most part like NumPy arrays and will generally do the right thing when asked. Knowing that ndarrays are at its core also helps when you are trying to frame problems for pandas—ultimately the requested data manipulation has to play nicely with NumPy. Now that we've got its building blocks in place, let's see how pandas extends the homogeneous NumPy array into the realm of heterogeneous data, where much of data visualization work takes place.

## CHAPTER 8

Introduction to pandas

pandas is a key element in our dataviz toolchain, as we will use it for both cleaning and exploring our recently scraped dataset (see Chapter 6). The last chapter introduced NumPy, the Python array processing library that is the foundation of pandas. Before we move on to applying pandas, this chapter will introduce its key concepts and show how it interacts with existing data files and database tables. The rest of your pandas learning will be on the job over the next couple of chapters.

Why pandas Is Tailor-Made for Dataviz

Take any dataviz, whether web-based or in print, and chances are that the data visualized was at one point stored in row-columnar form in a spreadsheet like Excel, a CSV file, or HDF5. There are certainly visualizations, like network graphs, for which row-columnar data is not the best form, but they are in the minority. pandas is tailor-made to manipulate row-columnar data tables with its core datatype, the DataFrame, which is best thought of as a very fast, programmatic spreadsheet.

Why pandas Was Developed

First revealed by Wes Kinney in 2008, pandas was built to solve a particular problem—namely, that while Python was great for manipulating data, it was weak in the area of data analysis and modeling, certainly compared with big hitters like R.

pandas is designed to work with the kind of heterogenous[1] data found in row-columnar spreadsheets, but cleverly manages to leverage some of the speed of

---

1 The columns in a typical spreadsheet will typically have different datatypes (dtypes), like floats, date-times, integers etc.

NumPy's homogeneous numeric arrays used by mathematicians, physicists, computer graphics, and the like. Combined with the Jupyter notebook and the Matplotlib plotting library (with auxiliary libraries like seaborn), pandas represents a first-class interactive data analysis tool. Because it's part of the NumPy ecosystem, its data modeling is easily enhanced by such libraries as SciPy, statsmodels, and scikit-learn, to name but a few.

Categorizing Data and Measurements

I'll cover the core concepts of pandas in the next section, focusing on the DataFrame and how to get your data into and out of it via the common datastores, CSV files, and SQL databases. But first let's take a little diversion to consider what we really mean by the heterogeneous datasets that pandas was designed to work with and that are the mainstay of data visualizers.

Chances are that a visualization, maybe a bar chart or line graph used to illustrate an article or a modern web dashboard, presents the results of measurements in the real world, the price of commodities as they change over time, changes in rainfall over a year, voting intentions by ethnic group, and so forth. These measurements can be broadly broken into two groups, numerical and categorical. Numerical values can be divided into interval and ratio scales, and categorical values can in turn be divided into nominal and ordinal measurements. This gives four broad categories of observation available to the data visualizer.

Let's take a set of tweets as an example in order to draw out these measurement categories. Each tweet has various data fields:

```
{
    "text": "#Python and #JavaScript sitting in a tree...", ❶
    "id": 2103303030333004303, ❶
    "favorited": true, ❷
    "filter_level":"medium", ❸
    "created_at": "Wed Mar 23 14:07:43 +0000 2015", ❹
    "retweet_count":23, ❺
    "coordinates":[-97.5, 45.3] ❻
    ...
}
```

❶ The text and id fields are unique indicators. The former might contain categorical information (e.g., the category of tweets containing the #Python hashtag), and the latter might be used to create a category (e.g., the set of all users retweeting this tweet), but they are not per se visualizable fields.

❷ favorited is Boolean, categorical information, dividing the tweets into two sets. This would count as a *nominal* category, as it can be counted but not ordered.

❸ `filter_level` is also categorical information, but it is ordinal. There is an order, low→medium→high, to the filter levels.

❹ The `created_at` field is a timestamp, a numerical value on an interval scale. We would probably want to order the tweets on this scale, something pandas does automatically, and then maybe box into broader intervals, say by the day or week. Again, pandas makes this trivial.

❺ `retweet_count` is likewise on a numerical scale, but it is a ratio one. A ratio scale, as opposed to an interval scale, has a meaningful concept of zero—in this case, no retweets. Our `created_at` timestamp, on the other hand, can have an arbitrary baseline (e.g., unixtime or Gregorian year 0), much in the same way as temperature scales, with 0 degrees Celsius being the same as 273.15 degrees Kelvin.

❻ `coordinates`, if available, has two numerical scales for longitude and latitude. Both are interval scales, though, as it doesn't make much sense to speak of ratios of degrees.

So a small subset of our humble tweet's fields contains heterogeneous information covering all the generally accepted divisions of measurement. Whereas the NumPy array is generally used for homogeneous, numerical number crunching, pandas is designed to deal with categorical data, time series, and items that reflect the heterogeneous nature of real-world data. This makes it a great fit for the data visualization.

Now that we know the type of data pandas is designed to deal with, let's look at the data structures it uses.

The DataFrame

The first step in a pandas session is usually to load some data into a DataFrame. We'll cover the various ways we can do this in a later section. For now, let's read our *nobel_winners.json* JSON data from a file. `read_json` returns a DataFrame, parsed from the JSON file specified. By convention, DataFrame variables start with `df`:

```
import pandas as pd

df = pd.read_json('data/nobel_winners.json')
```

With our DataFrame in hand, let's inspect its content. A quick way to get the row-columnar structure of the DataFrame is to use its `head` method to show (by default) the top five items. Figure 8-1 shows the output from a Jupyter notebook (*https://jupyter.org*), with key elements of the DataFrame highlighted.

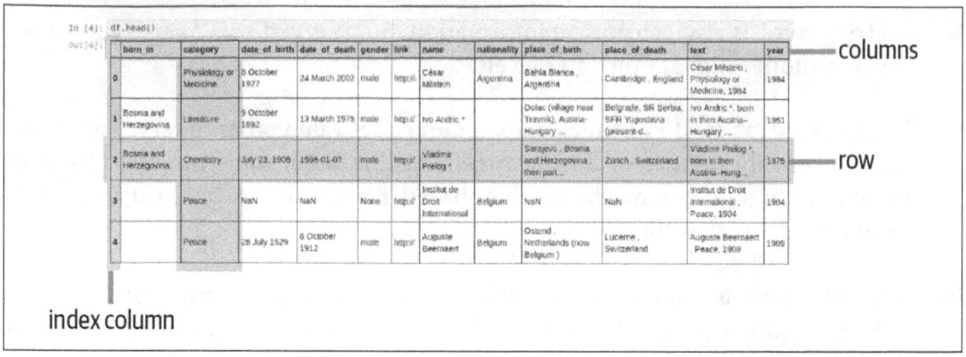

Figure 8-1. The key elements of a pandas DataFrame

Indices

The DataFrame's columns are indexed by a `columns` property, which is a pandas `index` instance. Let's select the columns in Figure 8-1:

```
In [0]: df.columns
Out[0]: Index(['born_in', 'category', ... ], dtype='object')
```

Initially, pandas rows have a single numeric index (pandas can handle multiple indices if necessary) that can be accessed by the `index` property. This is a memory-saving `RangeIndex` (*https://oreil.ly/7Qzia*) by default:

```
In [1]: df.index
Out[1]: RangeIndex(start=0, stop=1052, step=1)
```

As well as integers, row indices can be strings, `DatetimeIndices`, or `PeriodIndices` for time-based data, and so on. Often, to aid selections, a column of the DataFrame will be set to the index via the `set_index` method. In the following code, we first use the `set_index` method to set our Nobel DataFrame's index to the name column and then use the `loc` method to select a row by the index label (`name` in this case):

```
In [2] df = df.set_index('name')     ❶
In [3] df.loc['Albert Einstein']     ❷
Out[3]:
                born_in category     country date_of_birth date_of_death  \
name
Albert Einstein         Physics  Switzerland    1879-03-14    1955-04-18
Albert Einstein         Physics      Germany    1879-03-14    1955-04-18
[...]

df = df.reset_index()     ❸
```

❶ Set the index to the name column.

❷ You can now select a row by the `name` label.

❸ Return the index to original integer-based state.

Rows and Columns

The rows and columns of a DataFrame are stored as pandas Series (*https://oreil.ly/z7PF4*), a heterogeneous counterpart to NumPy's array. These are essentially a labeled one-dimensional array that can contain any datatype from integers, strings, and floats to Python objects and lists.

There are two ways to select a row from the DataFrame. We've seen the loc method, which selects by label. There's also an iloc method, which selects by position. So to select the row in Figure 8-1, we grab row number two:

```
In [4] df.iloc[2]
Out[4]:
name                          Vladimir Prelog *
born_in               Bosnia and Herzegovina
category                              Chemistry
country
date_of_birth                     July 23, 1906
...
year                                       1975
Name: 2, dtype: object
```

You can grab a column of your DataFrame using dot notation[2] or conventional array access by keyword string. This returns a pandas Series with all the column fields with their DataFrame indices preserved:

```
In [9] gender_col = df.gender # or df['gender']
In [10] type(gender_col)
Out[10] pandas.core.series.Series
In [11] gender_col.head() # grab the Series' first five items
Out[11]:
0    male #index, object
1    male
2    male
3    None
4    male
Name: gender, dtype: object
```

Selecting Groups

There are various ways we can select groups (or subsets of rows) of our DataFrame. Often we want to select all rows with a specific column value (e.g., all rows with category Physics). One way to do this is to use the DataFrame's groupby method to

---

2 Only if the column name is a string without spaces.

group a column (or list of columns) and then use the `get_group` method to select the required group. Let's use these two methods to select all Nobel Physics Prize winners:

```
cat_groups = df.groupby('category')
cat_groups
#Out[-] <pandas.core.groupby.generic.DataFrameGroupBy object ...>

cat_groups.groups.keys()
#Out[-]: dict_keys(['', 'Chemistry', 'Economics', 'Literature',\
#                   'Peace', 'Physics', 'Physiology or Medicine'])
 ...

In [14] phy_group = cat_groups.get_group('Physics')
In [15] phy_group.head()
Out[15]:
                name born_in category  country     date_of_birth  \
13   François Englert         Physics  Belgium  6 November 1932
19          Niels Bohr         Physics  Denmark  7 October 1885
23  Ben Roy Mottelson         Physics  Denmark       July 9, 1926
24          Aage Bohr         Physics  Denmark     19 June 1922
47     Alfred Kastler         Physics   France       3 May 1902
 ...
```

Another way to select row subsets is to use a Boolean mask to create a new Data-Frame. You can apply Boolean operators to all rows in a DataFrame in much the same way as you can to all members of a NumPy array:

```
In [16] df.category == 'Physics'
Out[16]:
0       False
1       False
...
1047    True
...
```

The resulting Boolean mask can then be applied to the original DataFrame to select a subset of its rows:

```
In [17]: df[df.category == 'Physics']
Out[17]:
                      name      born_in category   country  \
13           François Englert          Physics   Belgium
19                 Niels Bohr          Physics   Denmark
23          Ben Roy Mottelson          Physics   Denmark
24                 Aage Bohr          Physics   Denmark
...
1047         Brian P. Schmidt          Physics  Australia  ...
```

We'll cover a lot more examples of data selections in the coming chapters. For now, let's see how we create DataFrames from existing data and how to save the results of our data frame manipulations.

Creating and Saving DataFrames

The easiest way to create a DataFrame is to use a Python dictionary. It's also a way you won't be using very often, as you will likely be accessing your data from files or databases. Nevertheless, it has its use cases.

By default, we specify the columns separately, in the following example creating three rows with name and category columns:

```
df = pd.DataFrame({
    'name': ['Albert Einstein', 'Marie Curie',\
    'William Faulkner'],
    'category': ['Physics', 'Chemistry', 'Literature']
})
```

We can use the `from_dict` method to allow us to use our preferred record-based object arrays. `from_dict` has an `orient` argument to allow us to specify record-like data, but pandas is smart enough to work out the data form:

```
df = pd.DataFrame.from_dict([ ❶
    {'name': 'Albert Einstein', 'category':'Physics'},
    {'name': 'Marie Curie', 'category':'Chemistry'},
    {'name': 'William Faulkner', 'category':'Literature'}
])
```

❶ Here we pass in an array of objects, each corresponding to a row in our DataFrame.

The methods just shown produce an identical DataFrame:

```
df.head()
Out:
                name     category
0    Albert Einstein      Physics
1        Marie Curie    Chemistry
2   William Faulkner   Literature
```

As mentioned, you probably won't be creating DataFrames from Python containers directly. Instead, you will probably use one of the pandas data-reading methods.

pandas has an impressive array of `read_[format]`/`to_[format]` methods, covering most conceivable data-loading use cases, from CSV through binary HDF5 to SQL databases. We'll cover the subset most relevant to dataviz work. For a full list, see the pandas documentation (*https://oreil.ly/b3VFR*).

Note that by default pandas will try to convert the loaded data sensibly. The `con vert_axes` (try to convert the axes to the proper `dtypes`), `dtype` (guess datatype), and `convert_dates` arguments to the read methods are all `True` by default. See the pandas documentation (*https://oreil.ly/MkmIx*) for an example of the available options, in this case for reading JSON files into a DataFrame.

Let's cover file-based DataFrames first, then see how to interact with (No)SQL databases.

JSON

Loading data from our preferred JSON format is trivial in pandas:

```
df = pd.read_json('file.json')
```

There are various forms the JSON file can take, specified by an optional `orient` argument, one of [`split`, `records`, `index`, `columns`, `values`]. An array of records, our standard form, will be detected:

```
[{"name":"Albert Einstein", "category":"Physics", ...},
 {"name":"Marie Curie", "category":"Chemistry", ... } ... ]
```

The default for a JSON object is `columns`, in the form:

```
{"name":{"0":"Albert Einstein","1":"Marie Curie" ... },
 "category":{"1","Physics","2":"Chemistry" ... }}
```

As discussed, for web-based visualization work, particularly D3, record-based JSON arrays are the most common way of passing row-columnar data to the browser.

> Note that you will need valid JSON files to work with pandas because the `read_json` method and Python JSON parsers in general tend to be fairly unforgiving, and exceptions not as informative as they might be.[3] A common JSON error is failing to enclose keys in double-quote marks or using single quotes where double quotes are expected. The latter is particularly common for those coming from languages where single- and double-string quotes are essentially interchangeable and one reason why you should never build JSON documents yourself—always use an official or well-respected library.

There are various ways to store DataFrames in JSON, but the format that will play most nicely with any dataviz work is the array of records. This is the most common form of D3 data and the one I recommend outputting from pandas.[4] Writing a DataFrame as records to JSON is then simply a case of specifying the `orient` field in the `to_json` method:

```
df = pd.read_json('data.json')
# ... Perform data-cleaning operations
```

---

3 If you have problems, you might try a subset of your data in JSONLint's validator (*https://jsonlint.com*) for better feedback.

4 D3 takes a number of other data formats, such as hierarchical (tree type) data or node and link graph formats. Here's an example of a tree hierarchy specified in JSON (*https://oreil.ly/WsBCI*).

```
json = df.to_json('data_cleaned.json', orient='records') ❶
Out:
[{"name":"Albert Einstein", "category":"Physics", ...},
{"name":"Marie Curie", "category":"Chemistry", ... } ... ]
```

❶ Override the default save to store the JSON as dataviz-friendly records.

We also have the parameters `date_format` (*epoch* timestamp, *iso* for ISO8601, etc.), `double_precision`, and `default_handler` to call if the object cannot be converted into JSON using pandas's parser. Check the pandas documentation (*https://oreil.ly/wqnI0*) for more details.

CSV

As befits pandas's data-table ethos, its handling of CSV files is sophisticated enough to cope with pretty much all conceivable data. Conventional CSV files, which is the large majority, will load without parameters:

```
# data.csv:
# name,category
# "Albert Einstein",Physics
# "Marie Curie",Chemistry

df = pd.read_csv('data.csv')
df
Out:
              name    category
0  Albert Einstein     Physics
1      Marie Curie   Chemistry
```

Although you might expect all CSV files to be comma-separated, you will often find files with a CSV suffix with different delimiters such as semicolons or pipes (|). They may also use idiosyncratic quoting for strings containing spaces or special characters. In this case, we can specify any nonstandard elements in our read request. We'll use Python's handy `StringIO` module to emulate reading from a file:[5]

```
from io import StringIO

data = "  `Albert Einstein`| Physics \n`Marie Curie`|  Chemistry"

df = pd.read_csv(StringIO(data),
    sep='|', ❶
    names=['name', 'category'], ❷
    skipinitialspace=True, quotechar="`")

df
```

---

5 I recommend using this approach if you want to get a feel for the CSV or JSON parsers. It's much more convenient than managing local files.

```
Out:
              name    category
0   Albert Einstein    Physics
1       Marie Curie  Chemistry
```

 The fields are pipe-separated, not the default comma-separated.

❷ Here we provide the missing column headers.

We have the same degree of flexibility when saving CSV files, here setting the encoding to Unicode utf-8:

```
df.to_csv('data.csv', encoding='utf-8')
```

For full coverage of the CSV options, see the pandas documentation (*https://oreil.ly/QPCs1*).

Excel Files

pandas uses Python's xlrd module to read Excel 2003 (*.xls*) and the openpyxl module to read Excel 2007+ (*.xlsx*) files. The latter is an optional dependency that will need installing:

```
$ pip install openpyxl
```

Excel documents have multiple named sheets, each of which can be passed to a DataFrame. There are two ways to read a datasheet into a DataFrame. The first is by creating and then parsing an ExcelFile object:

```
dfs = {}
xls = pd.ExcelFile('data/nobel_winners.xlsx') # load Excel file
dfs['WinnersSheet1'] = xls.parse('WinnersSheet1', na_values=['NA']) ❶
dfs['WinnersSheet2'] = xls.parse('WinnersSheet2',
    index_col=1, ❷
    na_values=['-'], ❸
    skiprows=3 ❹
    )
```

❶ Grab a sheet by name and save to a dictionary.

❷ Specify the column, by position, to use as DataFrame's row labels.

❸ A list of additional strings to recognize as NaN.

❹ The number of rows (e.g., metadata) to skip before processing.

Alternatively you can use the read_excel method, which is a convenience method for loading multiple spreadsheets:

```
dfs = pd.read_excel('data/nobel_winners.xlsx', ['WinnersSheet1','WinnersSheet2'],
                    index_col=None, na_values=['NA'])
```

Let's check the content of the second Excel sheet using the resulting DataFrame:

```
In: dfs['WinnersSheet2'].head()
Out:
        category            nationality  year                name  gender
0          Peace               American  1906  Theodore Roosevelt    male
1     Literature           South African  1991      Nadine Gordimer  female
2      Chemistry  Bosnia and Herzegovina  1975      Vladamir Prelog    male
```

The only reason not to use `read_excel` is if you need different arguments for reading each Excel sheet.

You can specify sheets by index or name using the second (`sheetname`) parameter. `sheetname` can be a single name string or index (beginning at 0) or a mixed list. By default `sheetname` is 0, returning the first sheet. Example 8-1 shows some variations. Setting `sheetname` to `None` returns a sheetname-keyed dictionary of DataFrames.

Example 8-1. Loading Excel sheets

```
# return the first datasheet
df = pd.read_excel('nobel_winners.xls')

# return a named sheet
df = pd.read_excel('nobel_winners.xls', 'WinnersSheet3')

# first sheet and sheet named 'WinnersSheet3'
df = pd.read_excel('nobel_winners.xls', [0, 'WinnersSheet3'])

# all sheets loaded into a name-keyed dictionary
dfs = pd.read_excel('nobel_winners.xls', sheetname=None)
```

The `parse_cols` parameter lets you select the sheet columns to be parsed. Setting `parse_cols` to an integer value selects all columns up to that ordinal. Setting `parse_cols` to a list of integers allows you to select specific columns:

```
# parse up to the fifth column
pd.read_excel('nobel_winners.xls', 'WinnersSheet1', parse_cols=4)

# parse the second and fourth columns
pd.read_excel('nobel_winners.xls', 'WinnersSheet1', parse_cols=[1, 3])
```

For more information on `read_excel`, see the pandas documentation (*https://oreil.ly/Js7Le*).

You can save a DataFrame to the sheet of an Excel file with the `to_excel` method, giving the Excel filename and a sheetname, 'nobel_winners' and 'WinnersSheet1', respectively, in this example:

```
df.to_excel('nobel_winners.xlsx', sheet_name='WinnersSheet1')
```

There are various options similar to to_csv covered in the pandas docs (*https://oreil.ly/g15Al*). Because pandas Panels and Excel files can store multiple DataFrames, there is a Panel to_excel method to write all its DataFrames to an Excel file.

If you need to select multiple DataFrames to write to a shared Excel file, you can use an ExcelWriter object:

```
with pd.ExcelWriter('nobel_winners.xlsx') as writer:
    df1.to_excel(writer, sheet_name='WinnersSheet1')
    df2.to_excel(writer, sheet_name='WinnersSheet2')
```

SQL

By preference pandas uses Python's SQLAlchemy module to do the database abstraction. If using SQLAlchemy, you'll also need the driver library for your database.

The easiest way to load a database table or the results of an SQL query is with the read_sql method. Let's use our preferred SQLite database and read its winners table into a DataFrame:

```
import sqlalchemy

engine = sqlalchemy.create_engine(
                'sqlite:///data/nobel_winners.db') ❶
df = pd.read_sql('winners', engine) ❷
df
Out:
    index            category    country date_of_birth
0   4                Peace       Belgium  1829-07-26
...
                         name                        place_of_birth
0   Auguste Beernaert Ostend , Netherlands (now  Belgium )
...
```

❶ Here, we use an existing SQLite (file-based) database. SQLAlchemy can create engines for all the commonly used databases, for example *mysql://USER:PASSWORD@localhost/db*.

❷ Read the contents of the 'nobel_winners' SQL table into a DataFrame. read_sql is a convenience wrapper around the read_sql_table and read_sql_query methods and will do the right thing depending on its first argument.

Writing DataFrames to an SQL database is simple enough. Using the engine we just created, we can add a copy of the winners table to our SQLite database:

```
# save DataFrame df to nobel_winners SQL table
df.to_sql('winners_copy', engine, if_exists='replace')
```

If you encounter errors due to packet-size limitations, the chunksize parameter can set the number of rows to be written at a time:

```
# write 500 rows at a time
df.to_sql('winners_copy', engine, chunksize=500)
```

pandas will do the sensible thing and try to map your data to a suitable SQL type, inferring the datatype of objects. If necessary, the default type can be overridden in the load call:

```
from sqlalchemy.types import String
df.to_sql('winners_copy', engine, dtype={'year': String}) ❶
```

❶ Override pandas's inference, and specify year as a String column.

Further details of pandas-SQL interaction can be found in the pandas documentation (*https://oreil.ly/kiLyQ*).

MongoDB

For dataviz work, there's a lot to be said for the convenience of document-based NoSQL databases like MongoDB. In MongoDB's case, things are even better, as it uses a binary form of JSON for its datastore—namely BSON, short for binary JSON. Since JSON is our data glue of choice, as it connects our web dataviz with its backend server, there's a good reason to consider storing your datasets in Mongo. It also plays nicely with pandas.

As we've seen, pandas DataFrames convert nicely to and from JSON format, so getting a Mongo document collection into a pandas DataFrame is a pretty easy affair:

```
import pandas as pd
from pymongo import MongoClient

client = MongoClient() ❶

db = client.nobel_prize ❷
cursor = db.winners.find() ❸
df = pd.DataFrame(list(cursor)) ❹
df ❺
# _
```

❶ Create a Mongo client, using the default host and ports.

❷ Get the nobel_prize database.

❸ Find all documents in the winner collection.

❹ Load all documents from the cursor into a list and use to create a DataFrame.

⑤ The winners collection is empty at this point—let's fill it with some DataFrame data.

It's just as easy to insert a DataFrame's records into a MongoDB database. Here, we use the `get_mongo_database` method we defined in Example 3-5 to get our `nobel_prize` database and save the DataFrame to its winners collection:

```
db = get_mongo_database('nobel_prize')

records = df.to_dict('records') ❶
db[collection].insert_many(records) ❷
```

❶ Converts the DataFrame to a `dict`, using the `records` argument to convert the rows into individual objects.

❷ For PyMongo version 2, use the `insert` method.

pandas doesn't have MongoDB convenience methods comparable to `to_csv` or `read_csv`, but it's easy enough to roll a couple of utility functions to convert from MongoDB to DataFrames and back again:

```
def mongo_to_dataframe(db_name, collection, query={},\
                       host='localhost', port=27017,\
                       username=None, password=None,\
                        no_id=True):
    """ create a DataFrame from mongodb collection """

    db = get_mongo_database(db_name, host, port, username,\
     password)
    cursor = db[collection].find(query)
    df =  pd.DataFrame(list(cursor))

    if no_id: ❶
        del df['_id']

    return df

def dataframe_to_mongo(df, db_name, collection,\
                       host='localhost', port=27017,\
                       username=None, password=None):
    """ save a DataFrame to mongodb collection """
    db = get_mongo_database(db_name, host, port, username,\
     password)

    records = df.to_dict('records')
    db[collection].insert_many(records)
```

❶ Mongo's `_id` field will be included in the DataFrame. By default, remove the column.

Having inserted the DataFrame's records into Mongo, let's make sure they have been successfully stored:

```
db = get_mongo_database('nobel_prize')
list(db.winners.find())  ❶
[{'_id': ObjectId('62fcf2fb0e7fe50ac4393912'),
  'id': 1,
  'category': 'Physics',
  'name': 'Albert Einstein',
  'nationality': 'Swiss',
  'year': 1921,
  'gender': 'male'},
 {'_id': ObjectId('62fcf2fb0e7fe50ac4393913'),
  'id': 2,
  'category': 'Physics',
  'name': 'Paul Dirac',
  'nationality': 'British',
  'year': 1933,
  'gender': 'male'},
 {'_id': ObjectId('62fcf2fb0e7fe50ac4393914'),
  'id': 3,
  'category': 'Chemistry',
  'name': 'Marie Curie',
  'nationality': 'Polish',
  'year': 1911,
  'gender': 'female'}]
```

 The collection's find method returns a cursor, which we convert to a Python list to see the contents.

Another way to create DataFrames is to build them from a collection of Series. Let's have a look at that, taking the opportunity to explore Series in more detail.

Series into DataFrames

Series are the building block of pandas's DataFrames. They can be manipulated independently with methods that mirror those of the DataFrame and they can be combined to form DataFrames, as we'll see in the subsection.

The key idea with pandas Series is the index. These indices function as labels for the heterogeneous data contained in, say, a row of data. When pandas operates on more than one data object, these indices are used to align the fields.

Series can be created in one of three ways. The first is from a Python list or NumPy array:

```
s = pd.Series([1, 2, 3, 4]) # Series(np.arange(4))
Out:
0    1 # index, value
1    2
2    3
3    4
dtype: int64
```

Note that integer indices are automatically created for our Series. If we were adding a row of data to a DataFrame (table), we would want to specify the column indices by passing them as a list of integers or labels:

```
s = pd.Series([1, 2, 3, 4], index=['a', 'b', 'c', 'd'])
s
Out:
a    1
b    2
c    3
d    4
dtype: int64
```

Note that the length of the index array should match the length of the data array.

We can specify both data and index using a Python dict:

```
s = pd.Series({'a':1, 'b':2, 'c':3})
Out:
a    1
b    2
c    3
dtype: int64
```

If we pass an index array along with the dict, pandas will do the sensible thing, matching the indices to the data array. Any unmatched indices will be set to NaN (not a number), and any unmatched data discarded. Note one consequence of having fewer elements than indices is that the series is cast to a float64 type:

```
s = pd.Series({'a':1, 'b':2}, index=['a', 'b', 'c'])
Out:
a    1.0
b    2.0
c    NaN
dtype: float64

s = pd.Series({'a':1, 'b':2, 'c':3}, index=['a', 'b'])
Out:
a 1
b 2
dtype: int64
```

Finally, we can pass a single, scalar value as data to the Series, provided we also specify an index. The scalar value is then applied to all indices:

```
pd.Series(9, {'a', 'b', 'c'})
Out:
a    9
b    9
c    9
dtype: int64
```

Series are like NumPy arrays (ndarray), which means they can be passed to most NumPy functions:

```
s = pd.Series([1, 2, 3, 4], ['a', 'b', 'c', 'd'])
np.sqrt(s)
Out:
a    1.000000
b    1.414214
c    1.732051
d    2.000000
dtype: float64
```

Slicing operations work as they would with Python lists or ndarrays, but note that the index labels are preserved:

```
s[1:3]
Out:
b    2
c    3
dtype: int64
```

Unlike NumPy's arrays, pandas's series can take data of multiple types. Adding two series demonstrates this utility with numbers being added while strings are concatenated:

```
pd.Series([1, 2.1, 'foo']) + pd.Series([2, 3, 'bar'])
Out:
0         3 # 1 + 2
1       5.1 # 2.1 + 3
2    foobar # strings correctly concatenated
dtype: object
```

The ability to create and manipulate individual Series is particularly important when you are interacting with the NumPy ecosystem, manipulating data from a DataFrame, or creating visualizations outside of pandas's Matplotlib wrapper.

As Series are the building block of DataFrames, it's easy to join them together to create a DataFrame, using pandas's concat method:

```
names = pd.Series(['Albert Einstein', 'Marie Curie'],\
  name='name') ❶
categories = pd.Series(['Physics', 'Chemistry'],\
  name='category')

df = pd.concat([names, categories], axis=1) ❷
```

```
df.head()
Out:
             name     category
0    Albert Einstein    Physics
1       Marie Curie   Chemistry
```

 We use the `names` and `categories` series to provide the data and column names (the series `name` property) for a DataFrame.

❷ Concatenate the two Series using the `axis` argument of 1 to indicate that the Series are columns.

Along with the many ways to create DataFrames from files and databases just discussed, you should now have a solid grounding in getting data into and out of DataFrames.

Summary

This chapter laid a foundation for the two pandas-based chapters to come. The core concepts of pandas—the DataFrame, Index, and Series—were discussed and we saw why pandas is such a good fit with the type of real-world data that data visualizers deal with, extending the NumPy `ndarray` by allowing the storage of heterogeneous data and adding a powerful indexing system.

With pandas's core data structures under our belts, the next few chapters will show you how to use them to clean and process your dataset of Nobel Prize winners, extending your knowledge of the pandas toolkit and showing you how to go about applying it in a data visualization context.

Now that we know how to get data into and out of a DataFrame, it's time to see what pandas can do with it. We'll first see how to give your data a clean bill of health, discovering and fixing anomalies such as duplicate rows, missing fields, and corrupted data.

## CHAPTER 9

Cleaning Data with pandas

The previous two chapters introduced pandas and NumPy, the Numeric Python library it extends. Armed with basic pandas know-how, we're ready to start the cleaning stage of our toolchain, aiming to find and eliminate the dirty data in our scraped dataset (see Chapter 6). This chapter will also extend your pandas knowledge, introducing new methods in a working context.

In Chapter 8, we covered the core components of pandas: the DataFrame, a programmatic spreadsheet capable of dealing with the many different datatypes found in the real world, and its building block, the Series, a heterogeneous extension of NumPy's homogeneous ndarray. We also covered how to read from and write to different datastores, including JSON, CSV files, MongoDB, and SQL databases. Now we'll start to put pandas through its paces, showing how it can be used to clean dirty data. I'll introduce the key elements of data cleaning using our dirty Nobel Prize dataset as an example.

I'll take it slowly, introducing key pandas concepts in a working environment. Let's first establish why cleaning data is such an important part of a data visualizer's work.

Coming Clean About Dirty Data

I think it's fair to say that most people entering the field of data visualization underestimate, often by a fairly large factor, the amount of time they're going to spend trying to make their data presentable. The fact is that getting clean datasets that are a pleasure to transform into cool visualizations could well take over half your time. Data in the wild is very rarely pristine, often bearing the sticky paw prints of mistaken manual data entry, missing whole fields due to oversight or parsing errors and/or mixed datetime formats.

For this book, and to pose a properly meaty challenge, our Nobel Prize dataset has been scraped from Wikipedia, a manually edited website with fairly informal guidelines. In this sense, the data is bound to be dirty—humans make mistakes even when the environment is a good deal more forgiving. But even data from the official APIs of, for example, large social media sites, is often flawed, with missing or incomplete fields, scar tissue from countless changes to the data schemas, deliberate mis-entry, and the like.

So cleaning data is a fundamental part of the job of a data visualizer, stealing time from all the cool stuff you'd rather be doing—which is an excellent reason to get really good at it and free up that drudge time for more meaningful pursuits. And a large part of getting good at cleaning data is choosing the right toolset, which is where pandas comes in. It's a great way to slice and dice even fairly large datasets,[1] and being comfortable with it could save you a lot of time. That is where this chapter comes in.

To recap, scraping the Nobel data from Wikipedia using Python's Scrapy library (see Chapter 6) produced an array of JSON objects of the form:

```
{
  "category": "Physics",
  "name": "Albert Einstein",
  "gender": "male",
  "place_of_birth": "Ulm , Baden-W\u00fcrttemberg ,
    German Empire",
  "date_of_death": "1955-04-18",
  ...
}
```

The job of this chapter is to turn that array into as clean a data source as possible before we explore it with pandas in the next chapter.

There are many forms of dirty data, most commonly:

- Duplicate entries/rows
- Missing fields
- Misaligned rows
- Corrupted fields
- Mixed datatypes in a column

We'll now probe our Nobel Prize data for these kinds of anomalies.

---

1 *Large* is a very relative term, but pandas will take pretty much whatever will fit in your computer's RAM memory, which is where DataFrames live.

First, we need to load our JSON data into a DataFrame, as shown in the previous chapter (see "Creating and Saving DataFrames" on page 199). We can open the JSON data file directly:

```
import pandas as pd

df = pd.read_json(open('data/nobel_winners_dirty.json'))
```

Now that we've got our dirty scraped data into a DataFrame, let's get a broad overview of what we have.

Inspecting the Data

The pandas DataFrame has a number of methods and properties that give a quick overview of the data contained within. The most general is `info`, which gives a neat summary of the number of data entries by column:

```
df.info()
<class 'pandas.core.frame.DataFrame'>
RangeIndex: 1052 entries, 0 to 1051
Data columns (total 12 columns):
 #   Column          Non-Null Count  Dtype
---  ------          --------------  -----
 0   born_in         1052 non-null   object
 1   category        1052 non-null   object
 2   country         1052 non-null   object
 3   date_of_birth   1044 non-null   object
 4   date_of_death   1044 non-null   object
 5   gender          1040 non-null   object
 6   link            1052 non-null   object
 7   name            1052 non-null   object
 8   place_of_birth  1044 non-null   object
 9   place_of_death  1044 non-null   object
 10  text            1052 non-null   object
 11  year            1052 non-null   int64
dtypes: int64(1), object(11)
memory usage: 98.8+ KB
```

You can see that some fields are missing entries. For example, although there are 1,052 rows in our DataFrame, there are only 1,040 gender attributes. Note also the handy `memory_usage`—pandas DataFrames are held in RAM, so as datasets increase in size, this number gives a nice indication of how close we are to our machine-specific memory limits.

DataFrame's describe method gives a handy statistical summary of relevant columns:

```
df.describe()
Out:
              year
count  1052.000000
mean   1968.729087
std      33.155829
min    1809.000000
25%    1947.000000
50%    1975.000000
75%    1996.000000
max    2014.000000
```

As you can see, by default only numerical columns are described. Already we can see an error in the data, the minimum year being 1809, which is impossible when the first Nobel was awarded in 1901.

describe takes an include parameter that allows us to specify the column datatypes (dtypes) to be assessed. Other than year, the columns in our Nobel Prize dataset are all objects, which are pandas's default, catchall dtype, capable of representing any numbers, strings, data times, and more. Example 9-1 shows how to get their stats.

Example 9-1. Describing the DataFrame

```
In [140]: df.describe(include=['object']) ❶
Out[140]:
        born_in  category date_of_birth date_of_death gender  \
count      1052      1052          1044          1044   1040
unique       40         7           853           563      2
top                Physio..   9 May 1947                 male
freq        910       250             4           362    983

                          link       name  \
count                     1052       1052
unique                     893        998
top      http://eg/wiki/...     Daniel Kahneman
freq                         4          2

          country place_of_birth place_of_death  \
count        1052           1044           1044
unique         59            735            410
top    United States
freq          350             29            409
...
```

❶ The include argument is a list (or single item) of columnar dtypes to summarize.

There's quite a lot of useful information to be gleaned from the output of Example 9-1, such as that there are 59 unique nationalities with the United States, at 350, being the largest group.

One interesting tidbit is that of 1,044 recorded dates of birth, only 853 are unique, which could mean any number of things. Possibly some auspicious days saw the birth of more than one laureate or, wearing our data-cleaning hats, it's more likely that there are some duplicated winners or that some dates are wrong or have only recorded the year. The duplicated winners hypothesis is confirmed by the observation that of 1,052 name counts, only 998 are unique. Now there have been a few multiple winners but not enough to account for 54 duplicates.

DataFrame's `head` and `tail` methods provide another easy way to get a quick feel for the data. By default, they display the top or bottom five rows, but we can set that number by passing an integer as the first argument. Example 9-2 shows the result of using `head` with our Nobel DataFrame.

Example 9-2. Sampling the first five DataFrame rows

```
df.head()
Out:
                          born_in                    category   date_of_bi..
0                                   Physiology or Medicine  8 October 1..
1   Bosnia and Herzegovina                    Literature   9 October 1..❶
2   Bosnia and Herzegovina                     Chemistry   July 23, 1..
3                                                     Peace              ..
4                                                     Peace  26 July 1..

     date_of_death gender                                             ..
0   24 March 2002    male  http://en.wikipedia.org/wiki/C%C3%A..
1   13 March 1975    male         http://en.wikipedia.org/wi..
2      1998-01-07    male      http://en.wikipedia.org/wiki/Vl..❷
3             NaN    None  http://en.wikipedia.org/wiki/Institu..
4  6 October 1912    male  http://en.wikipedia.org/wiki/Auguste..

                            name country  \
0              César Milstein    Argentina
1                  Ivo Andric *              ❶
2              Vladimir Prelog *
3   Institut de Droit International      Belgium
4             Auguste Beernaert      Belgium
```

❶ These rows have an entry for the `born_in` field and an asterisk by their name.

❷ The `date_of_death` field has a different time format than the other rows.

The first five winners in Example 9-2 show a couple of useful things. First, we see the names in rows 1 and 2 are marked by an asterisk and have an entry in the born_in field ❶. Second, note that row 2 has a different time format for date_of_death than the others, and that there are both month-day and day-month time formats in the date_of_birth field ❷. This kind of inconsistency is a perennial problem for human-edited data, particularly dates and times. We'll see how to fix it with pandas later.

Example 9-1 gives an object count of 1,052 for the born_in field, indicating no empty fields, but head shows only rows 1 and 2 have content. This suggests that the missing fields are an empty string or space, both of which count as data to pandas. Let's change them to a noncounted NaN, which will make more sense of the numbers. But first we're going to need a little primer in pandas data selection.

Indices and pandas Data Selection

Before beginning to clean our data, let's do a quick recap of basic pandas data selection, using the Nobel Prize dataset as an example.

pandas indexes by rows and columns. Usually column indices are specified by the data file, SQL table, and so on, but, as shown in the last chapter, we can set or override these when the DataFrame is created by using the names argument to pass a list of column names. The columns index is accessible as a DataFrame property:

```
# Our Nobel dataset's columns
df.columns
Out: Index(['born_in', 'category', 'date_of_birth',
    ...
        'place_of_death', 'text', 'year'], dtype='object')
```

By default, pandas specifies a zero-base integer index for the rows, but we can override this by passing a list in the index parameter on creation of the DataFrame or afterward by setting the index property directly. More often we want to use one or more[2] of the DataFrame's columns as an index. We can do this using the set_index method. If you want to return to the default index, you can use the reset_index method, as shown in Example 9-3.

---

2 pandas supports multiple indices using the MultiIndex object. This provides a very powerful way of refining higher-dimensional data. Check out the details in the pandas documentation (*https://oreil.ly/itwDR*).

Example 9-3. Setting the DataFrame's index

```
# set the name field as index
df = df.set_index('name') ❶
df.head(2)
Out:
                                 born_in                   category  \
name ❷
César Milstein                                  Physiology or Medicine
Ivo Andric *     Bosnia and Herzegovina                     Literature
...

df.reset_index(inplace=True) ❸

df.head(2)
Out:
          name                    born_in                   category  \
0   César Milstein                          Physiology or Medicine ❹
1     Ivo Andric *   Bosnia and Herzegovina                  Literature
```

❶ Sets the frame's index to its name column. Set the result back to df.

❷ The rows are now indexed by name.

❸ Resets the index to its integer. Note that we change it in place this time.

❹ The index is now by integer position.

> There are two ways to change a pandas DataFrame or Series: by altering the data in place or by assigning a copy. There is no guarantee that in place is faster, plus method-chaining requires that the operation return a changed object. Generally, I use the df = df.foo(...) form, but most mutating methods have an inplace argument df.foo(..., inplace=True).

Now that we understand the row-columnar indexing system, let's start selecting slices of the DataFrame.

We can select a column of the DataFrame by dot notation (where no spaces or special characters are in the name) or square-bracket notation. Let's take a look at that born_in column:

```
bi_col = df.born_in # or bi = df['born_in']
bi_col
Out:
0
1      Bosnia and Herzegovina
```

```
2         Bosnia and Herzegovina
3
...
1051
Name: born_in, Length: 1052, dtype: object

type(bi_col)
Out: pandas.core.series.Series
```

Note that the column selection returns a pandas Series, with the DataFrame indexing preserved.

DataFrames and Series share the same methods for accessing rows/members. `iloc` selects by integer position, and `loc` selects by label. Let's use `iloc` to grab the first row of our DataFrame:

```
# access the first row
df.iloc[0]
Out:
name                          César Milstein
born_in
category                 Physiology or Medicine
...

# set the index to 'name' and access by name-label
df.set_index('name', inplace=True)
df.loc['Albert Einstein']
Out:
                    born_in category        country  ...
name
Albert Einstein             Physics  Switzerland  ...
Albert Einstein             Physics      Germany  ...
...
```

Selecting Multiple Rows

Standard Python array slicing can be used with a DataFrame to select multiple rows:

```
# select the first 10 rows
df[0:10]
Out:
                    born_in                   category   date_of_b..
0                          Physiology or Medicine  8 October ..
1  Bosnia and Herzegovina             Literature  9 October ..
...
9                                          Peace        1910-0..
# select the last four rows
df[-4:]
Out:
       born_in             category       date_of_birth date_..
1048                          Peace    November 1, 1878   May..
1049        Physiology or Medicine         1887-04-10    19..
```

```
1050              Chemistry           1906-9-6   1..
1051                  Peace  November 26, 1931   ..
```

The standard way to select multiple rows based on a conditional expression (e.g., is the value of the column `value` greater than x) is to create a Boolean mask and use it in a selector. Let's find all the Nobel Prize winners after the year 2000. First, we create a mask by performing a Boolean expression on each of the rows:

```
mask = df.year > 2000 ❶
mask
Out:
0      False
1      False
...
13     True
...
1047     True
1048     False
...
Name: year, Length: 1052, dtype: bool
```

❶ `True` for all rows where the `year` field is greater than 2000.

The resulting Boolean mask shares our DataFrame's index and can be used to select all `True` rows:

```
mask = df.year > 2000
winners_since_2000 = df[mask] ❶
winners_since_2000.count()
Out:
...
year            202 # number of winners since 2000
dtype: int64

winners_since_2000.head()
Out:
...
                                                  text  year
13                      François Englert , Physics, 2013  2013
32          Christopher A. Pissarides , Economics, 2010  2010
66                           Kofi Annan , Peace, 2001  2001
87                  Riccardo Giacconi *, Physics, 2002  2002
88     Mario Capecchi *, Physiology or Medicine, 2007  2007
```

❶ This will return a DataFrame containing only those rows where the Boolean mask array is `True`.

Boolean masking is a very powerful technique capable of selecting any subset of the data you need. I recommend setting a few targets to practice constructing the right Boolean expressions. Generally, we dispense with the intermediate mask creation:

```
winners_since_2000 = df[df.year > 2000]
```

Now that we can select individual and multiple rows by slicing or using a Boolean mask, in the next sections we'll see how we can change our DataFrame, purging it of dirty data as we go.

Cleaning the Data

Now that we know how to access our data, let's see how we can change it for the better, starting with what looks like empty born_in fields we saw in Example 9-2. If we look at the count of the born_in columns, it doesn't show any missing rows, which it would were any fields missing or NaN (not a number):

```
In [0]: df.born_in.describe()
Out[0]:
count      1052
unique       40
top
freq        910
Name: born_in, dtype: object
```

Finding Mixed Types

Note that pandas stores all string-like data using the dtype object. A cursory inspection suggests that the column is a mixture of empty and country-name strings. We can quickly check that all the column members are strings by mapping the Python type function (*https://oreil.ly/jj9hY*) to all members using the apply method and then making a set of the resulting list of column members by type:

```
In [1]: set(df.born_in.apply(type))
Out[1]: {str}
```

This shows that all of the born_in column members are strings of type str. Now let's replace any empty strings with an empty field.

Replacing Strings

We want to replace these empty strings with a NaN, to prevent them being counted.[3] The pandas replace method is tailor-made for this and can be applied to the whole DataFrame or individual Series:

```
import numpy as np

bi_col.replace('', np.nan, inplace=True)
bi_col
```

---

3 By default, pandas uses NumPy's NaN (not a number) float to designate missing values.

```
Out:
0                         NaN ❶
1     Bosnia and Herzegovina
2     Bosnia and Herzegovina
3                         NaN
...

bi_col.count()
Out: 142 ❷
```

❶ Our empty `''` strings have been replaced with NumPy's NaN.

❷ Unlike the empty strings, the NaN fields are discounted.

After replacing the empty strings with NaNs, we get a true count of 142 for the born_in field.

Let's replace all empty strings in our DataFrame with discounted NaNs:

```
df.replace('', np.nan, inplace=True)
```

pandas allows sophisticated replacement of strings (and other objects) in columns (e.g., allowing you to craft regular expressions or regexes (*https://oreil.ly/KK3b2*), which are applied to whole Series, typically DataFrame columns). Let's look at a little example, using the asterisk-marked names in our Nobel Prize DataFrame.

Example 9-2 showed that some of our Nobel Prize names are marked with an asterisk, denoting that these winners are recorded by country of birth, not country at the time of winning the prize:

```
df.head()
Out:
...

                             name country  \
0                  César Milstein    Argentina
1                     Ivo Andric *
2                 Vladimir Prelog *
3    Institut de Droit International      Belgium
4                 Auguste Beernaert      Belgium
```

Let's set ourselves the task of cleaning up those names by removing the asterisks and stripping any remaining whitespace.

pandas Series have a handy `str` member, which provides a number of useful string methods to be performed on the array. Let's use it to check how many asterisked names we have:

```
df[df.name.str.contains(r'\*')]['name'] ❶
Out:
1               Ivo Andric *
2           Vladimir Prelog *
```

```
...
1041        John Warcup Cornforth *
1046        Elizabeth H. Blackburn *
Name: name, Length: 142, dtype: object ❷
```

❶ We use str's contains method on the name column. Note that we have to escape the asterisk ('*') as this is a regex string. The Boolean mask is then applied to our Nobel Prize DataFrame and the resulting names listed.

❷ 142 of our 1,052 rows have a name containing *.

To clean up the names, let's replace the asterisks with an empty string and strip any whitespace from the resulting names:

```
df.name = df.name.str.replace('*', '', regex=True) ❶
# strip the whitespace from the names
df.name = df.name.str.strip()
```

❶ Removes all asterisks in the name fields and return the result to the DataFrame. Note that we have to explicitly set the regex flag to True.

A quick check shows that the names are now clean:

```
df[df.name.str.contains('\*')]
Out:
Empty DataFrame
```

pandas Series have an impressive number of string-handling functions, enabling you to search and adapt your string columns. You can find a full list of these in the API docs (*https://oreil.ly/2mCSZ*).

Removing Rows

To recap, the 142 winners with born_in fields are duplicates, having an entry in the Wikipedia biography page by both the country they were born in and their country when given the prize. Although the former could form the basis of an interesting visualization,[4] for our visualization we want each individual prize represented once only and so need to remove these from our DataFrame.

We want to create a new DataFrame using only those rows with a NaN born_in field. You might naively assume that a conditional expression comparing the born_in field to NaN would work here, but by definition[5] NaN Boolean comparisons always return False:

---

4 One interesting visualization might be charting the migration of Nobel Prize winners from their homelands.

5 See IEEE 754 and Wikipedia (*https://oreil.ly/5H3q2*).

```
np.nan == np.nan
Out: False
```

As a result, pandas provides the dedicated `isnull` method to check for discounted (null) fields:

```
df = df[df.born_in.isnull()] ❶
df.count()
Out:
born_in              0 # all entries now empty
category           910
...
dtype: int64
```

❶ `isnull` produces a Boolean mask with `True` for all rows with an empty `born_in` field.

The `born_in` column is no longer of use, so let's remove it for now:[6]

```
df = df.drop('born_in', axis=1) ❶
```

❶ `drop` takes a single label or index (or list of same) as a first argument and an `axis` argument to indicate row (`0` and default) or column (`1`) index.

Finding Duplicates

Now, a quick internet search shows that 889 people and organizations have received the Nobel Prize up to 2015. With 910 remaining rows, we still have a few duplicates or anomalies to account for.

pandas has a handy `duplicated` method for finding matching rows. This matches by column name or list of column names. Let's get the list of all duplicates by name:

```
dupes_by_name = df[df.duplicated('name')] ❶
dupes_by_name.count()
Out:
...
year                46
dtype: int64
```

❶ `duplicated` returns a Boolean array with `True` for the first occurrence of any rows with the same `name` field.

Now, a few people have won the Nobel Prize more than once but not 46, which means 40-odd winners are duplicated. Given that the Wikipedia page we scraped

---

6 As you'll see in the next chapter, the `born_in` fields contain some interesting information about the movements of Nobel Prize winners. We'll see how to add this data to the cleaned dataset at the end of this chapter.

listed prize winners by country, the best bet is winners being "claimed" by more than one country.

Let's look at some of the ways we can find duplicates by name in our Nobel Prize DataFrame. Some of these are pretty inefficient, but it's a nice way to demonstrate a few pandas functions.

By default, duplicated indicates (Boolean True) all duplicates after the first occurrence, but setting the keep option to *last* sets the first occurrence of duplicated rows to True. By combining these two calls using a Boolean *or* (|), we can get the full list of duplicates:

```
all_dupes = df[df.duplicated('name')\
                | df.duplicated('name', keep='last')]
all_dupes.count()
Out:
...
year            92
dtype: int64
```

We could also get all the duplicates by testing whether our DataFrame rows have a name in the list of duplicate names. pandas has a handy isin method for this:

```
all_dupes = df[df.name.isin(dupes_by_name.name)]  ❶
all_dupes.count()
Out:
...
year            92
dtype: int64
```

❶ dupes_by_name.name is a column Series containing all the duplicated names.

We can also find all duplicates by using pandas's powerful groupby method, which groups our DataFrame's rows by column or list of columns. It returns a list of key-value pairs with the column value(s) as key and list of rows as values:

```
for name, rows in df.groupby('name'):  ❶
    print('name: %s, number of rows: %d'%(name, len(rows)))

name: A. Michael Spence, number of rows: 1
name: Aage Bohr, number of rows: 1
name: Aaron Ciechanover, number of rows: 1
...
```

❶ groupby returns an iterator of (group name, group) tuples.

In order to get all duplicate rows, we merely need to check the length of the list of rows returned by key. Anything greater than one has name duplicates. Here we use pandas's concat method, which takes a list of row lists and creates a DataFrame with all the duplicated rows. A Python list constructor is used to filter for groups with more than one row:

```
pd.concat([g for _,g in df.groupby('name')]\  ❶
                      if len(g) > 1])['name']
```

```
Out:
121            Aaron Klug
131            Aaron Klug
615        Albert Einstein
844        Albert Einstein
...
489        Yoichiro Nambu
773        Yoichiro Nambu
Name: name, Length: 92, dtype: object
```

❶ Create a Python list by filtering the name row groups for those with more than one row (i.e., duplicated names).

Different Paths to the Same Goal

With a large library like pandas, there are usually a number of ways to achieve the same thing. With small datasets like our Nobel Prize winners, any one will do, but for large datasets there could be significant performance implications. Just because pandas will do what you ask doesn't mean it's necessarily efficient. With a lot of complex data manipulation going on behind the scenes, it's a good idea to be prepared to be flexible and alert to inefficient approaches.

Sorting Data

Now that we have our all_dupes DataFrame, with all duplicated rows by name, let's use it to demonstrate pandas's sort method.

pandas provides a sophisticated sort method for the DataFrame and Series classes, capable of sorting on multiple column names:

```
df2 = pd.DataFrame(\
    {'name':['zak', 'alice', 'bob', 'mike', 'bob', 'bob'],\
     'score':[4, 3, 5, 2, 3, 7]})
df2.sort_values(['name', 'score'],\  ❶
       ascending=[1,0])  ❷
```

```
Out:
     name  score
1   alice      3
5     bob      7
2     bob      5
4     bob      3
```

```
3    mike      2
0    zak       4
```

 Sorts the DataFrame first by name, then by score within those subgroups. Older pandas versions use sort, now deprecated.

 Sorts the names in alphabetical ascending order; sorts scores from high to low.

Let's sort the DataFrame of all_dupes by name and then look at the name, country, and year columns:

```
In [306]: all_dupes.sort_values('name')\
   [['name', 'country', 'year']]
Out[306]:
                           name         country  year
121                   Aaron Klug    South Africa  1982
131                   Aaron Klug  United Kingdom  1982
844              Albert Einstein         Germany  1921
615              Albert Einstein     Switzerland  1921
...
910                  Marie Curie          France  1903
919                  Marie Curie          France  1911
706       Marie Skłodowska-Curie          Poland  1903
709       Marie Skłodowska-Curie          Poland  1911
...
650                Ragnar Granit          Sweden  1967
960                Ragnar Granit         Finland  1809
...
396                Sidney Altman   United States  1990
995                Sidney Altman          Canada  1989
...
[92 rows x 3 columns]
```

This output shows that, as expected, some winners have been attributed twice for the same year with different countries. It also reveals a few other anomalies. Although Marie Curie did win a Nobel Prize twice, she's included here with both French and Polish nationalities.[7] The fairest thing here is to split the spoils between Poland and France while settling on the single compound surname. We have also found our anomalous year of 1809 at row 960. Sidney Altman is both duplicated and given the wrong year of 1990.

Removing Duplicates

Let's go about removing the duplicates we just identified and start compiling a little cleaning function.

---

7 While France was Curie's adopted country, she retained Polish citizenship and named her first discovered radioactive isotope *polonium* after her home country.

Views Versus Copies

It's very important when working with pandas to be clear whether you are altering a view or copy of your DataFrame, Series, and so on. The following seems like a natural way to change the country field of a row (Marie Curie's) but gives a potentially confusing warning:

```
df['country'][709] = 'France'  ❶
-c:1: SettingWithCopyWarning:
A value is trying to be set on a copy of a slice from a
DataFrame

See the caveats in the documentation:
    http://pandas.pydata.org/pandas-docs/stable/...
```

❶ Set the country of row 709, Marie Curie, from Poland to France.

This is all the more confusing when you find that it has worked as expected:

```
df['country'][709]
Out: 'France'
```

It turns out that such *chained* operations are discouraged by the pandas devs because it's easy to unintentionally alter a copy of the datatype, not the original (view).[8]

These warnings[9] are there to encourage best practice, which is to use the loc (by label) and iloc (by integer position) methods:

```
df.loc[709, 'country'] = 'France'
```

Changing rows by numeric index is fine if you know your dataset is stable and don't anticipate running any of your cleaning scripts again. But if, as in the case of our scraped Nobel Prize data, you may want to run the same cleaning script on an updated dataset, it's much better to use stable indicators (i.e., grab the row with name Marie Curie and year 1911, not index 919).

A more robust way of changing the country of a specific row is to use stable column values to select the row rather than its index. This means if the index value changes the cleaning script should still work. So to change Marie Curie's 1911 prize country to France, we can use a Boolean mask with the loc method to select a row and then set its country column to France. Note that we specify the Unicode for the Polish ł:

---

8 Some users dismiss such warnings as nannying paranoia. See the discussion on Stack Overflow (*https://oreil.ly/b7G9r*).

9 They can be turned off with pd.options.mode.chained_assignment = None # default=*warn*.

```
df.loc[(df.name == 'Marie Sk\u0142odowska-Curie') &\
    (df.year == 1911), 'country'] = 'France'
```

As well as changing Marie Curie's country, we want to remove or drop some rows from our DataFrame, based on column values. There are two ways we can do this, firstly by using the DataFrame's drop method, which takes a list of index labels, or by creating a new DataFrame with a Boolean mask that filters the rows we want to drop. If we use drop, we can use the inplace argument to change the existing DataFrame.

In the following code, we drop our duplicate Sidney Altman row by creating a DataFrame with the single row we want (remember, index labels are preserved) and passing that index to the drop method and changing the DataFrame in place:

```
df.drop(df[(df.name == 'Sidney Altman') &\
 (df.year == 1990)].index,
    inplace=True)
```

Another way to remove the row is to use the same Boolean mask with a logical *not* (~) to create a new DataFrame with all rows except the one(s) we're selecting:

```
df = df[~((df.name == 'Sidney Altman') & (df.year == 1990))]
```

Let's add this change and all current modifications to a clean_data method:

```
def clean_data(df):
    df = df.replace('', np.nan)
    df = df[df.born_in.isnull()]
    df = df.drop('born_in', axis=1)
    df.drop(df[df.year == 1809].index, inplace=True)
    df = df[~(df.name == 'Marie Curie')]
    df.loc[(df.name == 'Marie Sk\u0142odowska-Curie') &\
            (df.year == 1911), 'country'] = 'France'
    df = df[~((df.name == 'Sidney Altman') &\
     (df.year == 1990))]
    return df
```

We now have a mix of valid duplicates (those few multiple Nobel Prize winners) and those with dual country. For the purposes of our visualization, we want each prize to count only once, so we have to discard half the dual-country prizes. The easiest way is to use the duplicated method, but because we collected the winners alphabetically by country, this would favor those nationalities with first letters earlier in the alphabet. Short of a fair amount of research and debate, the fairest way seems to pick one out at random and discard it. There are various ways to do this, but the simplest is to randomize the order of the rows before using drop_duplicates, a pandas method that drops all duplicated rows after the first encountered or, with the take_last argument set to True, all before the last.

NumPy has a number of very useful methods in its random module, of which permuta tion is perfect for randomizing the row index. This method takes an array (or pandas index) of values and shuffles them. We can then use the DataFrame reindex method to apply the shuffled result. Note that we drop those rows sharing both name and year, which will preserve the legitimate double winners with different years for their prizes:

```
df = df.reindex(np.random.permutation(df.index)) ❶
df = df.drop_duplicates(['name', 'year'])         ❷
df = df.sort_index()                              ❸
df.count()
Out:
...
year               865
dtype: int64
```

❶ Create a shuffled version of df's index and reindex df with it.

❷ Drop all duplicates sharing name and year.

❸ Return the index to sorted-by-integer position.

If our data wrangling has been successful, we should have only valid duplicates left, those vaunted double-prize winners. Let's list the remaining duplicates to check:

```
In : df[df.duplicated('name') |
         df.duplicated('name', keep='last')]\ ❶
        .sort_values(by='name')\
        [['name', 'country', 'year', 'category']]
Out:
                        name        country  year   category
548        Frederick Sanger  United Kingdom  1958  Chemistry
580        Frederick Sanger  United Kingdom  1980  Chemistry
292            John Bardeen   United States  1956    Physics
326            John Bardeen   United States  1972    Physics
285          Linus C. Pauling  United States  1954  Chemistry
309          Linus C. Pauling  United States  1962      Peace
706  Marie Skłodowska-Curie          Poland  1903    Physics
709  Marie Skłodowska-Curie          France  1911  Chemistry
```

❶ We combine duplicates from the first with the last to get them all. If using an older version of pandas, you may need to use the argument take_last=True.

A quick internet check shows that we have the correct four double-prize winners.

Assuming we've caught the unwanted duplicates,[10] let's move on to other "dirty" aspects of the data.

---

10 Depending on the dataset, the cleaning phase is unlikely to catch all transgressors.

Dealing with Missing Fields

Let's see where we stand as far as *null* fields are concerned by counting our DataFrame:

```
df.count()
Out:
category          864 
country           865
date_of_birth     857
date_of_death     566
gender            857 
link              865
name              865
place_of_birth    831
place_of_death    524
text              865
year              865
dtype: int64
```

    A missing category field

❷   Eight missing gender fields

We appear to be missing a category field, which suggests a data entry mistake. If you remember, while scraping our Nobel Prize data we checked the category against a valid list (see Example 6-3). One of them appears to have failed this check. Let's find out which one it is by grabbing the row where the category field is null and showing its name and text columns:

```
df[df.category.isnull()][['name', 'text']]
Out:
                 name                        text
922  Alexis Carrel  Alexis Carrel , Medicine, 1912
```

We saved the original link text for our winners and, as you can see, Alexis Carrel was listed as winning the Nobel prize for Medicine, when it should have been Physiology or Medicine. Let's correct that now:

```
...
df.loc[df.name == 'Alexis Carrel', 'category'] =\
  'Physiology or Medicine'
```

We are also missing gender for eight winners. Let's list them:

```
df[df.gender.isnull()]['name']
Out:
3                            Institut de Droit International
156                             Friends Service Council
267       American Friends Service Committee  (The Quakers)
574                             Amnesty International
650                             Ragnar Granit
```

```
947                        Médecins Sans Frontières
1000        Pugwash Conferences on Science and World Affairs
1033                  International Atomic Energy Agency
Name: name, dtype: object
```

With the exception of Ragnar Granit, all these are genderless (missing person data) institutions. The focus of our visualization is on individual winners, so we'll remove these while establishing Ragnar Granit's gender[11]:

```
...
def clean_data(df):
    ...
    df.loc[df.name == 'Ragnar Granit', 'gender'] = 'male'
    df = df[df.gender.notnull()] # remove genderless entries
```

Let's see where those changes leave us by performing another count on our DataFrame:

```
df.count()
Out:
category        858
date_of_birth   857 # missing field
...
year            858
dtype: int64
```

Having removed all the institutions, all entries should have at least a date of birth. Let's find the missing entry and fix it:

```
df[df.date_of_birth.isnull()]['name']
Out:
782    Hiroshi Amano
Name: name, dtype: object
```

Probably because Hiroshi Amano is a very recent (2014) winner, his date of birth was not available to be scraped. A quick web search establishes Amano's date of birth, which we add to the DataFrame by hand:

```
...
    df.loc[df.name == 'Hiroshi Amano', 'date_of_birth'] =\
    '11 September 1960'
```

We now have 858 individual winners. Let's do a final count to see where we stand:

```
df.count()
Out:
category        858
country         858
date_of_birth   858
```

---

11 Although Granit's gender is not specified in the person data, his Wikipedia biography (*https://oreil.ly/PxUns*) uses the male gender.

```
date_of_death        566
gender               858
link                 858
name                 858
place_of_birth       831
place_of_death       524
text                 858
year                 858
dtype: int64
```

The key fields of `category`, `date_of_birth`, `gender`, `country`, and `year` are all filled and there's a healthy amount of data in the remaining stats. All in all, there's enough clean data to form the basis for a rich visualization.

Now let's put on the finishing touches by making our temporal fields more usable.

Dealing with Times and Dates

Currently the `date_of_birth` and `date_of_death` fields are represented by strings. As we've seen, Wikipedia's informal editing guidelines have led to a number of different time formats. Our original DataFrame shows an impressive variety of formats in the first 10 entries:

```
df[['name', 'date_of_birth']]
Out[14]:
                          name       date_of_birth
4             Auguste Beernaert       26 July 1829
                                            . . .
8             Corneille Heymans     28 March 1892
. . .                      . . .             . . .
1047            Brian P. Schmidt   February 24, 1967
1048    Carlos Saavedra Lamas     November 1, 1878
1049            Bernardo Houssay        1887-04-10
1050      Luis Federico Leloir          1906-9-6
1051    Adolfo Pérez Esquivel     November 26, 1931

[858 rows x 2 columns]
```

In order to compare the date fields (for example, subtracting the prize *year* from *date of birth* to give the winners' ages), we need to get them into a format that allows such operations. Unsurprisingly, pandas is good with parsing messy dates and times, converting them by default into the NumPy `datetime64` object, which has a slew of useful methods and operators.

Converting a time column to `datetime64`, we use pandas's `to_datetime` method:

```
pd.to_datetime(df.date_of_birth, errors='raise') ❶
Out:
4      1829-07-26
5      1862-08-29
          . . .
```

```
1050    1906-09-06
1051    1931-11-26
Name: date_of_birth, Length: 858, dtype: datetime64[ns]
```

❶ The errors default is ignore, but we want them flagged.

By default to_datetime ignores errors, but here we want to know if pandas has been unable to parse a date_of_birth, giving us the opportunity to fix it manually. Thankfully, the conversion passes without error.

Let's fix our DataFrame's date_of_birth column before moving on:

```
In: df.date_of_birth = pd.to_datetime(df.date_of_birth, errors='coerce')
```

Running to_datetime on the date_of_birth field raises a ValueError and an unhelpful one at that, giving no indication of the entry that triggered it:

```
In [143]: pd.to_datetime(df.date_of_death, errors='raise')
---------------------------------------------------------------
ValueError                      Traceback (most recent call last)
...
    301     if arg is None:

ValueError: month must be in 1..12
```

One naive way to find the bad dates would be to iterate through our rows of data, and catch and display any errors. pandas has a handy iterrows method that provides a row iterator. Combined with a Python try-except block, this successfully finds our problem date fields:

```
for i,row in df.iterrows():
    try:
        pd.to_datetime(row.date_of_death, errors='raise') ❶
    except:
        print(f"{row.date_of_death.ljust(30)}({row['name']}, {i})") ❷
```

❶ Run to_datetime on the individual row and catch any errors.

❷ We left-justify the date of death in a text column of width 30 to make the output easier to read. pandas rows have a masking Name property, so we use string-key access with ['name'].

This lists the offending rows:

```
1968-23-07              (Henry Hallett Dale, 150)
May 30, 2011 (aged 89)  (Rosalyn Yalow, 349)
living                  (David Trimble, 581)
Diederik Korteweg       (Johannes Diderik van der Waals, 746)
living                  (Shirin Ebadi, 809)
living                  (Rigoberta Menchú, 833)
1 February 1976, age 74 (Werner Karl Heisenberg, 858)
```

which is a good demonstration of the kind of data errors you get with collaborative editing.

Although the last method works, whenever you find yourself iterating through rows of a pandas DataFrame, you should pause for a second and try to find a better way, one that exploits the multirow array handling that is a fundamental aspect of pandas's efficiency.

A better way to find the bad dates exploits the fact that pandas's to_datetime method has a coerce argument, which, if True, converts any date exceptions to NaT (not a time), the temporal equivalent of NaN. We can then create a Boolean mask out of the resulting DataFrame based on the NaT date rows, producing Figure 9-1:

```
with_death_dates = df[df.date_of_death.notnull()] ❶
bad_dates = pd.isnull(pd.to_datetime(\
            with_death_dates.date_of_death, errors='coerce')) ❷
with_death_dates[bad_dates][['category', 'date_of_death',\
'name']]
```

❶ Gets all rows with non-null date fields.

❷ Creates a Boolean mask for all bad dates in with_death_dates by checking against null (NaT) after coercing failed conversions to NaT. For older pandas versions, you may need to use coerce=True.

	category	date_of_death	name
150	Physiology or Medicine	1968-23-07	Henry Hallett Dale
349	Physiology or Medicine	May 30, 2011 (aged 89)	Rosalyn Yalow
581	Peace	living	David Trimble
746	Physics	Diederik Korteweg	Johannes Diderik van der Waals
809	Peace	living	Shirin Ebadi
833	Peace	living	Rigoberta Menchú
858	Physics	1 February 1976, age 74	Werner Karl Heisenberg

Figure 9-1. The unparseable date fields

Depending on how fastidious you want to be, these can be corrected by hand or coerced to NumPy's time equivalent of NaN, NaT. We've got more than 500 valid dates of death, which is enough to get some interesting time stats, so we'll run to_datetime again and force errors to null:

```
df.date_of_death = pd.to_datetime(df.date_of_death,\
errors='coerce')
```

Now that we have our time fields in a usable format, let's add a field for the age of the winner on receiving his/her Nobel Prize. In order to get the year value of our new dates, we need to tell pandas that it's dealing with a date column, using the `DatetimeIndex` method. Note that this gives a crude estimation of award age and may be off by a year. For the purposes of the next chapter's dataviz exploration, this is more than adequate:

```
df['award_age'] = df.year - pd.DatetimeIndex(df.date_of_birth)\
.year ❶
```

❶ Convert the column to a `DatetimeIndex`, an `ndarray` of `datetime64` data, and use the `year` property.

Let's use our new `award_age` field to see the youngest recipients of the Nobel Prize:

```
# use +sort+ for older pandas
df.sort_values('award_age').iloc[:10]\
      [['name', 'award_age', 'category', 'year']]
Out:
                     name  award_age      category  year
725        Malala Yousafzai      17.0         Peace  2014 ❶
525  William Lawrence Bragg      25.0       Physics  1915
626    Georges J. F. Köhler      30.0  Phys...Medicine  1976
294           Tsung-Dao Lee      31.0       Physics  1957
858  Werner Karl Heisenberg      31.0       Physics  1932
247           Carl Anderson      31.0       Physics  1936
146             Paul Dirac      31.0       Physics  1933
877      Rudolf Mössbauer      32.0       Physics  1961
226        Tawakkol Karman      32.0         Peace  2011
804        Mairéad Corrigan      32.0         Peace  1976
```

❶ For activism for female education, I'd recommend reading more about Malala's inspirational story (*https://oreil.ly/26szS*).

Now that we have our date fields in a manipulable form, let's have a look at the full `clean_data` function, which summarizes this chapter's cleaning efforts.

The Full clean_data Function

For manually edited data like scraped Wikipedia datasets, it's unlikely that you'll catch all the errors on a first pass. So expect to pick up a few during the data exploration phase. Nevertheless, our Nobel Prize dataset is looking very usable. We'll declare it clean enough and the job of this chapter done. Example 9-4 shows the steps we used to achieve this cleaning feat.

Example 9-4. The full Nobel Prize dataset cleaning function

```python
def clean_data(df):
    df = df.replace('', np.nan)
    df_born_in = df[df.born_in.notnull()]  ❶
    df = df[df.born_in.isnull()]
    df = df.drop('born_in', axis=1)
    df.drop(df[df.year == 1809].index, inplace=True)
    df = df[~(df.name == 'Marie Curie')]
    df.loc[(df.name == 'Marie Sk\u0142odowska-Curie') &\
            (df.year == 1911), 'country'] = 'France'
    df = df[~((df.name == 'Sidney Altman') & (df.year == 1990))]
    df = df.reindex(np.random.permutation(df.index))
    df = df.drop_duplicates(['name', 'year'])  ❷
    df = df.sort_index()
    df.loc[df.name == 'Alexis Carrel', 'category'] =\
        'Physiology or Medicine'
    df.loc[df.name == 'Ragnar Granit', 'gender'] = 'male'
    df = df[df.gender.notnull()] # remove institutional prizes
    df.loc[df.name == 'Hiroshi Amano', 'date_of_birth'] =\
    '11 September 1960'
    df.date_of_birth = pd.to_datetime(df.date_of_birth)  ❸
    df.date_of_death = pd.to_datetime(df.date_of_death,\
    errors='coerce')
    df['award_age'] = df.year - pd.DatetimeIndex(df.date_of_birth)\
    .year
    return df, df_born_in  ❹
```

❶ Makes a DataFrame containing the rows with born_in fields.

❷ Removes duplicates from the DataFrame after randomizing the row order.

❸ Converts the date columns to the practical datetime64 datatype.

❹ We return a DataFrame with the deleted born_in field; this data will provide an interesting visualization in the next chapter.

Adding the born_in column

While cleaning the winners DataFrame we removed the born_in column (see "Removing Rows" on page 222). As we'll see in the next chapter, this column has some interesting data that can be correlated with the winners' country (of prize-winning origin) to tell an interesting story or two. The clean_data function returns the born_in data as a DataFrame. Let's see how we can add this data to our freshly cleaned DataFrame. First, we'll read in our original, dirty dataset and apply our data cleaning function:

```
df = pd.read_json(open('data/nobel_winners_dirty.json'))
df_clean, df_born_in = clean_data(df)
```

Now we'll clean up the name field of the df_born_in DataFrame by removing the asterisks, stripping any whitespace and then removing any duplicate rows by name. Finally, we'll set the index of the DataFrame to its name column:

```
# clean up name column: '* Aaron Klug' -> 'Aaron Klug'
df_born_in.name = dfbi.name.str.replace('*', '', regex=False) ❶
df_born_in.name = dfbi.name.str.strip()
df_born_in.drop_duplicates(subset=['name'], inplace=True)
df_born_in.set_index('name', inplace=True)
```

We now have a df_born_in DataFrame that we can query by name:

```
In: df_born_in['Eugene Wigner']
Out:
born_in                                          Hungary
category                                         Physics
...
year                                                1963
Name: Eugene Wigner, dtype: object
```

Now we'll write a little Python function to return the born_in field by name of our df_born_in DataFrame if it exists, otherwise returning a NumPy nan:

```
def get_born_in(name):
    try:
        born_in = df_born_in.loc[name]['born_in']
        # We'll print out these rows as a sanity-check
        print('name: %s, born in: %s'%(name, born_in))
    except:
        born_in = np.nan
    return born_in
```

We can now create a born_in column to our main DataFrame by applying this get_born_in function to each row, using the name field:

```
In: df_wbi = df_clean.copy()
In: df_wbi['born_in'] = df_wbi['name'].apply(get_born_in)
Out:
...
name: Christian de Duve, born in: United Kingdom
name: Ilya Prigogine, born in: Russia
...
name: Niels Kaj Jerne, born in: United Kingdom
name: Albert Schweitzer, born in: Germany
...
```

Finally, let's make sure we've successfully added a born_in column to our DataFrame:

```
In: df_wbi.info()
Out:
<class 'pandas.core.frame.DataFrame'>
```

```
Int64Index: 858 entries, 4 to 1051
Data columns (total 13 columns):
 #   Column          Non-Null Count  Dtype
---  ------          --------------  -----
 0   category        858 non-null    object
...
 12  born_in         102 non-null    object
dtypes: datetime64[ns](2), int64(2), object(9)
memory usage: 93.8+ KB
```

Note that if there were no duplicate names among our Nobel winners, we could create the born_in column by simply setting the index of df and df_born_in to *name* and creating the column directly:

```
# this won't work with duplicate names in our index
In: df_wbi['born_in'] = df_born_in.born_in
Out:
...
ValueError: cannot reindex from a duplicate axis
```

The use of apply can be inefficient for large datasets, but it provides a very flexible way of creating new columns based on the existing ones.

Merging DataFrames

At this point, we can also create a merged database of our clean winners data and the image and biography dataset we scraped in "Scraping Text and Images with a Pipeline" on page 173. This will provide a good opportunity to demonstrate pandas's ability to merge DataFrames. The following code shows how to merge df_clean and the bio dataset:

```
# Read the Scrapy bio-data into a DataFrame
df_winners_bios = pd.read_json(\
open('data/scrapy_nwinners_minibio.json'))

df_clean_bios = pd.merge(df_wbi, df_winners_bios,\
how='outer', on='link') ❶
```

❶ pandas's merge (*https://oreil.ly/T3ujJ*) takes two DataFrames and merges them based on shared column name(s) (link, in this case). The how argument specifies how to determine which keys are to be included in the resulting table and works in the same way as SQL joins. In this case, outer specifies a FULL_OUTER_JOIN.

Merging the two DataFrames results in redundancies in our merged dataset, with more than the 858 winning rows:

```
df_clean_bios.count()
Out:
award_age       1023
category        1023
```

```
...
bio_image          978
mini_bio          1086
```

We can easily remove these by using `drop_duplicates` to remove any rows that share a `link` and `year` field after removing any rows without a `name` field:

```
df_clean_bios = df_clean_bios[~df_clean_bios.name.isnull()]\
.drop_duplicates(subset=['link', 'year'])
```

A quick count shows that we now have the right number of winners with images for 770 and a `mini_bio` for all but one:

```
df_clean_bios.count()
award_age         858
category          858
...
born_in           102
bio_image         770
mini_bio          857
dtype: int64
```

While we're cleaning our dataset, let's see which winner is missing a `mini_bio` field:

```
df_clean_bios[df_clean_bios.mini_bio.isnull()]
Out:
...
                                        link        name  \
229  http://en.wikipedia.org/wiki/L%C3%AA_%C3...  Lê Đức Thọ
...
```

It turns out to be a Unicode error in creating the Wikipedia link for Lê Đức Thọ, the Vietnamese Peace Prize winner. This can be corrected by hand.

The `df_clean_bios` DataFrame includes an array of image URLs we scraped from Wikipedia. We won't be using these, and they would have to be converted to JSON in order to save them to SQL. Let's drop the `images_url` column to make our dataset as uncluttered as possible:

```
df_clean_bios.drop('image_urls', axis=1, inplace=True)
```

Now our dataset is cleaned and streamlined, let's save it in a couple of handy formats.

Saving the Cleaned Datasets

Now we have the datasets required for our upcoming exploration with pandas, let's save them in a couple of formats ubiquitous in data visualization, SQL and JSON.

First, we'll save our cleaned DataFrame with `born_in` field and merged biographies as a JSON file using pandas's handy `to_json` method:

```
df_clean_bios.to_json('data/nobel_winners_cleaned.json',\
        orient='records', date_format='iso') ❶
```

❶ We set the orient argument to records to store an array of row-objects and specify 'iso' as the string encoding for our date format.

Let's save a copy of our clean DataFrame to an SQLite nobel_prize database in a local *data* directory. We'll use this to demonstrate the Flask-based REST web API in Chapter 13. Three lines of Python and the DataFrame's to_sql method do the job succinctly (see "SQL" on page 204 for more details):

```
import sqlalchemy

engine = sqlalchemy.create_engine(\
        'sqlite:///data/nobel_winners_clean.db')
df_clean_bios.to_sql('winners', engine, if_exists='replace')
```

Let's make sure we've successfully created the database by reading the contents back into a DataFrame:

```
df_read_sql = pd.read_sql('winners', engine)
df_read_sql.info()
Out:
<class 'pandas.core.frame.DataFrame'>
RangeIndex: 858 entries, 0 to 857
Data columns (total 16 columns):
 #   Column          Non-Null Count  Dtype
---  ------          --------------  -----
 0   index           858 non-null    int64
 1   category        858 non-null    object
 2   country         858 non-null    object
 3   date_of_birth   858 non-null    datetime64[ns]
 [...]
 14  bio_image       770 non-null    object
 15  mini_bio        857 non-null    object
dtypes: datetime64[ns](2), float64(2), int64(1), object(11)
memory usage: 107.4+ KB
```

With our cleaned data in the database, we're ready to start exploring it in the next chapter.

Summary

In this chapter, you learned how to clean a fairly messy dataset, producing data that will be much nicer to explore and generally work with. Along the way, a number of new pandas methods and techniques were introduced to extend the last chapter's introduction to basic pandas.

In the next chapter, we will use our newly minted dataset to start getting a feel for the Nobel Prize recipients, their country, gender, age, and any interesting correlations (or lack thereof) we can find.

## CHAPTER 10

Visualizing Data with Matplotlib

As a data visualizer, one of the best ways to come to grips with your data is to visualize it interactively, using the full range of charts and plots that have evolved to summarize and refine datasets. Conventionally, the fruits of this exploratory phase are then presented as static figures, but increasingly they are used to construct more engaging interactive web-based charts, such as the cool D3 visualizations you have probably seen (one of which we'll be building in Part V).

Python's Matplotlib and its family of extensions (such as the statistically focused seaborn) form a mature and very customizable plotting ecosystem. Matplotlib plots can be used interactively by IPython (the Qt and notebook versions), providing a very powerful and intuitive way of finding interesting nuggets in your data. In this chapter, we'll introduce Matplotlib and one of its great extensions, seaborn.

pyplot and Object-Oriented Matplotlib

Matplotlib can be more than a little confusing, especially if you start randomly sampling examples online. The main complicating factor is that there are two main ways to create plots, which are similar enough to be confused but different enough to lead to a lot of frustrating errors. The first way uses a global state machine to interact directly with Matplotlib's pyplot module. The second, object-oriented approach uses the more familiar notion of figure and axes classes to provide a programmatic alternative. I'll clarify their differences in the sections ahead, but as a rough rule of thumb, if you're working interactively with single plots, pyplot's global state is a convenient shortcut. For all other occasions, it makes sense to explicitly declare your figures and axes using the object-oriented approach.

Starting an Interactive Session

We will be using a Jupyter notebook (*https://jupyter.org*) for our interactive visualization. Use the following command to start a session:

```
$ jupyter notebook
```

You can then use one of the Matplotlib magic commands (*https://oreil.ly/KhWbX*) within the IPython session to enable interactive Matplotlib. On its own, `%matplotlib` will use the default GUI backend to create a plotting window, but you can specify the backend directly. The following should work on standard and Qt console IPython:[1]

```
%matplotlib [qt | osx | wx ...]
```

To get inline graphics in the notebook or Qt console, you can use the `inline` directive. Note that with inline plots, you can't amend them after creation, unlike the standalone Matplotlib window:

```
%matplotlib inline
```

Whether you are using Matplotlib interactively or in Python programs, you'll use similar imports:

```
import numpy as np
import pandas as pd
import matplotlib.pyplot as plt
```

> You will find many examples of Matplotlib using `pylab`. `pylab` is a convenience module that bulk-imports `matplotlib.pyplot` (for plotting) and NumPy in a single namespace. `pylab` is pretty much deprecated now, but even were it not, I'd still recommend avoiding this namespace and merging and importing `pyplot` and `numpy` explicitly.

While NumPy and pandas are not mandatory, Matplotlib is designed to play well with them, handling NumPy arrays and, by association, pandas Series.

The ability to create inline plots is key to enjoyable interaction with Matplotlib, and we achieve this in IPython with the following "magic"[2] injunction:

```
In [0]: %matplotlib inline
```

---

1 If you have errors trying to start a GUI session, try changing the backend setting (e.g., if using macOS and `%matplotlib qt` doesn't work, try `%matplotlib osx`).

2 IPython has a large number of such functions to enable a whole slew of useful extras to the vanilla Python interpreter. Check them out on the IPython website (*https://oreil.ly/0gUSc*).

Your Matplotlib plots will now be inserted into your IPython workflow. This works with Qt and notebook versions. In notebooks, the plots are incorporated into the active cell.

Amending Plots

In inline mode, after a Jupyter notebook cell or (multiline) input has been run, the drawing context is flushed. This means you cannot change the plot from a previous cell or input using the gcf (get current figure) method but have to repeat all the plot commands with any additions or amendments in a new input/cell.

Interactive Plotting with pyplot's Global State

The pyplot module provides a global state that you can manipulate interactively.[3] This is intended for use in interactive data exploration and is best when you are creating simple plots, usually containing single figures. pyplot is convenient and many of the examples you'll see use it, but for more complex plotting Matplotlib's object-oriented API (which we'll see shortly) comes into its own. Before demoing use of the global plot, let's create some random data to display, courtesy of pandas's useful period_range method:

```
from datetime import datetime

x = pd.period_range(datetime.now(), periods=200, freq='d')❶
x = x.to_timestamp().to_pydatetime() ❷
y = np.random.randn(200, 3).cumsum(0) ❸
```

❶ Creates a pandas datetime index with 200 day (d) elements, starting from the current time (datetime.now()).

❷ Converts datetime index to Python datetimes.

❸ Creates three 200-element random arrays summed along the 0 axis.

We now have a y-axis with 200 time slots and three random arrays for the complementary x values. These are provided as separate arguments to the (line)plot method:

```
plt.plot(x, y)
```

This gives us the not particularly inspiring chart shown in Figure 10-1. Note how Matplotlib deals naturally with a multidimensional NumPy line array.

---

3 This was inspired by MATLAB (*https://oreil.ly/sw9KZ*).

Figure 10-1. Default line plot

Although Matplotlib's defaults are, by general consensus, less than ideal, one of its strengths is the sheer amount of customization you can perform. This is why there is a rich ecosystem of chart libraries that wrap Matplotlib with better defaults, more attractive color schemes, and more. Let's see some of this customization in action by using vanilla Matplotlib to tailor our default plot.

Configuring Matplotlib

Matplotlib provides a wide range of configurations (*https://oreil.ly/IbgVA*), which can be specified in a `matplotlibrc` file (*https://oreil.ly/knyiZ*) or dynamically, through the dictionary-like `rcParams` variable. Here we change the width and default color of our plot lines:

```
import matplotlib as mpl
mpl.rcParams['lines.linewidth'] = 2
mpl.rcParams['lines.color'] = 'r' # red
```

You can find a sample `matplotlibrc` file at the main site (*https://oreil.ly/LBqxb*).

As well as using the `rcParams` variable, you can use the `gcf` (get current figure) method to grab the currently active figure and manipulate it directly.

Let's see a little example of configuration, setting the current figure's size.

Setting the Figure's Size

If your plot's default readability is poor or the width-to-height ratio suboptimal, you will want to change its size. By default, Matplotlib uses inches for its plotting size. This makes sense when you consider the many backends (often vector-graphic-based) that Matplotlib can save to. Here we show two ways to use `pyplot` to set the figure size to eight by four inches, using `rcParams` and `gcf`:

```
# Two ways to set the figure size to 8 by 4 inches
plt.rcParams['figure.figsize'] = (8,4)
plt.gcf().set_size_inches(8, 4)
```

Points, Not Pixels

Matplotlib uses points, not pixels, to measure the size of its figures. This is the accepted measure for print-quality publications, and Matplotlib is used to deliver publication-quality images.

By default a point is approximately 1/72 of an inch wide, but Matplotlib allows you to adjust this by changing the dots-per-inch (dpi) for any figures generated. The higher this number, the better the quality of the image. For the purpose of the inline figures shown interactively during IPython sessions, the resolution is usually a product of the backend engine being used to generate the plots (e.g., Qt, WxAgg, tkinter). See the Matplotlib documentation (*https://oreil.ly/4ENnG*) for an explanation of backends.

Labels and Legends

Figure 10-1 needs, among other things, to tell us what the lines mean. Matplotlib has a handy legend box for line labeling, which, like most things Matplotlib, is heavily configurable. Labeling our three lines involves a little indirection as the `plot` method only takes one label, which it applies to all lines generated. Usefully, the `plot` command returns all `Line2D` objects created. These can be used by the `legend` method to set individual labels.

Because this plot will be appearing in black and white (if you're reading the print version of this book), we need a way to distinguish the lines other than the default colors. The easiest way to do this with Matplotlib is to create the lines sequentially, specifying *x* and *y* values and a line style.[4] We'll make our line styles solid (-), dashed (--), and dash-dotted (-.). Note the use of NumPy's column indexing (see Figure 7-1):

---

4 You can find details of Matplotlib's line styles in its documentation (*https://oreil.ly/iqlBE*).

```
#plots = plt.plot(x,y)
plots = plt.plot(x, y[:,0], '-', x, y[:,1], '--', x, y[:,2], '-.')
plots
Out:
[<matplotlib.lines.Line2D at 0x9b31a90>,
 <matplotlib.lines.Line2D at 0x9b4da90>,
 <matplotlib.lines.Line2D at 0x9b4dcd0>]
```

The legend method (*https://oreil.ly/2hEMc*) can set labels, suggest a location for the legend box, and configure a number of other things:

```
plt.legend(plots, ('foo', 'bar', 'baz'), ❶
           loc='best', ❷
           framealpha=0.5, ❸
           prop={'size':'small', 'family':'monospace'}) ❹
```

❶ Sets the labels for our three plots.

❷ Using the best location should avoid obscuring lines.

❸ Sets the legend's transparency.

❹ Here we adjust the font properties of the legend.[5]

Titles and Axes Labels

Adding a title and label for your axes is as easy as can be:

```
plt.title('Random trends')
plt.xlabel('Date')
plt.ylabel('Cum. sum')
```

You can add some text with the figtext method:[6]

```
plt.figtext(0.995, 0.01, ❶
            '© Acme designs 2022',
            ha='right', va='bottom') ❷
```

❶ The location of the text proportionate to figure size.

❷ Horizontal (ha) and vertical (va) alignment.

The complete code is shown in Example 10-1 and the resulting chart in Figure 10-2.

---

5 See the docs (*https://oreil.ly/upz5A*) for more details.

6 See the Matplotlib website (*https://oreil.ly/oD0lN*) for details.

Example 10-1. Customized line chart

```
plots = plt.plot(x, y[:,0], '-', x, y[:,1], '--', x, y[:,2], '-.')
plt.legend(plots, ('foo', 'bar', 'baz'), loc='best,
                   framealpha=0.25,
                   prop={'size':'small', 'family':'monospace'})
plt.gcf().set_size_inches(8, 4)
plt.title('Random trends')
plt.xlabel('Date')
plt.ylabel('Cum. sum')
plt.grid(True) ❶
plt.figtext(0.995, 0.01, '© Acme Designs 2021',
ha='right', va='bottom')
plt.tight_layout() ❷
```

❶ This will add a dotted grid to the figure, marking the axis ticks.

❷ The `tight_layout` method (*https://oreil.ly/roH2Z*) should guarantee that all your
   plot elements are within the figure box. Otherwise, you might find tick-labels or
   legends truncated.

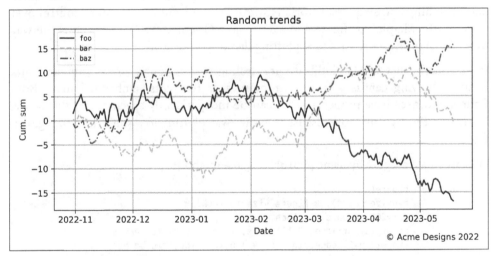

Figure 10-2. Customized line chart

We used the `tight_layout` method in Example 10-1 to prevent plot elements
from being obscured or truncated. `tight_layout` has been known to cause problems with some systems, particularly macOS. If you have any problems, this issue
thread (*https://oreil.ly/qGONZ*) may help. As of now, the best advice is to use the
`set_tight_layout` method on the current figure:

```
plt.gcf().set_tight_layout(True)
```

Saving Your Charts

One area where Matplotlib shines is in saving your plots, providing many output formats.[7] The available formats depend on the backends available, but generally PNG, PDF, PS, EPS, and SVG are supported. PNG stands for Portable Network Graphics and is the most popular format for distributing web images. The other formats are vector-based, which can scale smoothly without pixelation artifacts. For high-quality print work, this is probably what you want.

Saving is as simple as this:

```
plt.tight_layout() # force plot into figure dimensions
plt.savefig('mpl_3lines_custom.svg')
```

You can set the format explicitly using `format="svg"`, but Matplotlib understands the *.svg* suffix. To avoid truncated labels, use the `tight_layout` method.[8]

Figures and Object-Oriented Matplotlib

As just shown, interactively manipulating `pyplot`'s global state works fine for quick data sketching and single-plot work. However, if you want to have more control over your charts, Matplotlib's figure and axes Object-Oriented (OO) approach is the way to go. Most of the more advanced plotting demos you see will be done this way.

In essence, with OO Matplotlib we are dealing with a figure, which you can think of as a drawing canvas with one or more axes (or plots) embedded in it. Both figures and axes have properties that can be independently specified. In this sense, the interactive `pyplot` route discussed earlier was plotting to a single axis of a global figure.

We can create a figure by using `pyplot`'s `figure` method:

```
fig = plt.figure(
        figsize=(8, 4), # figure size in inches
        dpi=200, # dots per inch
        tight_layout=True, # fit axes, labels, etc. to canvas
        linewidth=1, edgecolor='r' # 1 pixel wide, red border
        )
```

As you can see, figures share a subset of properties with the global `pyplot` module. These can be set on creation of the figure or through similar methods (i.e., `fig.text()` as opposed to `plt.fig_text()`). Each figure can have multiple axes, each

---

7 As well as providing many formats, it also understands LaTeX math mode (*https://www.latex-project.org*), which is a language that will allow you to use mathematical symbols in the titles, legends, and the like. This is one of the reasons Matplotlib is much beloved by academics, as it is quite capable of journal-quality images.

8 More details are available on the Matplotlib website (*https://oreil.ly/GacYP*).

---

of which is analogous to the single, global plot state but with the considerable advantage that multiple axes can exist on one figure, each with independent properties.

Axes and Subplots

The figure.add_axes method allows precise control over the position of axes within a figure (e.g., enabling you to embed a smaller plot within the main). Positioning of plot elements uses a $0 \rightarrow 1$ coordinate system, where 1 is the width or height of the figure. You can specify the position using a four-element list or tuple to set bottom-left and top-right bounds:

```
# h = height, w = width
fig.add_axes([0.2, 0.2, #[bottom(h*0.2), left(w*0.2),
              0.8, 0.8])# top(h*0.8), right(w*0.8)]
```

Example 10-2 shows the code needed to insert smaller axes into larger ones, using our random test data. The result is shown in Figure 10-3.

Example 10-2. A plot insert with figure.add_axes

```
fig = plt.figure(figsize=(8,4))
# --- Main Axes
ax = fig.add_axes([0.1, 0.1, 0.8, 0.8])
ax.set_title('Main Axes with Insert Child Axes')
ax.plot(x, y[:,0]) ❶
ax.set_xlabel('Date')
ax.set_ylabel('Cum. sum')
# --- Inserted Axes
ax = fig.add_axes([0.15, 0.15, 0.3, 0.3])
ax.plot(x, y[:,1], color='g') # 'g' for green
ax.set_xticks([]); ❷
```

❶ This selects the first column of our random NumPy y-data.

❷ Removes the x ticks and labels from our embedded plot.

Although add_axes gives us a lot of scope for fine-tuning the appearance of our charts, most of the time Matplotlib's built-in grid-layout system makes life much easier.[9] The simplest option is to use figure.subplots, which allows you to specify row-column layouts of equal-sized plots. If you want a grid with different-sized plots, the gridspec module is your go-to.

---

9 The handy tight_layout option assumes grid-layout subplots.

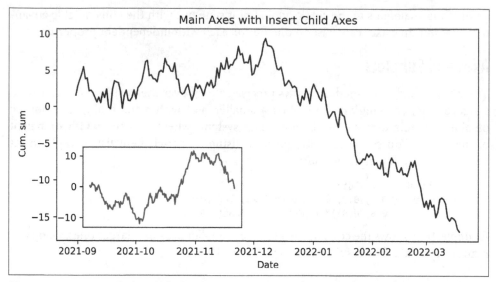

Figure 10-3. Inserted plot with `figure.add_axes`

Calling `subplots` without arguments returns a figure with single axes. This is closest in use to using the `pyplot` state machine shown in "Interactive Plotting with pyplot's Global State" on page 245. Example 10-3 shows the figure and axes equivalent to the `pyplot` demo in Example 10-1, producing the chart in Figure 10-2. Note the use of "setter" methods for figure and axes.

Example 10-3. Plotting with single figure and axes

```
figure, ax = plt.subplots()
plots = ax.plot(x, y, label='')
figure.set_size_inches(8, 4)
ax.legend(plots, ('foo', 'bar', 'baz'), loc='best', framealpha=0.25,
          prop={'size':'small', 'family':'monospace'})
ax.set_title('Random trends')
ax.set_xlabel('Date')
ax.set_ylabel('Cum. sum')
ax.grid(True)
figure.text(0.995, 0.01, '©  Acme Designs 2022',
            ha='right', va='bottom')
figure.tight_layout()
```

Calling `subplots` with arguments for number of rows (`nrows`) and columns (`ncols`) (as shown in Example 10-4) allows multiple plots to be placed on a grid layout (see the results in Figure 10-4). The call to `subplots` returns the figure and an array of axes, in row-column order. In the example, we specify one column so `axes` is a single array of three stacked axes.

Example 10-4. Using subplots

```
fig, axes = plt.subplots(
                    nrows=3, ncols=1, ❶
                    sharex=True, sharey=True, ❷
                    figsize=(8, 8))
labelled_data = zip(y.transpose(), ❸
                    ('foo', 'bar', 'baz'), ('b', 'g', 'r'))
fig.suptitle('Three Random Trends', fontsize=16)
for i, ld in enumerate(labelled_data):
    ax = axes[i]
    ax.plot(x, ld[0], label=ld[1], color=ld[2])
    ax.set_ylabel('Cum. sum')
    ax.legend(loc='upper left', framealpha=0.5,
            prop={'size':'small'})
axes[-1].set_xlabel('Date') ❹
```

❶ Specifies a subplot grid of three rows by one column.

❷ We want to share x- and y-axes, automatically adjusting limits for easy comparison.

❸ Switch y to row-column and zip the line data, labels, and line colors together.

❹ Labels the last of the shared x-axes.

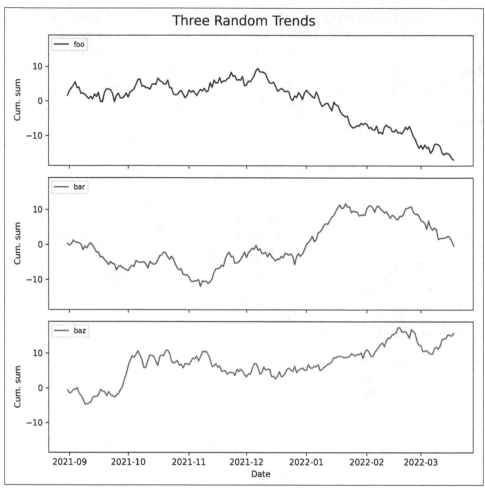

Figure 10-4. Three subplots

We make use of Python's handy `zip` method to produce three dictionaries with line data. `zip` (*https://oreil.ly/G8YGh*) takes lists or tuples of length *n* and returns *n* lists, formed by matching the elements by order:

```
letters = ['a', 'b']
numbers = [1, 2]
zip(letters, numbers)
Out:
[('a', 1), ('b', 2)]
```

In the `for` loop, we use `enumerate` to supply an index `i`, which we use to select an axis by row, using our zipped `labelled_data` to provide the plot properties.

Note the shared x- and y-axes specified in the `subplots` call in Example 10-4 (2). This allows easy comparison of the three charts, particularly on the now normalized y-axis. To avoid redundant x labels, we only call `set_xlabel` on the last row, using Python's handy negative indexing.

Now that we've covered the two ways in which IPython and Matplotlib engage interactively, using the global state (accessed through `plt`) and the object-oriented API, let's look at a few of the common plot types you'll use to explore your datasets.

Plot Types

As well as the line plot just demonstrated, Matplotlib has a number of plot types available. I'll now demonstrate a few of the ones commonly used in exploratory data visualization.

Bar Charts

The humble bar chart is a staple for a lot of visual data exploration. As with most of Matplotlib charts, there's a good deal of customization possible. We'll now run through a few variants to give you the gist.

The code in Example 10-5 produces the bar chart in Figure 10-5. Note that you have to specify your own bar and label locations. This kind of flexibility is beloved by hardcore Matplotlibbers and is pretty easy to get the hang of. Nevertheless, it's the sort of thing that can get tedious. It's trivial to write some helper methods here, and there are many libraries that wrap Matplotlib and make things a little more user-friendly. As we'll see in Chapter 11, pandas's built-in Matplotlib-based plots are quite a bit simpler to use.

Example 10-5. A simple bar chart

```
labels = ["Physics", "Chemistry", "Literature", "Peace"]
foo_data =    [3, 6, 10, 4]

bar_width = 0.5
xlocations = np.array(range(len(foo_data))) + bar_width  ❶
plt.bar(xlocations, foo_data, width=bar_width)
plt.yticks(range(0, 12))  ❷
plt.xticks(xlocations, labels)  ❸
plt.title("Prizes won by Fooland")
plt.gca().get_xaxis().tick_bottom()
plt.gca().get_yaxis().tick_left()
plt.gcf().set_size_inches((8, 4))
```

❶ Here we create the middle bar locations, two `bar_width`'s apart.

❷ We're hardcoding the x values for demonstration purposes—usually you will want to calculate ranges on the fly.

❸ This places tick labels at the middle of the bars.

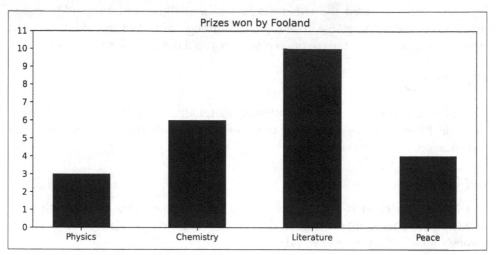

Figure 10-5. A simple bar chart

Bar charts with multiple groups are particularly useful. In Example 10-6, we add some more country data (for a mythical Barland) and use the `subplots` method to produce grouped bar charts (see Figure 10-6). Once again we specify the bar locations manually, adding two bar groups—this time with `ax.bar`. Note that our axes' x-limits are automatically rescaled in a sensible fashion, at increments of 0.5:

```
ax.get_xlim()
# Out: (-0.5, 3.5)
```

Use the respective setter methods (`set_xlim`, in this case) if autoscaling doesn't achieve the desired look.

Example 10-6. Creating a grouped bar chart

```
labels = ["Physics", "Chemistry", "Literature", "Peace"]
foo_data = [3, 6, 10, 4]
bar_data = [8, 3, 6, 1]

fig, ax = plt.subplots(figsize=(8, 4))
bar_width = 0.4 ❶
xlocs = np.arange(len(foo_data))
ax.bar(xlocs-bar_width, foo_data, bar_width,
       color='#fde0bc', label='Fooland') ❷
ax.bar(xlocs, bar_data, bar_width, color='peru', label='Barland')
```

```
#--- ticks, labels, grids, and title
ax.set_yticks(range(12))
ax.set_xticks(ticks=range(len(foo_data)))
ax.set_xticklabels(labels)
ax.yaxis.grid(True)
ax.legend(loc='best')
ax.set_ylabel('Number of prizes')
fig.suptitle('Prizes by country')
fig.tight_layout(pad=2) ❸
fig.savefig('mpl_barchart_multi.png', dpi=200) ❹
```

❶ With a width of 1 for our two-bar groups, this bar width gives 0.1 bar padding.

❷ Matplotlib supports standard HTML colors, taking hex values or a name.

❸ We use the pad argument to specify padding around the figure as a fraction of the font size.

❹ This saves the figure at the high resolution of 200 dots per inch.

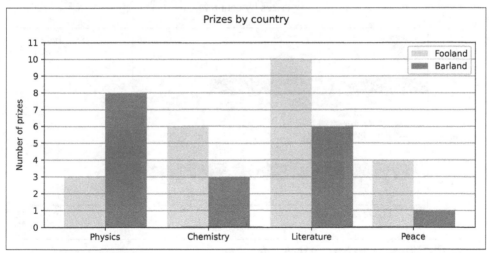

Figure 10-6. Grouped bar charts

It's often useful to use horizontal bars, particularly if there are a lot of them and/or you are using tick labels, which are likely to run into one another if placed on the same line. Turning Figure 10-6 on its side is easy enough, requiring only that we replace the bar method with its horizontal counterpart barh and switch the axis labels and limits (see Example 10-7 and the resulting chart Figure 10-7).

Example 10-7. Converting Example 10-6 to horizontal bars

```
# ...
ylocs = np.arange(len(foo_data))
ax.barh(ylocs-bar_width, foo_data, bar_width, color='#fde0bc',
        label='Fooland') ❶
ax.barh(ylocs, bar_data, bar_width, color='peru', label='Barland')
# --- labels, grids and title, then save
ax.set_xticks(range(12)) ❷
ax.set_yticks(ticks=ylocs-bar_width/2)
ax.set_yticklabels(labels)
ax.xaxis.grid(True)
ax.legend(loc='best')
ax.set_xlabel('Number of prizes')
# ...
```

❶   To create a horizontal bar chart, we use barh in place of bar.

❷   A horizontal chart necessitates swapping the horizontal and vertical axes.

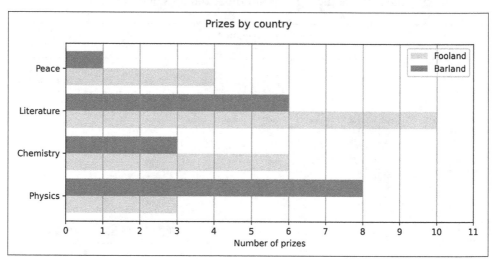

Figure 10-7. Turning the bars on their side

Stacked bars are easy to achieve in Matplotlib.[10] Example 10-8 converts Figure 10-6 to a stacked form; Figure 10-8 shows the result. The trick is to use the bottom argument to bar to set the bottom of the raised bars as the top of the previous group.

---

10 It's questionable whether stacked bar charts are a particularly good way of appreciating groups of data. See Solomon Messing's blog (*https://oreil.ly/nClO0*) for a nice discussion and one example of "good" use.

Example 10-8. Converting Example 10-6 to stacked bars

```
# ...
bar_width = 0.8
xlocs = np.arange(len(foo_data))
ax.bar(xlocs, foo_data, bar_width, color='#fde0bc',  ❶
       label='Fooland')
ax.bar(xlocs, bar_data, bar_width, color='peru',     ❷
       label='Barland', bottom=foo_data)
# --- labels, grids and title, then save
ax.set_yticks(range(18))
ax.set_xticks(ticks=xlocs)
ax.set_xticklabels(labels)
# ...
```

❶ The foo_data and bar_data bar groups share the same x-locations.

❷ The bottom of the bar_data group is the top of the foo_data, providing stacked bars.

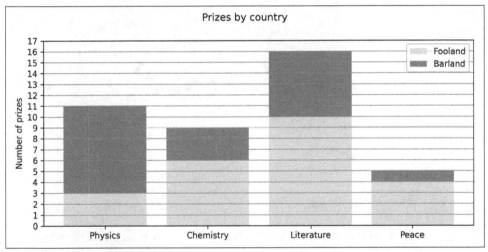

Figure 10-8. Stacked bar chart

Scatter Plots

Another useful chart is the scatter plot, which takes 2D arrays of points with options for point size, color, and more.

Example 10-9 shows the code for a quick scatter plot, using Matplotlib autoscaling for x and y limits. We create a noisy line by adding normally distributed random numbers (sigma of 10). Figure 10-9 shows the resulting chart.

Example 10-9. A simple scatter plot

```
num_points = 100
gradient = 0.5
x = np.array(range(num_points))
y = np.random.randn(num_points) * 10 + x*gradient ❶
fig, ax = plt.subplots(figsize=(8, 4))
ax.scatter(x, y) ❷

fig.suptitle('A Simple Scatterplot')
```

❶ randn gives normally distributed random numbers, which we scale to be within 0 and 10 and to which we then add an x-dependent value.

❷ The equally sized x and y arrays provide the point coordinates.

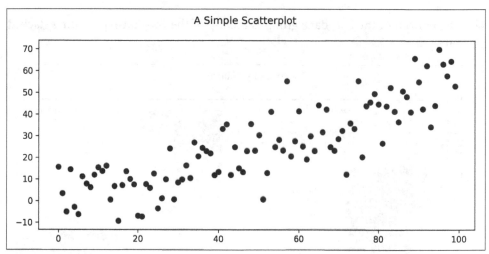

Figure 10-9. A simple scatter plot

We can adjust the size and color of individual points by passing an array of marker sizes and color indices to the current default colormap. One thing to note, which can be confusing, is that we are specifying the area of the markers' bounding boxes, not the circles' diameters. This means if we want points to double the diameter of the circles, we must increase the size by a factor of four.[11] In Example 10-10, we add size and color information to our simple scatter plot, producing Figure 10-10.

---

11 Setting marker size, rather than width or radius, is actually a good default, making it proportional to whatever value we are trying to reflect.

Example 10-10. Adjusting point size and color

```
num_points = 100
gradient = 0.5
x = np.array(range(num_points))
y = np.random.randn(num_points) * 10 + x*gradient
fig, ax = plt.subplots(figsize=(8, 4))
colors = np.random.rand(num_points) ❶
size = np.pi * (2 + np.random.rand(num_points) * 8) ** 2 ❷
ax.scatter(x, y, s=size, c=colors, alpha=0.5) ❸
fig.suptitle('Scatterplot with Color and Size Specified')
```

❶ This produces 100 random color values between 0 and 1 for the default color-map.

❷ We use the power notation ** to square values between 2 and 10, the width range for our markers.

❸ We use the alpha argument to make our markers half-transparent.

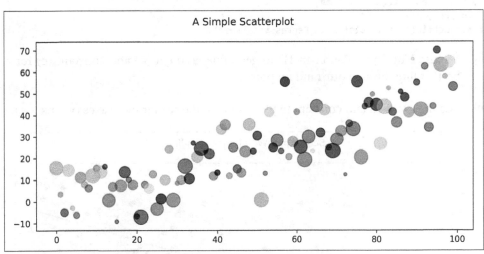

Figure 10-10. Adjusting point size and color

Matplotlib Colormaps

Matplotlib has a huge variety of colormaps available, the choice of which can significantly improve the quality of your visualization. See the colormap docs (*https://oreil.ly/g8Q9b*) for details.

Adding a regression line

A regression line is a simple predictive model of the correlation between two variables, in this case the x and y coordinates of our scatter plot. The line is essentially a best fit through the points of the plot, and adding one to a scatter plot is a useful dataviz technique and a good way to demo Matplotlib and NumPy interaction.

In Example 10-11 NumPy's very useful `polyfit` function is used to generate the gradient and constant of a best-fit line for the points defined by the x and y arrays. We then plot this line on the same axes as the scatter plot (see Figure 10-11).

Example 10-11. Scatter plot with regression line

```
num_points = 100
gradient = 0.5
x = np.array(range(num_points))
y = np.random.randn(num_points) * 10 + x*gradient
fig, ax = plt.subplots(figsize=(8, 4))
ax.scatter(x, y)
m, c = np.polyfit(x, y ,1) ❶
ax.plot(x, m*x + c) ❷
fig.suptitle('Scatterplot With Regression-line')
```

❶ We use NumPy's `polyfit` in 1D to get a line gradient (m) and constant (c) for a best-fit line through our random points.

❷ Use the gradient and constant to plot a line on the scatter plot's axes (y = mx + c).

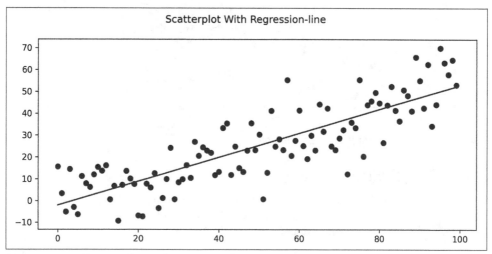

Figure 10-11. Scatter plot with regression line

It's generally a good idea to plot confidence intervals when doing line regression. This gives an idea of how reliable the line fit is, based on the number and distribution of the points. Confidence intervals can be achieved with Matplotlib and NumPy, but it is a little awkward. Luckily, there is a library built on Matplotlib that has extra, specialized functions for statistical analysis and data visualization and, in the opinion of many, looks a lot better than Matplotlib's defaults. That library is seaborn, which we are going to take a quick look at now.

seaborn

There are a number of libraries that wrap the powerful plotting abilities of Matplotlib in a more user-friendly guise[12] and, as important for us data visualizers, play nicely with pandas.

Bokeh (*https://bokeh.pydata.org/en/latest*) is an interactive visualization library with the web in mind, producing browser-rendered output and therefore playing very nicely with IPython notebook. It's a great achievement, with a design philosophy similar to D3's.[13]

But for the kind of interactive, exploratory dataviz necessary to get a feel for your data and suggest visualizations, I recommend seaborn (*https://oreil.ly/b2RpH*). seaborn extends Matplotlib with some powerful statistical plots and is well integrated with the PyData stack, playing nicely with NumPy, pandas, and the statistical routines found in SciPy and statsmodels (*https://oreil.ly/peqqT*).

One of the nice things about seaborn is that it doesn't hide the Matplotlib API, allowing you to tweak your charts with Matplotlib's extensive tools. In this sense, it's not a replacement for Matplotlib and the relevant skills, but a very impressive extension.

To work with seaborn, simply extend your standard Matplotlib imports:

```
import numpy as np
import pandas as pd
import seaborn as sns # relies on matplotlib
import matplotlib as mpl
import matplotlib.pyplot as plt
```

---

12 It's generally agreed that Matplotlib's defaults aren't that great and making them better is an easy win for any wrapper.

13 Both D3 and Bokeh tip their hats to the classic visualization text, Leland Wilkinson's *The Grammar of Graphics* (Springer).

Matplotlib provides a number of plotting styles that can be invoked by calling a use method with a style key. Let's set the current style to seaborn's default, which will provide a subtle gray grid to the charts:

```
matplotlib.style.use('seaborn')
```

You can check out all available styles and their visual effects in the Matplotlib documentation (*https://oreil.ly/9RTub*).

Many of seaborn's functions are designed to accept a pandas DataFrame, allowing you to specify, for example, the column values describing 2D scattered points. Let's take our existing x and y arrays from Example 10-9 and use them to make some dummy data:

```
data = pd.DataFrame({'dummy x':x, 'dummy y':y})
```

We now have some `data` with columns of x (`'dummy x'`) and y (`'dummy y'`) values. Example 10-12 demonstrates the use of seaborn's dedicated linear regression plot `lmplot`, which produces the chart in Figure 10-12. Note that for some seaborn plots, to adjust figure size we pass a size (height) in inches and an aspect ratio (width/ height). Note also that seaborn shares pyplot's global context.

Example 10-12. Linear regression plot with seaborn

```
data = pd.DataFrame({'dummy x':x, 'dummy y':y})
sns.lmplot(data=data, x='dummy x', y='dummy y',  ❶
           height=4, aspect=2)  ❷
plt.tight_layout()  ❸
plt.savefig('mpl_scatter_seaborn.png')  ❸
```

❶ The x and y arguments specify the column names of the DataFrame data that define the coordinates of the plot points.

❷ To set figure size, we provide the height in inches and an aspect ratio of width/ height. Here we'll use a ratio of two to better fit this book's page format.

❸ seaborn shares the pyplot global context, allowing you to save its plots as you would Matplotlib's.

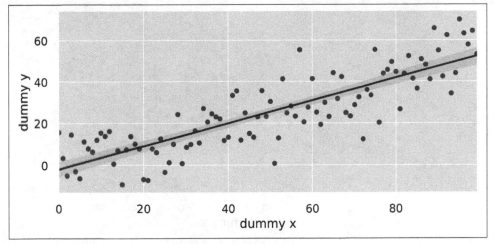

Figure 10-12. Linear regression plot with seaborn

As you would expect from a library that places an emphasis on attractive-looking plots, seaborn allows a lot of visual customization. Let's make a few changes to the look of Figure 10-12 and adjust the confidence interval to the standard error (*https://oreil.ly/gOLOo*) estimate of 68% (see Figure 10-13 for the result):

```
sns.lmplot(data=data, x='dummy x', y='dummy y', height=4, aspect=2,
        scatter_kws={"color": "slategray"}, ❶
        line_kws={"linewidth": 2, "linestyle":'--', ❷
                "color": "seagreen"},
        markers='D', ❸
        ci=68) ❹
```

❶ Provide the scatter plot component's keyword arguments, setting our points' color to slate gray.

❷ Provide the line plot component's keyword arguments, setting line width and style.

❸ Set the plot markers to diamonds using Matplotlib marker code *D*.

❹ We set a confidence interval of 68%, the standard error estimate.

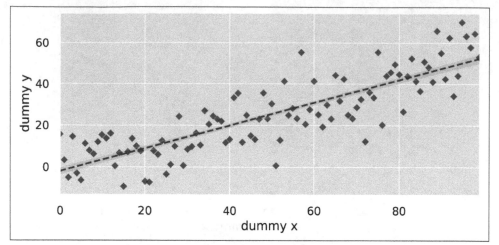

Figure 10-13. Customizing the seaborn scatter plot

seaborn offers a number of useful plots beyond Matplotlib's basic set. Let's take a look at one of the most interesting, using seaborn's FacetGrid to plot reflections of multidimensional data.

FacetGrids

Often referred to as "lattice" or "trellis" plotting, the ability to draw multiple instances of the same plot on different subsets of your dataset is a good way to get a bird's-eye view of your data. Large amounts of information can be presented in one plot, and relationships between the different dimensions can be quickly apprehended. This technique is related to the small multiples (*https://oreil.ly/Ck1fT*) popularized by Edward Tufte.

FacetGrids require the data to be in the form of a pandas DataFrame (see "The DataFrame" on page 195) and in a form referred to by Hadley Wickham, creator of ggplot2, as "tidy," meaning each column in the DataFrame should be a variable and each row an observation.

Let's use Tips, one of seaborn's test datasets,[14] to show a FacetGrid in action. Tips is a small set of data showing the distribution of tips by various dimensions, such as day of the week or whether the customer was a smoker.[15] First, let's load our Tips dataset into a pandas DataFrame using the load_dataset method:

---

14 seaborn has a number of handy datasets, which you can find on GitHub (*https://oreil.ly/clELR*).

15 The Tips dataset uses sex as a category, whereas the datasets in this book have used gender. In the past these tended to be used interchangeably, but this is no longer the case. See this Yale School of Medicine article (*https://oreil.ly/P0zWt*) for an explanation.

```
In [0]: tips = sns.load_dataset('tips')
Out[0]:
   total_bill   tip     sex smoker   day    time  size
0       16.99  1.01  Female     No   Sun  Dinner     2
1       10.34  1.66    Male     No   Sun  Dinner     3
2       21.01  3.50    Male     No   Sun  Dinner     3
3       23.68  3.31    Male     No   Sun  Dinner     2
...
```

To create a FacetGrid, we specify the `tips` DataFrame and a column of interest, such as the smoking status of the customer. This column will be used to create our plot groups. There are two categories in the smoker column (`'smoker=Yes'` and `'smoker=No'`), which means there will be two charts in our facet-grid. We then use the grid's `map` method to create multiple scatter plots of tip size against total bill:

```
g = sns.FacetGrid(tips, col="smoker", height=4, aspect=1)
g.map(plt.scatter, "total_bill", "tip") ❶
```

❶ `map` takes a plot class, in this case `scatter`, and two (`tips`) dimensions required for this scatter plot.

This produces the two scatter plots shown in Figure 10-14, one for each smoker status, with tips and total bills correlated.

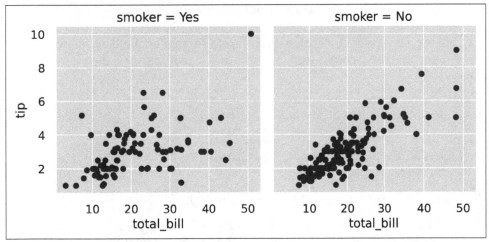

Figure 10-14. A seaborn FacetGrid using scatter plots

We can include another dimension of the `tips` data by specifying the marker to be used in our scatter plots. Let's make it a red diamond for females and a blue square for males:

```
pal = dict(Female='red', Male='blue')
g = sns.FacetGrid(tips, col="smoker",
                  hue="sex", hue_kws={"marker": ["D", "s"]}, ❶
```

```
                palette=pal, height=4, aspect=1, )
    g.map(plt.scatter, "total_bill", "tip", alpha=.4)
    g.add_legend();
```

 Adds a marker color (hue) for the sex dimension with diamond (D) and square
(s) shapes, and uses our color palette (pal) to make them red and blue.

You can see the resulting FacetGrid in Figure 10-15.

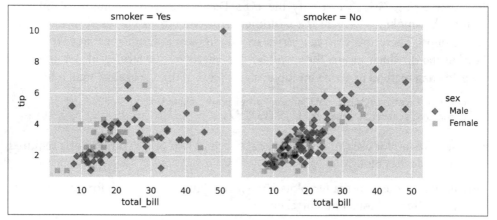

Figure 10-15. Scatter plot with diamond and square markers for sex

We can use rows as well as columns to create subsets of the data by dimension.
Combining the two allows, with the help of a `regplot`,[16] five dimensions to be
explored:

```
    pal = dict(Female='red', Male='blue')
    g = sns.FacetGrid(tips, col="smoker", row="time", ❶
                    hue="sex", hue_kws={"marker": ["D", "s"]},
                    palette=pal, height=4, aspect=1, )
    g.map(sns.regplot, "total_bill", "tip", alpha=.4)
    g.add_legend();
```

❶ Adds a time row to separate tips by lunch and dinner.

Figure 10-16 shows four `regplots` producing a linear-regression model fit with
confidence intervals for female and male hue-groups. The plot titles show the data
subset being used, each row having the same time and smoker status.

---

16 `regplot`, short for regression plot, is equivalent to `lmplot`, used in Example 10-12. The latter combines
`regplot` and FacetGrid for convenience.

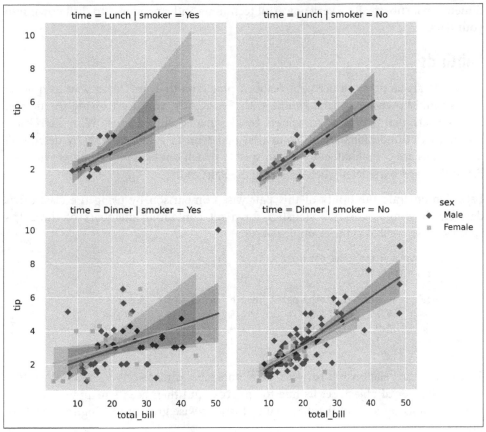

Figure 10-16. Visualizing five dimensions

We can achieve the same effect using the `lmplot` we saw in Example 10-12, which wraps the functionality of FacetGrid and `regplot` for convenience. The following code produces Figure 10-16:

```
pal = dict(Female='red', Male='blue')
sns.lmplot(x="total_bill", y="tip", hue="sex",
           markers=["D", "s"], ❶
           col="smoker", row="time", data=tips, palette=pal,
           height=4, aspect=1
           );
```

❶ Note the use of a `markers` keyword as opposed to the `kws_hue` dictionary we used with the FacetGrid plot.

`lmplot` offers a nice shortcut to producing FacetGrid `regplot`s, but FacetGrid's `map` allows you to use the full panoply of seaborn and Matplotlib charts to create plots on dimensional subsets. It's a very powerful technique and a great way to drill down into your data.

PairGrids

PairGrids are another rather cool seaborn plot type that provide a way to quickly assess multidimensional data. Unlike with FacetGrids, you don't divide the dataset into subsets that are then compared by designated dimensions. With PairGrids, the dataset's dimensions are all compared pair-wise in a square grid. By default all dimensions are compared, but you can specify which ones get plotted by providing a list to the `vars` parameter when declaring the PairGrid.[17]

Let's demonstrate the utility of this pair-wise comparison by using the classic Iris dataset, showing some vital statistics for a set containing members of three Iris species. First, we'll load the example dataset:

```
In [0]: iris = sns.load_dataset('iris')
In [1]: iris.head()
Out[1]:
   sepal_length sepal_width petal_length petal_width species
0         5.1         3.5          1.4         0.2   setosa
1         4.9         3.0          1.4         0.2   setosa
2         4.7         3.2          1.3         0.2   setosa
...
```

To capture the relationship between petal and sepal dimensions by species, we first create a `PairGrid` object, set its hue to `species`, and then use its mapping methods to create plots on and off the diagonal of the pair-wise grid, producing the charts in Figure 10-17:

```
sns.set_theme(font_scale=1.5) ❶
g = sns.PairGrid(iris, hue="species") ❷
g.map_diag(plt.hist) ❸
g.map_offdiag(plt.scatter) ❹
g.add_legend();
```

❶ Tweaks the font size using seaborn's `set_theme` method (see the documentation (*https://oreil.ly/rSmrH*) for the full list of available tweaks).

❷ Sets the markers and subbars to be colored by species.

❸ Places histograms of the species' dimensions on the grid's diagonal.

❹ Uses standard scatter plots to compare the dimensions of the diagonal.

---

17 There are also `x_vars` and `y_vars` parameters enabling you to specify nonsquare grids.

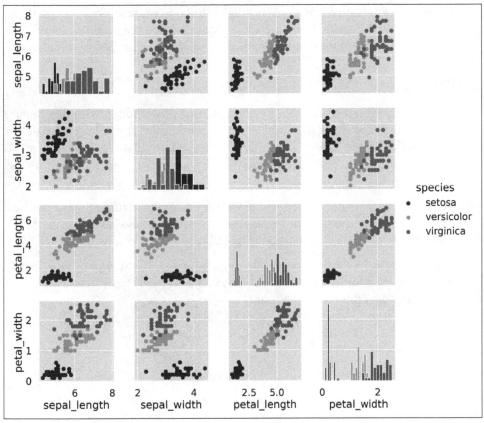

Figure 10-17. PairGrid summation of Iris measures

As you can see in Figure 10-17, a few lines of seaborn go a long way in creating a richly informative set of plots correlating the different Iris metrics. This plot is known as a scatter-plot matrix (*https://oreil.ly/UAJ8T*) and is a great way of finding linear correlations between pairs of variables in a multivariate set. As it stands, there is redundancy in the grid: for example, plots for `sepal_width-petal_length` and `petal_length-septal_width`. `PairGrid` gives you the opportunity to use the redundant plots above or below the main diagonal to provide a different reflection of the data. Check out some of the examples at the seaborn docs (*https://stanford.io/1YydS2V*) for more info.[18]

I've covered a few of the seaborn plots in this section, and you'll be seeing a few more when we explore our Nobel Prize dataset in the next chapter. But seaborn has a lot of other very handy and very powerful plotting tools, mainly of a statistical nature. For

---

18 For the curious, there's a D3 example that builds a scatter-plot matrix at the *bl.ocks.org* site (*https://oreil.ly/ox8VW*).

further investigation, I'd recommend starting with the main seaborn documentation (*https://stanford.io/28L8ezk*). There are some nice examples, a well-documented API, and some good tutorials that should complement what you've learned in this chapter.

Summary

This chapter introduced Matplotlib, Python's plotting powerhouse. It's a big, mature library with lots of documentation and an active community. If you have a particular customization in mind, chances are there's an example out there somewhere. I'd recommend firing up a Jupyter notebook (*https://jupyter.org*) and playing around with a dataset.

We saw how seaborn extends Matplotlib with some useful statistical methods and that it has what many consider to be superior aesthetics. It also allows access to the Matplotlib figure and axes internals, allowing full customization if required.

In the next chapter, we'll use Matplotlib along with pandas to explore our freshly scraped and cleaned Nobel dataset. We'll use some of the plot types demonstrated in this chapter and see a few useful new ones.

## CHAPTER 11

Exploring Data with pandas

In the previous chapter, we cleaned the Nobel Prize dataset that we scraped from Wikipedia in Chapter 6. Now it's time to start exploring our shiny new dataset, looking for interesting patterns, stories to tell, and anything else that could form the basis for an interesting visualization.

First off, let's try to clear our minds and take a long, hard look at the data to hand to get a broad idea of the visualizations suggested. Example 11-1 shows the form of the Nobel dataset, with categorical, temporal, and geographical data.

Example 11-1. Our cleaned Nobel Prize dataset

```
[{
 'category': 'Physiology or Medicine',
 'date_of_birth': '8 October 1927',
 'date_of_death': '24 March 2002',
 'gender': 'male',
 'link': 'http://en.wikipedia.org/wiki/C%C3%A9sar_Milstein',
 'name': 'César Milstein'
 'country': 'Argentina',
 'place_of_birth': 'Bahía Blanca,  Argentina',
 'place_of_death': 'Cambridge , England',
 'year': 1984,
 'born_in': NaN
 },
 ...
 ]
```

The data in Example 11-1 suggests a number of *stories* we might want to investigate, among them:

- Gender disparities among the prize winners
- National trends (e.g., which country has most prizes in Economics)
- Details about individual winners, such as their average age on receiving the prize or life expectancy
- Geographical journey from place of birth to adopted country using the born_in and country fields

These investigative lines form the basis for the coming sections, which will probe the dataset by asking questions of it, such as "How many women other than Marie Curie have won the Nobel Prize for Physics?", "Which countries have the most prizes per capita rather than absolute?", and "Is there a historical trend to prizes by nation, a changing of the guard from old (science) world (big European nations) to new (US and upcoming Asian nations)?" Before beginning our explorations, let's ready our tools and load our Nobel Prize dataset.

Starting to Explore

To start our exploration, let's fire up a Jupyter notebook from the command line:

```
$ jupyter notebook
```

We'll use the *magic* matplotlib command to enable inline plotting:

```
%matplotlib inline
```

Then import the standard set of data exploration modules:

```
import pandas as pd
import numpy as np
import matplotlib.pyplot as plt
import json
import matplotlib
import seaborn as sns
```

Now we'll make a few adjustments to the plotting parameters and the general look and feel of the charts. Make sure to change the style *before* adjusting figure sizes, fonts, and the rest:

```
matplotlib.style.use('seaborn')  ❶

plt.rcParams['figure.figsize'] = (8, 4)  ❷
plt.rcParams['font.size'] = '14'
```

❶ We'll use the seaborn theming for our charts, arguably more attractive than Matplotlib's default.

❷ Sets the default plotting size to eight inches by four.

At the end of Chapter 9, we saved our clean dataset as a JSON file. Let's load the clean data into a pandas DataFrame, ready to begin exploring.

```
df = pd.read_json(open('data/nobel_winners_cleaned.json'))
```

Let's get some basic information about our dataset's structure:

```
df.info()

<class 'pandas.core.frame.DataFrame'>
RangeIndex: 858 entries, 0 to 857
Data columns (total 13 columns):
 #   Column          Non-Null Count  Dtype
---  ------          --------------  -----
 0   category        858 non-null    object
 1   country         858 non-null    object
 2   date_of_birth   858 non-null    object
 3   date_of_death   559 non-null    object
 4   gender          858 non-null    object
 5   link            858 non-null    object
 6   name            858 non-null    object
 7   place_of_birth  831 non-null    object
 8   place_of_death  524 non-null    object
 9   text            858 non-null    object
 10  year            858 non-null    int64
 11  award_age       858 non-null    int64
 12  born_in         102 non-null    object
 13  bio_image       770 non-null    object
 14  mini_bio        857 non-null    object
dtypes: int64(2), object(13)
memory usage: 100.7+ KB
```

Note that our dates of birth and death columns have the standard pandas datatype of `object`. In order to make date comparisons, we'll need to convert those to the datetime type, `datetime64`. We can use pandas's `to_datetime` method (*https://oreil.ly/jjcoR*) to achieve this conversion:

```
df.date_of_birth = pd.to_datetime(df.date_of_birth)
df.date_of_death = pd.to_datetime(df.date_of_death)
```

Running `df.info()` should now show two datetime columns:

```
df.info()

...
date_of_birth    858 non-null    datetime64[ns, UTC] ❶
date_of_death    559 non-null    datetime64[ns, UTC]
...
```

❶ UTC (*https://oreil.ly/ZzSOR*) (Coordinated Universal Time in English) is the primary time standard by which the world regulates clocks and time. It's almost always desirable to work to this standard.

to_datetime usually works without needing extra arguments and should throw an error if given non time-based data, but it's worth checking the converted columns to make sure. In the case of our Nobel Prize dataset, everything checks out.

Plotting with pandas

Both pandas Series and DataFrames have integrated plotting, which wraps the most common Matplotlib charts, a few of which we explored in the last chapter. This makes it easy to get quick visual feedback as you interact with your DataFrame. And if you want to visualize something a little more complicated, the pandas containers will play nicely with vanilla Matplotlib. You can also adapt the plots produced by pandas using standard Matplotlib customizations.

Let's look at an example of pandas's integrated plotting, starting with a basic plot of gender disparity in Nobel Prize wins. Notoriously, the Nobel Prize has been distributed unequally among the genders. Let's get a quick feel for that disparity by using a bar plot on the *gender* category. Example 11-2 produces Figure 11-1, showing the huge difference, with males receiving 811 of the 858 prizes in our dataset.

Example 11-2. Using pandas's integrated plotting to see gender disparities

```
by_gender = df.groupby('gender')
by_gender.size().plot(kind='bar')
```

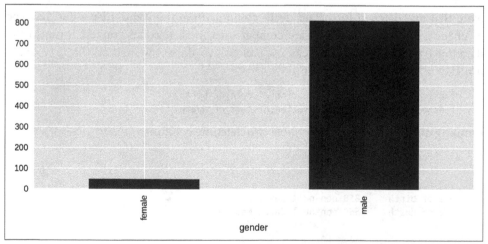

Figure 11-1. Prize counts by gender

In Example 11-2, the Series produced by the gender group's `size` method has its own integrated `plot` method, which turns the raw numbers into a chart:

```
by_gender.size()
Out:
gender
female    47
male      811
dtype: int64
```

In addition to the default line plot, the pandas `plot` method takes a `kind` argument to select among other possible plots. Among the more commonly used are:

- `bar` or `barh` (*h* for horizontal) for bar plots
- `hist` for a histogram
- `box` for a box plot
- `scatter` for scatter plots

You can find a full list of pandas's integrated plots in the docs (*https://oreil.ly/Zeo9f*) as well as some pandas plotting functions that take DataFrames and Series as arguments.

Let's extend our investigation into gender disparities and start extending our plotting know-how.

Gender Disparities

Let's break down the gender numbers shown in Figure 11-1 by category of prize. pandas's `groupby` method can take a list of columns to group by, with each group being accessed by multiple keys:

```
by_cat_gen = df.groupby(['category','gender'])

by_cat_gen.get_group(('Physics', 'female'))[['name', 'year']]  ❶
```

❶ Gets a group using a `category` and `gender` key:

```
Out:
                      name  year
269   Maria Goeppert-Mayer  1963
612  Marie Skłodowska-Curie  1903
```

Using the `size` method to get the size of these groups returns a Series with a `MultiIndex` that labels the values by both category and gender:

```
by_cat_gen.size()

Out:
category                  gender
Chemistry                 female      4
                          male      167
Economics                 female      1
                          male       74
...
Physiology or Medicine    female     11
                          male      191
dtype: int64
```

We can plot this multi-indexed Series directly, using hbar as the kind argument to produce a horizontal bar chart. This code produces Figure 11-2.

```
by_cat_gen.size().plot(kind='barh')
```

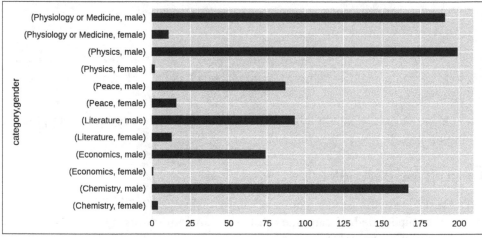

Figure 11-2. Plotting multikey groups

Figure 11-2 is a little crude and makes comparing gender disparities harder than it should be. Let's go about refining our charts to make those disparities clearer.

Unstacking Groups

Figure 11-2 isn't the easiest chart to read, even were we to improve the sorting of the bars. Handily, pandas Series has a cool unstack method that takes the multiple indices—in this case, gender and category—and uses them as columns and indices, respectively, to create a new DataFrame. Plotting this DataFrame gives a much more usable plot, as it compares prize wins by gender. The following code produces Figure 11-3:

```
by_cat_gen.size().unstack().plot(kind='barh')
```

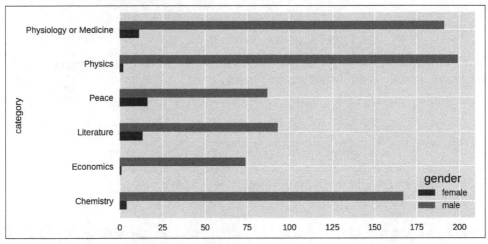

Figure 11-3. Unstacked Series of group sizes

Figure 11-3 shows a huge discrepancy between male and female prize numbers. Let's make the data a little more concrete by using pandas to produce a chart showing the percentage of female winners by category. We'll also order the category bars by prize haul.

First, we'll unstack the by_cat_gen group to produce a cat_gen_sz DataFrame:

```
cat_gen_sz = by_cat_gen.size().unstack()
cat_gen_sz.head()

gender      female  male
category
Chemistry        4   167
Economics        1    74
Literature      13    93
Peace           16    87
Physics          2   199
```

We'll do the pandas manipulation in two stages for demonstration purposes, using two new columns to store our new data. First, we'll make a column containing the ratio of female winners to the total number of winners:

```
cat_gen_sz['ratio'] = cat_gen_sz.female /\ ❶
                        (cat_gen_sz.female + cat_gen_sz.male)
cat_gen_sz.head()
```

❶ The awkward forward slash stops Python breaking, but this is a division operation.

```
ender      female  male    ratio
category
Chemistry       4   167  0.023392
Economics       1    74  0.013333
```

```
Literature        13    93  0.122642
Peace             16    87  0.155340
Physics            2   199  0.009950
```

With the ratio column in place, we can create a column containing percentage of female winners by multiplying that ratio by 100:

```
cat_gen_sz['female_pc'] = cat_gen_sz['ratio'] * 100
```

Let's plot these female percentages on a horizontal bar chart, setting an x-limit of 100 (%) and sorting the categories by prize number:

```
cat_gen_sz = cat_gen_sz.sort_values(by='female_pc', ascending=True)
ax = cat_gen_sz[['female_pc']].plot(kind='barh')
ax.set_xlim([0, 100])
ax.set_xlabel('% of female winners')
```

You can see the new plot in Figure 11-4, clearly showing the discrepancy in prize totals by gender.

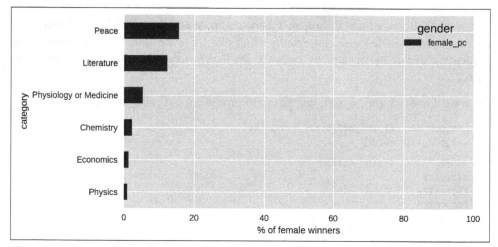

Figure 11-4. Percentage of winning females by prize category

Ignoring Economics, a recent and contentious addition to the Nobel Prize categories, Figure 11-4 shows that the largest discrepancy in the number of male and female prize winners is in Physics, with only two female winners. Let's remind ourselves who they are:

```
df[(df.category == 'Physics') & (df.gender == 'female')]\
   [['name', 'country','year']]

Out:
                      name      country  year
269     Maria Goeppert-Mayer  United States  1963
612  Marie Skłodowska-Curie         Poland  1903
```

While most people will have heard of Marie Curie, who is actually one of the four illustrious winners of two Nobel Prizes, few have heard of Maria Goeppert-Mayer.[1] This ignorance is surprising, given the drive to encourage women into science. I would want my visualization to enable people to discover and learn a little about Maria Goeppert-Mayer.

Historical Trends

It would be interesting to see if there has been any increase in female prize allocation in recent years. One way to visualize this would be as grouped bars over time. Let's run up a quick plot, using unstack as in Figure 11-3 but using the year and gender columns:

```
by_year_gender = df.groupby(['year','gender'])
year_gen_sz = by_year_gender.size().unstack()
year_gen_sz.plot(kind='bar', figsize=(16,4))
```

Figure 11-5, the hard-to-read plot produced, is only functional. The trend of female prize distributions can be observed, but the plot has many problems. Let's use Matplotlib's and pandas's eminent flexibility to fix them.

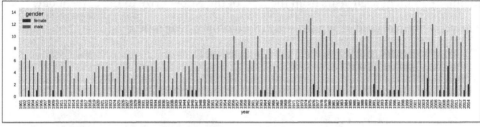

Figure 11-5. Prizes by year and gender

The first thing we need to do is reduce the number of x-axis labels. By default, Matplotlib will label each bar or bar group of a bar plot, which in the case of our hundred years of prizes creates a mess of labels. What we need is the ability to thin out the number of axis labels as desired. There are various ways to do this in Matplotlib; I'll demonstrate the one I've found to be most reliable. It's the sort of thing you're going to want to reuse, so it makes sense to stick it in a dedicated function. Example 11-3 shows a function to reduce the number of ticks on our x-axis.

---

1 Anecdotally, no one I have asked in person or in talk audiences has known the name of the *other* female Nobel Prize winner for Physics.

Example 11-3. Reducing the number of x-axis labels

```python
def thin_xticks(ax, tick_gap=10, rotation=45):
    """ Thin x-ticks and adjust rotation """
    ticks = ax.xaxis.get_ticklocs() ❶
    ticklabels = [l.get_text()
                    for l in ax.xaxis.get_ticklabels()] ❶
    # Sets the new tick locations and labels at an interval
    # of tick_gap (default +10+):
    ax.xaxis.set_ticks(ticks[::tick_gap])
    ax.xaxis.set_ticklabels(ticklabels[::tick_gap],
                    rotation=rotation) ❷
    ax.figure.show()
```

❶ Gets the existing locations and labels of the x-ticks, currently one per bar.

❷ Rotates the labels for readability, by default on an upward diagonal.

As well as needing to reduce the number of ticks, the x-axis in Figure 11-5 has a discontinuous range, missing the years 1939–1945 of WWII, during which no Nobel Prizes were presented. We want to see such gaps, so we need to set the x-axis range manually to include all years from the start of the Nobel Prize to the current day.

The current unstacked group sizes use an automatic year index:

```python
by_year_gender = df.groupby(['year', 'gender'])
by_year_gender.size().unstack()
Out:
gender  female  male
year
1901        NaN   6.0
1902        NaN   7.0
...
2014        2.0  11.0
[111 rows x 2 columns]
```

In order to see any gaps in the prize distribution, all we have to do is reindex this Series with one containing the full range of years:

```python
new_index = pd.Index(np.arange(1901, 2015), name='year') ❶
by_year_gender = df.groupby(['year','gender'])
year_gen_sz = by_year_gender.size().unstack()
    .reindex(new_index) ❷
```

❶ Here we create a full-range index named year, covering all the Nobel Prize years.

❷ We replace our discontinuous index with the new continuous one.

Another problem with Figure 11-5 is the excessive number of bars. Although we do get male and female bars side by side, it looks messy and has aliasing artifacts too. It's better to have dedicated male and female plots but stacked so as to allow easy comparison. We can achieve this using the subplotting method we saw in "Axes and Subplots" on page 251, using the pandas data but customizing the plot using our Matplotlib know-how. Example 11-4 shows how to do this, producing the plot in Figure 11-6.

Example 11-4. Stacked gender prizes by year

```
new_index = pd.Index(np.arange(1901, 2015), name='year')
by_year_gender = df.groupby(['year','gender'])

year_gen_sz = by_year_gender.size().unstack().reindex(new_index)

fig, axes = plt.subplots(nrows=2, ncols=1, ❶
            sharex=True, sharey=True, figsize=(16, 8)) ❷

ax_f = axes[0]
ax_m = axes[1]

fig.suptitle('Nobel Prize-winners by gender', fontsize=16)

ax_f.bar(year_gen_sz.index, year_gen_sz.female) ❸
ax_f.set_ylabel('Female winners')

ax_m.bar(year_gen_sz.index, year_gen_sz.male)
ax_m.set_ylabel('Male winners')

ax_m.set_xlabel('Year')
```

❶ Creates two axes, on a two (row) by one (column) grid.

❷ We'll share the x- and y-axes, which will make comparisons between the two plots sensible.

❸ We provide the axis's bar chart (bar) method with the continuous year index and the unstacked gender columns.

The take-home from our investigation into gender distributions is that there is a huge discrepancy but, as shown by Figure 11-6, a slight improvement in recent years. Moreover, with Economics being an outlier, the difference is greatest in the sciences. Given the fairly small number of female prize winners, there's not a lot more to be seen here.

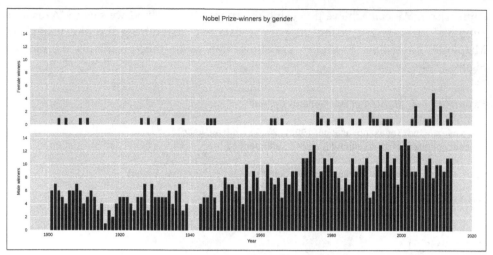

Figure 11-6. Prizes by year and gender, on two stacked axes

Let's now take a look at national trends in prize wins and see if there are any interesting nuggets for visualization.

National Trends

The obvious starting point in looking at national trends is to plot the absolute number of prize winners. This is easily done in one line of pandas, broken up here for ease of reading:

```
df.groupby('country').size().order(ascending=False)
       .plot(kind='bar', figsize=(12,4))
```

This produces Figure 11-7, showing the United States with the lion's share of prizes.

The absolute number of prizes will be bound to favor countries with large populations. Let's look at a fairer comparison, visualizing prizes per capita.

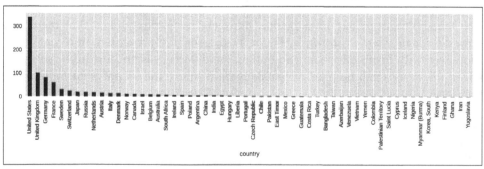

Figure 11-7. Absolute prize wins by country

Prize Winners Per Capita

The absolute number of prize winners is bound to favor larger countries, which raises the question, how do the numbers stack up if we account for population sizes? In order to test prize haul per capita, we need to divide the absolute prize numbers by population size. In "Getting Country Data for the Nobel Dataviz" on page 128, we downloaded some country data from the web and stored it as a JSON file. Let's retrieve it now and use it to produce a plot of prizes relative to population size.

First, let's get the national group sizes, with country names as index labels:

```
nat_group = df.groupby('country')
ngsz = nat_group.size()
ngsz.index
Out:
Index([u'Argentina', u'Australia', u'Austria', u'Azerbaijan',...])
```

Now let's load our country data into a DataFrame and remind ourselves of the data it contains:

```
df_countries = pd.read_json('data/winning_country_data.json',\
                            orient='index')

df_countries.loc['Japan'] # countries indexed by name

Out:
gini                    38.1
name                   Japan
alpha3Code               JPN
area                377930.0
latlng          [36.0, 138.0]
capital                Tokyo
population          127080000
Name: Japan, dtype: object
```

Our country dataset is already indexed to its `name` column. If we add to it the `ngsz` national group-size Series, which also has a country name index, the two will combine on the shared indices, giving our country data a new `nobel_wins` column. We can then use this new column to create a `nobel_wins_per_capita` by dividing it by population size:

```
df_countries = df_countries.set_index('name')
df_countries['nobel_wins'] = ngsz
df_countries['nobel_wins_per_capita'] =\
    df_countries.nobel_wins / df_countries.population
```

We now need only to sort the `df_countries` DataFrame by its new `nobel_wins_per_cap` column and plot the Nobel Prize wins per capita, producing Figure 11-8:

```
df.countries.sort_values(by='nobel_wins_per_capita',\
    ascending=False).nobel_per_capita.plot(kind='bar',\
    figsize=(12, 4))
```

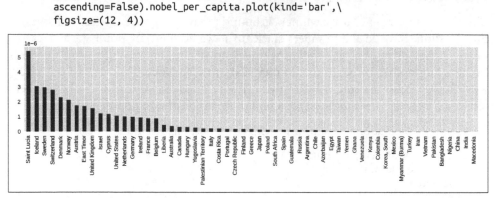

Figure 11-8. National prize numbers per capita

This shows the Caribbean island of Saint Lucia taking top place. Home to the Nobel Prize–winning poet Derek Walcott (*https://oreil.ly/OOYBc*), its small population of 175,000 gives it a high Nobel Prizes per capita.

Let's see how things stack up with the larger countries by filtering the results for countries that have won more than two Nobel Prizes:

```
df_countries[df_countries.nobel_wins > 2]\
    .sort_values(by='nobel_wins_per_capita', ascending=False)\
    .nobel_wins_per_capita.plot(kind='bar')
```

The results in Figure 11-9 show the Scandinavian countries and Switzerland punching above their weight.

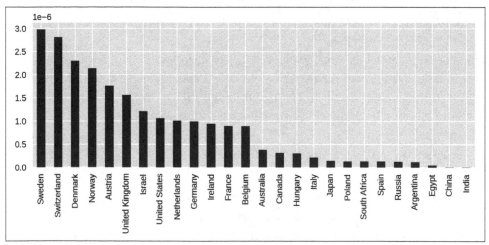

Figure 11-9. National prize numbers per capita, filtered for three or more wins

Changing the metric for national prize counts from absolute to per capita makes a big difference. Let's now refine our search a little and focus on the prize categories, looking for interesting nuggets there.

Prizes by Category

Let's drill down a bit into the absolute prize data and look at wins by category. This will require grouping by country and category columns, getting the size of those groups, unstacking the resulting Series and then plotting the columns of the resulting DataFrame. First, we get our categories with country group sizes:

```
nat_cat_sz = df.groupby(['country', 'category']).size()
.unstack()
nat_cat_sz
Out:
category      Chemistry  Economics  Literature  Peace  \...
country
Argentina             1        NaN         NaN      2
Australia           NaN          1           1    NaN
Austria               3          1           1      2
Azerbaijan          NaN        NaN         NaN    NaN
Bangladesh          NaN        NaN         NaN      1
```

We then use the `nat_cat_sz` DataFrame to produce subplots for the six Nobel Prize categories:

```
COL_NUM = 2
ROW_NUM = 3

fig, axes = plt.subplots(ROW_NUM, COL_NUM, figsize=(12,12))

for i, (label, col) in enumerate(nat_cat_sz.items()):  ❶
    ax = axes[i//COL_NUM, i%COL_NUM]  ❷
    col = col.order(ascending=False)[:10]  ❸
    col = col.sort_values(ascending=True)  ❹
    col.plot(kind='barh', ax=ax)
    ax.set_title(label)

plt.tight_layout()  ❺
```

❶ items returns an iterator for the DataFrames columns in form of (column_label, column) tuples.

❷ Python 3 acquired the handy integer division (*https://oreil.ly/X6QGK*) operator //, which returns the rounded-down integer value of the division.

❸ order orders the column's Series by first making a copy. It is the equivalent of sort(inplace=False).

Having sliced off the largest 10 countries, we now reverse the order to make the bar chart, which plots from bottom to top, presenting the largest countries at the top.

 `tight_layout` should prevent label overlaps among the subplots. If you have any problems with `tight_layout`, see the end of "Titles and Axes Labels" on page 248.

This produces the plots in Figure 11-10.

A couple of interesting nuggets from Figure 11-10 are the United States' overwhelming dominance of the Economics prize, reflecting a post-WWII economic consensus, and France's leadership of the Literature prize.

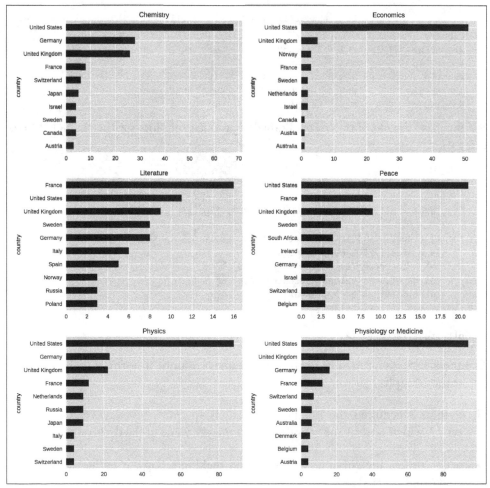

Figure 11-10. Prizes by country and category

Historical Trends in Prize Distribution

Now that we know the aggregate prize stats by country, are there any interesting historical trends to the prize distribution? Let's explore this with some line plots.

First, let's increase the default font size to 20 points to make the plot labels more legible:

```
plt.rcParams['font.size'] = 20
```

We're going to be looking at prize distribution by year and country, so we'll need a new unstacked DataFrame based on these two columns. As previously, we add a new_index to give continuous years:

```
new_index = pd.Index(np.arange(1901, 2015), name='year')

by_year_nat_sz = df.groupby(['year', 'country'])\
    .size().unstack().reindex(new_index)
```

The trend we're interested in is the cumulative sum of Nobel Prizes by country over its history. We can further explore trends in individual categories, but for now we'll look at the total for all. pandas has a handy cumsum method for just this. Let's take the United States column and plot it:

```
by_year_nat_sz['United States'].cumsum().plot()
```

This produces the chart in Figure 11-11.

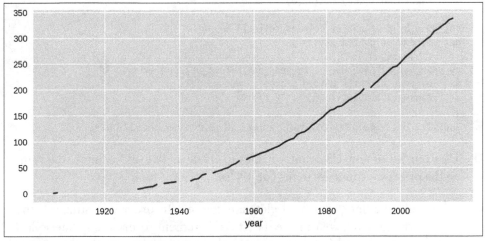

Figure 11-11. Cumulative sum of US prize winners over time

The gaps in the line plot are where the fields are NaN, years when the US won no prizes. The cumsum algorithm returns NaN here. Let's fill those in with a zero to remove the gaps:

```
by_year_nat_sz['United States'].fillna(0)
    .cumsum().plot()
```

This produces the cleaner chart shown in Figure 11-12.

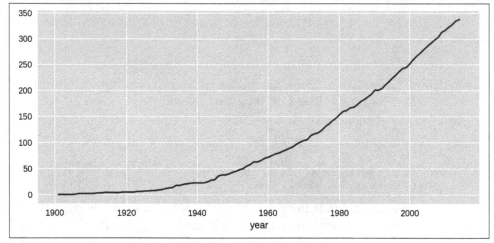

Figure 11-12. Cumulative sum of US prize winners over time

Let's compare the US prize rate with that of the rest of the world:

```
by_year_nat_sz = df.groupby(['year', 'country'])
    .size().unstack().fillna(0)

not_US = by_year_nat_sz.columns.tolist()   ❶
not_US.remove('United States')

by_year_nat_sz['Not US'] = by_year_nat_sz[not_US].sum(axis=1)   ❷
ax = by_year_nat_sz[['United States', 'Not US']]\
    .cumsum().plot(style=['-', '--'])   ❸
```

❶ Gets the list of country column names and removes United States.

❷ Uses our list of non-US country names to create a 'Not_US' column, the sum of all the prizes for countries in the not_US list.

❸ By default, the lines in pandas plots are colored. In order to distinguish them in the printed book, we can use the `style` argument to make one line solid (-) and the other dashed (--), using the Matplotlib line styles (see the docs (*https:// oreil.ly/dUw3x*) for details).

This code produces the chart shown in Figure 11-13.

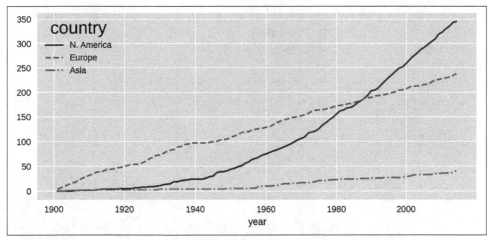

Figure 11-13. United States versus rest of world prize hauls

Where the `'Not_US'` haul shows a steady increase over the years of the prize, the US shows a rapid increase around the end of World War II. Let's investigate that further, looking at regional differences. We'll focus on the two or three largest winners for North America, Europe, and Asia:

```python
by_year_nat_sz = df.groupby(['year', 'country'])\
    .size().unstack().reindex(new_index).fillna(0)

regions = [ ❶
    {'label':'N. America',
     'countries':['United States', 'Canada']},
    {'label':'Europe',
     'countries':['United Kingdom', 'Germany', 'France']},
    {'label':'Asia',
     'countries':['Japan', 'Russia', 'India']}
]

for region in regions: ❷
    by_year_nat_sz[region['label']] =\
        by_year_nat_sz[region['countries']].sum(axis=1)

by_year_nat_sz[[r['label'] for r in regions]].cumsum()\
    .plot(style=['-', '--', '-.']) # solid, dashed, dash-dotted line style ❸
```

❶ Our continental country list created by selecting the biggest two or three winners in the three continents compared.

❷ Creates a new column with a region label for each `dict` in the `regions` list, summing its `countries` members.

❸ Plots the cumulative sum of all the new region columns.

This gives us the plot in Figure 11-14. The rate of Asia's prize haul has increased slightly over the years, but the main point of note is North America's huge increase in prizes around the mid-1940s, overtaking a declining Europe in total prizes around the mid-1980s.

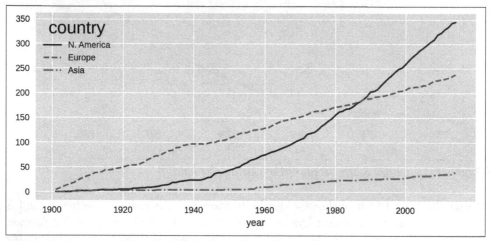

Figure 11-14. Historical prize trends by region

Let's expand the detail of the previous national plots by summarizing the prize rates for the 16 biggest winners, excluding the outlying United States:

```
COL_NUM = 4
ROW_NUM = 4

by_nat_sz = df.groupby('country').size()
by_nat_sz.sort_values(ascending=False,\
    inplace=True)  ❶

fig, axes = plt.subplots(COL_NUM, ROW_NUM,\  ❷
    sharex=True, sharey=True,  ❷
    figsize=(12,12))

for i, nat in enumerate(by_nat.index[1:17]):  ❸
    ax = axes[i/COL_NUM, i%ROW_NUM]
    by_year_nat_sz[nat].cumsum().plot(ax=ax)  ❹
    ax.set_title(nat)
```

❶ Sorts our country groups from highest to lowest win-hauls.

❷ Gets a 4×4 grid of axes with shared x- and y-axes for normalized comparison.

❸ Enumerates over the sorted index from the second row (1), excluding the US (0).

❹ Selects the `nat` country name column and plots its cumulative sum of prizes on the grid axis `ax`.

This produces Figure 11-15, which shows some nations like Japan, Australia, and Israel on the rise historically, while others flatten off.

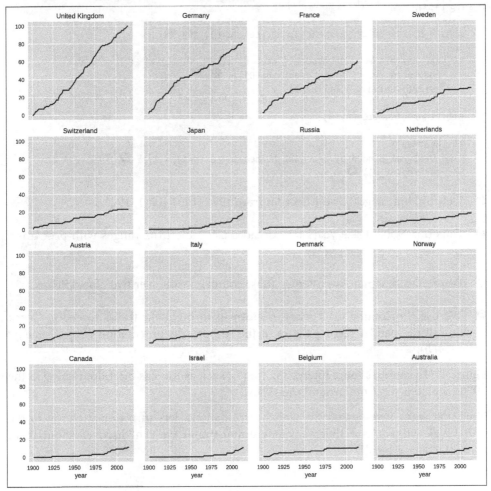

Figure 11-15. Prize rates for the 16 largest national winners after the US

Another good way to summarize national prize rates over time is by using a heatmap and dividing the totals by decade. The seaborn library provides a good heatmap. Let's import it and use its `set` method to increase the font size of its labels by scaling them:

```
import seaborn as sns

sns.set(font_scale = 1.3)
```

The division of data into chunks is also known as *binning* (*https://oreil.ly/SkFSj*), as it creates *bins* of data. pandas has a handy cut method for just this job, taking a column of continuous values—in our case, Nobel Prize years—and returning ranges of a specified size. You can supply the DataFrame's groupby method with the result of cut and it will group by the range of indexed values. The following code produces Figure 11-16:

```
bins = np.arange(df.year.min(), df.year.max(), 10) ❶

by_year_nat_binned = df.groupby('country',\
    [pd.cut(df.year, bins, precision=0)])\ ❷
    .size().unstack().fillna(0)

plt.figure(figsize=(8, 8))

sns.heatmap(\
    by_year_nat_binned[by_year_nat_binned.sum(axis=1) > 2],\ ❸
    cmap='rocket_r') ❹
```

❶ Gets our bin ranges for the decades from 1901 (1901, 1911, 1921…).

❷ Cuts our Nobel Prize years into decades using the bins ranges with precision set to 0, to give integer years.

❸ Before heatmapping, we filter for those countries with over two Nobel Prizes.

❹ We use the continuous rocket_r heatmap to highlight the differences. Check out all the pandas color palettes in the seaborn documentation (*https://oreil.ly/3FmHj*).

Figure 11-16 captures some interesting trends, such as Russia's brief flourishing in the 1950s, which petered out around the 1980s.

Now that we've investigated the Nobel Prize nations, let's turn our attention to the individual winners. Are there any interesting things we can discover about them using the data at hand?

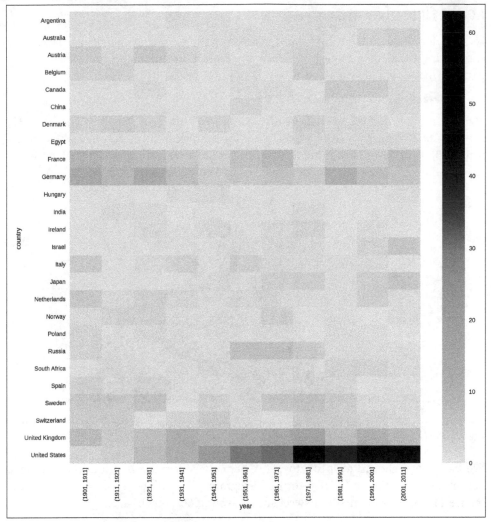

Figure 11-16. Nations' Nobel Prize hauls by decade

Age and Life Expectancy of Winners

We have the date of birth for all our winners and the date of death for 559 of them. Combined with the year in which they won their prizes, we have a fair amount of individual data to mine. Let's investigate the age distribution of winners and try to glean some idea of the winners' longevity.

Age at Time of Award

In Chapter 9, we added an `'award_age'` column to our Nobel Prize dataset by subtracting the winners' ages from their prize years. A quick and easy win is to use pandas's histogram plot to assess this distribution:

```
df['award_age'].hist(bins=20)
```

Here we require that the age data be divided into 20 bins. This produces Figure 11-17, showing that the early '60s is a sweet spot for the prize and if you haven't achieved it by 100, it probably isn't going to happen. Note the outlier around 20, which is the 17-year-old recipient of the Peace Prize, Malala Yousafzai (*https://oreil.ly/8ft8y*).

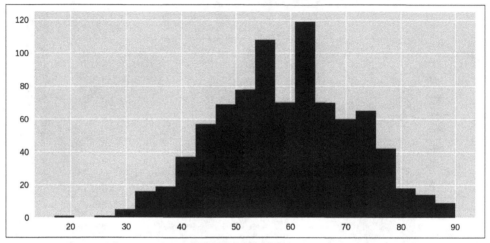

Figure 11-17. Distribution of ages at time of award

We can use seaborn's `displot` to get a better feel for the distribution, adding a kernel density estimate (KDE)[2] to the histogram. The following one-liner produces Figure 11-18, showing that our sweet spot is around 60 years of age:

```
sns.displot(df['award_age'], kde=True, height=4, aspect=2)
```

---

2 See Wikipedia (*https://oreil.ly/DUd3e*) for details. Essentially the data is smoothed and a probability density function derived.

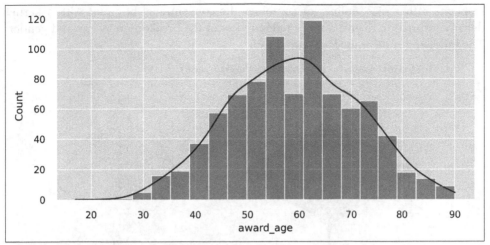

Figure 11-18. Distribution of ages at time of award with KDE superimposed

A box plot (*https://oreil.ly/EWFhx*) is a good way of visualizing continuous data, showing the quartiles, the first and third marking the edges of the box and the second quartile (or median average) marking the line in the box. Generally, as in Figure 11-19, the horizontal end lines (known as the whisker ends) indicate the max and min of the data. Let's use a seaborn box plot and divide the prizes by gender:

```
sns.boxplot(df, x='gender', y='award_age')
```

This produces Figure 11-19, which shows that the distributions by gender are similar, with women having a slightly lower average age. Note that with far fewer female prize winners, their statistics are subject to a good deal more uncertainty.

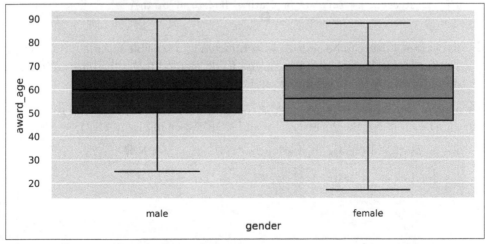

Figure 11-19. Ages of prize winners by gender

seaborn's rather nice violin plot combines the conventional box plot with a kernel density estimation to give a more refined view of the breakdown by age and gender. The following code produces Figure 11-20:

```
sns.violinplot(data=df, x='gender', y='award_age')
```

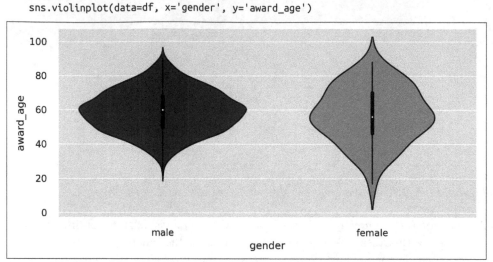

Figure 11-20. Violin plots of prize-age distribution by gender

Life Expectancy of Winners

Now let's look at the longevity of Nobel Prize winners, by subtracting the available dates of death from their respective dates of birth. We'll store this data in a new 'age_at_death' column:

```
df['age_at_death'] = (df.date_of_death - df.date_of_birth)\
                        .dt.days/365 ❶
```

❶ datetime64 data can be added and subtracted in a sensible fashion, producing a pandas timedelta column. We can use its dt method to get the interval in days, dividing this by 365 to get the age at death as a float.

We make a copy of the 'age_at_death' column,[3] removing all empty NaN rows. This can then be used to make the histogram and KDE shown in Figure 11-21:

```
age_at_death = df[df.age_at_death.notnull()].age_at_death ❶
```

```
sns.displot(age_at_death, bins=40, kde=True, aspect=2, height=4)
```

---

3 We are ignoring leap years and other subtle, complicating factors in deriving years from days.

❶ Removes all NaNs to clean the data and reduce plotting errors (e.g., `distplot` fails with NaNs).

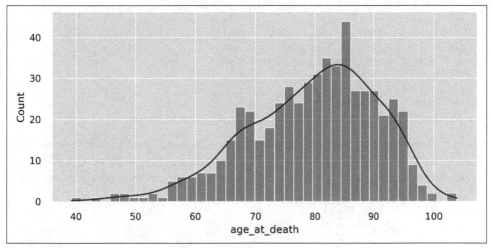

Figure 11-21. Life expectancy of the Nobel Prize winners

Figure 11-21 shows the Nobel Prize winners to be a remarkably long-lived bunch, with an average age in the early 80s. This is all the more impressive given that the large majority of winners are men, who have significantly lower average life expectancies[4] in the general population than women. One contributary factor to this longevity is the selection bias we saw earlier. Nobel Prize winners aren't generally honored until they're in their late 50s and 60s, which removes the subpopulation who died before having the chance to be acknowledged, pushing up the longevity figures.

Figure 11-21 shows some centenarians among the prize winners. Let's find them:

```
df[df.age_at_death > 100][['name', 'category', 'year']]
Out:
                       name                category  year
101            Ronald Coase               Economics  1991
328    Rita Levi-Montalcini  Physiology or Medicine  1986
```

---

4 Depending on the country, this is around five to six years. See Our World in Data (*https://oreil.ly/6xY9W*) for some stats.

Now let's superimpose a couple of KDEs to show differences in mortality for male and female recipients:

```
df_temp = df_temp[df.age_at_death.notnull()] ❶
sns.kdeplot(df_temp[df_temp.gender == 'male']
    .age_at_death, shade=True, label='male')
sns.kdeplot(df_temp[df_temp.gender == 'female']
    .age_at_death, shade=True, label='female')

plt.legend()
```

❶   Creates a DataFrame with only valid `'age_at_death'` fields.

This produces Figure 11-22, which, allowing for the small number of female winners and flatter distribution, shows the male and female averages to be close. Female Nobel Prize winners seem to live relatively shorter lives than their counterparts in the general population.

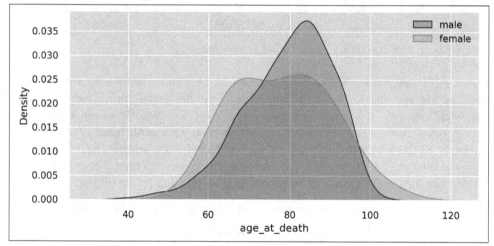

Figure 11-22. Nobel Prize winner life expectancies by gender

A violin plot provides another perspective, shown in Figure 11-23:

```
sns.violinplot(data=df, x='gender', y='age_at_death',\
                aspect=2, height=4)
```

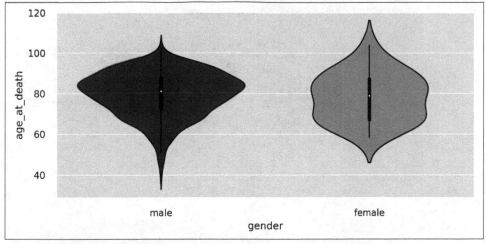

Figure 11-23. Winner life expectancies by gender

Increasing Life Expectancies over Time

Let's do a little historical demographic analysis by seeing if there's a correlation between the date of birth of our Nobel Prize winners and their life expectancy. We'll use one of seaborn's lmplots to provide a scatter plot and line-fitting with confidence intervals (see "seaborn" on page 263):

```
df_temp = df[df.age_at_death.notnull()] ❶
data = pd.DataFrame( ❷
    {'age at death':df_temp.age_at_death,
     'date of birth':df_temp.date_of_birth.dt.year})
sns.lmplot(data=data, x='date of birth', y='age at death',
   height=6, aspect=1.5)
```

❶ Creates a temporary DataFrame, removing all the rows with no 'age_at_death' field.

❷ Creates a new DataFrame with only the two columns of interest from the refined df_temp. We grab only the year from the date_of_birth, using its dt accessor (*https://oreil.ly/hGULX*).

This produces Figure 11-24, showing an increase in life expectancy of a decade or so over the prize's duration.

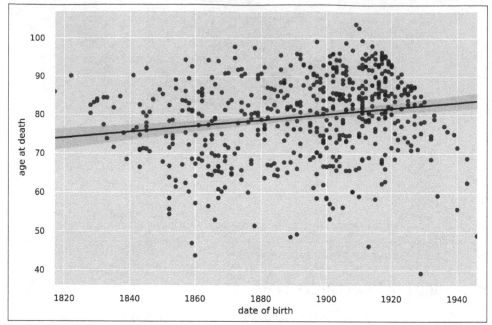

Figure 11-24. Correlating date of birth with age at death

The Nobel Diaspora

While cleaning our Nobel Prize dataset in Chapter 9, we found duplicate entries recording the winner's place of birth and country at time of winning. We preserved these, giving us 104 winners whose country at time of winning was different from their country of birth. Is there a story to tell here?

A good way to visualize the movement patterns from the winners' country of birth to their adopted country is by using a heatmap to show all born_in/country pairs. The following code produces the heatmap in Figure 11-25:

```
by_bornin_nat = df[df.born_in.notnull()].groupby(\ ❶
    ['born_in', 'country']).size().unstack()
by_bornin_nat.index.name = 'Born in' ❷
by_bornin_nat.columns.name = 'Moved to'
plt.figure(figsize=(12, 12))

ax = sns.heatmap(by_bornin_nat, vmin=0, vmax=8, cmap="crest",\ ❸
                 linewidth=0.5)
ax.set_title('The Nobel Diaspora')
```

❶ Selects all rows with a 'born_in' field, and forms groups on this and the country column.

❷ We rename the row index and column names to make them more descriptive.

❸ seaborn's `heatmap` attempts to set the correct bounds for the data, but in this case, we must manually adjust the limits (`vmin` and `vmax`) to see all the cells.

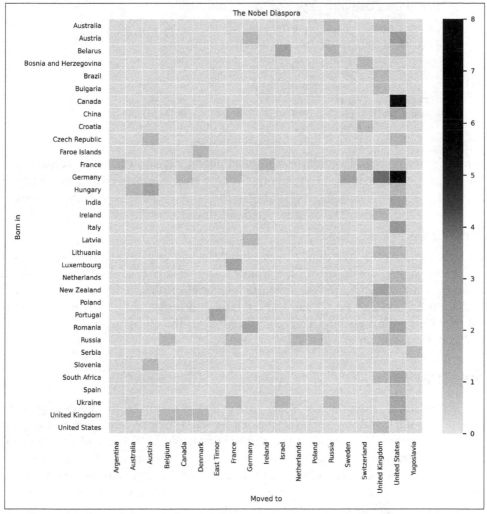

Figure 11-25. The Nobel Prize diaspora

Figure 11-25 shows some interesting patterns, which tell a tale of persecution and sanctuary. First, the United States is the overwhelming recipient of relocated Nobel winners, followed by the United Kingdom. Note that the biggest contingents for both (except cross-border traffic from Canada) are from Germany. Italy, Hungary, and Austria are the next largest groups. Examining the individuals in these groups shows that the majority were displaced as a result of the rise of antisemitic fascist regimes in the run-up to World War II and the increasing persecution of Jewish minorities.

To take an example, all four of the Nobel winners who moved from Germany to the United Kingdom were German research scientists with Jewish ancestry who moved in response to the Nazis' rise to power:

```
df[(df.born_in == 'Germany') & (df.country == 'United Kingdom')]
    [['name', 'date_of_birth', 'category']]

Out:
                   name date_of_birth             category
119   Ernst Boris Chain   1906-06-19  Physiology or Medicine
484    Hans Adolf Krebs   1900-08-25  Physiology or Medicine
486            Max Born   1882-12-11                 Physics
503        Bernard Katz   1911-03-26  Physiology or Medicine
```

Ernst Chain pioneered the industrial production of penicillin. Hans Krebs discovered the Krebs cycle, one of the most important discoveries in biochemistry, which regulates the energy production of cells. Max Born was one of the pioneers of quantum mechanics, and Bernard Katz uncovered the fundamental properties of synaptic junctions in neurons.

There are many such illustrious names among the winning emigrants. One interesting discovery is the number of prize winners who were part of the famous Kindertransport (*https://oreil.ly/tIzjj*), an organized rescue effort that took place nine months before the outbreak of WWII and saw ten thousand Jewish children from Germany, Austria, Czechoslovakia, and Poland transported to the United Kingdom. Of these children, four went on to win a Nobel Prize.

Summary

In this chapter, we explored our Nobel Prize dataset, probing the key fields of gender, category, country, and year (of prize) looking for interesting trends and stories we can tell or enable visually. We used a fair number of Matplotlib (by way of pandas) and seaborn's plots, from basic bar charts to more complicated statistical summaries like violin plots and heatmaps. Mastery of these tools and the others in the Python chart armory will allow you to quickly get the feel of your datasets, which is a prerequisite to building a visualization around them. We found more than enough stories in the data to suggest a web visualization. In the next chapter, we will imagine and design just such a Nobel Prize winner visualization, cherry-picking the nuggets gained in this chapter.

## PART IV

Delivering the Data

In this part of the book, we'll see how to deliver our select Nobel Prize dataset, recently cleaned and explored, to the browser, wherein JavaScript and D3 will turn it into an engaging, interactive visualization (see Figure IV-1).

The great thing about using a general-purpose library like Python is that you can as easily roll a web server in a few, impressively succinct lines, as mine your data with powerful data-processing libraries.

The key server tool in our toolchain is Flask, Python's powerful but lightweight web framework. In Chapter 12, we'll see how to serve your data statically (serving system files) and dynamically, usually as a database selection specified in the request. In Chapter 13, we'll see how two Flask-based libraries make creating a RESTful web API the work of a few lines of Python.

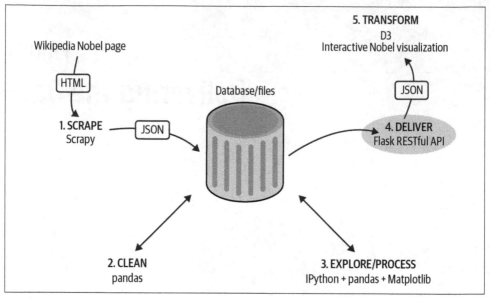

Figure IV-1. Delivering the data

You can find the code for this part of the book at the book's GitHub repo (*https://github.com/Kyrand/dataviz-with-python-and-js-ed-2*).

## CHAPTER 12

Delivering the Data

Chapter 6 showed how to grab your data of interest from the web with a web scraper. We used Scrapy to fetch a dataset of Nobel Prize winners and then in Chapters 9 and 11 we cleaned and explored the Nobel Prize dataset using pandas.

This chapter will show you how to deliver data statically or dynamically from a Python server to JavaScript on the client browser, using our Nobel Prize dataset as an example. This data is stored in the JSON format and consists of a list of Nobel Prize–winner objects like the one shown in Example 12-1.

Example 12-1. Our Nobel Prize JSON data, scraped and then cleaned

```
[
  {
    "category": "Physiology or Medicine",
    "country": "Argentina",
    "date_of_birth": "1927-10-08T00:00:00.000Z",
    "date_of_death": "2002-03-24T00:00:00.000Z",
    "gender": "male",
    "link": "http:\/\/en.wikipedia.org\/wiki\/C%C3%A9sar_Milstein",
    "name": "C\u00e9sar Milstein",
    "place_of_birth": "Bah\u00eda Blanca ,  Argentina",
    "place_of_death": "Cambridge , England",
    "text": "C\u00e9sar Milstein , Physiology or Medicine, 1984",
    "year": 1984,
    "award_age": 57,
    "born_in": "",
    "bio_image": "full/6bf65058d573e07b72231407842018afc98fd3ea.jpg",
    "mini_bio": "<p><b>César Milstein</b>, <a href='http://en.w..."
  }
  ['...']
]
```

As with the rest of this book, the emphasis will be on minimizing the amount of web development so you can get down to the business of building the web visualization in JavaScript.

 A good rule of thumb is to aim to do as much data manipulation as possible with Python—it's much less painful than equivalent operations in JavaScript. Following from this, the data delivered should be as close as possible to the form it will be consumed in (i.e., for D3 this will usually be a JSON array of objects, such as the one we produced in Chapter 9).

Serving the Data

You'll need a web server to process HTTP requests from the browser, for the initial static HTML and CSS files used to build the web page, and for any subsequent AJAX requests for data. During development, this server will typically be running on a port of localhost (on most systems this has an IP address of 127.0.0.1). Conventionally, an *index.html* HTML file is used to initialize the website or, in our case, the single-page application (SPA) (*https://oreil.ly/23h3Y*) constituting our web visualization.

The Single-Line Servers

While developing or running demos that depend on static content, it is often handy to have a little web server that just delivers the HTML, CSS, JavaScript, and JSON files to a browser running locally, usually on port 8000 or 8080. Python has a built-in solution with the `http.server` module, which can be fired up from the root directory of your project with:

```
$ python -m http.server 8000
Serving HTTP on 0.0.0.0 port 8000 (http://0.0.0.0:8000/) ...
```

Node provides an alternative dev server with `http-server`, installed using `npm install -g http-server` and run from your project root like so:

```
viz $ http-server
Starting up http-server, serving ./
...
Available on:
  http://127.0.0.1:8080
  ...
Hit CTRL-C to stop the server
```

Serving your SPA with a single-line server can be fine for visualization prototyping and sketching out ideas but gives you no control over even basic server functionality, such as URL routing or the use of dynamic templates. Thankfully, Python has a great little web server that provides all the functionality a web visualizer could need without sacrificing our aim to minimize the boilerplate standing between our Python-processed data and JavaScripted visualization masterwork. Flask is the mini web server in question and a worthy addition to our best-of-breed toolchain.

Organizing Your Flask Files

How to organize your project files is one of those really useful bits of information that is often neglected in tutorials and the like, possibly because things can get opinionated fast and at the end of the day, it's a personal preference. Nevertheless, good file organization can really pay off, especially when you start collaborating.

Figure 12-1 gives a rough idea of where your files should go as you move from the basic dataviz JavaScript prototype using a one-line server labeled basic, through a more complex project labeled basic+, to a typical, simple Flask setup labeled flask_project.

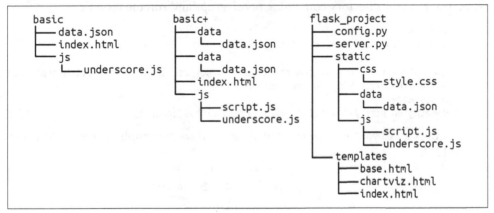

Figure 12-1. Organizing your server project files

The key thing with file organization is consistency. It helps enormously to have the position of files in your procedural memory.

Serving Data with Flask

If you're using Python's Anaconda packages (see Chapter 1), then Flask is already available to you. Otherwise, a simple pip install should make it available:

```
$ pip install Flask
```

With the Flask modules in hand, we can set up a server with a few lines to serve the universal programming greeting:

```
# server.py
from flask import Flask
app = Flask(__name__)

@app.route("/")  ❶
def hello():
    return "Hello World!"

if __name__ == "__main__":
    app.run(port=8000, debug=True)  ❷
```

❶ Flask routes allow you to direct your web traffic. This is the root route (i.e., *http://localhost:8000*).

❷ Sets the localhost port the server will run on (default 5000). In debug mode, Flask will provide useful logging to screen and in the event of an error, a browser-based report.

Now, just go to the directory containing *nobel_viz.py* and run the module:

```
$ python server.py
 * Serving Flask app 'server' (lazy loading)
 * Environment: production
   WARNING: This is a development server. Do not use it in a production deployment.
   Use a production WSGI server instead.
 * Debug mode: off
 * Running on http://127.0.0.1:8000/ (Press CTRL+C to quit)
```

You can now go to your web browser of choice and see the emphatic result shown in Figure 12-2.

Figure 12-2. A simple message served to the browser

Templating with Jinja2

By default, Flask uses the powerful and fairly intuitive Jinja2 templating library (*https://oreil.ly/lSA7g*), which can use Python variables to configure an HTML page. The following code shows a little template that loops through an array of winners to create an unordered list:

```
<!-- testj2.html -->
<!DOCTYPE html>
<meta charset="utf-8">

<body>
  <h2>\{{ heading \}}</h2>
```

```
    <ul>
        {% for winner in winners %}
        <li><a href="{{ 'http://wikipedia.com/wiki/'
            + winner.name }}">
            {{ winner.name }}</a>
            {{ ', category: ' + winner.category }}
        </li>
        {% endfor %}
    </ul>
</body>
```

When using Jinja2 with Flask, you will typically use the render_template method to produce an HTML response from a template in the project's *templates* (by default) directory. Any arguments made to render_template after its first template file reference are made available to the template. So with *testj2.html* in our project's template directory, the following code will render the template when the user visits the */demol-ist* address, producing the list shown in Figure 12-3:

```
# server_jinja.py
# ...
app = Flask(__name__)
# ...

winners = [
    {'name': 'Albert Einstein', 'category':'Physics'},
    {'name': 'V.S. Naipaul', 'category':'Literature'},
    {'name': 'Dorothy Hodgkin', 'category':'Chemistry'}
]

@app.route('/winners')
def winners_list():
    return render_template('testj2.html',
                           heading="A little winners' list",
                           winners=winners
                           )
```

Figure 12-3. A winners list rendered from the testj2.html template

Jinja2 is a powerful and mature templating language with comprehensive docs (*https://oreil.ly/lSA7g*), which makes it a cinch to use data to render HTML pages server-side.

As we'll see in "Dynamic Data with Flask APIs" on page 317, pattern matching with Flask routing makes it trivial to roll out a simple web API. It's also easy to use templates to generate dynamic web pages as shown in Figure 12-4. Templates can be useful in visualizations for composing essentially static HTML pages server-side, but generally you'll be delivering a simple HTML backbone on which to build a visualization with JavaScript. With the visualization being configured in JavaScript, the chief job of the server (aside from delivering the static files needed to seed the process) is to dynamically negotiate data (usually providing it) with the browser's and JavaScript AJAX requests.

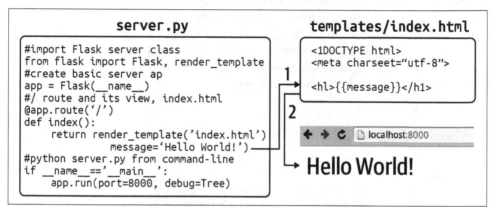

Figure 12-4. (1) An index.html template is used to create a web page using a message variable, which is then (2) served to the browser

Flask is perfectly capable of delivering full websites, with powerful HTML templating, blueprints (*https://oreil.ly/Y1PxL*) for modularizing large sites and supporting common usage patterns, and a slew of useful plug-ins and extensions. The Flask user's guide (*https://oreil.ly/aoqYy*) is a good starting point for learning more, and the API specifics can be found in this subsection of the guide (*https://oreil.ly/kpFpw*). The single-page apps that characterize most web visualizations don't need a lot of bells and whistles server-side to deliver the necessary static files. Our key interest in Flask is its ability to provide simple, efficient data servers, with robust RESTful web APIs available in a few lines of Python. But before dipping our toes in data APIs, let's look at how we deliver and use file-based data assets such as JSON and CSV files.

Delivering Data Files

Many websites that don't need the overhead of dynamically configured data choose to deliver their data in a *static* form, which essentially means that all the HTML files and, crucially, data (usually in JSON or CSV format), exist as files on the server's filesystem, ready to be delivered without, for example, making calls to a database.

Static pages are easy to cache, meaning their delivery can be much faster. It can also be more secure, as those database calls can be a common attack vector for nefarious hackers (e.g., injection attacks (*https://oreil.ly/SY92s*)). The price paid for this increased speed and security is a loss of flexibility. Being limited to a set of preassembled pages means prohibiting user interactions that might demand multivariate combinations of data.

For the budding data visualizer, there is an attraction in supplying static data. You can easily create a standalone project without needing a web API and are able to deliver your work (in progress) as a single folder of HTML, CSS, and JSON files.

The simplest example of data-driven web visualizations with static files is probably that seen in the many cool D3 examples at *https://bl.ocks.org/mbostock*.[1] They follow a similar structure to the basic page we discussed in "A Basic Page with Placeholders" on page 95.

Although the examples use `<script>` and `<style>` tags to embed JavaScript and CSS in the HTML page, I'd recommend keeping your CSS and JavaScript in separate files, where you get the advantages of a decent format-aware editor and easier debugging.

Example 12-2 shows such an *index.html* basic page with `<h2>` and `<div>` data placeholders and a `<script>` tag that loads a local *script.js* file. As we're only setting the `font-family` style, we'll inline the CSS in the page. With our *nobel_winners.json* dataset in a *data* subdirectory, this gives us the following file structure:

```
viz
├── data
│   └── nobel_winners.json
├── index.html
└── script.js
```

Example 12-2. A basic HTML page with data placeholders

```
<!DOCTYPE html>
<meta charset="utf-8">

<style>
  body{ font-family: sans-serif; }
</style>

<h2 id='data-title'></h2>
<div id='data'>
    <pre></pre>
</div>
```

---

[1] Mike Bostock, D3's creator, is a big advocate of examples. Here's a great talk (*https://oreil.ly/QsMfK*) where he emphasizes the role examples have played in the success of D3.

```
<script src="lib/d3.v7.min.js"></script>
<script src="script.js"></script>
```

The static data file for these examples consists of a single JSON file (*nobel_winners.json*) sitting in a *data* subdirectory. Consuming this data requires a JavaScript AJAX (*https://oreil.ly/5w6MQ*) call to our server. D3 provides convenient libraries for making AJAX calls, with D3's format-specific `json`, `csv`, and `tsv` methods being handier for web visualizers.

Example 12-3 shows how to load data with D3's `json` method using a callback function. Behind the scenes, D3 is using JavaScript's Fetch API (*https://oreil.ly/D5wut*) to fetch the data. This returns a JavaScript Promise (*https://oreil.ly/K570a*), which can be resolved using its `then` method, returning the data unless an error has occurred.

Example 12-3. Using D3's `json` method to load data

```
d3.json("data/nobel_winners_cleaned.json")
  .then((data) => {
  d3.select("h2#data-title").text("All the Nobel-winners");
  d3.select("div#data pre").html(JSON.stringify(data, null, 4)); ❶
});
```

❶ JavaScript's `JSON.stringify` method (*https://oreil.ly/65ZTd*) is a handy way to prettify a JavaScript object for output. Here we insert some whitespace to indent the output by four spaces.

If you run a one-line server (e.g., `python -m http.server`) in your *viz* directory and open the localhost page in your web browser, you should see something similar to Figure 12-5, indicating the data has been successfully delivered to JavaScript, ready to be visualized.

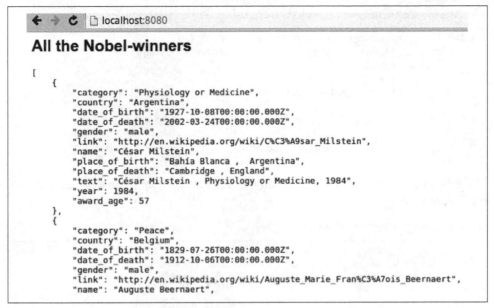

Figure 12-5. Delivering JSON to the browser

The *nobel_winners.json* dataset we're using isn't particularly large, but if we were to start adding biographical body text or other textual data, it could easily grow to a size that strains available browser bandwidth and starts to make the user wait uncomfortably. One strategy to limit loading times is to break the data down into subsets based on one of the dimensions. An obvious way to do this with our data is to store the winners by country. A few lines of pandas does the job of creating a suitable *data* directory:

```
import pandas as pd

df_winners = pd.read_json('data/nobel_winners.json')

for name, group in df_winners.groupby('country'): ❶
    group.to_json('data/winners_by_country' + name + '.json',\
                orient='records')
```

 Groups the winners DataFrame by country and iterates over the group name and members.

This should give us a winners_by_country *data* subdirectory:

```
$ ls data/winners_by_country
Argentina.json  Azerbaijan.json    Canada.json
Colombia.json   Czech Republic.json Egypt.json ...
```

We can now consume our data by country using a little tailor-made function:

```
let loadCountryWinnersJSON = function (country) {
    d3.json("data/winners_by_country/" + country + ".json")
      .then(function (data) {
        d3.select("h2#data-title").text(
          "All the Nobel-winners from " + country
        );
        d3.select("div#data pre").html(JSON.stringify(data, null, 4));
      })
      .catch((error) => console.log(error));
};
```

The following function call will select all the Australian Nobel Prize winners, producing Figure 12-6:

```
loadCountryWinnersJSON('Australia');
```

```
←  →  ⟳   🖹 localhost:8080
```

All the Nobel-winners from Australia

```
[
    {
        "award_age": 47,
        "category": "Physiology or Medicine",
        "country": "Australia",
        "date_of_birth": "1898-09-24T00:00:00.000Z",
        "date_of_death": "1968-02-21T00:00:00.000Z",
        "gender": "male",
        "link": "http://en.wikipedia.org/wiki/Howard_Walter_Florey",
        "name": "Sir Howard Florey",
        "place_of_birth": "Adelaide ,  South Australia",
        "place_of_death": "Oxford , United Kingdom",
        "text": "Sir Howard Florey , Physiology or Medicine, 1945",
        "year": 1945
    },
    {
        "award_age": 61,
        "category": "Physiology or Medicine",
        "country": "Australia",
```

Figure 12-6. Selecting winners by country

For the right visualization, the ability to select winners by country could reduce
the data bandwidth and subsequent lag, but what if we wanted winners by year or
gender? Each division by dimension (categorical, temporal, etc.) would require its
own subdirectory, creating a mess of files and all the bookkeeping that entails. What
if we wanted to make fine-grained requests for data (e.g., all US prize winners since
2000)? At this point, we need a data server that can respond dynamically to such
requests, usually driven by user interaction. The next section will show you how to
start crafting such a server with Flask.

Dynamic Data with Flask APIs

Delivering data to web pages with JSON or CSV files is the basis for many of the most impressive dataviz examples seen on the web and is perfect for small demos and prototypes. But there are constraints to the form, most obviously in the size of the datasets that can be realistically delivered. As the datasets increase in size and the files start to tip into megabytes, page loading slows down and user frustration mounts with every spin of the spinner. For much dataviz, particularly dashboards or exploratory charts, it makes sense to deliver the data as needed and in response to user requests generated by a user interface of some form. For this kind of data delivery a small data server is often perfect for the job, and Python's Flask has everything you need to craft one of these.

If we're delivering data dynamically, we're going to need some kind of API to enable our JavaScript to request data.

A Simple Data API with Flask

Using Dataset (see "Easier SQL with Dataset" on page 69), we can easily adapt our existing server for an SQL database. Here we use Dataset for convenience and the specialized JSON encoder (see Example 3-2) to convert Python datatimes to a JSON-friendly ISO string:

```python
# server_sql.py
from flask import Flask, request, abort
import dataset
import json
import datetime


app = Flask(__name__)
db = dataset.connect('sqlite:///data/nobel_winners.db')

@app.route('/api/winners')
def get_country_data():
    print 'Request args: ' + str(dict(request.args))
    query_dict = {}
    for key in ['country', 'category', 'year']: ❶
        arg = request.args.get(key) ❷
        if arg:
            query_dict[key] = arg

    winners = list(db['winners'].find(**query_dict)) ❸
    if winners:
        return dumps(winners)
    abort(404) # resource not found

class JSONDateTimeEncoder(json.JSONEncoder): ❹
    def default(self, obj):
```

```
        if isinstance(obj, (datetime.date, datetime.datetime)):
            return obj.isoformat()
        else:
            return json.JSONEncoder.default(self, obj)

    def dumps(obj):
        return json.dumps(obj, cls=JSONDateTimeEncoder)

    if __name__=='__main__':
        app.run(port=8000, debug=True)
```

❶ Restricts our database queries to keys in this list.

❷ `request.args` gives us access to the arguments of the request (e.g., `'?coun try=Australia&category=Chemistry'`).

❸ `dataset`'s `find` method requires our argument dictionary to be unpacked with `**` (i.e., `find(country='Australia', category='Literature')`). We convert the iterator to a list, ready to serialize.

❹ This is the specialized JSON encoder detailed in Example 3-2.

We can test this little API with curl (*https://curl.se*) after starting the server (`python server_sql.py`). Let's get all Japanese Physics prizewinners:

```
$ curl -d category=Physics -d country=Japan
  --get http://localhost:8000/api/

[{"index": 761, "category": "Physics", "country": "Japan",
"date_of_birth": "1907-01-23T00:00:00", "date_of_death": "1981-09-08T00:00:00",
"gender": "male", "link": "http://en.wikipedia.org/wiki/Hideki_Yukawa",
"name": "Hideki Yukawa", "place_of_birth": "Tokyo , Japan",
"place_of_death": "Kyoto , Japan", "text": "Hideki Yukawa , Physics, 1949",
"year": 1949, "award_age": 42}, {"index": 762, "category": "Physics",
"country": "Japan", "date_of_birth": "1906-03-31T00:00:00",
"date_of_death": "1979-07-08T00:00:00", "gender": "male", ... }]
```

You've now seen how easy it is to start creating a simple API. There are lots of ways one can extend it, but for fast and dirty prototyping, this is a handy little form.

But what if you want pagination, authentication, and a host of other things a sophisticated RESTful API would provide? In the next chapter, we'll see how easy it is to extend our simple data API into something more powerful and extendible, using some brilliant Python libraries like marmalade.

Using Static or Dynamic Delivery

When to use static or dynamic delivery is highly dependent on context and is an inevitable compromise. Bandwidths vary regionally and with devices. For example, if you're developing a visualization that should be accessible from a smartphone in a rural context, the data constraints are very different from those of an in-house data app running on a local network.

The ultimate guide is user experience. If a little wait at the beginning while the data caches leads to a lightning-fast JavaScript dataviz, then purely static delivery may well be the answer. If you are allowing the user to cut and slice a large, multivariate dataset, then this probably won't be possible without an annoyingly long wait time. As a rough rule of thumb, any dataset less than 200 KB should be fine with purely static delivery. As you move into the megabytes of data and beyond, you'll probably need a database-driven API from which to fetch your data.

Summary

This chapter explained the rudiments of static data delivery of files on the web server, and dynamic delivery of data, sketching the basis of a simple Flask-based RESTful web server. Although Flask makes rolling a basic data API pretty trivial, adding such bells and whistles as pagination, selective data queries, and the full complement of HTTP verbs requires a little more work. In the first edition of this book I turned to some off-the-shelf Python RESTful libraries, but these tend to have a short expiry date, probably because it's so easy to string together some single-purpose Python libraries to achieve the same end, with more flexibility. It's also a great way to learn those tools, so building just such a RESTful API is the topic of the next chapter.

## CHAPTER 13

RESTful Data with Flask

In "A Simple Data API with Flask" on page 317, we saw how to build a very simple data API with Flask and Dataset. For many simple data visualizations this kind of quick and dirty API is fine, but as the data demands become more advanced it helps to have an API that respects some conventions for retrieval and, sometimes, creation, update and delete.[1] In "Using Python to Consume Data from a Web API" on page 124, we covered the types of web API and why RESTful[2] APIs are acquiring a well-deserved prominence. In this chapter, we'll see how easy it is to combine a few Flask libraries into a flexible RESTful API.

The Tools for a RESTful Job

As seen in "A Simple Data API with Flask" on page 317, the basics of a data API are pretty simple. It needs a server, which accepts HTTP requests such as GET to retrieve or more advanced verbs like POST (to add) or DELETE. These requests are on routes like `api/winners` that are then dealt with by functions provided. In these functions data is retrieved from a backend database, possibly filtered using data parameters (e.g., strings like `?category=comic&name=Groucho` appended to the URL calls). This data then needs to be returned or serialized in some requested format, pretty much always JSON-based. For this round trip of data, the Flask/Python ecosystem provides some perfect libraries:

---

1 These create, read, update and delete methods form the CRUD acronym (*https://oreil.ly/0AkAw*).

2 Essentially, RESTful means resources being identified by a stateless, cacheable URI/URL and manipulated by HTTP verbs such as GET or POST. See Wikipedia's take (*https://oreil.ly/l0QhB*) and this Stack Overflow thread (*https://oreil.ly/6zxhv*) for a little debate.

- Flask to do the server work

- Flask SQLAlchemy (*https://oreil.ly/NVldl*), a Flask extension that integrates SQL-Alchemy (*https://sqlalchemy.org*), our preferred Python SQL library with object-relational mapper (ORM)

- Flask-Marshmallow (*https://oreil.ly/Vbgq3*), a Flask extension that adds support for marshmallow (*https://oreil.ly/AIySU*), a powerful Python library for object serialization

You can install the required extensions with `pip`:

```
$ pip install Flask-SQLALchemy flask-marshmallow marshmallow-sqlalchemy
```

Creating the Database

In "Saving the Cleaned Datasets" on page 239, we saw how easy it is to save a pandas DataFrame to SQL using the `to_sql` method. This is a very convenient way to store a DataFrame, but the table produced lacks a primary key field (*https://oreil.ly/x4OM6*), which uniquely specifies a table row. It's good form to have a primary key, and for the purposes of creating or deleting rows via our Web API, is pretty much essential. For this reason we'll create our SQL table by another route.

First, we build an SQLite database with SQLAlchemy, adding a primary-key ID to the winners table:

```
from sqlalchemy import Column, Integer, String, Text
from sqlalchemy.ext.declarative import declarative_base
from sqlalchemy.orm import sessionmaker

Base = declarative_base()


class Winner(Base):
    __tablename__ = 'winners'
    id = Column(Integer, primary_key=True) ❶
    category = Column(String)
    country = Column(String)
    date_of_birth = Column(String) # string form dates
    date_of_death = Column(String)
    # ...

# create SQLite database and start a session
engine = sqlalchemy.create_engine('sqlite:///data/nobel_winners_cleaned_api.db')
Base.metadata.create_all(engine)
Session = sessionmaker(bind=engine)
session = Session()
```

❶ We specify the all-important primary key to disambiguate our winners.

Note that we are going to store the dates as strings to limit any problems serializing datetime objects. We'll convert those DataFrame columns before committing the rows to the database:

```
df['date_of_birth'] = df['date_of_birth'].astype(str)
df['date_of_death'] = dl['date_of_death'].astype(str)
df.date_of_birth
#0      1927-10-08
#4      1829-07-26
#5      1862-08-29
..
```

We can now iterate through our DataFrame's rows, adding them to the database as dictionary records and then commit all of them, relatively efficiently, as one transaction:

```
for d in df_tosql.to_dict(orient='records'):
    session.add(Winner(**d))
session.commit()
```

With our well-formed database to hand, let's see how to easily serve it with Flask.

A Flask RESTful Data Server

This will be a standard Flask server, similar to the one seen in "Serving Data with Flask" on page 309. First, we import the standard Flask modules along with the SQLALchemy and marshmallow extensions and create our Flask app:

```
from flask import Flask, request, jsonify
from flask_sqlalchemy import SQLAlchemy
from flask_marshmallow import Marshmallow

# Init app
app = Flask(__name__)
```

Now some database-specific declarations, initializing SQLAlchemy with the Flask app:

```
app.config['SQLALCHEMY_DATABASE_URI'] =\
    'sqlite:///data/nobel_winners_cleaned_api_test.db'

db = SQLAlchemy(app)
```

We can now use the db instance to define our winners table, subclassed from the base declarative model. This matches the schema used to create the winners table in the last section:

```
class Winner(db.Model):
    __tablename__ = 'winners'
    id = db.Column(db.Integer, primary_key=True)
    category = db.Column(db.String)
    country = db.Column(db.String)
```

```
    date_of_birth = db.Column(db.String)
    date_of_death = db.Column(db.String)
    gender = db.Column(db.String)
    link = db.Column(db.String)
    name = db.Column(db.String)
    place_of_birth = db.Column(db.String)
    place_of_death = db.Column(db.String)
    text = db.Column(db.Text)
    year = db.Column(db.Integer)
    award_age = db.Column(db.Integer)

    def __repr__(self):
        return "<Winner(name='%s', category='%s', year='%s')>"\
            % (self.name, self.category, self.year)
```

Serializing with marshmallow

marshmallow is a really useful little Python library that does one job and does it well. To quote the documentation (*https://oreil.ly/kLTVF*):

> marshmallow is an ORM/ODM/framework-agnostic library for converting complex datatypes, such as objects, to and from native Python datatypes.

marshmallow uses Schemas, similar to SQLALchemy's, to enable deserializing input data to app-level objects and validation of that input data. For our purposes here its key asset is its ability to take data from our SQLite database, provided by SQL-Alchemy, and turn it into JSON-compliant data.

To use Flask-Marshmallow we first create a marshmallow instance (ma), initialized with the Flask app. We then use this to create a marshmallow schema, using the SQLAlchemy Winner model as its base. The schema also has a fields property that allows you to specify which (database) fields to serialize:

```
ma = Marshmallow(app)

class WinnerSchema(ma.Schema):
    class Meta:
        model = Winner
        fields = ('category', 'country', 'date_of_birth', 'date_of_death', ❶
                  'gender', 'link', 'name', 'place_of_birth', 'place_of_death',
                  'text', 'year', 'award_age')

winner_schema = WinnerSchema() ❷
winners_schema = WinnerSchema(many=True)
```

❶ The database fields to serialize.

❷ We declare two schema instances, one for returning single records and one for multiple records.

Adding our RESTful API Routes

Now the backbone is in place, let's craft a few Flask routes to define a small RESTful API. For a first test, we'll make a route that returns all the Nobel winners in our database table:

```
@app.route('/winners/')
def winner_list():
    all_winners = Winner.query.all()  ❶
    result = winners_schema.jsonify(all_winners)  ❷
    return result
```

❶ Database query for all rows in the winners table.

❷ The marshmallow schema for many rows takes the all-winners result and serializes it to JSON.

We'll test the API with some command-line curl:

```
$ curl http://localhost:5000/winners/
[
  {
    "award_age": 57,
    "category": "Physiology or Medicine",
    "country": "Argentina",
    "date_of_birth": "1927-10-08",
    "date_of_death": "2002-03-24",
    "gender": "male",
    "link": "http://en.wikipedia.org/wiki/C%C3%A9sar_Milstein",
    "name": "C\u00e9sar Milstein",
    "place_of_birth": "Bah\u00eda Blanca , Argentina",
    "place_of_death": "Cambridge , England",
    "text": "C\u00e9sar Milstein , Physiology or Medicine, 1984",
    "year": 1984
  },
  {
    "award_age": 80,
    "category": "Peace" , ...
  }...
]
```

So we now have an API endpoint to return all the winners. What about being able to retrieve individuals by ID (our primary key for the winners table)? To do this, we retrieve the ID from the API call, using Flask's route pattern-matching, and use it to make a specific database query. We then serialize this to JSON using our single-row marshmallow schema:

```
@app.route('/winners/<id>/')
def winner_detail(id):
    winner = Winner.query.get_or_404(id)  ❶
```

```
    result = winner_schema.jsonify(winner)
    return result
```

 Flask-SQLAlchemy provides a default 404 error message, which can be serialized to JSON by marshmallow if the query is invalid.

Testing with curl shows the expected single JSON object returned:

```
$ curl http://localhost:5000/winners/10/
{
  "award_age": 60,
  "category": "Chemistry",
  "country": "Belgium",
  "date_of_birth": "1917-01-25",
  "date_of_death": "2003-05-28",
  "gender": "male",
  "link": "http://en.wikipedia.org/wiki/Ilya_Prigogine",
  "name": "Ilya Prigogine",
  "place_of_birth": "Moscow ,  Russia",
  "place_of_death": "Brussels ,  Belgium",
  "text": "Ilya Prigogine ,  born in Russia , Chemistry, 1977",
  "year": 1977
}
```

Being able to retrieve all the winners on a single API call isn't particularly useful. Let's add the ability to filter those results with some arguments provided on the request. These arguments are the ones found on the URL query string, starting with a ? and separated by &s, which follows the endpoint, e.g., `http://nobel.net/api/winners?category=Physics&year=1980`. Flask provides a `request.args` object that has a `to_dict` method, returning a dictionary of URL arguments.[3] We can use this to specify our data table filters, which can be applied as key-value pairs using SQLAlchemy's `to_filter` method, which can be applied to queries. Here's a simple implementation:

```
@app.route('/winners/')
def winner_list():
    valid_filters = ('year', 'category', 'gender', 'country', 'name') ❶
    filters = request.args.to_dict()

    args = {name: value for name, value in filters.items()
            if name in valid_filters} ❷
    # This for loop does the same job as the dict
    # comprehension above
    # args = {}
    # for vf in valid_filters:
```

---

3 Technically URL query strings form a multidictionary, which allows multiple occurrences of the same key. For the purposes of our API we expect to have only one instance of each key, making conversion to a dictionary fine.

```
#      if vf in filters:
#          args[vf] = filters.get(vf)
app.logger.info(f'Filtering with the fields: {args}')
all_winners = Winner.query.filter_by(**args) ❸
result = winners_schema.jsonify(all_winners)
return result
```

❶ These are the fields we will allow filtering on.

❷ We iterate through the filter fields provided and use the valid ones to create our filter dictionary. Here we use a Python dictionary comprehension (*https://oreil.ly/ wmy3c*) to construct the `args` dictionary.

❸ Use Python's dictionary unpacking to specify method parameters.

Let's test our filtering abilty with curl, using the `-d` (data) arguments to specify our query parameters:

```
$ curl -d category=Physics -d year=1933 --get http://localhost:5000/winners/

[
  {
    "award_age": 31,
    "category": "Physics",
    "country": "United Kingdom",
    "date_of_birth": "1902-08-08",
    "date_of_death": "1984-10-20",
    "gender": "male",
    "link": "http://en.wikipedia.org/wiki/Paul_Dirac",
    "name": "Paul Dirac",
    "place_of_birth": "Bristol , England",
    "place_of_death": "Tallahassee, Florida , US",
    "text": "Paul Dirac , Physics, 1933",
    "year": 1933
  },
  {
    "award_age": 46,
    "category": "Physics",
    "country": "Austria",
    "date_of_birth": "1887-08-12",
    "date_of_death": "1961-01-04",
    "gender": "male",
    "link": "http://en.wikipedia.org/wiki/Erwin_Schr%C3%B6dinger",
    "name": "Erwin Schr\u00f6dinger",
    "place_of_birth": "Erdberg, Vienna, Austria",
    "place_of_death": "Vienna, Austria",
    "text": "Erwin Schr\u00f6dinger , Physics, 1933",
    "year": 1933
  }
]
```

We now have fairly fine-grained filtering on our winners dataset, and for many data visualizations, that would be enough to provide a large, user-driven dataset, fetching data from the RESTful API as required. The ability to post or create data entries from the API or a web form is one of those requirements that crops up now and again and is a good *to know*. It means you can use the API as a central data pool and add to it from various locations. It's also very easy to do with Flask and our extensions.

Posting Data to the API

Flask routes take an optional methods argument, which specifies the HTTP verbs accepted. The GET verb is the default, but by setting it to POST we can post data to this route with the packet available on the request object, in this case as JSON encoded data.

We add another /winners endpoint, with a methods array containing POST, then use the JSON data to make a winner_data dict that is used to create an entry in the winners table. This is then added to the database session and finally committed. The new entry is returned using marshmallow's serializing:

```
@app.route('/winners/', methods=['POST'])
def add_winner():
    valid_fields = winner_schema.fields

    winner_data = {name: value for name,
                    value in request.json.items() if name in valid_fields}
    app.logger.info(f"Creating a winner with these fields: {winner_data}")
    new_winner = Winner(**winner_data)
    db.session.add(new_winner)
    db.session.commit()
    return winner_schema.jsonify(new_winner)
```

Testing with curl returns the expected result:

```
$ curl http://localhost:5000/winners/ \
    -X POST \
    -H "Content-Type: application/json" \
    -d '{"category":"Physics","year":2021,
        "name":"Syukuro Manabe","country":"Japan"}' ❶
{
  "award_age": null,
  "category": "Physics",
  "country": "Japan",
  "date_of_birth": null,
  "date_of_death": null,
  "gender": null,
  "link": null,
  "name": "Syukuro Manabe",
  "place_of_birth": null,
  "place_of_death": null,
  "text": null,
```

```
    "year": 2021
  }
```

❶ The input data is a JSON encoded string.

Perhaps more useful for data management is an API endpoint enabling a winner's data to be updated. For this we can use the HTTP PATCH verb called on an individual URL. As with the POST to create a new winner, we cycle through the request.json dictionary and use any valid fields, in this case all available to marshmallow's serializer, to update the attributes of the winner by ID:

```
@app.route('/winners/<id>/', methods=['PATCH'])
def update_winner(id):
    winner = Winner.query.get_or_404(id)
    valid_fields = winner_schema.fields
    winner_data = {name: value for name, value
                   in request.json.items() if name in valid_fields}
    app.logger.info(f"Updating a winner with these fields: {winner_data}")
    for k, v in winner_data.items():
        setattr(winner, k, v)
    db.session.commit()
    return winner_schema.jsonify(winner)
```

Here we use this API patch point to update, for the purposes of demonstration, the name and prize year of a Nobel winner:

```
$ curl http://localhost:5000/winners/3/ \
    -X PATCH \
    -H "Content-Type: application/json" \
    -d '{"name":"Morris Maeterlink","year":"1912"}'
{
  "award_age": 49,
  "category": "Literature",
  "country": "Belgium",
  "date_of_birth": "1862-08-29",
  "date_of_death": "1949-05-06",
  "gender": "male",
  "link": "http://en.wikipedia.org/wiki/Maurice_Maeterlinck",
  "name": "Morris Maeterlink",
  "place_of_birth": "Ghent ,  Belgium",
  "place_of_death": "Nice ,  France",
  "text": "Maurice Maeterlinck , Literature, 1911",  ❶
  "year": 1912
}
```

❶ The original details.

At this point we have built a useful, targeted API able to fetch data according to fine-grained filters and update or create winners. If you wanted to add more endpoints covering a few more database tables, the Flask routing boilerplate and associated methods can get a little messy. Flask MethodViews provide a way of encapsulating our endpoint API calls in a single class instance, making things cleaner and more extendible. It's easy to transfer our existing API to MethodViews and the reduced cognitive load will pay off as your APIs get more involved.

Extending the API with MethodViews

We can reuse the bulk of our API's code, and shifting it to MethodViews loses a pleasing amount of boilerplate too. MethodViews encapsulate endpoints and their associated HTTP verbs (GET, POST, etc.) in a single class instance, which can be easily extended and adapted. To shift our winners table to a dedicated resource, we can just lift the existing Flask route methods into a `MethodView` class and make a few minor adjustments. First, we'll need to import the `MethodView` class:

```
#...
from flask.views import MethodView
#...
```

The SQLAlchemy model and marshmallow schemas don't need changing. Now we create a `MethodView` instance for our winners collection with methods for the relevant HTTP verbs. We can reuse the existing route methods. We then use the Flask app's `add_url_rule` method to provide an endpoint, which the view will handle:

```
class WinnersListView(MethodView):

    def get(self):
        valid_filters = ('year', 'category', 'gender', 'country', 'name')
        filters = request.args.to_dict()
        args = {name: value for name, value in filters.items()
                if name in valid_filters}
        app.logger.info('Filtering with the %s fields' % (str(args)))
        all_winners = Winner.query.filter_by(**args)
        result = winners_schema.jsonify(all_winners)
        return result

    def post(self):
        valid_fields = winner_schema.fields
        winner_data = {name: value for name,
                       value in request.json.items() if name in valid_fields}
        app.logger.info("Creating a winner with these fields: %s" %
                        str(winner_data))
        new_winner = Winner(**winner_data)
        db.session.add(new_winner)
        db.session.commit()
        return winner_schema.jsonify(new_winner)

app.add_url_rule("/winners/",
                 view_func=WinnersListView.as_view("winners_list_view"))
```

To create HTTP methods for individual table entries follows the same pattern. We'll add a delete method for good measure. Successful HTTP deletes should return the 204 (no content) HTTP code and an empty content package:

```
class WinnerView(MethodView):

    def get(self, winner_id):
        winner = Winner.query.get_or_404(winner_id)
        result = winner_schema.jsonify(winner)
        return result

    def patch(self, winner_id):
        winner = Winner.query.get_or_404(winner_id)
        valid_fields = winner_schema.fields
        winner_data = {name: value for name,
                        value in request.json.items() if name in valid_fields}
        app.logger.info("Updating a winner with these fields: %s" %
                        str(winner_data))
        for k, v in winner_data.items():
            setattr(winner, k, v)
        db.session.commit()
        return winner_schema.jsonify(winner)

    def delete(self, winner_id):
        winner = Winner.query.get_or_404(winner_id)
        db.session.delete(winner)
        db.session.commit()
        return '', 204

app.add_url_rule("/winners/<winner_id>",
                view_func=WinnerView.as_view("winner_view")) ❶
```

❶ The named, pattern-matched arguments are passed to all the MethodViews methods.

Let's use curl to delete one of our winners, specifying a verbose output:

```
$ curl http://localhost:5000/winners/858 -X DELETE -v
*   Trying 127.0.0.1...
* Connected to localhost (127.0.0.1) port 5000 (#0)
> DELETE /winners/858 HTTP/1.1
> Host: localhost:5000
> User-Agent: curl/7.47.0
> Accept: */*
>
* HTTP 1.0, assume close after body
< HTTP/1.0 204 NO CONTENT
< Content-Type: application/json
< Server: Werkzeug/2.0.2 Python/3.8.9
< Date: Sun, 27 Mar 2022 15:35:51 GMT
<
* Closing connection 0
```

By using MethodViews on dedicated endpoints, we cut out a lot of Flask's routing boilerplate and make the codebase easier to work with and extend. By way of example, let's see how to add a very handy API feature, the ability to paginate or chunk data.

Paginating the Data Returns

If you have large datasets and anticipate large result sets, the ability to receive that data in paginated chunks is a very useful API feature; for many use cases, a vital one.

SQLAlchemy has a handy `paginate` method that can be called on queries to return pages of data of a specified page size. To add pagination to our winners API, we just need to add a couple of query parameters to specify the page and page size. We'll use `_page` and `_page-size` and prefix them with an underscore to distinguish them from any filter queries we may apply.

Here's the adapted `get` method:

```
class WinnersListView(MethodView):

    def get(self):
        valid_filters = ('year', 'category', 'gender', 'country', 'name')
        filters = request.args.to_dict()
        args = {name: value for name, value in filters.items()
                if name in valid_filters}

        app.logger.info(f'Filtering with the {args} fields')

        page = request.args.get("_page", 1, type=int)  ❶
        per_page = request.args.get("_per-page", 20, type=int)

        winners = Winner.query.filter_by(**args).paginate(page, per_page)  ❷
        winners_dumped = winners_schema.dump(winners.items)

        results = {
            "results": winners_dumped,
            "filters": args,
            "pagination":  ❸
            {
                "count": winners.total,
                "page": page,
                "per_page": per_page,
                "pages": winners.pages,
            },
        }

        make_pagination_links('winners', results)  ❹

        return jsonify(results)
    # ...
```

❶ The pagination parameters with sensible defaults.

❷ Here we use SQLAlchemy's `paginate` method with our `page` and `per_page` pagination variables.

❸ We return our paginated results and anything else that makes sense. In the `pagination` dict we provide useful feedback—the page being returned and the size of the total dataset.

❹ We'll use this function to add some handy URLs to fetch previous or next pages.

By convention it's useful to return URL endpoints for previous and next pages, to allow easy consumption of the total dataset. We have a little `make_pagination_links` function for this, which adds these convenient URLs to the pagination dictionary. We'll use Python's *urllib* library to construct our URL's query string:

```
#...
import urllib.parse
#...
def make_pagination_links(url, results):
    pag = results['pagination']
    query_string = urllib.parse.urlencode(results['filters'])  ❶

    page = pag['page']
    if page > 1:
        prev_page = url + '?_page=%d&_per-page=%d%s' % (page-1,
                                                        pag['per_page'],
                                                        query_string)
    else:
        prev_page = ''

    if page < pag['pages']:  ❷
        next_page = url + '?_page=%d&_per-page=%d%s' % (page+1,
                                                        pag['per_page'],
                                                        query_string)
    else:
        next_page = ''

    pag['prev_page'] = prev_page
    pag['next_page'] = next_page
```

❶ We'll remake our query string from the filter queries, e.g., &category=Chemistry&year=1976. *urllib*'s parse module turns the filters dict into a correctly formatted URL query.

❷ Add previous and next page URLs where applicable, appending any filter queries to the result.

Let's use curl to test our paginated data. We'll add a filter to get all the Nobel Prize–winning physicists:

```
$ curl -d category=Physics  --get http://localhost:5000/winners/

{
  "filters": {
    "category": "Physics"
  },
  "pagination": {
    "count": 201,
    "next_page": "?_page=2&_per-page=20&category=Physics",  ❶
    "page": 1,
    "pages": 11,
    "per_page": 20,
    "prev_page": ""
  },
  "results": [  ❷
    {
      "award_age": 81,
      "category": "Physics",
      "country": "Belgium",
      "date_of_birth": "1932-11-06",
      "date_of_death": "NaT",
      "gender": "male",
      "link": "http://en.wikipedia.org/wiki/Fran%C3%A7ois_Englert",
      "name": "Fran\u00e7ois Englert",
      "place_of_birth": "Etterbeek ,  Brussels ,  Belgium",
      "place_of_death": null,
      "text": "Fran\u00e7ois Englert , Physics, 2013",
      "year": 2013
    },
    {
      "award_age": 37,
      "category": "Physics",
      "country": "Denmark",
      "date_of_birth": "1885-10-07",
      "date_of_death": "1962-11-18",
      "gender": "male",
      "link": "http://en.wikipedia.org/wiki/Niels_Bohr",
      "name": "Niels Bohr",
      ...
    }]}
```

❶ This is a first page, so no previous pages are available, but the next page's URL is provided to allow easy consumption of the data.

❷ A results array containing the first 20 physicists in the winners table.

With powerful libraries like marshmallow integrated as Flask extensions, it's easy enough to roll your own API without needing to resort to a dedicated RESTful Flask library which, experience suggests, might not be around too long.

Deploying the API Remotely with Heroku

Having a local development data server like the one we just built is great for prototyping, testing data flow, and all number of dataviz things dealing with datasets too large to comfortably be consumed as a JSON (or equivalent) file. But it does mean that anyone trying out visualization needs to run a local data server, which is just one more thing to think about. This is where it can be very useful to put the data server on the web as a remote resource. There are various ways this can be done, but possibly the favorite among Pythonistas, including myself, is Heroku (*https://oreil.ly/V4Q6h*), a cloud service that makes deploying a Flask server pretty trivial. Let's demo this by putting our Nobel data server on the web.

First, you'll need to create a free Heroku account (*https://signup.heroku.com*). You'll then need to install the Heroku client tools (*https://oreil.ly/wutXG*) for your OS.

With the tools installed, you can log into Heroku by running `login` from the command line:

```
$ heroku login
heroku: Press any key to open up the browser to login or q to exit
 ›   Warning: If browser does not open, visit
 ›   https://cli-auth.heroku.com/auth/browser/***
heroku: Waiting for login...
Logging in... done
Logged in as me@example.com
```

Now you're logged in, we're going to create a Heroku app and deploy it to the web. First, we create an app directory (*heroku_api*) and put our Flask API *api_rest.py* file in it. We'll also need a Procfile, a *requirements.txt* file, and the `nobel_win ners_cleaned_api.db` SQLite database to be served:

```
heroku_api
├── api_rest.py
├── data
│   ├── nobel_winners_cleaned_api.db
├── Procfile
└── requirements.txt
```

The Procfile is used by Heroku to know what and how to deploy. In this case we're going to use Python's Gunicorn WSGI HTTP server (*https://oreil.ly/yBTdb*) to negotiate web traffic with our Flask app and run it as a Heroku app. The Procfile looks like this:

```
web: gunicorn api_rest:app
```

As well as the Procfile, Heroku needs to know the Python libraries to install for the app. These are found in the *requirements.txt* file:

```
Flask==2.0.2
gunicorn==20.1.0
Flask-Cors==3.0.10
flask-marshmallow==0.14.0
Flask-SQLAlchemy==2.5.1
Jinja2==3.0.1
marshmallow==3.15.0
marshmallow-sqlalchemy==0.28.0
SQLAlchemy==1.4.26
Werkzeug==2.0.2
```

With the Heroku config files in place, we can create a Heroku app by running `create` from the command line.

We'll now use `git` to initialize a Git directory and add the existing files:

```
$ git init
$ git add .
$ git commit -m "First commit"
```

With `git` initialized, we just create our Heroku app:[4]

```
$ heroku create flask-rest-pyjs2
```

To deploy to Heroku is now just a `git` push away:

```
$ git push heroku master
```

Every time you make changes to the local codebase, just push them to Heroku and the site will update.

Let's test the API with curl by getting the first page of the Physics winners:

```
$ curl -d category=Physics --get
                         https://flask-rest-pyjs2.herokuapp.com/winners/
{"filters":{"category":"Physics"},"pagination":{"count":201,
"next_page":"winners/?_page=2&_per-page=20&category=Physics","page":1,
"pages":11,"per_page":20,"prev_page":""},"results":[{"award_age":81,
"category":"Physics","country":"Belgium","date_of_birth":"1932-11-06",
"date_of_death":"NaT","gender":"male","link":"http://en.wikipedia.org/wiki/
Fran%C3%A7ois_Englert","name":"Fran\u00e7ois Englert", ... }
```

CORS

In order to consume the API from a web browser, we'll need to handle Cross-Origin Resource Sharing (CORS) (*https://oreil.ly/ECpu0*) constraints on server data requests.

---

4 You can do this from the Heroku dashboard and then use `git remote - <app_name>` to attach the current Git directory to the app.

We'll use a Flask CORS extension and run it in default, allowing requests from any domain to access the data server. This just requires adding a couple of lines to our Flask app:

```
# ...
from flask_cors import CORS
# Init app
app = Flask(__name__)
CORS(app)
```

The Flask-CORS library (*https://oreil.ly/bCKME*) can be used to specify which domains are allowed to access which resources. We're allowing general access here.

Consuming the API Using JavaScript

To use the data server from a web app/page, we just use `fetch` to request the data. This example consumes all the paginated data by continuing to fetch pages until the `next_page` property is an empty string:

```
let data
async function init() {
  data = await getData('winners/?category=Physics&country=United States')  ❶
  console.log(`${data.length} US Physics winners:`, data)
  // Send the data to a suitable charting function
  drawChart(data)
}

init()

async function getData(ep='winners/?category=Physics'){  ❶
  let API_URL = 'https://flask-rest-pyjs2.herokuapp.com/'
  let data = []
  while(true) {
    let response = await fetch(API_URL + ep)  ❷
    .then(res => res.json())  ❸
    .then(data => {
      return data
    })

    ep = response.pagination.next_page
    data = data.concat(response.results) // add the page results
    if(!ep) break // no next-page so break out of the loop
  }
  return data
}
```

❶ The data coming from the server is asynchronous, so we use async functions to consume it.

❷ await (*https://oreil.ly/EWHec*) waits for the asynchronous Promise to resolve itself, providing its value.

❸ We convert the response data to JSON, passing it on the next then call, which returns the server data.

The JS call outputs the expected result to console:

```
89 US Physics winners:
[{
    award_age: 42
    category: "Physics"
    country: "United States"
    date_of_birth: "1969-12-16"
    date_of_death: "NaT"
    gender: "male"
    link: "http://en.wikipedia.org/wiki/Adam_G._Riess"
    name: "Adam G. Riess"
    place_of_birth: "Washington, D.C., United States"
    place_of_death: null
    text: "Adam G. Riess , Physics, 2011"
    year: 2011
  }, ...
}]
```

We now have a web-based RESTful data API that can be accessed from anywhere (subject to our CORS restrictions). As you've seen, the low overhead and ease of use make Heroku hard to beat. It's been going a while and has become a very refined setup.

Summary

I hope this chapter has demonstrated that with a handful of powerful extensions it's easy to roll your own RESTful API. It would take a lot more work and a few tests to make it industrial standard, but for most dataviz assignments this API would provide the ability to deal with large datasets and allow the user free exploration. At the very least it shows how easy it is to throw together a development server, allowing you to quickly test out visualization approaches for user-refined datasets. Dashboards is one area where this kind of remote fetching of data is expected.

The ability to easily deploy the API remotely with Heroku means large datasets can be sliced and diced without having to run local data servers—perfect for demonstrating ambitious dataviz to clients or colleagues.

## PART V

Visualizing Your Data with D3 and Plotly

In this part of the book, we take our hard-won Nobel Prize dataset, scraped from the web in Chapter 6 and cleaned in Chapter 9, and turn it into a modern, engaging, interactive web visualization using the Python- and JS-based Plotly library and D3, the heavyweight JS dataviz library (see Figure V-1).

We'll cover the realization of the D3 Nobel Prize dataviz in some detail, acquiring D3 and JavaScript knowledge as we go. First, let's imagine what our visualization should be, using insights gained in Chapter 11.

You can find the Python and JavaScript source code for this visualization in the *nobel_viz* directory of the book's GitHub repo (see "The Accompanying Code" on page 3 for details).

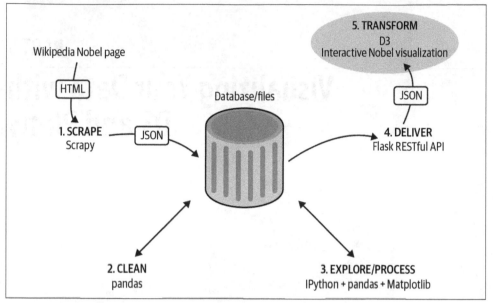

Figure V-1. Our dataviz toolchain: getting the data

You can find the code for this part of the book at the book's GitHub repo (*https://github.com/Kyrand/dataviz-with-python-and-js-ed-2*).

Bringing Your Charts to the Web with Matplotlib and Plotly

In this chapter, we'll see how to bring the fruits of your pandas data cleaning and exploration to the web. Often a good static visualization is a great way to present data, and we'll start by showing how you can use Matplotlib to do just that. Sometimes user interaction can really enrich a data visualization—we'll see how Python's Plotly library can be used to create interactive visualizations in a Jupyter notebook and transfer these, user interactions (UI) and all, to a web page.

We'll also see how learning Plotly's Python library gives you competence with a native JavaScript library, which can really extend the possibilities of your web dataviz. We'll demonstrate this by creating some simple JS UIs to update our native Plotly charts.

Static Charts with Matplotlib

Often the best chart for the job is a static chart where full editorial control lies with the creator. One of Matplotlib's strengths is its ability to produce print-quality charts in a comprehensive range of formats, from high-definition web PNGs to SVG renderings, with vector primitives that scale perfectly with document size.

For web graphics the ubiquitous, recommended format is the portable network graphics (PNG) format which, as the name suggests, was designed for the job. Let's select a few charts from our Nobel exploration (see Chapter 11) and deliver them to the web as PNGs, making a little presentation on the way.

In "National Trends" on page 284, we saw that measuring national prize hauls by absolute numbers gave a very different picture of a per-capita measurement, taking into account population sizes. We produced a couple of bar charts showing this. Now let's turn this exploratory find into a presentation. We'll use vertical bar charts to make the country names easier to read.

We take the Matplotlib axis returned by the pandas plot method and use it to make a few adaptations, changing its face color to light gray (#eee) and adding a label or two:

```python
ax = df_countries[df_countries.nobel_wins > 2]\ ❶
    .sort_values(by='nobel_wins_per_capita', ascending=True)\
    .nobel_wins_per_capita.plot(kind='barh',\ ❷
        figsize=(5, 10), title="Relative prize numbers")
ax.set_xlabel("Nobel prizes per capita")
ax.set_facecolor("#eee")
plt.tight_layout() ❸
plt.savefig("country_relative_prize_numbers.png")
```

❶ Threshold for countries with at least three prizes.

❷ We want a horizontal bar chart of kind barh.

❸ Using the tight_layout method reduces the chances of chart elements being lost in the saved figure.

We perform the same operation for the absolute numbers, producing two horizontal bar chart PNGs. To present these on the web, we'll use some of the HTML and CSS taught in Chapter 4:

```html
<!-- index.html -->
<div class="main">
  <h1 class='title'>The Nobel Prize</h1>
  <h2>A few exploratory nuggets</h2>

  <div class="intro">
    <p>Some nuggets of data mined from a dataset of Nobel prize
    winners (2016).</p>
  </div>

  <div class="container" id="by-country-container">

    <div class="info-box">
      <p>These two charts compare Nobel prize winners by
        country. [...] that Sweden, winner by a relative
          metric, hosts the prize.</p>
    </div>

    <div class="chart-wrapper" id="by-country">

      <div class="chart">
        <img src="images/country_absolute_prize_numbers.png" ❶
          alt="">
      </div>
```

```
    <div class="chart">
      <img src="images/country_relative_prize_numbers.png"
       alt="">
    </div>

  </div>
 </div>
</div>
```

 The images are in a subdirectory relative to *index.html*

After title, subtitle, and intro, we have a main container, within which there is a chart-wrapper div with two charts and an information box.

We'll use a little CSS to size, position, and style the content. The key CSS is the use of flex-boxes to distribute the charts and info-box in a row and make them of equal width by giving the chart-wrapper a flex weight of two and the info-box a flex weight of one:

```
html,
body {
  height: 100%;
  font-family: Georgia, serif;
  background: #fff1e5;
  font-size: 1.2em;
}

h1.title {
  font-size: 2.1em;
}

.main {
  padding: 10px;
  padding-bottom: 100px;
  min-width: 800px;
  max-width: 1200px;
}

.container {
  display: flex;
}

.chart-wrapper {
  display: flex; ❶
  flex: 2; ❷
}

.chart {
  flex: 1;
  padding: 0 1.5em;
}
```

```
.chart img {
  max-height: 600px;
}

.info-box {
  font-family: sans-serif;
  flex: 1; ❷
  font-size: 0.7em;
  padding: 0 1.5em;
  background: #ffebd9;
}
```

❶   The chart and info-box children of this container are under flex control.

❷   Chart-wrapper is twice the width of the info-box.

Figure 14-1 (left) shows the resulting web page.

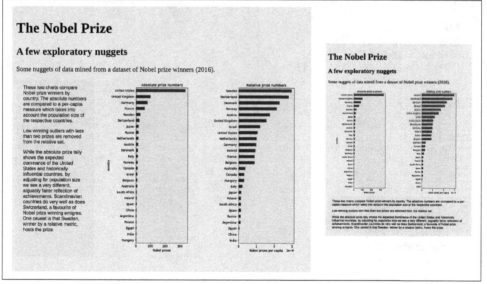

Figure 14-1. A couple of static charts

Adapting to Screen Sizes

One challenge for modern web development and associated dataviz is adapting to the many devices now used to access the web. Much of the time the ability of smartphones and tablets to pan and pinch/zoom means the same visualization can be used on all devices. Making visualizations adaptable is not easy and suffers from combinatorial explosion quite quickly. Often a compromise composition is the best way to proceed.

But there are occasions where an easy win is achievable using the CSS `media` property to adapt style to device screen size, usually using changing screen width to trigger the use of specialized styles. We'll use the Nobel web page we just created to demonstrate this.

The default chart layout in Figure 14-1 is fine for most laptop or PC screens, but as the width of the device is reduced, the charts and info-box become a little cluttered and the info-box elongates to contain the text. By triggering a flex-box change at a set width of 1,000 pixels, we can make the visualization easier to consume on a small screen device.

Here we add a media-screen trigger to apply a different `flex-direction` value to devices 1,000 or less pixels wide. Rather than displaying info-box and charts in a row, we display them in a column and reverse the order to put the info-box on the bottom. The result is shown in Figure 14-1 (right):

```
/* When the browser is 1000 pixels wide or less */
@media screen and (max-width: 1000px) {
  #by-country-container {
    flex-direction: column-reverse;
  }
}
```

Using Remote Images or Assets

You can use remote assets such as Dropbox or Google-hosted images by getting their shared link and using it as the image source. For example, the following `img` tags use Dropbox images for Figure 14-1 rather than locally hosted ones:

```
<div class="chart">
  <img src="https://www.dropbox.com/s/422ugyhvfc0zg99/
  country_absolute_prize_numbers.png?raw=1" alt="">
</div>

<div class="chart">
  <img src="https://www.dropbox.com/s/n6rfr9kvuvir7gi/
  country_relative_prize_numbers.png?raw=1" alt="">
</div>
```

Charting with Plotly

For static charts, presented as PNGs or SVGs, Matplotlib is eminently customizable, though its API could be more intuitive. But if you want your charts to have any dynamic/interactive elements, for example the ability to change or filter the dataset with buttons or selectors, then you will need a different charting library, and this is where Plotly[1] comes in.

Plotly (*https://plotly.com/python*) is a Python- (and other languages) based charting library that, like Matplotlib, can be used during interactive Jupyter notebook sessions. It offers a wide range of chart forms, some of which aren't found in the Matplotlib stable, and is arguably easier to configure than Matploblib. For this reason alone it's a useful tool to have, but where Plotly shines is its ability to export these charts, along with any scripted interactive widgets, to the web.

As mentioned, user interactions and dynamic charts are often surplus to requirements, but even in this case Plotly has some nice value-adds like tool-tipped information which, for example, gives specific information about a bar-group on mouse-over.

Basic Charts

Let's see how Plotly does things by replicating one of the Matploblib charts from "Historical Trends in Prize Distribution" on page 289. First, we'll create a DataFrame from the Nobel Prize dataset showing cumulative prizes for three geographical regions:

```
new_index = pd.Index(np.arange(1901, 2015), name='year')

by_year_nat_sz = df.groupby(['year', 'country'])\
    .size().unstack().reindex(new_index).fillna(0)

# Our continental country list created by selecting the biggest
# two or three winners in the three continents compared.
regions = [
{'label':'N. America',
 'countries':['United States', 'Canada']},
{'label':'Europe',
 'countries':['United Kingdom', 'Germany', 'France']},
{'label':'Asia',
 'countries':['Japan', 'Russia', 'India']}
]
# Creates a new column with a region label for each dict in the
# regions list, summing its countries members.
for region in regions:
    by_year_nat_sz[region['label']] =\
    by_year_nat_sz[region['countries']].sum(axis=1)
# Creates a new DataFrame using the cumulative sum of the
# new region columns.
df_regions = by_year_nat_sz[[r['label'] for r in regions]].\
    cumsum()
```

---

1 Bokeh (*https://bokeh.org*) is a worthy alternative.

This gives us a df_regions DataFrame with columnar cumulative sums:

```
df_regions
country  N. America  Europe  Asia
year
1901            0.0     4.0   0.0
1902            0.0     7.0   0.0
1903            0.0    10.0   0.0
1904            0.0    13.0   1.0
1905            0.0    15.0   1.0
...             ...     ...   ...
2010          327.0   230.0  36.0
2011          333.0   231.0  36.0
...
```

Plotly Express

Plotly provides an express module (*https://oreil.ly/bJRlf*) that enables fast chart sketches, great for exploratory iteration in a notebook. This module has high-level objects for line charts, bar charts, etc. and can take pandas DataFrames as arguments interpreting columnar data.[2] The regional DataFrame we just created can be used directly by Plotly Express to build a line chart in a couple of lines. This produces the chart in Figure 14-2 (left):

```
# load the express module
import plotly.express as px
# use the line method with a suitable DataFrame
fig = px.line(df_regions)
fig.show()
```

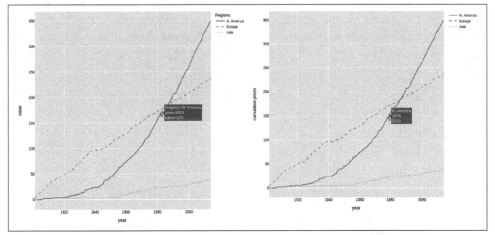

Figure 14-2. Cumulative prizes with Plotly

---

2 You can easily transpose your DataFrames to the required columnar form using the DataFrame's T operator.

Note the row index label that is used for the x-axis by default and the tooltip that appears on mouse-over showing, in this case, information about the line section.

Another thing to note is that the legend label is taken from the grouping index, in this case country. We can easily fix this by relabeling it to something more sensible, in this case Regions:

```
fig = px.line(df_regions, labels={'country': 'Regions'})
        line_dash='country', line_dash_sequence=['solid', 'dash', 'dot']) ❶
)
fig.show()
```

❶ Plotly colors the lines by default, but in order to distinguish them in the print version of this book, we can adjust their styles. To do this, we set the line_dash argument to the country group and the line_dash_sequence to the line styles we want.[3]

Plotly Express is easy to use and brings some novel charts into play.[4] For quick data sketches it competes with pandas's Matplotlib wrapper, which works directly on DataFrames. But if you want more control over your plots and to really exploit Plotly's advantages, I recommend focusing on using Plotly figures and graph-objects. This API is more complex but significantly more powerful. It is also mirrored by the JavaScript API, which means you're essentially learning two libraries—a very useful thing as we'll see later in the chapter.

Plotly Graph-Objects

Using Plotly graph-objects involves a little more boilerplate code, but the pattern is essentially the same whether creating bar charts, violin plots, maps, etc. The idea is to use an array of graph-objects such as scattered points (lines in line mode), bars, candles, boxes, etc., as data for the figure. A layout object is used to provide other chart features.

The following code produces the chart in Figure 14-2 (right). Note the customized tooltip on mouse-over:

```
import plotly.graph_objs as go


traces = [] ❶
for region in regions:
    name = region['label']
    traces.append(
        go.Scatter(
```

---

3 See *https://oreil.ly/zUyxK* for Plotly's line style options.

4 See the Plotly site (*https://plotly.com/python*) for some demos.

```
            x=df_regions.index, # years
            y=df_regions[name], # cum. prizes
            name=name,
            mode="lines",  ❷
            hovertemplate=f"{name}<br>%{{x}}<br>$%{{y}}<extra></extra>"  ❸
            line=dict(dash=['solid', 'dash', 'dot'][len(traces)])  ❹
        )
    )
layout = go.Layout(height=600, width=600,\  ❺
    xaxis_title="year", yaxis_title="cumulative prizes")
fig = go.Figure(traces, layout)  ❻
fig.show()
```

❶ We'll create an array of line graph-objects to use as our figure's data.

❷ In line mode scatter objects points are connected.

❸ You can provide an HTML string template that will appear on mouse-hover. x and y variables at that point are provided.

❹ The Scatter object has a *line* property that allows you to set various line properties like color, line style, line shape, etc.[5] In order to distinguish our lines in the black-and-white print book, we want to set their style. To do this we use the size (len) of the traces array as an index to an array of styles, setting the line styles in sequence.

❺ As well as data, we provide a layout object, defining things like the chart's dimension, x-axis titles, and much more.

❻ Create a figure using our array of graph-objects and the layout.

Mapping with Plotly

Another of Plotly's big strengths is its mapping libraries and particularly its ability to integrate the Mapbox ecosystem (*https://oreil.ly/965Zv*), one of the most powerful tile-based mapping resources for the web. Mapbox's tiling system is fast and efficient and opens up the possibility of ambitious mapping visualizations.

Let's demonstrate some Plotly mapping using our Nobel Prize dataset and aiming to visualize the global distribution of prizes.

First, we'll make a DataFrame with the prizes tallies by category for the winning countries and add a Total column by aggregating the category numbers:

---

5 See *https://oreil.ly/8UDgA* for further details.

```
df_country_category = df.groupby(['country', 'category'])\
    .size().unstack()
df_country_category['Total'] = df_country_category.sum(1)
df_country_category.head(3) # top three rows
#category   Chemistry Economics Literature  Peace  Physics  \
#country
#Argentina       1.0       NaN        NaN    2.0      NaN
#Australia       NaN       1.0        1.0    NaN      1.0
#Austria         3.0       1.0        1.0    2.0      4.0
#
#category   Physiology or Medicine  Total
#country
#Argentina                    2.0    5.0
#Australia                    6.0    9.0
#Austria                      4.0   15.0
```

We'll use that `Total` column to threshold the rows, limiting the countries to those that have won the Nobel at least three times. We'll make a copy of this slice to avoid any pandas DataFrame errors if trying to change a view:

```
df_country_category = df_country_category.\
    loc[df_country_category.Total > 2].copy()
df_country_category
```

With the prize tallies by country to hand we need some geographical data, namely the coordinates of the centroids (centers) of the countries. This is an opportunity to demo Geopy (*https://github.com/geopy/geopy*), a cool little Python library that does just that job, among many geographical others.

First, install with `pip` or equivalent:

```
!pip install geopy
```

Now we can use the `Nominatim` module to provide locations based on our country name strings. We create a geolocator by providing a user-agent string:

```
from geopy.geocoders import Nominatim

geolocator = Nominatim(user_agent="nobel_prize_app")
```

Using the geolocator, we can loop through a few countries in the DataFrame index to show the geo date available:

```
for name in df_country_category.index[:5]:
    location = geolocator.geocode(name)
    print("Name: ", name)
    print("Coords: ", (location.latitude, location.longitude))
    print("Raw details: ", location.raw)
#Name: Argentina
#Coords: (-34.9964963, -64.9672817)
#Raw details: {'place_id': 284427148, 'licence': 'Data ©
#OpenStreetMap contributors, ODbL 1.0. https://osm.org/
#copyright', 'osm_type': 'relation', 'osm_id': 286393,
```

```
#'boundingbox': ['-55.1850761', '-21.7808568', '-73.5605371',
#[...] }
```

Let's add geographic latitude (Lat) and longitude (Lon) columns to our DataFrame using our geolocator:

```
lats = {}
lons = {}
for name in df_country_category.index:
    location = geolocator.geocode(name)
    if location:
        lats[name] = location.latitude
        lons[name] = location.longitude
    else:
        print("No coords for %s"%name)

df_country_category.loc[:,'Lat'] = pd.Series(lats)
df_country_category.loc[:,'Lon'] = pd.Series(lons)
df_country_category
#category   Chemistry Economics Literature Peace  Physics \
#country
#Argentina       1.0       NaN        NaN   2.0      NaN
#Australia       NaN       1.0        1.0   NaN      1.0
#
#category  Physiology or Medicine  Total        Lat        Lon
#country
#Argentina                    2.0    5.0 -34.996496 -64.967282
#Australia                    6.0    9.0 -24.776109 134.755000
```

We're going to use some map markers to reflect the prize numbers for various countries. We want the size of the circle to reflect the prize sum, so we will need a little function to get the appropriate radius. We'll have a `scale` parameter to allow hand-tweaking of the marker size:

```
def calc_marker_radius(size, scale=5):
    return np.sqrt(size/np.pi) * scale
```

As with the basic charts, there is a Plotly Express mapping option, which allows for fast map creation using a pandas DataFrame. Express has a dedicated `scatter_map` box method that returns a figure object. Here we use this figure to make some updates to the map layout, using one of the free map styles (carto-positron) provided by Plotly (see Figure 14-3):

```
import plotly.express as px
init_notebook_mode(connected=True)

size = df_country_category['Total'].apply(calc_marker_radius, args=(16,)) ❶
fig = px.scatter_mapbox(df_country_category, lat="Lat", lon="Lon", ❷
                        hover_name=df_country_category.index, ❸
                        hover_data=['Total'],
                        color_discrete_sequence=["olive"],
                        zoom=0.7, size=size)
```

```
fig.update_layout(mapbox_style="carto-positron", width=800, height=450) ❹
fig.update_layout(margin={"r":0,"t":0,"l":0,"b":0})
fig.show()
```

❶ Create an array of sizes for the radii of the circular markers.

❷ The mapbox takes an array of latitudes and longitudes for marker placement, as well as our calculated size array. Zoom indicates the position of the camera above the Earth with 0.7 as a standard global default.

❸ hover_name gives the title of the mouse-over tooltip and data any extra info we want, in this case the Total column.

❹ Plotly provides a number of free-to-use mapping style tile-sets (https://oreil.ly/NbTg1).

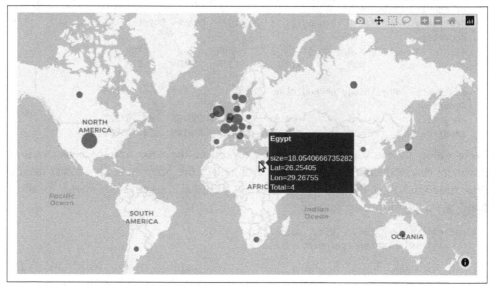

Figure 14-3. Fast mapping with Plotly Express

As with basic charts Plotly also offers a more powerful data+layout mapping option that follows the familiar recipe, creating an array of charts *traces* and a layout to specify things like legend boxes, titles, map zoom, etc. Here's how to make our Nobel map:

```
mapbox_access_token = "pk.eyJ1Ij...JwFsbg" ❶

df_cc = df_country_category

site_lat = df_cc.Lat ❷
site_lon = df_cc.Lon
```

```
totals = df_cc.Total
locations_name = df_cc.index

layout = go.Layout(
    title='Nobel prize totals by country',
    hovermode='closest',
    showlegend=False,
    margin ={'l':0,'t':0,'b':0,'r':0},
    mapbox=dict(
        accesstoken=mapbox_access_token,
        # we can set map details here including center, pitch and bearing..
        # try playing  with these.
#         bearing=0,
# #         center=dict(
# #             lat=38,
# #             lon=-94
# #         ),
#         pitch=0,
        zoom=0.7,
        style='light'
    ),
    width=875, height=450
)

traces = [
            go.Scattermapbox(
            lat=site_lat,
            lon=site_lon,
            mode='markers',
            marker=dict(
                size=totals.apply(calc_marker_radius, args=(7,)),
                color='olive',
                opacity=0.8
            ),
            text=[f'{locations_name[i]} won {int(x)} total prizes'\
                for i, x in enumerate(totals)],
            hoverinfo='text'
             )
]

fig = go.Figure(traces, layout=layout)
fig.show()
```

❶ Plotly offers a number of free, open-streetmap-based mapsets, but to use Mapbox-specific layers, you need to get a Mapbox access token (*https://oreil.ly/ 7zzug*). These tokens are free to use for personal use.

❷ We'll store the DataFrame's columns and index in a more user-friendly form.

The map produced is shown in Figure 14-4 (left). Note the customized tooltip, produced on mouse-over. Figure 14-4 (right) shows the result of some user interaction, panning and zooming to highlight European prize distributions.

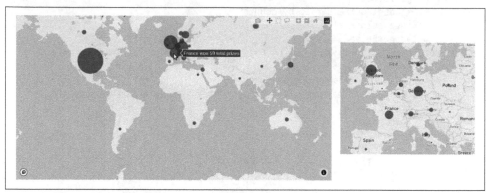

Figure 14-4. Mapping with Plotly's graph-objects

Let's extend the map to add some custom controls, using buttons to select prize categories to visualize.

Adding Custom Controls with Plotly

One of the cool features of Plotly's interactive maps is the ability to add custom controls (*https://oreil.ly/xo62V*) in Python that can be ported to the web as HTML+JS controls. The control API is a little clunky, in my opinion, and limited to a small set of controls, but the ability to add dataset selectors, sliders, filters, and the like is a great asset. Here we'll add a few buttons to our Nobel map, allowing the user to filter the dataset by category.

Before proceeding we need to replace the non-numbers from the prizes by country and category DataFrame with zero to avoid Plotly labeling errors. You can see these in the first two rows:

```
df_country_category.head(2)
# Out:
# category    Chemistry  Economics  Literature  Peace  Physics  \
# country
# Argentina      1.0        NaN        NaN        2.0      NaN
# Australia      NaN        1.0        1.0        NaN      1.0
```

A single line of pandas fills these NaNs with zero, making the change in place:

```
df_country_category.fillna(0, inplace=True)
```

This will involve a slightly different Plotly pattern than the one used up to now. We'll first create our figure with layout and then add the data traces using add_trace by iterating through the Nobel categories, adding buttons to the button array as we go.

We'll then add these buttons to the layout using its `update` method:

```
# ...
categories = ['Total', 'Chemistry',  'Economics', 'Literature',\
    'Peace', 'Physics','Physiology or Medicine',]
# ...
colors = ['#1b9e77','#d95f02','#7570b3','#e7298a','#66a61e','#e6ab02','#a6761d']
buttons = []
# ... DEFINE LAYOUT AS BEFORE
fig = go.Figure(layout=layout)
default_category = 'Total'

for i, category in enumerate(categories):
    visible = False
    if category == default_category:  ❶
        visible = True
    fig.add_trace(
        go.Scattermapbox(
            lat=site_lat,
            lon=site_lon,
            mode='markers',
            marker=dict(
                size=df_cc[category].apply(calc_marker_radius, args=(7,)),
                color=colors[i],
                opacity=0.8
            ),
            text=[f'{locations_name[i]} prizes for {category}: {int(x)}'\
                for i, x in enumerate(df_cc[category])],
            hoverinfo='text',
            visible=visible
            ),
    )
    # We start with a mask array of Boolean False, one for each category (inc. Total)
    # In Python [True] * 3 == [True, True, True]
    mask = [False] * len(categories)
    # We now set the mask index corresponding to the current category to True
    # i.e. button 'Chemistry' has mask [False, True, False, False, False, False]
    mask[categories.index(category)] = True
    # Now we can use that Boolean mask to add a button to our button list
    buttons.append(
            dict(
                label=category,
                method="update",
                args=[{"visible": mask}],  ❷
            ),
    )

fig.layout.update(  ❸
    updatemenus=[
        dict(
            type="buttons",
```

```
                direction="down",
                active=0,
                x=0.0,
                xanchor='left',
                y=0.65,
                showactive=True, # show the last button clicked
                buttons=buttons
            )
        ]
    )

fig.show()
```

❶ The category marker sets are initially invisible—only the default Total is shown.

❷ We use the mask to set a visibility array for this button that will only make the associated category data markers visible.

❸ We now add the buttons to our layout, adjusting direction (down) and position-ing using x and y to place the center of the button group vertically, with the button-box anchored on the left.

Clicking on a button (see Figure 14-5) shows the data markers associated with that category by applying the button's visibility mask. While this feels a little awkward, it is a solid way to filter the data by button-press. Unlike the JavaScript+HTML controls we'll look at later in the chapter, there's not a lot you can do in the way of styling to the buttons.

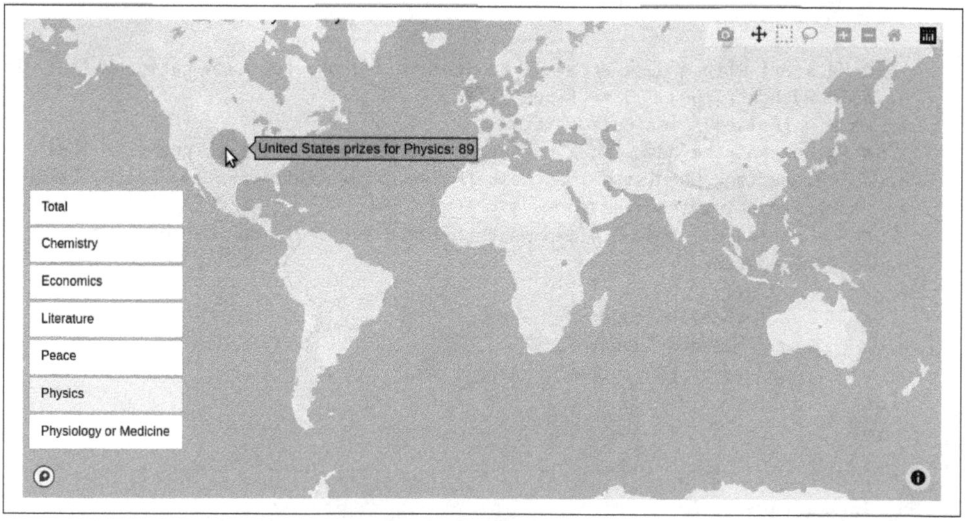

Figure 14-5. Adding custom controls to a Plotly map

From Notebook to Web with Plotly

Now we've got our Plotly charts displaying in the notebook, let's see how to transfer them to a little web presentation. We're going to use the `plot` function from Plotly's `offline` module to generated the embeddable HTML+JS required, so let's first import it:

```python
from plotly.offline import plot
```

Using `plot`, we can create an embeddable string from the figure that can be lifted straight to the web. It contains the necessary HTML and JavaScript tags to bootstrap Plotly's JavaScript library and create the chart:

```python
embed_string = plot(fig, output_type='div', include_plotlyjs="cdn")
embed_string
#'<div>                        <script type="text/javascript">window.PlotlyConfig
#= {MathJaxConfig: \'local\'};</script>\n        <script src="https://cdn.plot.ly/
#plotly-2.9.0.min.js"></script>              <div
#id="195b2d71-f59d-4f8a-a40a-3b8c797a918b" class="plotly-graph-div"
#style="height:600px; width:600px;"></div>            <script type="text/
#javascript"> [...]     </script>
#</div>'
```

If we tidy up that string we see it breaks down to four components, an HTML `div` tag with the chart's ID and some JavaScript, containing the `newPlot` call with data and layout passed in as parameters:

```html
<div>
  <!-- (1) JavaScript Plotly config, placed with JavaScript (.js) file -->
  <script type="text/javascript">window.PlotlyConfig = {MathJaxConfig: 'local'};
  </script>
  <!-- (2) Place bottom of HTML file to import the Plotly library
          from the cloud (content delivery network) -->
  <script src="https://cdn.plot.ly/plotly-2.9.0.min.js"></script>
  <!-- create a content div for the chart, with ID tag (to be inflated)
     (3) !! Put this div in the HTML section of the code-pen !! -->
  <div id="4dbeae4f-ed9b-4dc1-9c69-d4bb2a20eaa7" class="plotly-graph-div"
      style="height:100%; width:100%;"></div>

  <script type="text/javascript">
    // (4) Everything within this tag goes to a JavaScript (.js) file -->
    window.PLOTLYENV=window.PLOTLYENV || {};
    // Grab the 'div' tag above by ID and call Plotly's JS API on it, using the
    // embedded data and annotations
    if (document.getElementById("4dbeae4f-ed9b-4dc1-9c69-d4bb2a20eaa7"))
    {                    Plotly.newPlot("4dbeae4f-ed9b-4dc1-9c69-d4bb2a20eaa7",
                  [{"mode":"lines","name":"Korea, South",
                  "x": [0,1,2,3,4,5,6,7,8,9,10,11,12,...]}])
              };
  </script>
</div>
```

Although we could just paste the HTML+JS into a web page and see the chart rendered, it's better practice to separate JS and HTML concerns. First, we place the chart div in a little web page with a few headers, add some containers for info-boxes, etc.:

```
<!-- index.html -->
<div class="main">
  <h1 class='title'>The Nobel Prize</h1>
  <h2>From notebook to the web with Plotly</h2>

  <div class="intro">
    <p>Some nuggets of data mined [...]</p>
  </div>

  <div class="container" id="by-country-container">

    <div class="info-box">
      <p>This chart shows the cumulative Nobel prize wins by region, taking the
      two or three highest winning countries from each.[...]</p>
    </div>

    <div class="chart-wrapper" id="by-country">
      <div id="bd54c166-3733-4b20-9bb9-694cfff4a48e"  ❶
      class="plotly-graph-div" style="height:100%; width:100%;"></div>
    </div>
  </div>
</div>

<script scr="scripts/plotly_charts.js"></script>
<script src="https://cdn.plot.ly/plotly-2.9.0.min.js"></script> ❷
```

❶ The div container produced by Plotly with an ID corresponding to the JavaScripted chart.

❷ The script tag produced by Plotly to import the JS charting library.

We take the content of the remaining two JavaScript tags and place it in a *plotly_charts.js* JS file:

```
// scripts/plotly_charts.js
  window.PLOTLYENV=window.PLOTLYENV || {};
  if (document.getElementById("bd54c166-3733-4b20-9bb9-694cfff4a48e")){ ❶
    Plotly.newPlot("bd54c166-3733-4b20-9bb9-694cfff4a48e", ❷
      [{"hovertemplate":"N. America<br>%{x}<br>$%{y}<extra></extra>", ❸
        "mode":"lines","name":"N. America",
        "x":[1901,1902,1903,1904,1905,1906,1907,1908,1909,1910,1911,1912,1913,
            1914,1915,1916,1917,1918,1919,1920,1921,1922,...]
    }])
  }
```

❶ Checks that the div with correct ID is present.

❷   Plotly's `newPlot` method will build the chart in the identified container.

❸   An array of chart-objects, in this case containing all the data (x and y arrays) necessary to transfer the chart from notebook to web page.

On page load the Plotly library's `newPlot` method is run using the embedding data and layout and the chart built with JS in the `div` container specified by ID. This produces the web page shown in Figure 14-6.

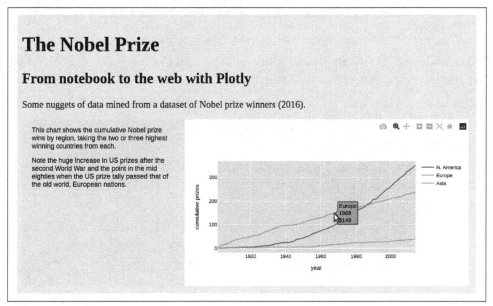

Figure 14-6. From notebook to web with Plotly

All charts produced in Python with Plotly can be transferred to the web in this way. If you plan on using more than a couple, I recommend having separate JS files for each chart as the embedded data can lead to very long files.

Native JavaScript Charts with Plotly

Being able to easily shift a favored chart from notebook to web is great, but if you need to make refinements it involves moving back and forth from notebook to webdev. This can get annoying after a while. One really cool thing about Plotly is that you are learning a JavaScript charting library for free, as it were. The Python and JS figure patterns are very similar, so it's easy to both convert chart code from Python to JS and start writing JS charts from scratch. Let's demonstrate this by converting a seaborn chart to JavaScripted Plotly.

In "Age at Time of Award" on page 296, we produced some violin plots using seaborn. To transfer these to the web, we'll first need some data. One useful method for shifting small datasets is to convert a refined dataset to JSON and just copy the string produced, pasting it into a JS file and then parsing the string to a JS object. First, we use pandas to create a small dataset with only the award_age and gender columns, then produce the required JSON array of objects:

```
df_select = df[['gender', 'award_age']]
df_select.to_json(orient='records')
#'[{"gender":"male","award_age":57},{"gender":"male","award_age":80},
#{"gender":"male","award_age":49},{"gender":"male","award_age":59},
#{"gender":"male","award_age":49},{"gender":"male","award_age":46},...}]'
```

We can take the JSON string, paste it into a JS file, and use the built-in JSON library to parse the string into a JS array of objects:

```
let data = JSON.parse('[{"gender":"male","award_age":57}
',{"gender":"male","award_age":80},'
'{"gender":"male","award_age":49},{"gender":"male","award_age":59},'
'{"gender":"male","award_age":48}, ... ]')
```

With the data to hand, we'll need a little HTML scaffold with a chart container, ID award_age, to contain the Plotly chart:

```
<div class="main">
  <h1 class='title'>The Nobel Prize</h1>
  <!-- ... -->
    <div class="chart-wrapper">
      <div class='chart' id='award_age'></div> ❶
  </div>

</div>

<script src="https://cdn.plot.ly/plotly-2.9.0.min.js"></script>
```

❶   We'll use this container's ID to tell Plotly where to build the chart.

We can now build our first JS-native Plotly chart. The pattern matches that seen with the Python Plotly plots in our notebook. First, we create a data array (traces) with some chart-objects, then a layout to provide titles, labels, colors, etc. Then we use newPlot to build the chart. The main difference with Python is that the first parameter of newPlot is the ID of the container within which to build the chart:

```
var traces = [{ ❶
  type: 'violin',
  x: data.map(d => d.gender), ❷
  y: data.map(d => d.award_age),
  points: 'none',
  box: {
    visible: true
  },
```

```
    line: {
      color: 'green',
    },
    meanline: {
      visible: true
    },
  }]

  var layout = {
    title: "Nobel Prize Violin Plot",
    yaxis: {
      zeroline: false
    }
  }

  Plotly.newPlot('award_age', traces, layout);  ❸
```

❶ As per the usual Plotly pattern, we first create an array of chart-objects.

❷ We use the JS array's `map` method with shorthand arrow functions to produce arrays of winners' genders and ages.

❸ Plotly will render the chart to our `div` container with ID `'award_age'`.

The violin chart produced is shown in Figure 14-7.

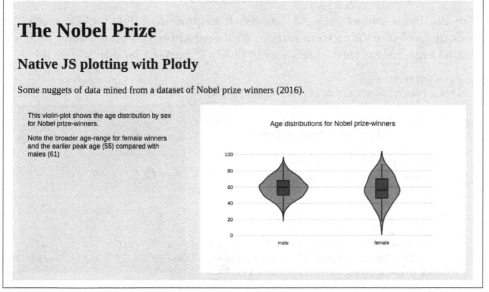

Figure 14-7. Violin plot with Plotly JS

As you can see, the Plotly's JS API matches the Python one and is, if anything, more succinct. Separating data delivery from chart construction makes the codebase much easier to work with and means tweaking and refinement don't require a return to the Python API. For small data sketches, parsing JSON strings gets the job done fast.

But if you want to have larger datasets to hand and to really leverage the power of the JS web context, the standard data delivery is through JSON files.[6] For datasets of a few megabytes, this offers the most flexibility for datavizzers.

Fetching JSON Files

Another way of getting data to your web pages is to export a DataFrame to JSON and then use JavaScript to fetch it, do any necessary further processing, and then pass it on to a native JS chart library (or D3). This is a very flexible workflow and provides the most freedom for JS data visualizations.

The separation of powers, allowing Python to focus on its data-processing strength and JavaScript its superior data-visualizing ability, provides a dataviz sweet spot and is the most common way of producing ambitious web dataviz.

First, we'll save our Nobel winners DataFrame to JSON using the dedicated method. Generally we'll want the data in the form of arrays of objects, which requires an `orient` parameter of `'records'`:

```
df.to_json('nobel_winners.json', orient='records')
```

With the JSON dataset to hand, lets use it to produce a Plotly chart using the JavaScript API as in the previous section. We'll need a little HTML, including an ID'ed container to build the chart in and a script link to import our JS code:

```
<!-- index.html -->
<link rel="stylesheet" href="styles/index.css">

<div class="main">
  <h1 class='title'>The Nobel Prize</h1>
  <!-- ... -->
    <div class="chart-wrapper">
      <div class='chart' id='gender-category'> </div> ❶
    </div>
  </div>
</div>

<script src="https://cdn.plot.ly/plotly-2.9.0.min.js"></script>
<script src="https://cdnjs.cloudflare.com/ajax/libs/d3/7.4.2/d3.min.js"></script>
<script src="scripts/index.js"></script> ❷
```

---

6 For more advanced, user-driven dataviz with large datasets, a data server with API is another route.

---

❶ We'll use the ID to tell Plotly where to build the chart.

❷ Import the index JS file from scripts folder.

In our JS entry point we use D3's `json` utility method to import the Nobel winners dataset and convert it to an array of JS objects. We then hand off the data to a `makeChart` function where Plotly will work its magic:

```
// scripts/index.js
d3.json('data/nobel_winners.json').then(data => {
  console.log("Dataset: ", data)
  makeChart(data)
})
```

The console shows our array of winners:

```
[
  {category: 'Physiology or Medicine', country: 'Argentina',
   date_of_birth: -1332806400000, date_of_death: 1016928000000,
   gender: 'male', …},
  {category: 'Peace', country: 'Belgium',
   date_of_birth: -4431715200000, date_of_death: -1806278400000,
   gender: 'male', …}
  [...]
]
```

In the `makeChart` function we use D3's very handy rollup method (*https://oreil.ly/wLVAZ*) to group our Nobel dataset by gender and category, and then provide the group sizes by taking the length of the arrays of members returned:

```
function makeChart(data) {
  let cat_groups = d3.rollup(data, v => v.length, ❶
                     d=>d.gender, d=>d.category)
  let male = cat_groups.get('male')
  let female = cat_groups.get('female')
  let categories = [...male.keys()].sort() ❷

  let traceM = {
    y: categories,
    x: categories.map(c => male.get(c)), ❸
    name: "male prize total",
    type: 'bar',
    orientation: 'h'
  }
    let traceF= {
    y: categories,
    x: categories.map(c => female.get(c)),
    name: "female prize total",
    type: 'bar',
    orientation: 'h'
  }
```

```
    let traces = [traceM, traceF]
    let layout = {barmode: 'group', margin: {l:160}} ❹

    Plotly.newPlot('gender-category', traces, layout)
}
```

❶ From the array of winner objects, `rollup` groups by gender, then category, and
then gives the array size/length of the resulting groups as a JS Map: `{male:
{Physics: 199, Economics: 74, ...}, female: {...}}`.

❷ We use the JS `...` spread operator (*https://oreil.ly/ZsIzM*) to produce an array
from the category keys, which is then sorted to produce our horizontal bar chart's
y values.

❸ We map the sorted categories to their group values to provide the bar chart
heights.

❹ We increase the left margin for our horizontal bar chart to accommodate long
labels.

The bar chart produced is shown in Figure 14-8. With the full Nobel winners dataset
available, it's easy to spin off a whole range of charts without having to switch context
from Python to JS. The Plotly API is pretty intuitive and discoverable, making it a
great addition to the dataviz toolset. Let's see how easy it is to extend it with a few
HTML+JS custom controls.

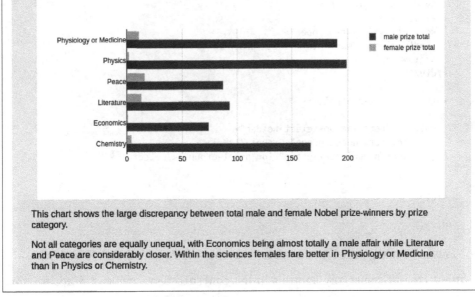

The Nobel Prize

From notebook to the web with Plotly

Some nuggets of data mined from a dataset of Nobel prize winners (2016).

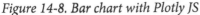

This chart shows the large discrepancy between total male and female Nobel prize-winners by prize category.

Not all categories are equally unequal, with Economics being almost totally a male affair while Literature and Peace are considerably closer. Within the sciences females fare better in Physiology or Medicine than in Physics or Chemistry.

Figure 14-8. Bar chart with Plotly JS

User-Driven Plotly with JavaScript and HTML

As we saw in "Adding Custom Controls with Plotly" on page 354, Plotly allows you to add custom controls such as buttons or dropdowns in Python, which can be transferred to the web as JS-driven HTML controls. Although this is a really useful feature of Plotly, it is a little limited, particularly in terms of placement and styling of these widgets. An alternative way to update Plotly web charts is to use native JS+HTML controls to change the charts, filtering the datasets or adapting the styling. It turns out this is pretty easy to do and, with a little JS know-how, it represents a more flexible and powerful control setup.

Let's demonstrate some JS custom control using one of the charts we just built in "Native JavaScript Charts with Plotly" on page 359. We'll add a dropdown to allow the user to change the x-axis group shown. The two obvious options are the existing breakdown by gender and one grouping the ages by prize category.

First, we'll add an HTML dropdown (`select`) to the page and center it using some flex-box CSS:

```
<div class="main">
  <h1 class='title'>The Nobel Prize</h1>
  <h2>From notebook to the web with Plotly</h2>

  <!-- ... -->
  <div class="container">
  <!-- ... -->
    <div class="chart-wrapper">
      <div class='chart' id='violin-group'> </div>
    </div>
  </div>

  <div id="chart-controls">

    <div id="nobel-group-select-holder">
      <label for="nobel-group">Group:</label>
      <select name="nobel-group" id="nobel-group"></select> ❶
    </div>

  </div>

</div>
```

❶ This `select` tag with contain `option` tags that will be added with JS and D3.

A little CSS will center any controls in the `controls` container and adapt the font style:

```
#chart-controls {
  display: flex;
  justify-content: center;
  font-family: sans-serif;
  font-size: 0.7em;
  margin: 20px 0;
}

select {
  padding: 2px;
}
```

Now that we've some HTML to build upon, we'll use some JS and D3 to add the `select` tags to our group controls. But first we'll adapt the Plotly charting function to allow it to be updated with new groups. The JSON data is imported as before, but now the data is stored as a local variable and used to update a Plotly violin chart. This `updateChart` function uses Plotly's `update` method (*https://oreil.ly/tayov*) to create the plot. This works like `newPlot` but is intended to be called when data or layout changes, efficiently redrawing the plot to reflect any changes.

We also have a new `selectedGroup` variable, which will be used in the dropdown `select` to change the field being plotted:

```
let data
d3.json("data/nobel_winners.json").then((_data) => {
  console.log(_data);
  data = _data
  updateChart();
});

let selectedGroup = 'gender' ❶

function updateChart() {
  var traces = [
    {
      type: "violin",
      x: data.map((d) => d[selectedGroup]), ❶
      y: data.map((d) => d.award_age),
      points: "none",
      box: {
        visible: true
      },
      line: {
        color: "green"
      },
      meanline: {
        visible: true
      }
    }
  ];

  var layout = {
    title: "Age distributions of the Nobel prizewinners",
    yaxis: {
      zeroline: false
    },
    xaxis: {
      categoryorder: 'category ascending' ❷
    }
  };

  Plotly.update("violin-group", traces, layout); ❸
}
```

❶ The `selectedGroup` variable allows the x-axis group to be changed by the user.

❷ We want the prize groups to be presented in alphabetical order (starting with *Chemistry*), so make this change to the layout.

❸ In place of `newPlot` we call `update`, which has the same signature but is used to reflect changes to data (`traces`) or layout.

With the `updateChart` method to hand, we now need to add the select options and a callback function to be called when the user changes the prize group:

```
let availableGroups = ['gender', 'category']
availableGroups.forEach((g) => {
  d3.select("#nobel-group") ❶
    .append("option")
    .property("selected", g === selectedGroup) ❷
    .attr("value", g)
    .text(g);
});

d3.select("#nobel-group").on("change", function (e) {
  selectedGroup = d3.select(this).property("value"); ❸
  updateChart();
});
```

❶ For each of the available groups, we use D3 to select the dropdown by ID and append an `<option>` tag with text and value set to the group string.

❷ This ensures that the initial selection is the value of `selectedGroup` by setting the `selected` attribute to true.

❸ We use D3 to add a callback function when a selection is made. Here we get the value of the option (*gender* or *category*) and use it to set the `selectedGroup` variable. We then update the chart to reflect this change.

With the wiring now complete, we have a group dropdown that changes the violin plot to reflect the group chosen. Figure 14-9 shows the result of selecting the prize category group. Note that Plotly helpfully rotates the category group labels to prevent overlap.

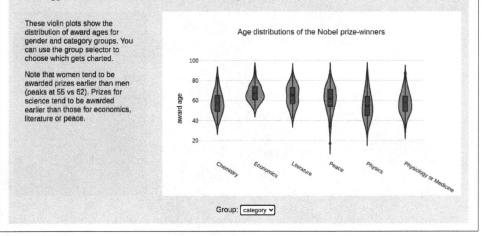

Figure 14-9. Adding a dropdown to control Plotly

We'll be seeing more HTML controls in action in later chapters where buttons and radio-boxes are demoed. Creating controls in JS is a lot more flexible than the Python-driven options at the cost of a small amount of web-dev fu.

Summary

In this chapter, we've seen how to turn the best charts from your notebook explorations into a web presentation. There are many options available, from static PNGs, with maybe some extra Matplotlib styling, to interactive Plotly charts, using custom JavaScript controls. Data can be embedded in the Plotly chart calls, produced using Plotly's offline library, or imported as a JSON string (nice for data sketches) or file.

Plotly is a good charting library, and in learning the Python API you pretty much learn the JS API as well—a big plus. For conventional and some specialized (e.g., machine learning) charts, it's a great option. For anything a little more bespoke or complex, D3 offers a lot more power, as we'll see in the upcoming chapters.

## CHAPTER 15

Imagining a Nobel Visualization

In Chapter 13, we explored the Nobel Prize dataset, looking for interesting stories to tell based on aspects of the data that should engage and educate. We found some interesting nuggets, among them:

- Maria Goeppert, the only female physicist other than Marie Curie to win a Physics Nobel
- The post-WWII surge of American Nobel prizes, passing the declining tallies of the three biggest European winners: the UK, Germany, and France
- The difference in continental prize distributions
- The dominance of the Scandinavian countries when prize tallies are adjusted for population size

These and a number of other narratives require particular types of visualization. Comparison of Nobel Prize numbers by nation is probably best achieved by means of a conventional bar chart, whereas geographic prize distributions demand a map. In this chapter, we will try to design a modern, interactive visualization that incorporates some of the key stories we discovered while exploring the dataset.

Who Is It For?

The first consideration when imagining a visualization is its target audience. A visualization intended for display in a gallery or museum will likely be very different from one intended for an in-house dashboard, even though they could use the same dataset. The Nobel Prize visualization anticipated for this book has as its chief constraint that it teach a key subset of D3 and the JavaScript needed to create a modern interactive web visualization. It is a fairly informal dataviz and should entertain and inform. It does not require a specialist audience.

Choosing Visual Elements

The first constraint on our Nobel Prize visualization is that it be simple enough to teach and provide a set of the key D3 skills. But even if that constraint was not in place, it is probably sensible to limit the scope of any visualization. This scope depends very much on the context,[1] but, as in many learning contexts, less is often more. Too much interactivity risks overwhelming the user and diluting the impact of any stories we might wish to tell.

With this in mind, let's look at the key elements we want to include and how these are to be visually arranged.

A menu bar of some sort is a must, allowing the user to engage with the visualization and manipulate the data. Its functionality will depend on the stories we choose to tell, but it will certainly provide some way to explore or filter the dataset.

Ideally, the visualization should display each prize by year and this display should update itself as the user refines the data through the menu bar. Given that national and regional trends are of interest, a map should be included, highlighting the prize-winning countries selected and giving some indication of their tally. A bar chart is the best way to compare the number of prizes by country, and this too should adapt dynamically to any data changes. There should also be a choice of measuring the absolute number of prizes by country or per capita, taking into account the respective population sizes.

In order to personalize the visualization, we should be able to select individual winners, showing any available picture and the short biography we scraped from Wikipedia. This requires a list of currently selected winners and a window in which to display the selected individual.

The aforementioned elements provide enough scope to tell the key stories we discovered in the last chapter, and with a bit of finessing should fit into a standard form factor.[2]

Our Nobel Prize visualization uses a fixed size for all devices, which means compromising larger devices with higher resolutions in order to accommodate smaller ones, such as last-generation smartphones or tablets. I find that for a lot of visualization work, a fixed size gives you much-needed control over specific placement of visual content blocks, information boxes, labels, and so on. For some visualizations, particularly multielement dashboards, a different approach may be required. Responsive

---

1 A specialized dashboard, designed for experts, could tolerate more functionality than a general-purpose educational visualization.

2 With a pixel measure, it's worth keeping track of changing device resolutions. As of May 2022, pretty much all devices will accommodate a 1,000×800 pixel visualization.

web design (RWD) (*https://oreil.ly/AURTe*) attempts to adapt the look and feel of your visualization to optimize for the specific device. Some popular CSS libraries such as Bootstrap (*https://getbootstrap.com*) detect the device size (e.g., a tablet with resolution of 1,280×800 pixels) and change the stylesheet applied in order to get the most out of the available screen real estate. Specifying a fixed size for your visualization and using absolute positioning within it is the way to go if you require pinpoint control of the placement of your visual elements. However, you should be aware of the challenges of RWD, particularly when required to build multicomponent dashboards and the like.

Now let's aim to pin down the look, feel, and requirements of the individual elements of our Nobel Prize visualization, beginning with the main user control, the menu bar.

Menu Bar

An interactive visualization is driven by the user selecting from options, clicking on things, manipulating sliders, and so on. These allow the user to define the scope of the visualization, which is why we'll deal with them first. Our user controls will appear as a toolbar at the top of the visualization.

A standard way to drive interesting discoveries is to allow the user to filter the data in key dimensions. The obvious options for our Nobel Prize visualization are category, gender, and country, the focus of our exploration in the last chapter. These filters should be cumulative, so, for example, selecting gender female and category Physics should return the two winning female physicists. In addition to those filters, we should have a radio button to choose between absolute and per capita numbers of national prize winners.

Figure 15-1 shows a menu bar that meets our requirements. Placed at the top of our visualization, it has selectors to filter our required dimensions and a radio button to select our national winner metric, either absolute or per capita.

Figure 15-1. The user's controls

The menu bar will sit atop the key component of our visualization, a chart showing all the Nobel Prizes over time. Let's describe that next.

Prizes by Year

The last chapter showed a lot of interesting historical trends in the Nobel Prizes by country. We also saw that although female recipients have increased recently, they are way behind in the sciences. One way of allowing these trends to be discovered is to show all the Nobel Prizes on a timeline and provide a filter to select the prizes by gender, country, and category (using the menu bar just discussed).

If we make our visualization 1,000 pixels wide, then, with 114 years of prizes to cover, we are allowed around 8 pixels per prize, enough to differentiate them. The highest number of prizes awarded in any one year is 14, in the year 2000, giving a minimal height for this element of 8×14 pixels, around 120. A circle, color-coded by category, seems a good way to represent the individual prizes, giving us a chart something like the one shown in Figure 15-2.

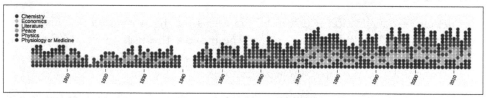

Figure 15-2. A timeline of Nobel Prizes by year, color-coded by category

The individual prizes are the essence of the visualization, so we'll place this timeline prominently at the top above our central element, which should be a map, reflecting the international nature of the prize and allowing the user to see any global trends.

A Map Showing Selected Nobel Countries

Mapping is one of D3's strengths, with many global projections available, from the classic Mercator to 3D spherical presentations.[3] Though maps are obviously engaging, they are also often overused and inappropriate when presenting nongeographical data. For example, unless you're careful, large geographical areas, such as countries in Europe or states of the US, tend to outweigh smaller ones even when the latter have far larger populations. When you are presenting demographic information, this skew is hard to avoid and misrepresentation can result.[4]

But the Nobel Prize is an international one and the distribution of prizes by continent is of interest, making a global map a good way to depict the filtered data. If we

---

3 These 3D orthographic projections are "fake" in the sense that they do not use a 3D graphics context, such as WebGL. There are some nice examples from Jason Davies (*https://oreil.ly/E7Rf3*), observablehq (*https://oreil.ly/mi2TC*), and nullschool (*https://oreil.ly/dLUlD*).

4 See xkcd (*https://xkcd.com/1138*) for an example.

---

superimpose a filled circle at the center of each country to reflect the prize measure (absolute or per capita), then we avoid skewing in favor of the larger land masses. In Europe, with many relatively small countries by land mass, these circles will intersect. By making them slightly transparent,[5] we can still see the superimposed circles and, by adding the opacities, give a sense of prize density. Figure 15-3 demonstrates this.

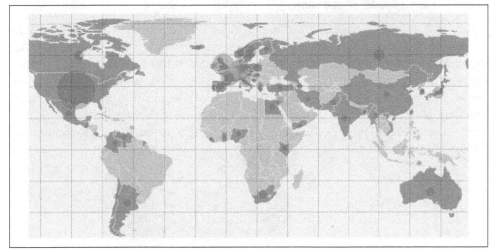

Figure 15-3. Global distribution of prizes

We'll provide a little tooltip for the map, both as a way of demonstrating how to build this handy visual component and also to help a little with naming the countries. Figure 15-4 shows what we're aiming for.

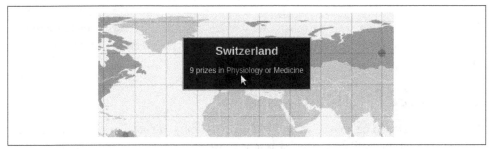

Figure 15-4. A simple tooltip for our Nobel Prize map

The last of the larger elements will be placed below the map: a bar chart allowing the user to make clear comparisons of the number of Nobel Prizes by country.

---

5 By adjusting the alpha channel in the RGBA code with the CSS property `opacity`, from 0 (none) to 1 (full).

A Bar Chart Showing Number of Winners by Country

There is a lot of evidence that bar charts are great for making numeric comparisons.[6] A reconfigurable bar chart gives our visualization a lot of flexibility, allowing it to present the results of user-directed data filtering, choice of metric (i.e., absolute versus per capita counts), and more.

Figure 15-5 shows the bar chart we'll use to compare the prize hauls of chosen countries. Both the axes ticks and bars should respond dynamically to user interaction, driven by the menu bar (see Figure 15-1). An animated transition between bar chart states would be good and (as we'll see in "Transitions" on page 432) pretty much comes free with D3. As well as being attractive, there's reason to think such transitions are also effective communicators. See this Stanford University paper (*https://stanford.io/1Ue3cBR*) on the effectiveness of animated transitions in data visualization for some insights.

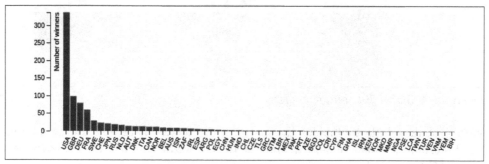

Figure 15-5. A bar chart component

To the side of the map and bar chart, we'll place a list of currently selected winners and a biography box, allowing the user to discover something about individual winners.

A List of the Selected Winners

We want the user to be able to select individual winners, displaying a mini-biography and picture when available. The easiest way to achieve this is to have a list box, showing the currently selected winners, filtered from the full dataset using the menu bar selectors. Ordering these by year, in descending order, is a sensible default. And although we could allow the list to be sorted by column, it seems an unnecessary complication.

---

6 See Stephen Few's insightful blog post (*https://oreil.ly/TAK5T*).

A simple HTML table with column headers should do the job here. It will look something like Figure 15-6.

Selected winners

Year	Category	Name
2014	Physics	Shuji Nakamura
2014	Chemistry	Eric Betzig
2014	Chemistry	William E. Moerner
2014	Physiology or Medicine	John O'Keefe
2014	Peace	Malala Yousafzai
2014	Physiology or Medicine	Edvard Moser
2014	Physiology or Medicine	May-Britt Moser
2014	Physics	Isamu Akasaki
2014	Physics	Hiroshi Amano
2014	Peace	Kailash Satyarthi
2014	Chemistry	Stefan Hell
2014	Literature	Patrick Modiano
2014	Economics	Jean Tirole
2013	Chemistry	Arieh Warshel
2013	Chemistry	Michael Levitt
2013	Chemistry	Martin Karplus
2013	Physiology or Medicine	Randy Schekman
2013	Physiology or Medicine	Thomas C. Südhof
2013	Physiology or Medicine	James Rothman
2013	Economics	Eugene F. Fama

Figure 15-6. A list of selected winners

The list will have clickable rows, allowing the user to select an individual winner to be displayed in our last element, a small biography box.

A Mini-Biography Box with Picture

The Nobel Prize is given to individuals, each with a story to tell. To both humanize and enrich our visualization, we should use the individual mini-biographies and images we scraped from Wikipedia (see Chapter 6) to display the result of selecting an individual from our list element.

Figure 15-7 shows a biography box with a colored top border indicating the category of prize, with colors shared by our time chart (Figure 15-2), a top-right photograph (when available), and the first few paragraphs of Wikipedia's biographic entry.

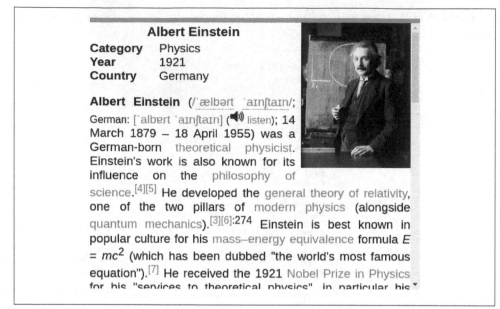

Albert Einstein

Category Physics
Year   1921
Country Germany

Albert Einstein (/ˈælbərt ˈaɪnʃtaɪn/;
German: [ˈalbɛʁt ˈaɪnʃtaɪn] (🔊 listen); 14
March 1879 – 18 April 1955) was a
German-born theoretical physicist.
Einstein's work is also known for its
influence on the philosophy of
science.[4][5] He developed the general theory of relativity,
one of the two pillars of modern physics (alongside
quantum mechanics).[3][6]:274 Einstein is best known in
popular culture for his mass–energy equivalence formula E
$= mc^2$ (which has been dubbed "the world's most famous
equation").[7] He received the 1921 Nobel Prize in Physics
for his "services to theoretical physics" in particular his

Figure 15-7. A mini-biography of the selected winner with picture, if available

The bio-box completes our set of visual components. We can now put them together in our specified 1,000×800 pixel frame.

The Complete Visualization

Figure 15-8 shows our complete Nobel Prize visualization with the five key elements plus the topmost user controls arranged to fit in a 1,000×800 pixel frame. Because we decided our timeline should take pride of place and the global map rather demanded the center, the other elements order themselves. The bar chart needs extra width to accommodate the labeled bars of all 58 countries, while the list of selected winners and mini-bio fit nicely to the right.

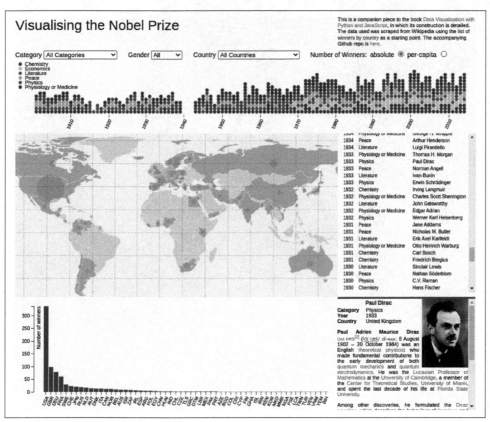

Figure 15-8. The complete Nobel Prize visualization

Let's summarize our imaginings before proceeding to the next chapter, where we'll see how to realize them.

Summary

In this chapter, we imagined our Nobel visualization, establishing a minimal set of visual elements necessary to tell the key stories discovered during our explorations of the last chapter. These fit neatly into our complete creation, shown in Figure 15-8. In the next chapters, I will show you how to build the individual elements and how to stitch them together to form a modern, interactive web visualization. We'll start with a gentle introduction to D3, by way of the simple story of a bar chart.

## CHAPTER 16

Building a Visualization

In Chapter 15, we used the results of our pandas exploration of the Nobel Prize dataset (see Chapter 11) to imagine a visualization. Figure 16-1 shows the visualization we imagined, and in this chapter we'll see how to go about building it, leveraging the power of JavaScript and D3.

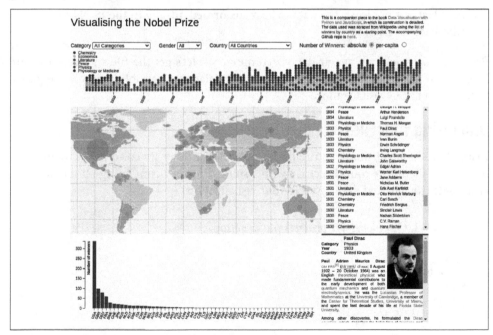

Figure 16-1. Our target, a Nobel Prize visualization

I'll show how the visual elements we conceived combine to transform our freshly cleaned and processed Nobel dataset into an interactive web visualization, deployable to billions of devices at the flick of a switch. But before going into the details, let's have a look at the core components of a modern web visualization.

Preliminaries

Before beginning to build the Nobel visualization, let's consider the core components that will be used and how we will organize our files.

Core Components

As we saw in "A Basic Page with Placeholders" on page 95, building a modern web visualization requires four key components:

- An HTML skeleton upon which to hang our JavaScripted creation
- One or more CSS files to govern the look and feel of the dataviz
- The JavaScript files themselves, including any third-party libraries you might need (D3 being our biggest dependency)
- And last but not least, the data to be transformed, ideally in the JSON or CSV (if wholly static data) format

Before we start looking at our dataviz components, let's get the file structure for our Nobel Prize visualization (Nobel-viz) project in place and establish how we're going to feed data to our visualization.

Organizing Your Files

Example 16-1 shows the structure of our project directory. By convention we have an *index.html* file in the root directory with a *static* directory containing all the libraries and assets (images and data) used for our visualization.

Example 16-1. Our Nobel-viz project's file structure

```
nobel_viz
├── index.html
└── static
    ├── css
    │   └── style.css
    ├── data                ❶
    │   ├── nobel_winners_biopic.json
    │   ├── winning_country_data.json
    │   ├── world-110m.json
    │   └── world-country-names-nobel.csv
    ├── images
```

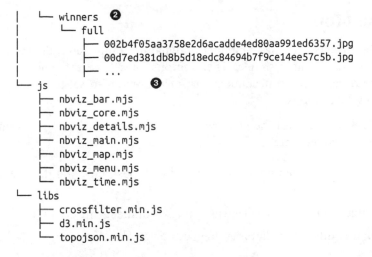

```
        │     └── winners  ❷
        │           └── full
        │                 ├── 002b4f05aa3758e2d6acadde4ed80aa991ed6357.jpg
        │                 ├── 00d7ed381db8b5d18edc84694b7f9ce14ee57c5b.jpg
        │                 ├── ...
        └── js                  ❸
              ├── nbviz_bar.mjs
              ├── nbviz_core.mjs
              ├── nbviz_details.mjs
              ├── nbviz_main.mjs
              ├── nbviz_map.mjs
              ├── nbviz_menu.mjs
              └── nbviz_time.mjs
        └── libs
              ├── crossfilter.min.js
              ├── d3.min.js
              └── topojson.min.js
```

❶ The static data files we'll be using, including a TopoJSON world map (see Chapter 19) and the country data we grabbed from the web (see "Getting Country Data for the Nobel Dataviz" on page 128).

❷ The Nobel Prize winners' photos we scraped using Scrapy in "Scraping Text and Images with a Pipeline" on page 173.

❸ The *js* subdirectory contains our Nobel-viz JavaScript module files (*.mjs*), separated into core elements and starting with *nbviz_*.

Serving the Data

The full Nobel dataset with the mini-biographies that we scraped in Chapter 6 amounts to around three megabytes of data, considerably less when compressed for web transport. By the standards of modern web pages, that's not a huge amount of data. In fact, average web page size is somewhere around 2MB to 3MB.[1] Nevertheless it's approaching a point where we might consider breaking it into smaller chunks that could be loaded on a need-to-use basis. We could also serve the data dynamically from a web server (see Chapter 13) with a database like SQLite. As it is, the small inconvenience of an initial wait time is compensated by speedy performance thereafter, as all the data is cached by the browser. It also makes things a lot simpler having just one initial fetching of data.

For our Nobel visualization we'll serve all the data from a data directory (see Example 16-1, #2), fetched as the app is initialized.

---

[1] See these SpeedCurve (*https://oreil.ly/ngdOJ*) and Web Almanac (*https://oreil.ly/qIvox*) posts for some analysis of average web page size.

The HTML Skeleton

Although our Nobel visualization has a number of dynamic components, the HTML skeleton required is surprisingly simple. This demonstrates a core theme of the book—that you need very little conventional web development to set the stage for programming data visualizations.

The *index.html* file, which creates the visualization on loading, is shown in Example 16-2. The three components are:

1. A CSS stylesheet *style.css*, setting fonts, content-block positions, and the like, is imported.

2. HTML placeholders for our visual elements with IDs of the form `nobel-[foo]`.

3. The JavaScript; first third-party libraries, then our original scripts.

We'll cover the individual HTML sections in detail in the coming chapters, but I wanted you to see what is essentially the entire nonprogrammatic element of the Nobel Prize visualization. With this skeleton in place, you can then turn to the job of creative programming, something D3 encourages and excels at. As you get used to defining your content blocks in HTML, and fixing dimensions and positioning with CSS, you'll find you spend more and more time doing what you love best: manipulating data with code.

 I find it helpful to treat the identified placeholders, such as the map holder `<div id="nobel-map"></div>`, as panels *owned* by their respective elements. We set the dimension and relative positioning of these frames in the main CSS or JS[2] file and the elements, such as our dynamic map, adapt themselves to the size of their frame. This allows a nonprogramming designer to change the look and feel of the visualization through CSS styling.

Example 16-2. The index.html access file to our single-page visualization

```
<!DOCTYPE html>
<meta charset="utf-8">
<title>Visualizing the Nobel Prize</title>
<!-- 1. IMPORT THE visualization'S CSS STYLING -->
<link rel="stylesheet" href="static/css/style.css"
media="screen" />
<body>
  <div id='chart'>
    <!-- 2. A HEADER WITH TITLE AND SOME EXPLANATORY INFO -->
```

---

2 I would advise saving JavaScripted styling for special occasions, doing as much as possible with vanilla CSS.

```html
<div id='title'>Visualizing the Nobel Prize</div>
<div id="info">
  This is a companion piece to the book <a href='http://'>
  Data visualization with Python and JavaScript</a>, in which
  its construction is detailed. The data used was scraped
  Wikipedia using the <a href=
  'https://en.wikipedia.org/wiki
  /List_of_Nobel_laureates_by_country'>
  list of winners by country</a> as a starting point. The
  accompanying GitHub repo is <a href=
  'http://github.com/Kyrand/dataviz-with-python-and-js-ed-2'>
  here</a>.
</div>
<!-- 3. THE PLACEHOLDERS FOR OUR VISUAL COMPONENTS  -->
<div id="nbviz">
  <!-- BEGIN MENU BAR -->
  <div id="nobel-menu">
    <div id="cat-select">
      Category
      <select></select>
    </div>
    <div id="gender-select">
      Gender
      <select>
        <option value="All">All</option>
        <option value="female">Female</option>
        <option value="male">Male</option>
      </select>
    </div>
    <div id="country-select">
      Country
      <select></select>
    </div>
    <div id='metric-radio'>
      Number of Winners: 
      <form>
        <label>absolute
          <input type="radio" name="mode" value="0" checked>
        </label>
        <label>per-capita
          <input type="radio" name="mode" value="1">
        </label>
      </form>
    </div>
  </div>
  <!-- END MENU BAR  -->
  <!-- BEGIN NOBEL-VIZ COMPONENTS -->
  <div id='chart-holder' class='_dev'>
    <!-- TIME LINE OF PRIZES -->
    <div id="nobel-time"></div>
    <!-- MAP AND TOOLTIP -->
    <div id="nobel-map">
```

```html
          <div id="map-tooltip">
            <h2></h2>
            <p></p>
          </div>
        </div>
        <!-- LIST OF WINNERS -->
        <div id="nobel-list">
          <h2>Selected winners</h2>
          <table>
            <thead>
              <tr>
                <th id='year'>Year</th>
                <th id='category'>Category</th>
                <th id='name'>Name</th>
              </tr>
            </thead>
            <tbody>
            </tbody>
          </table>
        </div>
        <!-- BIOGRAPHY BOX -->
        <div id="nobel-winner">
          <div id="picbox"></div>
          <div id='winner-title'></div>
          <div id='infobox'>
            <div class='property'>
              <div class='label'>Category</div>
              <span name='category'></span>
            </div>
            <div class='property'>
              <div class='label'>Year</div>
              <span name='year'></span>
            </div>
            <div class='property'>
              <div class='label'>Country</div>
              <span name='country'></span>
            </div>
          </div>
          <div id='biobox'></div>
          <div id='readmore'>
            <a href='#'>Read more at Wikipedia</a>
          </div>
        </div>
        <!-- NOBEL BAR CHART -->
        <div id="nobel-bar"></div>
      </div>
      <!-- END NOBEL-VIZ COMPONENTS -->
    </div>
  </div>
  <!-- 4. THE JAVASCRIPT FILES -->
  <!-- THIRD-PARTY JAVASCRIPT LIBRARIES, MAINLY D3  -->
  <script src="libs/d3.min.js"></script>
```

```
<!-- ... -->
<!-- THE MAIN JAVASCRIPT MODULE FOR OUR NOBEL ELEMENTS -->
<script src="static/js/nbviz_main.mjs" ></script>
</body>
```

The HTML skeleton (Example 16-2) defines the hierarchical structure of our Nobel-viz components, but their visual sizing and positioning are set in the *style.css* file. In the next section, we'll see how this is done and look at the general styling of our visualization.

CSS Styling

We'll deal with the styling of the individual chart components of our chart (Figure 16-1) in their respective chapters. This section will cover the remaining nonspecific CSS, most importantly the sizing and positioning of our elements' content blocks (*panels*).

The size of a visualization can be a tricky choice. There are many more device formats out there these days, with smartphones, tablets, mobile devices, etc. having a variety of different resolutions, such as "retina,"[3] and full HD (1,920×1,080). So pixel sizes are much more varied than they used to be, and pixel density becomes a more meaningful metric. Most devices perform pixel scaling to compensate for this, which is why you can still read the text on a smartphone even though it has as many pixels as a large desktop monitor. Also, most handheld devices have pinch-and-zoom and pan, allowing the user to easily focus on regions of a larger dataviz. For our Nobel dataviz we'll choose a compromise resolution of 1,280×800 pixels, which should look OK on most desktop monitors and be usable in landscape mode on a mobile device, including our 50-pixel-high top-most user controls.

First, we set some general styles we want applied to the whole document using the body selector; a sans-serif font, an off-white background, and some link detailing are specified. We also set the width of the visualization and its margins:

```
body {
    font-family: "Helvetica Neue", Helvetica, Arial, sans-serif;
    background: #fefefe; ❶
    width: 1000px;
    margin: 0 auto; /* top and bottom 0, left and right auto */
}

a:link {
    color: royalblue;
    text-decoration: none; ❷
}
```

---

3 Currently around 2,560×1,600 pixels.

```
a:hover {
    text-decoration: underline;
}
```

 This color is just off full-white (#ffffff) and should help to make the page slightly less bright and easier on the eyes.

❷ The default underlined hyperlinks look a bit fussy in my opinion, so we remove decoration.

There are three main div content blocks to our Nobel-viz, which we position absolutely within the #chart div (their relative parent). These are the main title (#title), some information on the visualization (#info), and the main container (#nbviz). The title and info are placed by eye and the main container is placed 90 pixels from the page top to allow them room, and given a width of 100% to make it expand to the available space. The following CSS achieves this:

```
#nbviz {
    position: absolute;
    top: 90px;
    width: 100%;
}

#title {
    position: absolute;
    font-size: 30px;
    font-weight: 100;
    top: 20px;
}

#info {
    position: absolute;
    font-size: 11px;
    top: 18px;
    width: 300px;
    right: 0px;
    line-height: 1.2;
}
```

The chart-holder is given a height of 750 px, a width of 100% its parent, and a position property of relative, meaning the absolute positioning of its child panels will be relative to its top-left corner. The bottom of our charts is padded by 20 pixels:

```
#chart-holder {
    width: 100%;
    height: 750px;
    position: relative;
    padding: 0 0 20px 0; /* top right bottom left */
}

#chart-holder svg { ❶
    width: 100%;
    height: 100%;
}
```

❶   We want the SVG contexts for our components to expand to fit their containers.

Allowing for the Nobel-viz's height constraint of 750 pixels, the width/height ratio of two for our equirectangular map,[4] and the need to fit over 100 years' worth of Nobel Prize circular indicators into our time chart, playing with the dimensions suggests Figure 16-2 as a good compromise for the size of our visual elements.

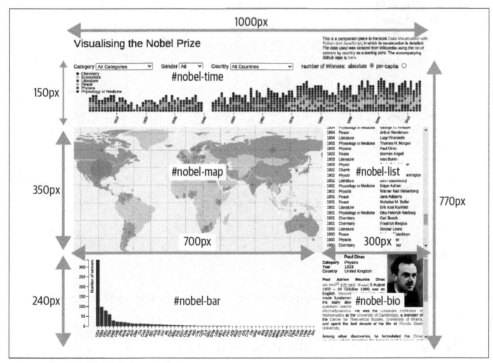

Figure 16-2. The Nobel-viz's dimensions

---

4 See "Projections" on page 458 for a comparison of the different geometric projections. Given the constraint of showing all Nobel Prize–winning countries, the equirectangular projection proved most effective.

This CSS positions and sizes the components as shown in Figure 16-2:

```css
#nobel-map, #nobel-winner, #nobel-bar, #nobel-time, #nobel-list{
    position:absolute; ❶
}

#nobel-time {
    top: 0;
    height: 150px;
    width: 100%; ❷
}

#nobel-map {
    background: azure;
    top: 160px;
    width: 700px;
    height: 350px;
}

#nobel-winner {
    top: 510px;
    left: 700px;
    height: 240px;
    width: 300px;
}

#nobel-bar {
    top: 510px;
    height: 240px;
    width: 700px;
}

#nobel-list {
    top: 160px;
    height: 340px;
    width: 290px;
    left: 700px;
    padding-left: 10px; ❸
}
```

❶ We want absolute, manually adjusted positioning, relative to the chart-holder parent container.

❷ The timeline runs the full width of the visualization.

❸ You can use padding to let the components "breathe."

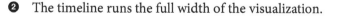

The other CSS styles are specific to the individual components and will be covered in their respective chapters. With the preceding CSS, we have an HTML skeleton on which to flesh out our visualization with JavaScript.

The JavaScript Engine

With a visualization of any size, it's good to start imposing some modularity early on. Many of the D3 examples on the web[5] are one-page solutions, combining HTML, CSS, JS, and even data on one page. Though this is great for teaching by example, as the codebase increases, things will degenerate fast, making changes a slog and increasing the chance of namespace collisions and the like.

Importing the Scripts

We include the JavaScript files for our visualization using <script> tags placed at the bottom of the <body> tag in our entry *index.html* file, as shown in Example 16-2:

```
<!DOCTYPE html>
<meta charset="utf-8">
...
<body>
...
  <!-- THIRD-PARTY JAVASCRIPT LIBRARIES, MAINLY D3 BASED  --> ❶
  <script src="static/libs/d3.min.js"></script>
  <script src="static/libs/topojson.min.js"></script>
  <script src="static/libs/crossfilter.min.js"></script>
  <!-- THE JAVASCRIPT FOR OUR NOBEL ELEMENTS -->
  <script src="static/js/nbviz_main.mjs"></script> ❷
</body>
```

❶ We use local copies of the third-party libraries.

❷ The main entry point for our Nobel app, where it requests its first datasets and sets the display ball rolling. This module imports all the others used by the visualization.

---

5 See the collection at D3's GitHub (*https://oreil.ly/khvac*).

Modular JS with Imports

In the first edition of this book, a common but rather hacky pattern was used to establish an nbviz namespace within which to place functions, variables, constants, etc. used by the various components of the Nobel dataviz. Here's an example, as you may well run into similar patterns in the wild:

```
/* js/nbviz_core.js
/* global $, _, crossfilter, d3  */ ❶
(function(nbviz) {
    //... MODULES PRIVATE VARS ETC..
    nbviz.foo = function(){ //... ❷
    };
}(window.nbviz = window.nbviz || {})); ❸
```

❶ Defining variables as global will prevent them triggering JSLint errors (*https://www.jslint.com*).

❷ Exposes this function to other scripts as part of shared nbviz namespace.

❸ Uses the nbviz object if available, and creates it otherwise.

Each JS script was encapsulated with this pattern and all required scripts were included with a <script> tag in the main *index.html* entry point. With the arrival of cross-browser support for JS modules, we have a much cleaner, modern way of including our JavaScript with modular imports familiar to any Pythonista (see "JavaScript Modules" on page 18).

We now have only to include our main JS module in *index.html*, and that will import all the other modules required:

```
// static/js/nbviz_main.mjs
import nbviz from './nbviz_core.mjs'
import { initMenu } from './nbviz_menu.mjs'
import { initMap } from './nbviz_map.mjs'
import './nbviz_bar.mjs' ❶
import './nbviz_details.mjs'
import './nbviz_time.mjs'
```

 These are imported to initialize their update callbacks. We'll see how that works later in the chapter.

In the coming chapters, the JavaScript/D3 used to produce the visualization's elements will be explained in detail. First, we'll deal with the flow of data through the Nobel-viz, from the (data) server to the client browser and within the client, driven by user interaction.

Basic Data Flow

There are many ways to deal with data in a project of any complexity. For interactive apps, and particularly data visualizations, I find the most robust pattern is to have a central data object to cache current data. In addition to the cached data, we also have some active reflections or subsets of this dataset, stored in the main data object. For example, in our Nobel-viz a user can select a number of subsets of the data (e.g., only those winners in the Physics category).

If a different data reflection is triggered by the user, such as by choosing the per capita prize metric, a flag[6] is set (in this case, valuePerCapita is set to 0 or 1). We then update all the visual components, and those that depend on valuePerCapita adapt accordingly. The size of the map indicators changes and the bar chart reorganizes.

The key idea is to make sure the visual elements are synchronized to any user-driven data changes. A reliable way to do this is to have a single update method (here called onDataChange) that is called whenever a user does something to change the data. This method alerts all the active visual elements to the changed data and they respond accordingly.

Let's now see how the app's code fits together, starting with the shared core utilities.

The Core Code

The first JavaScript file loaded is *nbviz_core.js*. This script contains any code we might want to share among the other scripts. For example, we have a categoryFill method that returns a specific color for each category. This is used by both the timeline

---

6 In our app, I'm keeping things as simple as possible; as the number of UI options increases, it's sensible to store flags, ranges, etc. in a dedicated object.

component and as a border in the biography box. This core code includes functions we might want to isolate for testing, or simply to make other modules less cluttered.

 Often in programming we use string constants as dictionary keys and comparatives, and in generated labels. It's easy to slip into the bad habit of typing these strings when required, but a much better way is to define a constant variable instead. For example, rather than `'if option === "All Categories"'`, we use `'if option === nbviz.ALL_CATS'`. In the former option, mistyping `'All Cat egories'` will not flag an error, an accident waiting to happen. Having a `const` also means only one edit is needed to change all occurrences of the string. JavaScript has a newish `const` keyword that makes enforcing constancy a bit easier, though it only prevents variables from being reassigned. See the Mozilla documentation (*https://oreil.ly/AlEbm*) for some examples and a breakdown of `const` limitations.

Example 16-3 shows the code shared between the other modules. Anything intended to be used by other modules is attached to the shared `nbviz` namespace.

Example 16-3. Shared codebase in nbviz_core.js

```
let nbviz = {}
nbviz.ALL_CATS = 'All Categories'
nbviz.TRANS_DURATION = 2000 // time in ms for our visual transitions
nbviz.MAX_CENTROID_RADIUS = 30
nbviz.MIN_CENTROID_RADIUS = 2
nbviz.COLORS = { palegold: '#E6BE8A' } // any named colors used

nbviz.data = {} // our main data store
nbviz.valuePerCapita = 0 // metric flag
nbviz.activeCountry = null
nbviz.activeCategory = nbviz.ALL_CATS

nbviz.CATEGORIES = [
    "Chemistry", "Economics", "Literature", "Peace",
    "Physics", "Physiology or Medicine"
];
// takes a category like Physics and returns a color
nbviz.categoryFill = function(category){
    var i = nbviz.CATEGORIES.indexOf(category);
    return d3.schemeCategory10[i]; ❶
};

let nestDataByYear = function(entries) {          ❷
//...
};
```

```
nbviz.makeFilterAndDimensions = function(winnersData){
//...
};

nbviz.filterByCountries = function(countryNames) {
//...
};

nbviz.filterByCategory = function(cat) {
//...
};

nbviz.getCountryData = function() {
// ...
};

nbviz.callbacks = []
nbviz.onDataChange = function () {  ❸
  nbviz.callbacks.forEach((cb) => cb())
}

export default nbviz  ❹
```

❶ We use one of D3's built-in color schemes to provide our prize category
colors. `schemeCategory10` is an array of 10 color hex codes (`['#1f77b4',
'#ff7f0e',...]`), which we access using the category indices.

❷ This and the following empty methods will be explained in detail in the following
chapters in a use context.

❸ This function is called when the dataset changes (after initialization of the app,
this is user-driven) to update the Nobel-viz elements. Update callbacks set by
the component modules and stored in the `callbacks` array are called in turn,
triggering any necessary visual changes. See "Basic Data Flow" on page 393 for
details.

❹ The `nbviz` object, with utility functions, constants, and variables, is the default
export for this module, imported by other modules, thus `import nbviz from
./nbviz_core`.

With the core code at hand, let's see how our app is initialized by fetching static
resources using D3's utility methods.

Initializing the Nobel Prize Visualization

In order to start the app, we need some data. We use D3's `json` and `csv` helper
functions to load the data and convert it to JavaScript objects and arrays. The

`Promise.all`[7] method is used to fire off these data fetches simultaneously, wait for all four to be resolved, and then deliver the data to a specified handler function, in this case `ready`:

```
// static/js/nbviz_main.mjs
//...
  Promise.all([ ❶
    d3.json('static/data/world-110m.json'),
    d3.csv('static/data/world-country-names-nobel.csv'),
    d3.json('static/data/winning_country_data.json'),
    d3.json('static/data/nobel_winners_biopic.json'),
  ]).then(ready)

  function ready([worldMap, countryNames, countryData, winnersData]) { ❷
    // STORE OUR COUNTRY-DATA DATASET
    nbviz.data.countryData = countryData
    nbviz.data.winnersData = winnersData
    //...
}
```

❶ Fire off simultaneous requests for the four data files. The static files consist of a world map (110m resolution) and some country data we'll be using in the visualization.

❷ The array returned to `ready` uses JavaScript destructuring (*https://oreil.ly/ RZzXm*) to assign the sequential data to its respective variables.

If our data requests are successful, the `ready` function receives the requested data and we're ready to start sending data to the visual elements.

Ready to Go

After the deferred requests for data made by the `Promise.all` method are resolved, it calls the specified `ready` function, passing the datasets as arguments in the order in which they were added.

The `ready` function is shown in Example 16-4. If the data has downloaded without error, we use the winners' data to create the active filter (courtesy of the Crossfilter library) we will use to allow the user to select subsets of the Nobel winners based on category, gender, and country. We then call some initializer methods, and finally use the `onDataChange` method to trigger a drawing of the visual elements of dataviz, updating bar chart, map, timeline, and so on. The schematic in Figure 16-3 shows the way in which data changes propagate.

---

7 You can read more about `Promise.all` in the Mozilla documentation (*https://oreil.ly/67Odo*).

Example 16-4. The ready function is called when the initial data requests have resolved

```
//...
    function ready([worldMap, countryNames, countryData, winnersData]) {
        // STORE OUR COUNTRY-DATA DATASET
        nbviz.data.countryData = countryData
        nbviz.data.winnersData = winnersData
        // MAKE OUR FILTER AND ITS DIMENSIONS
        nbviz.makeFilterAndDimensions(winnersData) ❶
        // INITIALIZE MENU AND MAP
        initMenu()
        initMap(worldMap, countryNames)
        // TRIGGER UPDATE WITH FULL WINNERS' DATASET
        nbviz.onDataChange()
    }
```

❶ This method uses the freshly loaded Nobel Prize dataset to create the filter we will use to allow the user to select subsets of the data to visualize. See "Filtering Data with Crossfilter" on page 400 for details.

We'll see how the `makeFilterAndDimensions` method (Example 16-4, ❶) works when we cover the Crossfilter library in "Filtering Data with Crossfilter" on page 400. For now, we'll assume we have a means of getting the data currently selected by the user via some menu selectors (e.g., selecting all female winners).

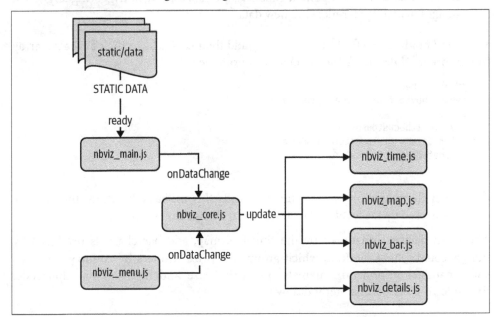

Figure 16-3. The app's main data flow

Data-Driven Updates

After the menu and map have been initialized in the ready function (we'll see how that works in their respective chapters: Chapter 19 for the map and Chapter 21 for the menu), we trigger an update of the visual elements with the onDataChange method defined in *nbviz_core.js*. onDataChange (see Example 16-5) is a shared function that is called whenever the set of displayed data changes in response to user interaction, or when the user chooses a different country prize metric (e.g., measuring per capita rather than absolute numbers).

Example 16-5. Function called to update the visual elements when selected data is changed

```
// nbviz_core.js
nbviz.callbacks = [] ❶

nbviz.onDataChange = function () {
  nbviz.callbacks.forEach((cb) => cb()) ❷
}
```

❶ Each component module that needs updating appends its callback to this array.

❷ On data change the component callbacks are called in turn, triggering any visual changes necessary to reflect the new data.

When the modules are first imported, they add their callbacks to the callbacks array in the core module. Here's the bar chart, for example:

```
// nbviz_bar.mjs
import nbviz from './nbviz_core.mjs'
// ...
nbviz.callbacks.push(() => {
  let data = nbviz.getCountryData()
  updateBarChart(data) ❶
})
```

❶ When the main core update function calls this callback function, the country data is used by the local update function to change the bar chart.

The main dataset, consumed by the timeline, map, and bar chart, is produced by the getCountryData method, which groups the prize winners by country and adds some national information, namely population size and international alphacode. Example 16-6 breaks this method down.

Example 16-6. Creating the main country dataset

```
nbviz.getCountryData = function() {
    var countryGroups = nbviz.countryDim.group().all(); ❶

    // make main data-ball
    var data = countryGroups.map( function(c) { ❷
        var cData = nbviz.data.countryData[c.key]; ❸
        var value = c.value;
        // if per capita value then divide by pop. size
        if(nbviz.valuePerCapita){
            value = value / cData.population; ❹
        }
        return {
            key: c.key, // e.g., Japan
            value: value, // e.g., 19 (prizes)
            code: cData.alpha3Code, // e.g., JPN
        };
    })
        .sort(function(a, b) { ❺
            return b.value - a.value; // descending
        });

    return data;
};
```

❶ countryDim is one of our Crossfilter dimensions (see "Filtering Data with Crossfilter" on page 400), here providing group key, value counts (e.g., {key:Argentina, value:5}).

❷ We use the array's map method to create a new array with added components from our country dataset.

❸ Fetches country data using our group key (e.g., Australia).

❹ If the valuePerCapita radio-switch is on then we divide the number of prizes by the size of the country's population, giving a *fairer*, relative prize tally.

❺ Uses Array's sort method to make the array descending by value.

The update methods of our Nobel-viz elements all make use of data filtered by the Crossfilter library. Let's see how that's done now.

Filtering Data with Crossfilter

Developed by D3's creators, Mike Bostock and Jason Davies, Crossfilter[8] is a highly optimized library for exploring large, multivariate datasets using JavaScript. It's very fast and can easily handle datasets far larger than our Nobel Prize dataset. We'll be using it to filter our dataset of winners by the dimensions of category, gender, and country.

The choice of Crossfilter is slightly ambitious, but I wanted to show it in action as I've found it to be so useful personally. It's also the basis of *dc.js* (*https://dc-js.github.io/dc.js*), the very popular D3 charting library, which testifies to its usefulness. Although Crossfilter can be a little difficult to grasp, especially when we start intersecting dimensional filters, most use cases follow a basic pattern that is quickly absorbed. If you ever find yourself trying to cut and slice large datasets, Crossfilter's optimizations will prove a boon.

Creating the filter

On initializing the Nobel-viz, the `makeFilterAndDimensions` method defined in *nbviz_core.js* is called from the `ready` method in *nbviz_main.js* (see "Ready to Go" on page 396). `makeFilterAndDimensions` uses the freshly loaded Nobel Prize dataset to create a Crossfilter filter and some dimensions (e.g., prize category) based on it.

We first create our filter using the dataset of Nobel Prize winners fetched on initialization. Let's remind ourselves what that looks like:

```
[{
  name:"C\u00e9sar Milstein",
  category:"Physiology or Medicine",
  gender:"male",
  country:"Argentina",
  year: 1984
  },
  {
  name:"Auguste Beernaert",
  category:"Peace",
  gender:"male",
  country:"Belgium",
  year: 1909
  },
  ...
}];
```

---

8 See this Square page (*https://square.github.io/crossfilter*) for an impressive example.

To create our filter, call the `crossfilter` function with the array of winner objects:

```
nbviz.makeFilterAndDimensions = function(winnersData){
    // ADD OUR FILTER AND CREATE CATEGORY DIMENSIONS
    nbviz.filter = crossfilter(winnersData);
    //...
};
```

Crossfilter works by allowing you to create dimensional filters on your data. You do so by applying a function to the objects. At its simplest, this creates a dimension based on a single category—for example, by gender. Here we create the gender dimension we'll use to filter Nobel Prizes:

```
nbviz.makeFilterAndDimensions = function(winnersData){
//...
    nbviz.genderDim = nbviz.filter.dimension(function(o) {
        return o.gender;
    });
//...
}
```

This dimension now has an efficient ordering of our dataset by the gender field. We can use it like this, to return all objects with gender female:

```
nbviz.genderDim.filter('female'); ❶
var femaleWinners = nbviz.genderDim.top(Infinity); ❷
femaleWinners.length // 47
```

❶ `filter` takes a single value or, where appropriate, a range (e.g., [5, 21]—all values between 5 and 21). It can also take a Boolean function of the values.

❷ Once the filter is applied, top returns the specified number of ordered objects. Specifying `Infinity`[9] returns all the filtered data objects.

Crossfilter really comes into its own when we start applying multiple dimensional filters, allowing us to slice and dice the data into any subsets we require, all achieved with impressive speed.[10]

Let's clear the gender dimension and add a new one, filtering by prize-winning category. To reset a dimension,[11] apply the `filter` method without arguments:

```
nbviz.genderDim.filter();
nbviz.genderDim.top(Infinity) //  the full Array[858] of objects
```

---

9 JavaScript's `Infinity` (*https://oreil.ly/Ll5xV*) is a numeric value representing infinity.

10 Crossfilter was designed to update millions of records in real time, in response to user input.

11 This will clear all the filters on this dimension.

We'll now create a new prize category dimension:

```
nbviz.categoryDim = nbviz.filter.dimension(function(o) {
    return o.category;
});
```

We can now filter the gender and category dimensions in sequence, allowing us to find, for example, all female Physics prize winners:

```
nbviz.genderDim.filter('female');
nbviz.categoryDim.filter('Physics');
nbviz.genderDim.top(Infinity);
// Out:
// [
//  {name:"Marie Sklodowska-Curie", category:"Physics",...
//  {name:"Maria Goeppert-Mayer", category:"Physics",...
// ]
```

Note that we can turn the filters on and off selectively. So, for example, we can remove the Physics category filter, meaning the gender dimension now contains all the female Nobel Prize winners:

```
nbviz.categoryDim.filter();
nbviz.genderDim.top(Infinity); // Array[47] of objects
```

In our Nobel-viz, these filter operations will be driven by the user making selections from the topmost menu bar.

As well as returning the filtered subsets, Crossfilter can perform grouping operations on the data. We use this to get the national prize aggregates for the bar chart and map indicators:

```
nbviz.genderDim.filter(); // reset gender dimension
var countryGroup = nbviz.countryDim.group(); ❶
countryGroup.all(); ❷

// Out:
// [
//  {key:"Argentina", value:5}, ❸
//  {key:"Australia", value:9},
//  {key:"Austria", value:14},
// ...]
```

❶ Group takes an optional function as an argument, but the default is generally what you want.

❷ Returns all groups by key and value. Do not modify the returned array.[12]

---

12 See the Crossfilter GitHub page (*https://oreil.ly/saEpG*).

❸ value is the total number of Nobel Prize winners for Argentina.

To create our Crossfilter filter and dimensions, we use the makeFilterAndDimensions method, defined in *nbviz_core.js*. Example 16-7 shows the whole method. Note that the order in which the filters are created isn't important—their intersection will still be the same.

Example 16-7. Making our Crossfilter filter and dimensions

```
nbviz.makeFilterAndDimensions = function(winnersData){
    // ADD OUR FILTER AND CREATE CATEGORY DIMENSIONS
    nbviz.filter = crossfilter(winnersData);
    nbviz.countryDim = nbviz.filter.dimension(function(o){ ❶
        return o.country;
    });

    nbviz.categoryDim = nbviz.filter.dimension(function(o) {
        return o.category;
    });

    nbviz.genderDim = nbviz.filter.dimension(function(o) {
        return o.gender;
    });
};
```

❶ We're using the full JavaScript functions for teaching clarity, but these days the shortened form would likely be used: o => o.country.

Running the Nobel Prize Visualization App

To run the Nobel visualization we need a web server that can access the root *index.html* file. For development purposes we can make use of Python's built-in http module to kick off the required server. In the root directory containing our index file, run:

```
$ python -m http.server 8080
Serving HTTP on 0.0.0.0 port 8080 ...
```

Now open up a browser window and go to *http:localhost:8080* and you should see Figure 16-4.

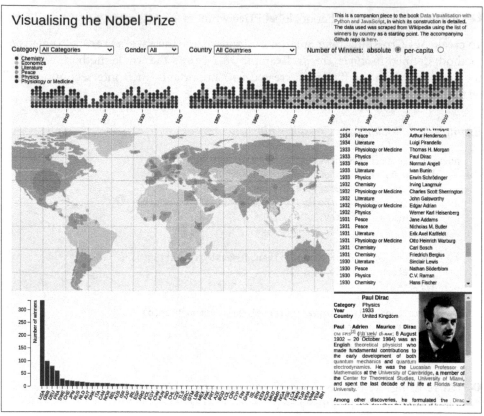

Figure 16-4. The finished Nobel-viz app

Summary

In this chapter, we sketched out how to implement the visualization we imagined in Chapter 15. The backbone was assembled from HTML, CSS, and JavaScript building blocks, and the data feed to the app and data flow within it described. In the following chapters, we'll see how the individual components of our Nobel-viz use the data sent to them to create our interactive visualization. We'll start with a big chapter, which will introduce the fundamentals of D3 while showing how to build the bar chart component of our app. This should set you up for the subsequent D3-focused chapters.

## CHAPTER 17

Introducing D3—The Story of a Bar Chart

In Chapter 16, we imagined our Nobel Prize visualization by breaking it into component elements. In this chapter, I will gently introduce you to D3 by showing you how to build the bar chart we need (Figure 17-1).

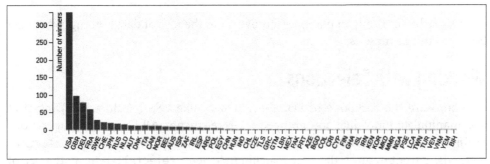

Figure 17-1. This chapter's target bar chart

D3 is much more than a charting library. It's a library you use to build charting libraries, among other things. So why am I introducing you to D3 by way of that ultra-conventional visualization, the bar chart? First, because there should be a little thrill in crafting one from scratch for the first time, having total control over the look and feel of the chart and being unconstrained by whatever prejudices a particular charting library has. And second, because it just happens to be a great way to cover the fundamental elements of D3, particularly data joining and the enter-exit-remove update pattern, now nicely encapsulated by D3's newish join method. If you get those fundamentals in place, you're well on your way to employing the full power and expressivity D3 offers, and producing something more novel than a bar chart.

We'll be using some of the webdev covered in Chapter 4, particularly the SVG graphics that are D3's specialty (see "Scalable Vector Graphics" on page 105). You can try out the code snippets using an online editor like CodePen's (*https://codepen.io*) or VizHub's (*https://vizhub.com*) (which also has a huge number of curated dataviz examples).

Before we begin building the bar chart, let's consider its elements.

Framing the Problem

A bar chart has three key components: the axes, legends, and labels, and, of course, the bars. As we're producing a modern, interactive bar chart component, we'll need the axes and bars to transform in response to user interaction—namely, filtering the set of prize winners via the top selectors (see Figure 15-1).

We'll build the chart one step at a time, ending with D3 transitions, which can make your D3 creations more engaging and attractive. But first we'll cover the basics of D3:

- Selecting DOM elements in your web page
- Getting and setting their attributes, properties, and styles
- Appending and inserting DOM elements

With these basics firmly in place, we'll move on to the joys of data binding, where D3 begins to flex its muscles.

Working with Selections

Selections are the backbone of D3. Using jQuery-like CSS selectors, D3 can select and manipulate individual and grouped DOM elements. All D3 chained operations begin by selecting a DOM element or set of elements using the `select` and `selectAll` methods. `select` returns the first matching element; `selectAll` returns the set of matching elements.

Figure 17-2 shows examples of D3 selections, using the `select` and `selectAll` methods. These selections are used to change the `height` attribute of one or more bars. The `select` method returns the first `rect` (ID `barL`) with class `bar`, whereas `selectAll` can return any combination of the `rects` depending on the query provided.

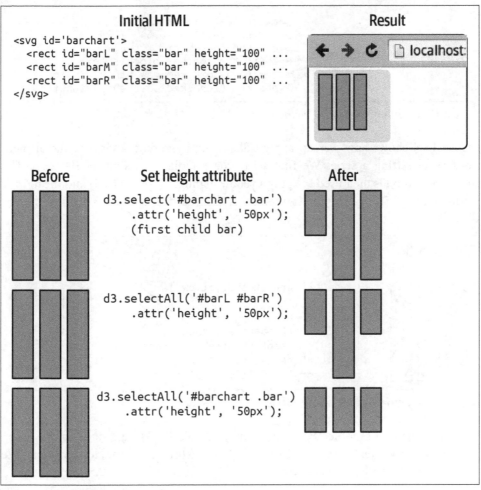

Figure 17-2. Selecting elements and changing attributes: three rectangles are built with the initial HTML. Selections are then made and the height attributes of one or more bars are adjusted.

In addition to setting attributes (the named strings on the DOM elements; e.g., id or class), D3 allows you to set elements' CSS styles, properties (e.g., whether a checkbox is checked), text, and HTML.

Figure 17-3 shows all the ways in which a DOM element can be changed with D3. With these few methods, you can achieve pretty much any look and feel you want.

Figure 17-3. Changing a DOM element with D3

Figure 17-4 shows how we can apply CSS styling by adding a class to the element or directly setting a style. We first select the middle bar using its ID barM. The classed method is then used to apply a yellow highlight (see the CSS) and the height attribute set to 50 px. The style method is then used to apply a red fill to the bar directly.

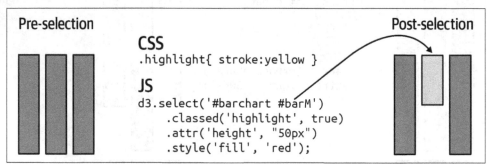

Figure 17-4. Setting attributes and style

D3's text method sets the text content of applicable DOM tags, such as div, p, h* headers, and SVG text elements. To see the text method in action, let's create a little title placeholder with some HTML:

```
<!DOCTYPE html>
<meta charset="utf-8">

<style>font-family: sans-serif;</style>

<body>
  <h2 id="title">title holder</h2>
</body>
```

Figure 17-5 (before) shows the resulting browser page.

Now let's create a fancy-title CSS class with a large, bold font:

```
.fancy-title {
    font-size: 24px;
    font-weight: bold;
}
```

We can now use D3 to select the title header, add the fancy-title class to it, and then set its text to My Bar Chart:

```
d3.select('#title')
  .classed('fancy-title', true)
  .text('My Bar Chart');
```

Figure 17-5 (after) shows the resulting enlarged and emboldened title.

Figure 17-5. Setting text and style with D3

In addition to setting the properties of DOM elements, we can use selections to get those properties. Leaving out the second argument to one of the methods listed in Figure 17-3 allows you to get information about the web page's setup.

Figure 17-6 shows how to get the key properties from an SVG rectangle. As we'll see, getting attributes like width and height from an SVG element can be very useful for programmatic adaptation and adjustment.

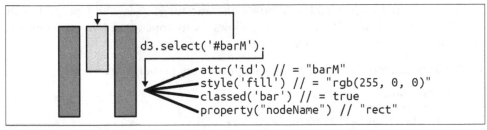

Figure 17-6. Getting a rect bar's details

Figure 17-7 demonstrates the html and text getter methods. After creating a little list (ID silly-list), we use D3 to select it and get various properties. The html method returns the HTML of the list's child <li> tags, while the text method returns the text contained in the list, with the HTML tags stripped. Note that for parent tags, the formatting of any text returned is a little messy, but maybe good enough for a string search or two.

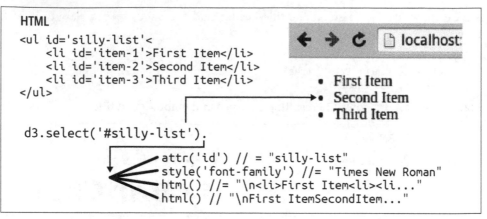

```
HTML
<ul id='silly-list'<
    <li id='item-1'>First Item</li>
    <li id='item-2'>Second Item</li>
    <li id='item-3'>Third Item</li>
</ul>

d3.select('#silly-list').
             attr('id') // = "silly-list"
             style('font-family') //= "Times New Roman"
             html() //= "\n<li>First Item<li><li..."
             html() // "\nFirst ItemSecondItem..."
```

Figure 17-7. Getting HTML and text from a list *tag*

So far we've been manipulating the attributes, styles, and properties of existing DOM elements. This is a useful skill, but D3 comes into its own when we start creating DOM elements programmatically using its append and insert methods. Let's look at these now.

Adding DOM Elements

We've seen how to select and manipulate the attributes, styles, and properties of DOM elements. Now we'll see how D3 allows us to append and insert elements, programmatically adapting the DOM tree.

We'll start with a little HTML skeleton containing a nobel-bar placeholder:

```
<!DOCTYPE html>
<meta charset="utf-8">
<link rel="stylesheet" href="style.css" />

<body>
  <div id='nobel-bar'></div>

  <script
    src="https://cdnjs.cloudflare.com/ajax/libs/d3/7.3.1/d3.min.js">
  </script>
  <script type="text/javascript" src="script.js"></script> ❶
</body>
```

❶ The *script.js* file is where we'll add our bar chart's JavaScript code.

Let's set the size of the nobel-bar element with a little CSS, placed in *style.css*:

```
#nobel-bar {
  width: 600px;
  height: 400px;
```

```
}
.bar {
    fill: blue; /* blue bars for the chapter */
}
```

Usually the first thing one does when creating a chart with D3 is to provide an SVG frame for it. This involves appending an <svg> canvas element to a div chartholder and then appending a <g> group to the <svg> to hold specific chart elements (in our case, the chart bars). This group has margins to accommodate axes, axes labels, and titles.

Getting the Dimensions of an Element

It's very common when programming in D3, or any other JavaScript visualization library, to require the width and height of an SVG or HTML element to use as the basis for setting the size of component elements. One way of doing this is to use D3's style component to grab the CSS dimensions and then use the parseInt function to get an integer value:

```
/* CSS: #nobel-bar { width: 600px }; */

var width = parseInt(d3.select('#nobel-bar')
                    .style('width'), 10); ❶
```

 The result of calling the style method is the string '600px', which we can convert to the number 600 using the parseInt function.

This method works pretty well as a rule, although the parseInt feels a bit hacky, turning the string '600px' into the number 600. It will also fail if the width is specified by a percentage of the parent container.

Arguably, a better, more robust approach is to get the dimensions of the bounding box of the HTML or SVG element in question. These give both the width, height, and relative position of the element, using the node method to get the DOM element:

```
let ele = d3.select("#chart-holder")
// For an HTML element, starting with the D3 +ele+ selection
let bRect = ele.node().getBoundingClientRect();
// e.g., bRect is {width: 600, height: 400, ... }
// For an SVG element use the getBBox method:
let bBox = eleSVG.node().getBBox();
// e.g., bBox is {width: 600, height: 400, x: 100, y: 100}
```

Conventionally, you will specify the margin of your chart in a `margin` object and then use that and the CSS-specified width and height of the chart container to derive the width and height of your chart group. The required JavaScript looks like Example 17-1.

Example 17-1. Getting our bar chart's dimensions

```
var chartHolder = d3.select("#nobel-bar");

var margin = {top:20, right:20, bottom:30, left:40};

var boundingRect = chartHolder.node()
  .getBoundingClientRect(); ❶
var width = boundingRect.width - margin.left - margin.right,
height = boundingRect.height - margin.top - margin.bottom;
```

❶ Gets the bounding rectangle for our Nobel bar chart's panel, using it to set the width and height of its bar container group.

With the width and height of our bar group in hand, we use D3 to build our chart's frame, appending the required `<svg>` and `<g>` tags and specifying the size of the SVG canvas and translation of the bar group:

```
d3.select('#nobel-bar').append("svg")
    .attr("width", width + margin.left + margin.right)
    .attr("height", height + margin.top + margin.bottom)
    .append("g").classed('chart', true)
    .attr("transform", "translate(" + margin.left + ","
                            + margin.top + ")");
```

This changes the HTML of the `nobel-bar` content block:

```
...
    <div id="nobel-bar">
      <svg width="600" height="400">
        <g class="chart" transform="translate(40, 20)"></g>
      </svg>
    </div>
...
```

The resulting SVG framework is shown in Figure 17-8. The `<svg>` element's width and height are the sum of its child group and the surrounding margins. The child group is offset using `transform` to translate it `margin.left` pixels to the right and `margin.top` pixels down (by SVG convention, in the positive y direction).

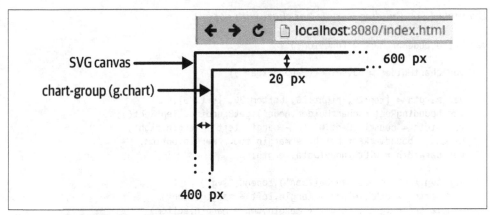

Figure 17-8. Building our bar chart's frame

With our frame in place, let's use append to add a few bars. We'll use a little dummy data: an array of objects with the top slice of Nobel Prize–winning countries by prize number:

```
var nobelData = [
    {key:'United States', value:336},
    {key:'United Kingdom', value:98},
    {key:'Germany', value:79},
    {key:'France', value:60},
    {key:'Sweden', value:29},
    {key:'Switzerland', value:23},
    {key:'Japan', value:21},
    {key:'Russia', value:19},
    {key:'Netherlands', value:17},
    {key:'Austria', value:14}
];
```

To build a crude bar chart,[1] we can iterate through the nobelData array, appending a bar to the chart group as we go. Example 17-2 demonstrates this. After building a basic frame for our chart, we iterate through the nobelData array, using the value fields to set the bar's height and y-position. Figure 17-9 shows how the object values are used to append bars to our chart group. Note that because SVG uses a downward y-axis, you have to displace the bars by the height of the bar chart minus that of the bar in order to put the bar chart the right way up. As we'll see later, by using D3's scales, we can limit such geometric bookkeeping.

---

1 We'll be dealing with axes, labels, and the like later in the chapter when we put D3 into top gear and start binding data.

Example 17-2. Building a crude bar chart with append

```
var buildCrudeBarchart = function() {

    var chartHolder = d3.select("#nobel-bar");

    var margin = {top:20, right:20, bottom:30, left:40};
    var boundingRect = chartHolder.node().getBoundingClientRect();
    var width = boundingRect.width - margin.left - margin.right,
    height = boundingRect.height - margin.top - margin.bottom;
    var barWidth = width/nobelData.length;

    var svg = d3.select('#nobel-bar').append("svg")
        .attr("width", width + margin.left + margin.right)
        .attr("height", height + margin.top + margin.bottom)
        .append("g").classed('chart', true)
        .attr("transform", "translate(" + margin.left + ","
        + margin.top + ")");

    nobelData.forEach(function(d, i) { ❶
        svg.append('rect').classed('bar', true)
            .attr('height', d.value)
            .attr('width', barWidth)
            .attr('y', height - d.value)
            .attr('x', i * (barWidth));
    });
};
```

❶ Iterates through each of the objects in `nobelData`, the `forEach` method providing object and array index to an anonymous function.

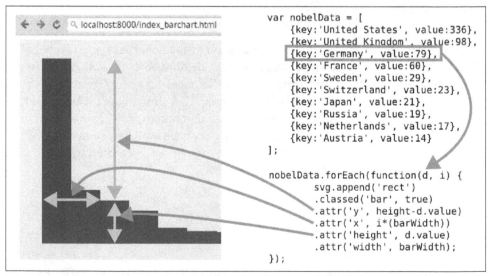

Figure 17-9. Programming a basic bar chart with D3

The other way in which D3 can add elements to the DOM tree is with its `insert` method. `insert` works like append but adds a second selector argument to allow you to place elements before a particular position in an sequence of tags, such as at the beginning of an ordered list. Figure 17-10 demonstrates the use of `insert`: list items in the `silly-list` are selected just like append and then a second argument (e.g., `':first-child'`) specifies the element to insert before.

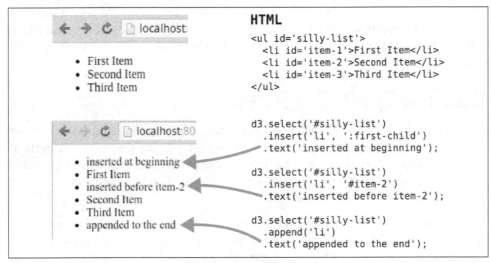

Figure 17-10. Using D3's `insert` method to add list items

For SVG elements, positioned directly within their parent group using x and y coordinates, `insert` might seem redundant. But, as discussed in "Layering and Transparency" on page 115, DOM ordering is important in SVG as elements are layered, meaning that the last element in the DOM tree overlays any previous. We'll see an example of this in Chapter 19 where we have a grid overlay (or `graticule`) for our world map. We want this grid to be drawn above all other map elements so use `insert` to place those elements before it.

Our crude bar chart in Figure 17-9 is crying out for a little refinement. Let's see how we can improve things, first with D3's powerful `scale` objects and then with D3's biggest idea, data binding.

Leveraging D3

In Example 17-2, we built a basic, no-frills bar chart with D3. This chart had a number of problems. First, looping through the data array is a bit clunky. What if we wanted to adapt the dataset for our chart? We'd need some way of adding or removing bars in response and then updating the resulting bars with the new data and redrawing everything. We'd also need to keep scaling the bar dimensions in x and y to reflect the different number of bars and a different maximum bar value. That's quite a lot of bookkeeping already, and things could get messy fast. Also, where do we keep the changing datasets? Every data-driven change to our chart would require passing the dataset around and then constructing a loop to iterate over elements. It feels as if the data exists outside the chained D3 workflow when it really needs to be integral to it.

The solution to elegantly integrating our dataset with D3 lies in the concept of data binding, D3's biggest idea. The scaling problems are sorted by one of D3's most useful utility libraries: scale. We'll take a look at these now and then unleash the power of D3 with some data binding.

Measuring Up with D3's Scales

The fundamental idea behind D3's scales is a mapping from an input domain to an output range. This simple procedure can remove a lot of the persnickety aspects of building charts, visualizations, and the like. As you get more comfortable with scales, you'll find more and more situations where you can apply them. Mastering them is a key component to relaxed, effortless D3.

D3 provides a lot of scales, dividing them into three main categories: quantitative, ordinal, and time[2] scales. There are exotic mappings to suit most conceivable situations, but you'll probably find yourself using the linear and ordinal scales much of the time.

In use, D3 scales can appear slightly strange because they are part object, part function. What this means is that after creating your scale, you can call various methods on it to set its properties (e.g., `domain` to set its domain), but you can also call it as a function with a domain argument to return a range value. The following example should make the distinction clear:

```
var scale = d3.scaleLinear(); // create a linear scale
scale.domain([0, 1]).range([0, 100]); ❶
scale(0.5) // returns 50 ❷
```

❶ We use the scale's `domain` and `range` methods to map from 0 → 1 to 0 → 100.

❷ We call the scale like a function with a domain argument of `0.5`, returning a range value of `50`.

Let's look at the two main D3 scales, the quantitative and the ordinal, showing how we use them to build our bar chart as we go.

---

2 See D3's GitHub page (*https://oreil.ly/xiKUs*) for a comprehensive list.

Quantitative Scales

A D3 quantitative scale you'll usually employ when building line charts, bar charts, scatter plots, and the like is linear, mapping a continuous domain to a continuous range. For example, we want our bar heights to be a linear function of the nobelData values. The range of values to be mapped to is between the maximum and minimum height of the bars in pixels (400 pixels to 0 pixels) and the domain to be mapped from is between the smallest conceivable value (0) and, in our case, the largest value in the array (336 US winners). In the following code, we first use D3's max method to get the largest value in our nobelData array, using that to specify the end of our domain:

```
let maxWinners = d3.max(nobelData, function(d){
            return +d.value; ❶
        });

let yScale = d3.scaleLinear()
            .domain([0, maxWinners]) /* [0, 336] */
            .range([height, 0]);
```

❶ If there's a chance, as is common with JSON encoded data, that the value is a string, prefixing + coerces it to a number.

One little trick to note is that our range decreases from its maximum. This is because we want to use it to specify a positive displacement along the SVG downward y-axis in order to make the bar chart's y-axis point upward (i.e., the smaller the bar height, the larger the y displacement required). Conversely, you can see that the largest bar (the US winners tally) isn't displaced at all (see Figure 17-11).

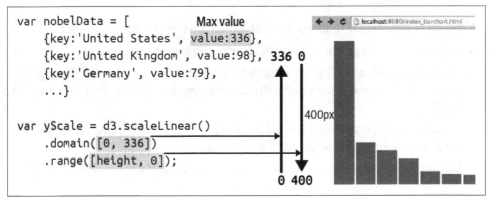

Figure 17-11. Using D3's linear scale to fix the domain and range of our bar chart's y-axis

We're using the simplest possible linear scale for our bar chart's y-axis, mapping from one numeric range to another, but D3's linear scales can do a lot more. The key to understanding this is D3's `interpolate` method.[3] This takes two values and returns an `interpolator` between them. So, for the range of our `yScale` in Figure 17-11, `interpolate` returns a numeric `interpolator` for the values 400 and 0:

```
var numInt = d3.interpolate(400, 0);

numInt(0);   //   400 ❶
numInt(0.5); // 200
numInt(1);   //     0
```

❶ Interpolators have a default domain of [0,1].

The `interpolate` method can deal with more than just numbers. Strings, color codes, and even objects are handled sensibly. You can also specify more than two numbers for your domain array—just make sure that domain and range arrays are the same size.[4] We can combine these two facts to create a useful colormap:[5]

```
var color = d3.scaleLinear()
    .domain([-1, 0, 1])
    .range(["red", "green", "blue"]);

color(0)   // "#008000" green's hex code
color(0.5) // "004080" slate blue
```

D3's linear scales have a lot of useful utility methods and rich functionality. The numeric maps will probably be your workhorse scale, but I recommend reading the D3 docs (*https://oreil.ly/lZy94*) to fully appreciate how flexible the linear scales are. On that web page, you'll find D3's other quantitative scales, to suit almost every quantitative occasion:

- Power scales, similar to linear but with exponential transform (e.g., `sqrt`).
- Log scales, similar to linear but with logarithmic transform.
- Quantize scales, a variant of linear with a discrete range; that is, although the input is continuous, the output is divided into segments or buckets (e.g., [1, 2, 3, 4, 5]).
- Quantile scales, often used for color palettes, are similar to quantize scales but have discrete or bucketed domains as well as ranges.
- Identity scales, linear with the same domain and range (fairly esoteric).

---

3 See the D3 docs (*https://oreil.ly/2IXaF*) for full details.

4 D3 will truncate whichever is bigger.

5 D3 has many built-in colormaps and sophisticated color handling with RGB, HCL, etc. We'll see a few of these in action in the coming chapters.

Quantitative scales are great for manipulating continuously valued quantities, but often we want to get values based on a discrete domain (e.g., names or categories). D3 has a specialized set of ordinal scales to meet this need.

Ordinal Scales

Ordinal scales take an array of values as their domain and map these to discrete or continuous ranges, producing a single mapped value for each. To explicitly create a one-to-one mapping, we use the scale's range method:

```
var oScale = d3.scaleOrdinal()
               .domain(['a', 'b', 'c', 'd', 'e'])
               .range([1, 2, 3, 4, 5]);

oScale('c'); // 3
```

In the case of our bar chart, we want to map an array of indices to a continuous range, to provide our bars' x-coordinates. For this, we can use the band scale `scaleBand` range or the `rangeRound` methods, the latter snapping output values to individual pixels. Here, we use `rangeRound` to map an array of numbers to a continuous range, rounding to integer pixel values:

```
var oScale = d3.scaleBand()
               .domain([1, 2, 3, 4, 5])
               .rangeRound([0, 400]);

oScale(3) // 160
oScale(5) // 320
```

In building our original crude bar chart (Example 17-2), we used a `barWidth` variable to size the bars. Implementing padding between the bars would have required a padding variable and necessary adjustments to `barWidth` and the bar positions. With our new ordinal band scale, we get these things for free, removing the fiddly book-keeping. Calling the `xScale`'s bandwidth method provides the calculated bar widths. We can also use the scale's `padding` method to specify the padding between the bars as a fraction of the space occupied by each bar. The `bandwidth` value is adjusted accordingly. Here are some examples of this in action:

```
var oScale = d3.scaleBand()
               .domain([1, 2]); ❶

oScale.rangeRound([0, 100]); ❷
oScale(2); // 50
oScale.bandwidth(); // 50


oScale.rangeRound([0, 100]);
oScale.padding(0.1) // pBpBp ❸
oScale(1); // 5
```

```
oScale(2); // 52
oScale.bandwidth(); // 42, the padded bar width
```

❶ Stores the scale with a fixed domain; useful if we anticipate the range changing.

❷ rangeRound snaps (rounds) the output values to integers.

❸ We specify a padding (p) factor of 0.1 * allocated bar(B)-space.

Figure 17-12 shows our bar chart's band x-scale with a padding factor of 0.1. The continuous range is 600 (pixels), which is the width of the bar chart, and the domain is an array of integers representing the individual bars. As shown, providing xScale with a bar's index number returns its position on the x-axis.

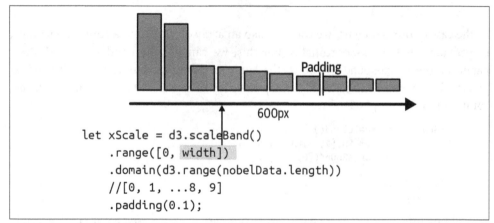

Figure 17-12. Setting the domain and range of our bar chart's x-scale, using a padding factor of 0.1

Armed with our D3 scales, let's turn to D3's central concept, binding data to the DOM in order to drive changes to it.

Unleashing the Power of D3 with Data Binding/Joining

D3 stands for *Data-Driven Documents*, and up to now we haven't really been driving with our data. In order to unleash D3, we need to embrace its big idea, which is binding or joining (both terms are used online) the data in our dataset to its respective DOM elements and updating the web page (document) based on this integration. This small step of joining data to the DOM enables a huge amount of functionality when combined with the most powerful D3 methods, enter and exit.

After a number of iterations, D3 (version 5 and above) now provides the `join` method, which considerably simplifies the use of `enter` and `exit`. The `join` method will be the focus of this chapter.

In order to interpret the thousands of examples online that use the older `enter`, `exit`, `remove` update patterns, it helps to know a little more about what's going on under the hood when D3 joins data. See Appendix A for details.

Updating the DOM with Data

I think it's fair to say that using D3 to update the DOM with new data has not been particularly easy to grasp historically (footnote: You really appreciate this when you try to teach it or write a book chapter on it). There have been a number of implementations such as the general update pattern (*https://oreil.ly/sYrAG*) that have themselves gone through a number of incompatible forms. This means a lot of popular examples on the web, using older version of D3, will steer you down the wrong path.

 Although you may anticipate building one-off charts, with a single data-binding process, it's good to get into the habit of asking yourself, "What if I need to change the data dynamically?" If the answer is not immediately obvious, you have probably implemented a bad D3 design. Catching yourself in the act means you can do a little code audit and make the necessary changes before things start to deteriorate. It's good to kick yourself out of this habit, but also, because D3 is somewhat of a craft skill, constantly reaffirming that best practice will pay off when you need it.

The good news is that recent versions of D3 have solidified the basic methods and made them a lot simpler as well. So employing `enter`, `exit`, and `remove`, the three key D3 methods used in data-joining, can now be done with a single `join` method, which has sensible defaults. In this section, we'll see how to use these four methods to update our bar chart in response to new data, in this case Nobel Prize–winning countries.

Probably the most fundamental concept behind D3 is that of the data-join. In essence, a dataset (usually an array of data objects) is used to create some visual elements, e.g., the rectangular bars of a bar chart. Any change to this data is reflected in a changing visualization, e.g., the number of bars in the bar chart or the heights or placement of existing bars. We can break this operation into three stages:

1. Create a visual element for any data without one using `enter`.

2. Update the attributes and styles of these and, if required, any existing elements.

3. Remove any old visual elements that no longer have any data joined to them using the `exit` and `remove` methods.

Whereas in the past D3 required you to implement the update pattern yourself, using `enter`, `exit`, and (briefly) a `merge` method, the new `join` (*https://oreil.ly/4mg8b*) method combines these methods in one user-friendly package. Often you can just call it with a single argument, specifying the visual element to be joined to the data (e.g., an SVG rect or circle), but it also has more fine-grained control, allowing you to pass in `enter`, `exit`, and `update` callback functions.

Let's see how easy it now is to join data and visual elements by joining some horizontal bars, constructed of SVG rectangles, to our dummy Nobel dataset. We'll join the following dataset to the group of rectangles and use it to create some horizontal bars. You can find a working code example in CodePen (*https://oreil.ly/YOnzx*).

```
let nobelData = [
  { key: "United States", value: 336 },
  { key: "United Kingdom", value: 98 },
  { key: "Germany", value: 79 },
  { key: "France", value: 60 },
  { key: "Sweden", value: 29 },
  { key: "Switzerland", value: 23 },
  { key: "Japan", value: 21 }
];
```

We'll use a little HTML and CSS to create an SVG group to put the bars in and a bar class with blue fill:

```
<div id="nobel-bars">
  <svg width="600" height="400">
    <g class="bars" transform="translate(40, 20)"></g>
  </svg>
</div>

<style>
.bar {
  fill: blue;
}
</style>
```

With data and HTML scaffold to hand, let's see D3's `join` in action. We'll create an `updateBars` function that will accept a data array of key-value countries and join it to some SVG rectangles.

The updateBars function accepts a data array and first adds it to a selection of class 'bar' using the data method. As seen in Example 17-3, it then joins this bars selection to some SVG rectangles, using the join method.

Example 17-3. Joining our country data to some SVG bars

```
function updateBars(data) {
  // select and store the SVG bars group
  let svg = d3.select("#nobel-bars g");
  let bars = svg.selectAll(".bar").data(data);

  bars
    .join("rect") ❶
    .classed("bar", true) ❷
    .attr("height", 10)
    .attr("width", d => d.value)
    .attr("y", function (d, i) {
      return i * 12;
    });
}
```

❶ This joins all existing bars data to SVG rect elements.

❷ join returns all existing rects, which we then update using their joined data.

After calling the join method, D3 is doing the sensible thing, using enter, exit, and remove to keep the data and visual elements in sync. Let's demonstrate this by calling the updateBars function a few times with changing data. First, we'll slice the first four members of our Nobel dataset and use those to update the bars:

```
updateBars(nobelData.slice(0, 4));
```

That produces the bars shown here:

Now let's update the data-join, using only the first two members of the Nobel data array:

```
updateBars(nobelData.slice(0, 2));
```

Calling this method produces the two bars shown in the preceding image. Behind the scenes, D3's bookkeeping has removed the redundant rectangles which, with a smaller dataset, are no longer joined to any data.

Now let's go the other way and see what happens if we use a bigger dataset, this time the first six members of the Nobel array:

```
updateBars(nobelData.slice(0, 6));
```

Once again, D3 does the expected thing (see preceding image), this time appending new rectangles to join to the new data objects.

Having demonstrated that D3's join successfully keeps data and visual elements in sync, adding and removing rectangles as required, we have the basis for our Nobel bar chart.

Putting the Bar Chart Together

Now let's put together what we've currently learned in this chapter and build the main elements of our bar chart. We'll be putting D3's scales to good use here.

First, we'll select the container for our bar chart by ID *#nobel-bar* and use its dimensions (from `boundingClientRectangle`) and some margin settings to get the width and height of the chart:

```
let chartHolder = d3.select('#nobel-bar')
let margin = { top: 20, right: 20, bottom: 35, left: 40 }
let boundingRect = chartHolder.node().getBoundingClientRect()
let width = boundingRect.width - margin.left - margin.right,
height = boundingRect.height - margin.top - margin.bottom
// some left-padding for the y-axis label
var xPaddingLeft = 20
```

Now we'll set our scales using the width and height:

```
let xScale = d3.scaleBand()
  .range([xPaddingLeft, width]) // left-padding for y-label
  .padding(0.1)

let yScale = d3.scaleLinear().range([height, 0])
```

Now we'll create our SVG chart group using width, height, and margins and store it to a variable:

```
var svg = chartHolder
    .append('svg')
    .attr('width', width + margin.left + margin.right)
    .attr('height', height + margin.top + margin.bottom)
    .append('g')
    .attr('transform', 'translate(' + margin.left + ',' + margin.top + ')')
```

With our HTML and SVG scaffold in place, let's adapt the `updateBars` function (see Example 17-3) to respond to changes in our real Nobel data. The update function will receive a data array of the form:

```
[ {key: 'United States', value: 336, code: 'USA'}
  {key: 'United Kingdom', value: 98, code: 'GBR'}
  {key: 'Germany', value: 79, code: 'DEU'} ... ]
```

On being called with new data, the `updateBarchart` function first filters out any zero prize-winning countries and then updates the x and y scale domains to reflect the number of bars/countries and the maximum prizes won, as seen in Example 17-4.

Example 17-4. Updating the bar chart

```
let updateBarChart = function (data) {
  // filter out any countries with zero prizes by value
  data = data.filter(function (d) {
    return d.value > 0
  })
  // change the scale domains to reflect the newly filtered data
  // this produces an array of country codes: ['USA', 'DEU', 'FRA' ...]
  xScale.domain(
    data.map(d => d.code)
  )
  // we want to scale the highest number of prizes won, e.g., USA: 336
  yScale.domain([
    0,
    d3.max(data, d => d.value)
  ])
// ...
}
```

With updated scales we can use a data-join to create the bars necessary for the data provided. This is essentially the same as the function shown in Example 17-3 but using scales to size the bars and with a customized `entry` method, to add a class and left-padding to newly minted bars:

```
let bars = svg
    .selectAll('.bar')
    .data(data)
    .join(
      (enter) => {  ❶
        return enter
          .append('rect')
          .attr('class', 'bar')
          .attr('x', xPaddingLeft)
      }
    )
    .attr('x', d => xScale(d.code))
    .attr('width', xScale.bandwidth())
```

```
        .attr('y', d => yScale(d.value))
        .attr('height', d => height - yScale(d.value))
```

❶ We customize the enter method to add a bar` class to the rectangle. Note that we need to return the enter object to use after the join call.

We now have a bar chart that responds to changes in the data, initiated in this case by the user. Filtering the data for all Chemistry prizes shows the result in Figure 17-13. Although lacking a few crucial elements, the hard work has been done building a bar chart. Now let's add axes and some cool transitional effects to make the finishing touches.

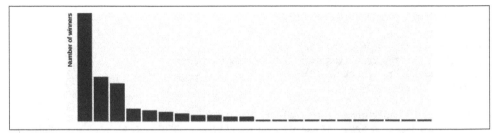

Figure 17-13. Final bar chart

Axes and Labels

Now that we have a working update pattern, we will add the axes and axes labels that any self-respecting bar chart needs.

D3 doesn't offer a lot in the way of high-level chart elements, encouraging you to roll your own. But it does provide a convenient axis object, which takes the sting out of having to craft the SVG elements yourself. It's easy to use and, as you would expect, plays nicely with our data update patterns, allowing for axes ticks and labels that change in response to the data presented.

D3 Axes

D3 axes can be confusing at first, feeling just a little bit magical. It's best to think of them as a plug-in[6] that generates the correct axis HTML (lines, ticks, tick labels, etc.) for you and which can respond sensibly to changes in data (i.e., if you change the range of your scales, the axes can change in response using nice, smooth transitions that look pretty cool).

---

6 Axes follow a similar pattern to that proposed by Mike Bostock in *Towards Reusable Charts* (*https://oreil.ly/ FOEoe*), using the JavaScript objects' call (*https://oreil.ly/4vVp3*) method to build HTML on the selected DOM element(s).

Generally with a D3 axis, you will create an SVG group to hold it and then call the axis on it, having set the scale it will represent. During the call, the axis object will *stamp* the correct HTML on the DOM. So, as a simple demo, the following code describes a simple chart setup with an SVG x-axis group and a D3 axis. Calling the axis on the axis group generates the HTML lines and text needed for an axis (find a working example in CodePen (*https://oreil.ly/pYb4c*)).

```html
<!DOCTYPE html>
<meta charset="utf-8">
<script src="static/libs/d3.min.js">
</script>
<style>
  svg {
    width: 600px;
    height: 400px
  }
</style>

<body>
  <svg>
    <g id='chart' transform='translate(20,20)'>
      <g id='x-axis'></g>
    </g>
  </svg>
  <script>
    var scale = d3.scaleLinear()
      .domain([0, 10]).range([0, 400]) ❶
    var xaxis = d3.axisBottom().scale(scale) ❷
    d3.select('#x-axis').call(xaxis) ❸
  </script>
</body>
```

❶ Creates a scale with a domain of 0 to 10 and a range of 400 (pixels).

❷ Creates a D3 bottom axis, using the scale just defined.

❸ Calling the D3 axis on our x-axis group creates the axis HTML branch shown in Figure 17-15, which looks like Figure 17-14.

0 1 2 3 4 5 6 7 8 9 10

Figure 17-14. A simple D3 axis

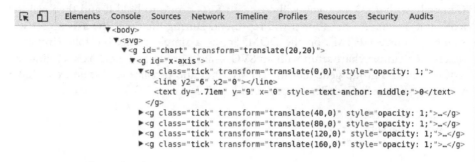

Elements Console Sources Network Timeline Profiles Resources Security Audits
▼<body>
  ▼<svg>
    ▼<g id="chart" transform="translate(20,20)">
      ▼<g id="x-axis">
        ▼<g class="tick" transform="translate(0,0)" style="opacity: 1;">
            <line y2="6" x2="0"></line>
            <text dy=".71em" y="9" x="0" style="text-anchor: middle;">0</text>
          </g>
        ►<g class="tick" transform="translate(40,0)" style="opacity: 1;">…</g>
        ►<g class="tick" transform="translate(80,0)" style="opacity: 1;">…</g>
        ►<g class="tick" transform="translate(120,0)" style="opacity: 1;">…</g>
        ►<g class="tick" transform="translate(160,0)" style="opacity: 1;">…</g>

Figure 17-15. The HTML branch created by a D3 axis instance

Using the `call` method on a selection is a common D3 technique to create plug-ins such as tooltips and brushes. There are loads of examples on *bl.ocks.org* like this one (*https://oreil.ly/J0Hrd*) by Charl Botha. The main takeaway is that it's not magic and it's certainly important that you understand the basics of what's happening during that `call` method.

In order to define our x and y axes, we need to know what ranges and domains we want our axes to represent. In our case, it's the same one as the ranges and domains of our x and y scales, so we supply these to the axes' `scale` method. D3 axes also allow you to specify their orientation, which will fix the relative position of ticks and tick labels. With our bar chart, we want the x-axis on the bottom and the y-axis on the left. Our ordinal x-axis will have a label for each bar, but with our y-axis, the choice of tick numbers is arbitrary. Ten seems like a reasonable number, so we set that using the `ticks` method. The following code shows how we declare our bar chart's axes:

```
let xAxis = d3.axisBottom().scale(xScale)

let yAxis = d3
  .axisLeft()
  .scale(yScale)
  .ticks(10)
  .tickFormat(function (d) {
    if (nbviz.valuePerCapita) { ❶
      return d.toExponential()
    }
    return d
  })
```

❶ We want the format of our tick labels to change with our chosen metric, per capita or absolute. Per capita produces a very small number that is best represented in exponential form (e.g., 0.000005 → 5e-6). The `tickFormat` method allows you to take the data value at each tick and return the desired tick string.

We'll also need a little bit of CSS to style the axes correctly, removing the default fill, setting the stroke color to black, and making the shape render crisply. We'll also specify the font size and family while we're at it:

```
/* style.css */
.axis { font: 10px sans-serif; }
.axis path, .axis line {
    fill: none;
    stroke: #000;
    shape-rendering: crispEdges;
}
```

Now that we have our axis generators, we need a couple of SVG groups to hold the axes they produce. Let's add these to our main svg selector as groups with sensible class names:

```
svg.append("g")
    .attr("class", "x axis")
    .attr("transform", "translate(0," + height + ")"); ❶

svg.append("g")
        .attr("class", "y axis");
```

❶ By SVG's convention, y is measured from the top down, so we want our *bottom*-oriented x-axis translated from the chart's top by *height* pixels.

Our bar chart's axes have fixed ranges (the width and height of the chart), but their domains will change as the user filters the dataset. For example, the number of (country) bars will be reduced if the user filters the data by Economics category: this will change the domain of the ordinal x-scale (number of bars) and the quantitative y-scale (maximum number of winners). We want the displayed axes to change with these changing domains, with a nice transition for good measure.

Example 17-5 shows how the axes are updated. First, we update our scale domains using the new data (A). These new scale domains are reflected when the axes generators (which are linked to them) are called on their respective axis groups.

Example 17-5. Updating our bar chart's axes

```
let updateBarChart = function(data) {
    // A. Update scale domains with new data
    xScale.domain( data.map(d => d.code) );
    yScale.domain([0, d3.max(data, d => +d.value)])
    // B. Use the axes generators with the new scale domains
    svg.select('.x.axis')
        .call(xAxis) ❶
        .selectAll("text") ❷
        .style("text-anchor", "end")
        .attr("dx", "-.8em")
```

```
        .attr("dy", ".15em")
        .attr("transform", "rotate(-65)");

    svg.select('.y.axis')
        .call(yAxis);
    // ...
}
```

 Calling the D3 `axis` on our x-axis group element builds all the necessary axis SVG in it, including ticks and tick labels. D3 `axis` uses an internal update pattern to enable transitions to newly bound data.

❷ After creating the x-axis, we perform some SVG manipulations of the text labels generated. First, we select the `text` elements of the axis, the tick labels. We then place their text anchors at the end of the element and shift their position a bit. This is because the text is rotated about its anchor and we want to rotate about the end of the country labels, now positioned under the tick lines. The result of our manipulations is shown in Figure 17-16. Note that without rotating our labels, they would merge into one another.

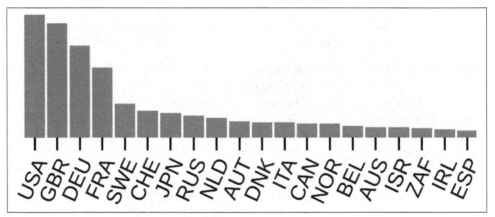

Figure 17-16. Reoriented tick labels on the x-axis

Now that we have our working axes, let's add a little label to the x-axis and then see how the bar chart copes with our real data:

```
let xPaddingLeft = 20 ❶

let xScale = d3.scaleBand()
    .range([xPaddingLeft, width])
    .padding(0.1)
//...
svg.append("g")
    .attr("class", "y axis")
    .append("text")
```

```
.attr('id', 'y-axis-label')
.attr("transform", "rotate(-90)")  ❷
.attr("y", 6)
.attr("dy", ".71em")  ❸
.style("text-anchor", "end")
.text('Number of winners');
```

❶ A left padding constant, in pixels, to make way for the y-axis label.

❷ Rotates the text anticlockwise to the upright position.

❸ dy is a relative coordinate [relative to the *y* coordinate just specified (6)]. By using the em unit (relative to font size), we can make handy adjustments to the text margin and baseline.

Figure 17-17 shows the result of filtering our Nobel Prize winners dataset for Chemistry winners, using our category selector filter. The bar widths increase to reflect the reduced number of countries, and both axes adapt to the new dataset.

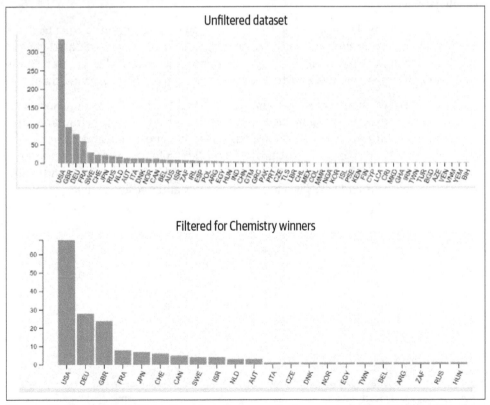

Figure 17-17. The Nobel Prize bar chart before and after we apply the category filter for Chemistry winners

We now have a working bar chart, using the update pattern to adjust itself as the user-driven dataset changes. But although it's functional, the transition in response to data change is visually stark, even jarring. One way to make the change much more engaging and even informative would be to have the chart update continuously over a short time period, with preserved country bars moving from their old to new position while simultaneously adapting their height and width. Such continuous transitions really add life to a visualization and are seen in many of the most impressive D3 pieces. The good news is that transitions are tightly integrated into D3's workflow, which means you can achieve these cool visual effects for the cost of a few lines of code.

Transitions

As it stands, our bar chart is perfectly functional. It responds to data changes by adding or removing bar elements and then updating them using the new data. But the immediate change from one reflection of the data to another feels a little stark and visually jarring.

D3's transitions provide the ability to smooth the visual update of our elements, making them change continuously over a set time period. This can be both aesthetically appealing and, on occasion, informative.[7] The important thing is that D3 transitions can be very engaging for the user, which is reason enough to want to master them.

Figure 17-18 shows the effect we are aiming at. When the bar chart is updated with a newly selected dataset, we want the bars of any countries present before and after the transition to morph smoothly from their old to new positions and dimensions.[8] So in Figure 17-18 the bar for France grows from start to finish over the course of the transition—say, a couple of seconds—with intermediate bars of increasing width and height. The axes ticks and labels will adapt too as the x and y scales change.

---

7 For example, when we change our measurement of Nobel Prize wins by country from absolute to per capita, the large amount of movement displayed as the country bars change their order emphasizes the difference between the two metrics.

8 In animation and computer graphics circles, this effect is known as *tweening* (see this Wikipedia page (*https:// oreil.ly/vr9QY*)).

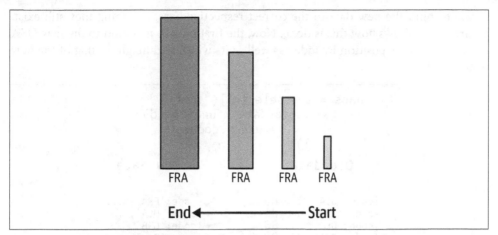

Figure 17-18. Smooth bar transitions on update

The effect shown in Figure 17-18 is surprisingly easy to achieve but involves under-standing the precise way data is joined in D3. By default, when new data is bound to existing DOM elements, it is done by array index. Figure 17-19 shows how this works, using our selected bars as an example. The first bar (B0), previously bound to the USA's data, is now bound to France's. It stays in first position and updates its size and tick label. Essentially, the USA's bar becomes France's.[9]

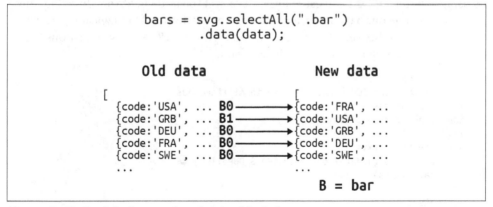

Figure 17-19. By default, new data is joined by index

In order to get continuity during our transitions (i.e., for the USA bar to move to its new position while changing to its new height and width), we need the new data to be bound by a unique key, not the index. D3 allows you to specify a function as a second argument to the data method, which returns a key from the object data

---

9 See Mike Bostock's nice demonstration of object constancy at his site (*https://oreil.ly/QZuYK*).

to use to bind the new data to the correct respective bars, assuming they still exist. Figure 17-20 shows how this is done. Now, the first bar (0) is bound to the new USA data, changing its position by index as well as its width and height to that of the new American bar.

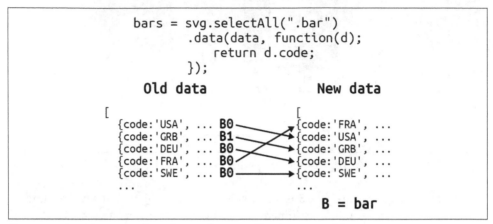

Figure 17-20. Using an object key to join new data

Joining the data by key gives us the correct start and endpoints for our national bars. Now all we need is a way to create a smooth transition between them. We can do this by using a couple of D3's coolest methods, `transition` and `duration`. By calling these before we change our bar dimension and position attributes, D3 magically performs a smooth transition between them, as shown in Figure 17-18. Adding transitions to our bar chart update requires only a few lines of code:

```
// nbviz_core.mjs
nbviz.TRANS_DURATION = 2000 // time in milliseconds
// nbviz_bar.mjs
import nbviz from ./nbviz_core.mjs
//...
svg.select('.x.axis')
    .transition().duration(nbviz.TRANS_DURATION) ❶
    .call(xAxis) //...
//...
svg.select('.y.axis')
    .transition().duration(nbviz.TRANS_DURATION)
    .call(yAxis);
//...
var bars = svg.selectAll(".bar")
    .data(data, d => d.code) ❷
//...
let bars = svg.selectAll('.bar')
  .data(data, (d) => d.code)
  .join(
   // ...
  )
```

```
  .classed('active', function (d) {
    return d.key === nbviz.activeCountry
  })
  .transition()
  .duration(nbviz.TRANS_DURATION)
  .attr("x", (d) => xScale(d.code)) ❸
  .attr("width", xScale.bandwidth())
  .attr("y", (d) => yScale(d.value))
  .attr("height", (d) => height - yScale(d.value));
```

❶ A transition with duration of two seconds, which is our `TRANS_DURATION` constant of 2000 (ms).

❷ Using the data object's `code` property to make the continuous data-joins.

❸ The x, y, width, and height attributes will be smoothly morphed from current values to those defined here.

Transitions will work on most obvious attributes and styles of an existing DOM element.[10]

The transitions just shown perform a smooth change of the attributes from starting point to end goal, but D3 allows for a lot of tuning for these effects. You can, for example, use the `delay` method to specify the time before the transition starts. This delay can also be a function of the data.

Probably the most useful extra transitioning method is `ease`, which allows you to specify the way in which the elements' attributes are updated over the transition's duration. The default easing function is `CubicInOut` (*https://oreil.ly/zP5FO*), but you can also specify things like `quad`, which speeds things up as the transition progresses, or `bounce` and `elastic`, which do pretty much what it says on the tin, giving a bouncy feel to the change. There's also `sin`, which speeds up at the beginning and slows down toward the end. See *easings.net* for a nice description of different easing functions and observablehq (*https://oreil.ly/crI0I*) for a comprehensive runthrough of D3's easing functions, assisted by interactive charts.

If the easing functions available to D3 don't suit your needs or you're feeling particularly ambitious, as with most things D3 you can roll your own to fit any subtle requirements. The `tween` method provides the fine-grained control you might need.

With a working `join`-based update pattern and some cool transitions, we have completed our Nobel-viz bar chart. There's always room for refinement, but this bar chart

---

10 Transitions only apply to existing elements—you can't fade in the creation of a DOM element, for example. You could, however, fade it in and out using the `opacity` CSS style.

will more than do the job. Let's summarize what we've learned in this rather large chapter before moving on to the other components of our Nobel Prize visualization.

Updating the Bar Chart

When the bar chart module is imported, it appends a callback function to the callbacks array in the core module. When data is updated in response to user interaction, this callback function is called and the bar chart updated with new country data:

```
nbviz.callbacks.push(() => {  ❶
  let data = nbviz.getCountryData()
  updateBarChart(data)
})
```

❶ This anonymous function is called in the core module when data is updated.

Summary

This has been a large and quite challenging chapter. D3 isn't the easiest library to learn, but I have smoothed the learning curve by breaking things down into digestible chunks. Take your time absorbing the fundamental ideas and, crucially, start setting yourself little objectives to stretch your D3 knowledge. I think D3 is very much an art form and, more than most libraries, one learns while doing.

The key elements to understanding D3 and applying it effectively are the update pattern and the data binding involved. If you understand this at a fundamental level, most of D3's other pyrotechnics slot nicely into place. Focus on the data, enter, exit, and remove methods and make sure you really understand what's going on. It's the only way to advance from much of the cut-and-paste style of D3 programming, which is initially productive (there being so many cool examples out there), but will eventually frustrate. Use your browser's developer console (currently Chrome and Chromium have the best tools here) to inspect DOM elements, to see what data is bound to them via the __data__ variable. If it doesn't match your expectations, you'll learn a lot by finding out why.

You should now have a pretty good grounding in D3's core techniques. In the next chapter, we'll aim to challenge those new skills with a rather more ambitious chart, our Nobel Prize timeline.

## CHAPTER 18

Visualizing Individual Prizes

In Chapter 17 you learned the basics of D3, how to select and change DOM elements, how to add new ones, and how to apply the data update pattern, which is the axis around which interactive D3 spins. In this chapter, I will expand on what you've learned so far and show you how to build a fairly novel visual element, showing all the individual Nobel Prizes by year (Figure 18-1). This Nobel timeline will allow us to expand on the knowledge of the last chapter, demonstrating a number of new techniques including more advanced data manipulation.

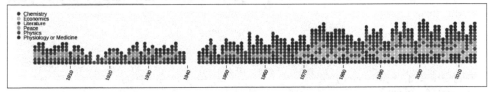

Figure 18-1. This chapter's target chart, a timeline of Nobel Prizes

Let's start by showing how we build the HTML framework for our timeline chart.

Building the Framework

Our target chart's construction is similar to that of our Nobel Prize bar chart, which we covered in detail in the last chapter. We first use D3 to select our <div> container with ID nobel-time, then use the width and height of the container, along with our specified margins, to create our svg chart group:

```
import nbviz from './nbviz_core.mjs'

let chartHolder = d3.select('#nobel-time');

let margin = {top:20, right:20, bottom:30, left:40};
```

```
let boundingRect = chartHolder.node()
  .getBoundingClientRect();
let width = boundingRect.width - margin.left
- margin.right,
height = boundingRect.height - margin.top - margin.bottom;

let svg = chartHolder.append("svg")
        .attr("width", width + margin.left + margin.right)
        .attr("height", height + margin.top
        + margin.bottom)
        .append('g')
          .attr("transform",
                  "translate(" + margin.left + ","
                  + margin.top + ")");
    // ...
})
```

With our svg chart group in place, let's add the scales and axes.

Scales

To place the circular indicators, we use two ordinal scales (Example 18-1). The x-scale uses the `rangeRoundBands` method to specify a 10% padding between the circles. Because we use the x-scale to set the circles' diameters, the height of our y-scale's range is manually adjusted to accommodate all the indicators, allowing a little padding between them. We use `rangeRoundPoints` to round to integer pixel coordinates.

Example 18-1. The chart's two ordinal band scales, for x and y axes

```
let xScale = d3.scaleBand()
  .range([0, width])
  .padding(0.1) ❶
  .domain(d3.range(1901, 2015))

let yScale = d3.scaleBand()
  .range([height, 0]).domain(d3.range(15)) ❷
```

❶ We're using a padding factor of 0.1, which is approximately 10% of an indicator's diameter.

❷ The domain is [0, …, 15] with 15 being the historical maximum number of prizes given in any one year.

Unlike our bar chart from the last chapter, both ranges and domains of this chart are fixed. The domain of the xScale is the years over which the Nobel Prize has run, and that of the yScale is from zero to the maximum number of prizes in any given year

---

(14 in the year 2000). Neither of these will change in response to user interaction, so we define them outside the `update` method.

Axes

With a maximum of 14 prizes in any one year and with a circular indicator for each, it is easy to make a prize count by eye if necessary. Given this, the emphasis on providing a relative indicator of prize distribution (e.g., showing the spurt in post-WWII US science prizes), and the long length of the chart, a y-axis is redundant for our chart.

For the x-axis, labeling the decades' starts seems about right. It reduces visual clutter and is also the standard human way of charting historical trends. Example 18-2 shows the construction of our x-axis, using D3's handy `axis` object. We override the tick values using the `tickValues` method, filtering the domain range (1900–2015) to return only those dates ending with zero.

Example 18-2. Making the x-axis, with tick labels per decade

```
let xAxis = d3.axisBottom()
    .scale(xScale)
    .tickValues(
      xScale.domain().filter(function (d, i) {
        return !(d % 10) ❶
      })
    )
```

❶ We only want to tick every 10th year, so we create tick values by filtering the x-scale domain values and using their index to select only those that are divisible by 10. These give 0 for modulus (%) 10, to which we apply the not Boolean operator (!) to produce `true`, which passes the filter.

This returns `true` for years ending in 0, giving a tick label at the start of every decade.

As with the scales, we don't anticipate the axes changing,[1] so we can add them before receiving the dataset in the `updateTimeChart` function:

```
svg.append("g") // group to hold the axis
    .attr("class", "x axis")
    .attr("transform", "translate(0," + height + ")")
    .call(xAxis) ❶
    .selectAll("text") ❷
```

---

1 D3 has some handy brushes that make selecting portions of the x- or y-axis easy. Combined with transitions, this can make for an engaging and intuitive way to increase the resolution of large datasets. See this *bl.ocks.org* page (*https://oreil.ly/2Q0j7*) for a good example.

```
        .style("text-anchor", "end")
        .attr("dx", "-.8em")
        .attr("dy", ".15em")
        .attr("transform", "rotate(-65)");
```

 Calls our D3 axis on the svg group, with the axis object taking care of building the axis elements.

 As in "Axes and Labels" on page 426, we rotate the axis tick labels to place them diagonally.

With axes and scales taken care of, we need only add a little legend with our colored category labels before moving on to the cool, interactive elements of the chart.

Category Labels

The last of our *static* components is a legend, containing the category labels shown in Figure 18-2.

● Chemistry
● Economics
● Literature
● Peace
● Physics
● Physiology or Medicine

Figure 18-2. Categories legend

To create the legend, we first create a group, class labels, to hold the labels. We bind our nbviz.CATEGORIES data to a label selection on this labels group, enter the bound data, and attach a group for each category, displaced on the y-axis by index:

```
let catLabels = chartHolder.select('svg').append('g')
        .attr('transform', "translate(10, 10)")
        .attr('class', 'labels')
        .selectAll('label').data(nbviz.CATEGORIES) ❶
        .join('g')
        .attr('transform', function(d, i) {
            return "translate(0," + i * 10 + ")"; ❷
        });
```

❶ We join our array of categories (["Chemistry", "Economics", …]) to the label group using the standard data followed by join methods.

 Creates a group for each category, spaced vertically 10 pixels apart.

Now that we have our `catLabels` selection, let's add a circular indicator (matching those seen in the timeline) and text label to each of its groups:

```
catLabels.append('circle')
    .attr('fill', (nbviz.categoryFill)) ❶
    .attr('r', xScale.bandwidth()/2); ❷

catLabels.append('text')
    .text(d => d)
    .attr('dy', '0.4em')
    .attr('x', 10);
```

❶ We use our shared `categoryFill` method to return a color based on the bound category.

❷ The x scales `bandwidth` method returns the distance between two category labels. We will use half of this to get the radius for our circular label markers.

The `categoryFill` function (Example 18-3) is defined in *nbviz_core.js* and is used by the app to provide colors for the categories. D3 provides a number of color schemes in the form of arrays of color hex codes, which can be used as our SVG fill colors. You can see a demo of the color schemes on Observable (*https://oreil.ly/sblXu*). We are dealing with categories, so we'll use the Category10 set.

Example 18-3. Setting the category colors

```
// nbviz_core.js
nbviz.CATEGORIES = [
    "Physiology or Medicine", "Peace", "Physics",
    "Literature", "Chemistry", "Economics"];

nbviz.categoryFill = function(category){
    var i = nbviz.CATEGORIES.indexOf(category);
    return d3.schemeCategory10[i]; ❶
};
```

❶ D3's `schemeCategory10` is an array of 10 color hex codes (`['#1f77b4', '#ff7f0e',...]`) that we can apply using the prize category index.

Now that we've covered all the static elements of our time chart, let's look at how we knock it into usable form with D3's *nest* library.

Nesting the Data

In order to create this timeline component, we need to reorganize our flat array of winners objects into a form that will allow us to bind it to the individual Nobel Prizes in our timeline. What we need, to make binding this data with D3 as smooth as possible, is an array of prize objects by year, with the year groups available as arrays. Let's demonstrate the conversion process with our Nobel Prize dataset.

The following is the flat Nobel Prize dataset we begin with, ordered by year:

```
[
  {"year":1901,"name":"Wilhelm Conrad R\\u00f6ntgen",...},
  {"year":1901,"name":"Jacobus Henricus van \'t Hoff",...},
  {"year":1901,"name":"Sully Prudhomme",...},
  {"year":1901,"name":"Fr\\u00e9d\\u00e9ric Passy",...},
  {"year":1901,"name":"Henry Dunant",...},
  {"year":1901,"name":"Emil Adolf von Behring",...},
  {"year":1902,"name":"Theodor Mommsen",...},
  {"year":1902,"name":"Hermann Emil Fischer",...},
  ...
];
```

We want to take this data and convert it to the following nested format, an array of objects with year keys and winners-by-year values:

```
[
  {"key":"1901",
   "values":[
    {"year":1901,"name":"Wilhelm Conrad R\\u00f6ntgen",...},
    {"year":1901,"name":"Jacobus Henricus van \'t Hoff",...},
    {"year":1901,"name":"Sully Prudhomme",...},
    {"year":1901,"name":"Fr\\u00e9d\\u00e9ric Passy",...},
    {"year":1901,"name":"Henry Dunant",...},
    {"year":1901,"name":"Emil Adolf von Behring",...}
   ]
  },
  {"key":"1902",
   "values":[
    {"year":1902,"name":"Theodor Mommsen",...},
    {"year":1902,"name":"Hermann Emil Fischer",...},
    ...
   ]
  },
  ...
];
```

We can iterate through this nested array and join the year groups in turn, each one represented by a column of indicators in our timeline.

We can make use of one D3 group utility method in order to group the Nobel prizes by year. group takes an array of data and returns an object grouped by the property specified in a callback function, in our case the year of the prize. So we group our entries by year like this:

```
let nestDataByYear = function (entries) {
    let yearGroups = d3.group(entries, d => d.year) ❶
        // ...
}
```

 Here we use a modern JavaScript lambda shorthand function, equivalent to `function(d) { return d.year }`.

This grouping returns the array of entries of the form:

```
[ // yearGroups
    {1913: [{year: 1913, ...}, {year: 1913, ...}, ...]},
    {1921: [{year: 1921, ...}, {year: 1921, ...}, ...]},
    ...
]
```

Now in order to convert this map to the required array of key-values objects, we'll make use of JavaScript's `Array` object and its `from` method. We pass in our `yearGroups` map and a converter function that takes the individual groups in the form of a [key, values] array and converts them to a {key: key, values: values} object. We are again using the destructuring assignment syntax (*https://oreil.ly/rREpC*) to map our key and values:

```
let keyValues = Array.from(yearGroups, [key, values] => {key, values})
```

We now have the required function to group our filtered winning prize entries by year in the key-values form required:

```
nbviz.nestDataByYear = function (entries) {
    let yearGroups = d3.group(entries, (d) => d.year);
    let keyValues = Array.from(yearGroups, ([key, values]) => {
        let year = key;
        let prizes = values;
        prizes = prizes.sort(
            (p1, p2) => (p1.category > p2.category ? 1 : -1)); ❶
        return { key: year, values: prizes };
    });
    return keyValues;
};
```

❶ We use the JavaScript array's `sort` method (*https://oreil.ly/VA1ot*) to sort the prizes alphabetically by category. This will make it easier to compare year with year. `sort` expects a positive or negative numerical value, which we produce using the Boolean alphanumeric string comparison.

Adding the Winners with a Nested Data-Join

In "Putting the Bar Chart Together" on page 424 of the last chapter, we saw how D3's newish `join` method makes it easy to synchronize changes in data, in that case number of prizes by country, with the visualization of that data, in that case bars in a bar chart. Our winners-by-year chart is essentially a bar chart where the individual bars are represented by prizes (circle markers). Now we'll see how this can easily be accomplished by using two data-joins and the nested dataset produced in the last section.

The nested data is first passed from `onDataChange` to our time chart's `updateTimeChart` method. We then use our first data-join to create the year groups, positioning them using our ordinal x scale, which mapped years to pixel positions (see Example 18-1) and naming them by year:

```
nbviz.updateTimeChart = function (data) {

  let years = svg.selectAll('.year').data(data, d => d.key) ❶

  years
    .join('g') ❷
    .classed('year', true)
    .attr('name', d => d.key)
    .attr('transform', function (year) {
      return 'translate(' + xScale(+year.key) + ',0)'
    })
    //...
}
```

❶ We want to join the year data to its respective column by its year key, not the default array index, which will change if there are year gaps in our nested array, as there often will be for the user-selected datasets.

❷ Our first data-join uses the key-values array to produce the circle-bar groups by year.

Let's use Chrome's Elements tab to see the changes we've made from this first data-join. Figure 18-3 shows our year groups nestled nicely in their parent chart group.

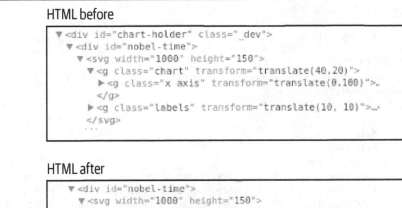

HTML before

```
▼<div id="chart-holder" class="_dev">
  ▼<div id="nobel-time">
    ▼<svg width="1000" height="150">
      ▼<g class="chart" transform="translate(40,20)">
        ▶<g class="x axis" transform="translate(0,100)">..
        </g>
      ▶<g class="labels" transform="translate(10, 10)">...<
      </svg>
      ...
```

HTML after

```
▼<div id="nobel-time">
  ▼<svg width="1000" height="150">
    ▼<g class="chart" transform="translate(40,20)">
      ▶<g class="x axis" transform="translate(0,100)">...</g>
        <g class="year" name="1901" transform="translate(18,0)
        <g class="year" name="1902" transform="translate(26,0)
        <g class="year" name="1903" transform="translate(34,0)
        <g class="year" name="1904" transform="translate(42,0)
        <g class="year" name="1905" transform="translate(50,0)
```

Figure 18-3. The result of creating our year groups during the first data-join

Let's check to make sure our nested data has been bound correctly to its respective year groups. In Figure 18-4, we select a group element by its year name and inspect it. As required, the correct data has been bound by year, showing an array of data objects for the six Nobel Prize winners of 1901.

Having joined our year group data to their respective groups, we can now join those values to the circular marker groups representing each year. The first thing we need to do is select all the year groups with the key-values data we just added and bind the values array (the prizes for that year) to some *winner* placeholders, which will soon be joined to some circle markers. This is achieved by the following D3 calls:

```
let winners = svg
    .selectAll('.year')
    .selectAll('circle') ❶
    .data(
      d => d.values, ❷
      d => d.name ❸
    );
```

❶ We'll be creating a circle marker for each prize in the values array.

❷ We'll use the values array to create the circles with D3's join.

❸ We use an optional key to track the circles/winners by name—this will be useful for transition effects, as we'll see later on.

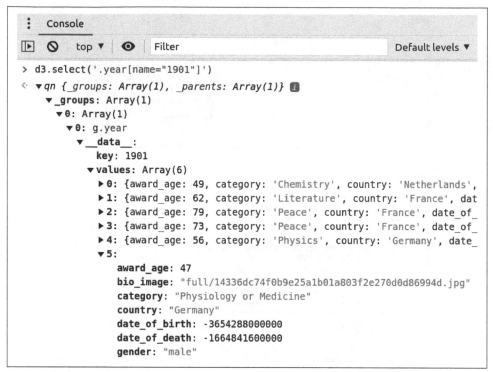

```
>  d3.select('.year[name="1901"]')
<  ▼qn {_groups: Array(1), _parents: Array(1)} ℹ
     ▼_groups: Array(1)
       ▼0: Array(1)
         ▼0: g.year
           ▼__data__:
               key: 1901
             ▼values: Array(6)
               ▶0: {award_age: 49, category: 'Chemistry', country: 'Netherlands',
               ▶1: {award_age: 62, category: 'Literature', country: 'France', dat
               ▶2: {award_age: 79, category: 'Peace', country: 'France', date_of_
               ▶3: {award_age: 73, category: 'Peace', country: 'France', date_of_
               ▶4: {award_age: 56, category: 'Physics', country: 'Germany', date_
               ▼5:
                   award_age: 47
                   bio_image: "full/14336dc74f0b9e25a1b01a803f2e270d0d86994d.jpg"
                   category: "Physiology or Medicine"
                   country: "Germany"
                   date_of_birth: -3654288000000
                   date_of_death: -1664841600000
                   gender: "male"
```

Figure 18-4. Checking the results of our first data-join with Chrome's console

Now that we've created our *circle* placeholders with winning entry data, it only remains to join these to a circle using D3's `join` method. This will keep track of any changes to the data and make sure circles are created and destroyed in sync. The rest of the impressively succinct code required is as follows in Example 18-4.

Example 18-4. A second data-join to produce the prizes' circle indicators

```
winners
    .join((enter) => {
      return enter.append('circle') ❶
              .attr('cy', height)
    })
    .attr('fill', function (d) {
      return nbviz.categoryFill(d.category) ❷
    })
    .attr('cx', xScale.bandwidth() / 2) ❸
    .attr('r', xScale.bandwidth() / 2)
    .attr("cy", (d, i) => yScale(i));
```

❶ A custom `enter` method is used to append any new circles needed and give them a default y position at the bottom (y is down for SVG) of the chart.

❷   A little helper method returns a color given the prize's category.

❸   The year group already has the correct x position, so we only need to use the bandwidth of the bars to set the radius and center the circle in the middle of the bar. The y-scale is used to set the height of the bar by index i in the winners array.

The code in Example 18-4 does the job of building our prize time chart, creating new indicator circles if required and placing them, along with any existing ones, at their correct position, as designated by their array index (see Figure 18-5).

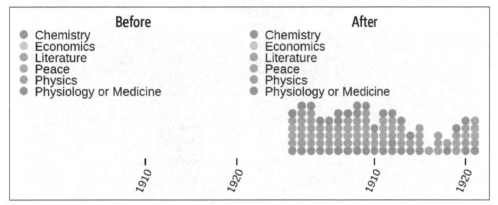

Figure 18-5. The result of our successful second data-join

Although we have produced a perfectly usable timeline, which will respond to user-driven changes in the data, the transition is a little stark and unengaging.[2] Let's now see a great demonstration of D3's power: how the addition of two lines of code can buy a rather cool visual effect as our timeline changes state.

A Little Transitional Sparkle

As things stand, when the user selects a new dataset,[3] the update pattern in Example 18-4 instantly sets the position of the relevant circles. What we now want to do is to animate this repositioning, smoothing it out over a couple of seconds.

Any user-driven filtering will either leave some existing indicators (e.g., when we select only the Chemistry prizes from all categories), add some new ones (e.g., changing our category from Physics to Chemistry), or do both. An edge case is when

---

2 As discussed in "Transitions" on page 432, the visual transition from one dataset to another can be both informative and lend a sense of continuity to the visualization, making it more appealing.

3 For example, filtering the prizes by category to show only the Physics winners.

the filtering leaves nothing (e.g., selecting female Economics winners). This means we need to decide what existing indicators should do and how to animate the positioning of new indicators.

Figure 18-6 shows what we want to happen on selecting a subset of the existing data, in this case filtering all Nobel Prizes to include only those Physics winners. On the user's selection of the Physics category, all indicators except the Physics ones are removed by the exit and remove methods. Meanwhile, the existing Physics indicators begin a two-second transition from their current position to an end position, dictated by their array index.

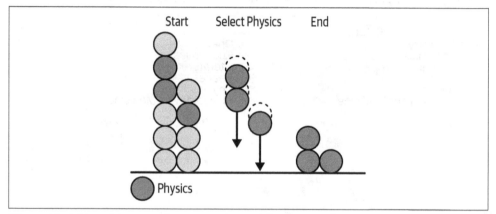

Figure 18-6. Transition on selecting a subset of the existing data

It may surprise you to discover that both these visual effects, moving existing bars smoothly into their new place and growing any new bars from the bottom of the chart, can be achieved by the addition of only two lines to our existing code. This is a big testimony to the power of D3's data-joining concept and its mature design.

To achieve the required transitions, we add calls to transition and duration methods before setting the y position (*cy* attribute) of the circle marker. These smooth the repositioning of the circle, easing it in over two seconds (2000ms):

```
winners
  .join((enter) => {
    return enter.append('circle').attr('cy', height) ❶
  })
  .attr('fill', function (d) {
    return nbviz.categoryFill(d.category)
  })
  .attr('cx', xScale.bandwidth() / 2)
  .attr('r', xScale.bandwidth() / 2)
  .transition() ❷
  .duration(2000)
  .attr("cy", (d, i) => yScale(i));
```

❶ Any new circles start at the bottom of the chart.

❷ All circles are eased into their y position over a duration of 2000ms.

As you can see, D3 makes it really easy to add cool visual effects to your data transitions. This is a testimony to its solid theoretical foundations. We now have our complete timeline chart, which transitions smoothly in response to data changes initiated by the user.

Updating the Bar Chart

When the time chart module is imported, it appends a callback function to the callbacks array in the core module. When data is updated in response to user interaction, this callback function is called and the time chart updated with new country data, nested by year:

```
nbviz.callbacks.push(() => { ❶
  let data = nbviz.nestDataByYear(nbviz.countryDim\
              .top(Infinity))
  updateTimeChart(data)
})
```

❶ This anonymous function is called in the core module when data is updated.

Summary

Following on from the bar chart in Chapter 17, this chapter extended the update pattern, showing how to use a second data-join on nested data to create a novel chart. It's important to emphasize that this ability to create novel visualizations is D3's great strength: you are not tied to the particular functionality of a conventional charting library but can achieve unique transformations of your data. As our Nobel Prize bar chart showed, it's easy to build conventional dynamic charts, but D3 allows for so much more.

We also saw how easy it is to liven up your visualizations with engaging transformations once a solid update pattern is in place.

In the next chapter, we will build the map component of our Nobel-viz using D3's impressive topographic library.

## CHAPTER 19

Mapping with D3

Building and customizing map visualizations is one of D3's core strengths. It has some very sophisticated libraries, allowing for all kinds of projections, from the workhorse Mercator and orthographic to more esoteric ones such as Conic Equidistant. Mapping seems to be something of an obsession for Mike Bostock and Jason Davies, D3's core devs, and their attention to detail is striking. If you have a mapping problem, chances are D3 can do the heavy lifting required.[1] In this chapter, we'll use our Nobel Prize visualization (Nobel-viz) map (Figure 19-1) to introduce the core D3 mapping concepts.

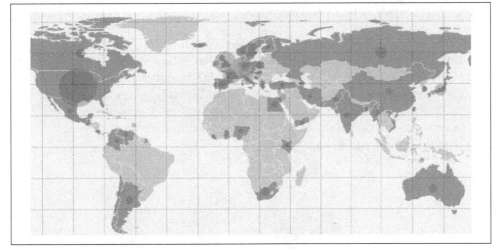

Figure 19-1. This chapter's target element

---

1 The math of geometric projections, for example, can get complicated fast.

Available Maps

The most popular mapping format is the aging shapefile (*https://oreil.ly/XV4Cb*), developed for geographic information system (GIS) software. There are many free and proprietary desktop programs[2] to manipulate and produce shapefiles.

Unfortunately, shapefiles were not designed for the web, which would far rather deal in a JSON-based map format, and demands small, efficient representations to limit bandwidth and related lag.

The good news is that there are many convenient ways to convert shapefiles to our preferred TopoJSON format,[3] meaning you can manipulate your shapefiles in software and then convert them to a web-friendly format. The standard way of finding maps for web dataviz is to first look for TopoJSON or GeoJSON versions, then search among the richer pool of shapefiles, and, as a last resort, roll your own using a shapefile, or equivalent, editor. Depending on how much map visualization you intend to do, there will probably be an off-the-shelf solution. For things like world maps or continental projections (e.g., the popular Albers USA), you can usually find a number of solutions with different degrees of accuracy.

For our Nobel map, we want a global mapping, at least showing all 58 Nobel Prize–winning nations, with labeled shapes for pretty much all of them. Luckily, D3 provides a number of example world maps, one at 50m grid resolution, the other a smaller 110m resolution map. The latter is fine for our fairly crude requirements.[4]

D3's Mapping Data Formats

D3 makes use of two JSON-based geometric data formats, GeoJSON (*https://geojson.org*) and TopoJSON (*https://oreil.ly/709GD*), an extension of GeoJSON devised by Mike Bostock that encodes topology. GeoJSON is more intuitive to read, but TopoJSON is far more efficient in most cases. Typically, maps are converted to TopoJSON for web delivery, where size is an important consideration. The TopoJSON is then converted to GeoJSON via D3 on the browser, to simplify SVG path creation, feature optimization, and so on.

---

2 I use and thoroughly recommend the open source QGIS (*https://www.qgis.org/en/site*).

3 Python's *topojson.py* and the TopoJSON command-line program.

4 As we'll see, it does lack a couple of our Nobel Prize countries, but these are too small to be clickable and we have the coordinates of their centers, allowing for a visual cue to be overlaid.

There is a nice summation of the differences between TopoJSON and GeoJSON on Stack Overflow (*https://oreil.ly/DvcaG*).

Let's have a look at the two formats now. Understanding their basic structure is important and a little effort there will pay off, especially as your mapping endeavors become more ambitious.

GeoJSON

GeoJSON files contain one `type` object, one of Point, MultiPoint, LineString, MultiLineString, Polygon, MultiPolygon, GeometryCollection, Feature, or FeatureCollection. The case of the type member values must be CamelCase (*https://oreil.ly/wS4q9*), as shown here. They may also contain a `crs` member, specifying a particular coordinate reference system.

FeatureCollections are the largest GeoJSON container, and maps with more than one region are usually specified with these. FeatureCollections contain a `features` array, each element of which is a GeoJSON object of a type listed in the previous paragraph.

Example 19-1 shows a typical FeatureCollection containing an array of country maps, the boundaries of which are specified by Polygons.

Example 19-1. The GeoJSON mapping data format

```
{
  "type": "FeatureCollection", ❶
  "features": [ ❷
    {
      "type": "Feature",
      "id": "AFG",
      "properties": {
        "name": "Afghanistan"
      },
      "geometry": { ❸
        "type": "Polygon",
        "coordinates": [
          [
            [
              61.210817, ❹
              35.650072
            ],
            [
              62.230651,
              35.270664
            ],
            ...
```

```
          ]
        ]
      }
    },
    ...
    {
      "type": "Feature",
      "id": "ZWE",
      "properties": {
        "name": "Zimbabwe"
      },
      "geometry": {
        "type": "Polygon",
        "coordinates": [
          [
            [...] ] ]
      }
    }
  ]
}
```

❶ Each GeoJSON file contains a single object with a type and containing…

❷ …an array of features—in this case, country objects…

❸ …with coordinate-based, polygonal geometry.

❹ Note that the geographic coordinates are given in [longitude, latitude] pairs, the reverse of conventional geographic positioning. This is because GeoJSON uses an [X,Y] coordinate scheme.

Although GeoJSON is more succinct than shapefiles and in the preferred JSON format, there is a lot of redundancy in the encoding of maps. For example, shared boundaries are specified twice and the floating-point coordinate format is fairly inflexible and, for many jobs, too precise. The TopoJSON format was designed to address these issues and produce a far more efficient way of delivering maps to the browser.

TopoJSON

Developed by Mike Bostock, TopoJSON is an extension to GeoJSON that encodes topology, stitching geometries together from a shared pool of line segments called arcs. Because they reuse these arcs, TopoJSON files are typically 80% smaller than their GeoJSON equivalents! In addition, taking a topological approach to map representation enables a number of techniques that use topology. One of these is topology-preserving shape simplification,[5] which can eliminate 95% of map points while retaining sufficient detail. Cartograms and automatic map coloring are also facilitated. Example 19-2 shows the structure of a TopoJSON file.

Example 19-2. Structure of our TopoJSON world map

```
{
    "type": "Topology",    ❶
    "objects":{            ❷
      "countries":{
        "type": "GeometryCollection",
        "geometries": [{
        "_id":24, "arcs":[[6,7,8],[10,11,12]], ... ❸
      ...}]},
      "land":{...},
    },
    "arcs":[[[67002,72360],[284,-219],[209..]], /*<-- arc*/ number 0 ❹
           [[70827,73379],[50,-165]], ...        /*<-- arc number 1*/
        ]
    "transform":{          ❺
      "scale":[
          0.003600036...,
          0.001736468...,
        ],
        "translate":[
          -180,
          -90
        ]
    }
}
```

❶ TopoJSON objects have a `Topology` type and must contain an `objects` object and an array of `arcs`.

❷ In this case, the objects are `countries` and `land`, both being arc-defined `Geometry Collections`.

❸ Each geometry (in this case defining a country shape) is defined by a number of arc paths, comprising continuous arcs referenced by their index in the `arcs` array ❹.

❹ An array of component arcs used to construct the objects. The arcs are referenced by index.

---

5 See this site by Mike Bostock (*https://bost.ocks.org/mike/simplify*) for a very cool example.

⑤ Numbers needed to quantize positions as integers rather than floats.

The smaller size of the TopoJSON format is obviously a big advantage if you have to fetch it to your web browser. Often only the GeoJSON format is available, so the ability to convert this to TopoJSON is a handy one. D3 provides a small command-line utility to do just this. Called `geo2topo`, it is part of the TopoJSON package and can be installed via `node`.

Converting Maps to TopoJSON

You can install TopoJSON via the `node` repositories (see Chapter 1), using the `-g` flag to make it a global[6] install:

```
$ npm install -g topojson
```

With `topojson` installed, converting an existing GeoJSON into TopoJSON is as easy as can be. Here we call `geo2topo` from the command line on a GeoJSON *geo_input.json* file, specifying an output file *topo_output.json*:

```
$ geo2topo -o topo_output.json geo_input.json
```

Alternatively, you can pipe the result to a file:

```
$ geo2topo geo_input.json > topo_output.json
```

`geo2topo` has a number of useful options, such as quantization, which allows you to specify your map's precision. Playing around with this option can result in a much smaller file with little perceptible reduction in quality. You can see the full spec on the geo2topo command-line reference (*https://oreil.ly/mp0RN*). If you want to convert your map files programmatically, there is a handy Python library for the job, *topojson.py*. You can find it on GitHub (*https://oreil.ly/8t7Ko*).

Now that we've got our map data in a light, efficient, web-optimized format, let's see how we use JavaScript to turn it into interactive web maps.

D3 Geo, Projections, and Paths

D3 has a client-side *topojson* library, dedicated to dealing with TopoJSON data. This converts the optimized, arc-based TopoJSON to the coordinate-based GeoJSON, ready to be manipulated by D3's `projections` and `paths`, objects in the *d3.geo* library.

Example 19-3 shows the process of extracting the GeoJSON features needed by our Nobel map from the TopoJSON *world-100m.json* map. This provides us with the coordinate-based polygons representing our countries and their borders.

---

6 By installing globally, you can use the `geo2topo` command in any directory.

In order to extract the GeoJSON features we require from the TopoJSON world object just delivered to the browser, we use *topojson*'s feature and mesh methods. feature returns the GeoJSON Feature or FeatureCollection for the specified object and mesh the GeoJSON MutliLineString geometry object representing the mesh for the specified object.

The feature and mesh methods take as their first argument the TopoJSON object and as their second a reference to the feature we want to extract (land and countries in Example 19-3). In our world map, countries is a FeatureCollection with a features array of countries (Example 19-3, ❷).

The mesh method has a third argument, which specifies a filter function, taking as arguments the two geometry objects (a and b) sharing the mesh arc. If the arc is unshared, then a and b are the same, allowing us to filter out external borders in our world map (Example 19-3, ❸).

Example 19-3. Extracting our TopoJSON features

```
// nbviz_main.mjs
import { initMap } from './nbviz_map.mjs'

Promise.all([
    d3.json('static/data/world-110m.json'), ❶
    d3.csv('static/data/world-country-names-nobel.csv'),
    // ...
 ]).then(ready)

function ready([worldMap, countryNames, countryData, winnersData]) {
    // ...
    nbviz.initMap(worldMap, countryNames)
}
// nbviz_map.mjs
export let initMap = function(world, names) {
    // EXTRACT OUR REQUIRED FEATURES FROM THE TOPOJSON
    let land = topojson.feature(world, world.objects.land),
        countries = topojson.feature(world, world.objects.countries)
                    .features, ❷
        borders = topojson.mesh(world, world.objects.countries,
                    function(a, b) { return a !== b; }); ❸
    // ...
}
```

❶ Load the map data using D3's helper functions and send on to a ready function to initiate the map chart.

❷ Uses topojson to extract our desired features from the TopoJSON data, delivering them in the GeoJSON format.

❸ Filters for only internal borders, shared between countries. If an arc is only used by one geometry (in this case, a country), then a and b are identical.

Map presentation in D3 generally follows a standard pattern. We first create a D3 `projection`, using one of D3's many and varied alternatives. We then create a `path` using this `projection`. This `path` is then used to convert the features and meshes extracted from our TopoJSON object into the SVG paths displayed in the browser window. Let's now look at the rich subject of D3 `projections`.

Projections

Probably the chief challenge for maps, since the time it was appreciated that the Earth is spheroidal, is that of representing a three-dimensional globe, or significant parts of it, in a two-dimensional form. In 1569, the Flemish cartographer Gerardus Mercator famously resolved this by extending lines from the Earth's center to significant boundary coordinates and then projecting them onto a surrounding cylinder. This had the useful property of representing lines of constant course, known as *rhumb lines*, as straight line segments, a very useful feature for the seafaring navigators intended to use the map. Unfortunately, the projection process distorts distances and size, magnifying the scale as one moves from the equator to the pole. As a result of this, the huge African continent appears not much bigger than Greenland when in reality it is around 14 times the size.

All projections are, like Mercator's, a compromise, and what's great about D3 is that the rich array of choices means one can balance these compromises to find the right projection for the job.[7] Figure 19-2 shows some alternative `projections` for our Nobel map, including the equirectangular one chosen for the final visualization. The constraint was to show all Nobel Prize–winning countries within the rectangular window and to try to maximize the space available, particularly in Europe where there are many countries that are small geographically but have a relatively large prize haul.

To create a D3 `projection`, just use one of the applicable *d3.geo* methods:

```
let projection = d3.geoEquirectangular()
// ...
```

D3 projections have a number of useful methods. It's common to use the `trans late` method to translate the map by half the width and height of the container, overriding the default of [480, 250]. You can also set the precision, which affects the degree of *adaptive resampling* used in the `projection`. Adaptive resampling is

---

7 The extended set of D3 projections (*https://oreil.ly/14vLd*) is part of an extension of D3, not in the main library.

a clever technique to increase the accuracy of projected lines while still performing efficiently.[8] The scale of the map and its center's longitude and latitude can be set by the scale and center methods.

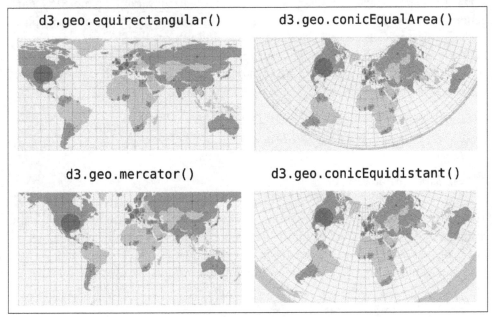

Figure 19-2. Some alternative mapping projections for the Nobel map

Putting the projection methods together, the following code is that used by our Nobel-viz world equirectangular map. Note that it's hand-tweaked to maximize the space given to Nobel Prize–winning countries. The two poles are truncated, there being no winners in either the Arctic or Antarctic (note that equirectangular maps assume a width/height ratio of 2):

```
let projection = d3.geoEquirectangular()
    .scale(193 * (height/480)) ❶
    .center([15,15]) ❷
    .translate([width / 2, height / 2])
    .precision(.1);
```

❶ Enlarged slightly; the default height is 480 and scale 153.

❷ Centered at 15 degrees east, 15 degrees north.

With our equirectangular projection defined, let's see how you use it to create a path, which will in turn be used to create the SVG maps.

---

8 See *https://oreil.ly/oAppn* for a nice demonstration.

Paths

Once you've settled on an appropriate projection for your map, you use it to create a D3 geographic path generator, which is a specialized variant of the SVG path generator (d3.svg.path). This path takes any GeoJSON feature or geometry object, such as a FeatureCollection, Polygon, or Point, and returns the SVG path data string for the d element. For example, with our map borders object, the geographic border coordinates describing a MultiLineString are converted into path coordinates for SVG.

Generally, we create our path and set its projection in one go:

```
var projection = d3.geoEquirectangular()
// ...

var path = d3.geoPath()
            .projection(projection);
```

Typically, we use the path as a function to generate the d attribute to an SVG path, using GeoJSON data bound using the datum method (used to bind a single object—not array—and shorthand for data([object])). So to use the borders data we just extracted using topojson.mesh to draw our country borders, we use the following:

```
// BOUNDRY MARKS
svg.insert("path", ".graticule")  ❶
    .datum(borders)
    .attr("class", "boundary")
    .attr("d", path);
```

 We want to insert the borders SVG before (below) the map's graticule (grid) overlay.

Figure 19-3 shows output from the Chrome Console for the TopoJSON borders object, extracted from our world-map data, and the resultant path generated by our *d3.geo* path, using the equirectangular projection.

The geo-path generator is the mainstay of D3 map presentations. I recommend playing around with different projections with simple geometries to get a feel for things, investigating the astonishing number of examples found at *bl.ocks.org* (*https://bl.ocks.org/mbostock*) and the docs on D3's GitHub page (*https://oreil.ly/2qgyf*), and checking out this great little demo (*https://oreil.ly/NansT*).

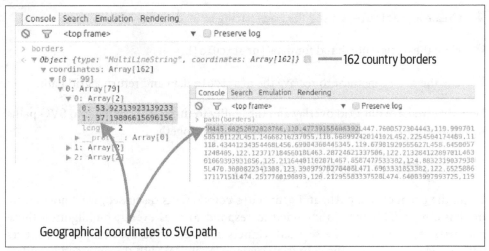

Figure 19-3. Path generator, from geometry to SVG path

Now let's look at one of the useful *d3.geo* components you'll use in your maps, the graticule (or map grid).

graticules

A useful component of *d3.geo* and one used in our Nobel map is the graticule, one of the geo shape generators.[9] This creates a global mesh of meridians (lines of longitude) and parallels (lines of latitude), spaced by default at 10 degrees. When our path is applied to this graticule, it generates a suitably projected grid, as shown back in Figure 19-1.

Example 19-4 shows how to add a graticule to your map. Note that if you want your grid to overlay your map paths, then its SVG path should come after the map paths in the DOM tree. As you'll see, you can use D3's insert method to enforce this order.

Example 19-4. Creating a graticule

```
var graticule = d3.geo.graticule()
                .step([20, 20]); ❶

svg.append("path")
    .datum(graticule) ❷
    .attr("class", "graticule")
    .attr("d", path); ❸
```

---

9 See the D3 GitHub (*https://oreil.ly/KqnF6*) for a full list.

❶ Create a `graticule`, setting the grid spacing to 20 degrees.

❷ Note the `datum` shorthand for data(`[graticule]`).

❸ Use the `path` generator to receive the `graticule` data and return a grid path.

Now that we have our grid overlay and the ability to turn our map file into SVG paths with the required `projection`, let's put the elements together.

Putting the Elements Together

Using the `projection`, `path`, and `graticule` components discussed, we'll now create the basic map. This map is intended to respond to user events, highlighting those countries represented by the selected winners, and reflecting the number of winners with a filled red circle at the countries' centers. We'll deal with this interactive update separately.

Example 19-5 shows the code required to build a basic global map. It follows what should now be a familiar pattern, getting the `mapContainer` from its `div` container (ID `nobel-map`), appending an `<svg>` tag to it, and then proceeding to add SVG elements, which in this case are D3-generated map paths.

Our map has fixed components (e.g., the choice of `projection` and `path`) that are not dependent on any data change and are defined outside the initializing `nbviz.initMap` method. `nbviz.initMap` is called when the visualization is initialized with data from the server. It receives the TopoJSON `world` object and uses it to build the basic map with the `path` object. Figure 19-4 shows the result.

Example 19-5. Building the map basics

```
// DIMENSIONS AND SVG
let mapContainer = d3.select('#nobel-map');
let boundingRect = mapContainer.node().getBoundingClientRect();
let width = boundingRect.width
    height = boundingRect.height;
let svg = mapContainer.append('svg');
// OUR CHOSEN PROJECTION
let projection = d3.geo.equirectangular()
    .scale(193 * (height/480))
    .center([15,15])
    .translate([width / 2, height / 2])
    .precision(.1);
// CREATE PATH WITH PROJECTION
let path = d3.geoPath().projection(projection);
// ADD GRATICULE
var graticule = d3.geoGraticule().step([20, 20]);
```

```
svg.append("path").datum(graticule)
    .attr("class", "graticule")
    .attr("d", path);
// A RADIUS SCALE FOR OUR CENTROID INDICATORS
var radiusScale = d3.scaleSqrt()
    .range([nbviz.MIN_CENTROID_RADIUS, nbviz.MAX_CENTROID_RADIUS]);
// OBJECT TO MAP COUNTRY NAME TO GEOJSON OBJECT
var cnameToCountry = {};
// INITIAL MAP CREATION, USING DOWNLOADED MAP DATA
export let initMap = function(world, names) { ❶
    // EXTRACT OUR REQUIRED FEATURES FROM THE TOPOJSON
    var land = topojson.feature(world, world.objects.land),
        countries = topojson.feature(world, world.objects.countries)
                        .features,
        borders = topojson.mesh(world, world.objects.countries,
                    function(a, b) { return a !== b; });
    // CREATE OBJECT MAPPING COUNTRY NAMES TO GEOJSON SHAPES
    var idToCountry = {};
    countries.forEach(function(c) {
        idToCountry[c.id] = c;
    });

    names.forEach(function(n) {
        cnameToCountry[n.name] = idToCountry[n.id]; ❷
    });
    // MAIN WORLD MAP
    svg.insert("path", ".graticule") ❸
        .datum(land)                 ❹
        .attr("class", "land")
        .attr("d", path)
    ;
    // COUNTRY PATHS
    svg.insert("g", ".graticule")
        .attr("class", 'countries');
    // COUNTRIES VALUE-INDICATORS
    svg.insert("g")
        .attr("class", "centroids");
    // BOUNDARY LINES
    svg.insert("path", ".graticule")
        .datum(borders)
        .attr("class", "boundary")
        .attr("d", path);
};
```

❶ world TopoJSON object with the country features with a names array connecting country names to country feature IDs (e.g., {id:36, name: 'Australia'}).

❷ Object that, if given country-name key, returns its respective GeoJSON geometry.

❸ Note that we insert this `path` before the `graticule` grid, keeping the grid overlay on top.

❹ Uses `datum` to assign the whole `land` object to our `path`.

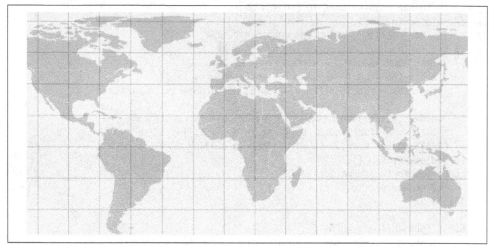

Figure 19-4. The basic map

With our map shapes in place, we can use a little CSS to style Figure 19-4, adding a light azure for the oceans and light gray for the land. The `graticule` is a half-transparent dark gray and the country boundaries white:

```
/* NOBEL-MAP STYLES */
#nobel-map {
    background: azure;
}

.graticule {
    fill: none;
    stroke: #777;
    stroke-width: .5px;
    stroke-opacity: .5;
}

.land {
    fill: #ddd;
}

.boundary {
    fill: none;
    stroke: #fff;
    stroke-width: .5px;
}
```

With the SVG map assembled, let's see how we use the winners dataset to draw the Nobel Prize–winning countries and the red indicator for number of wins.

Updating the Map

The first time our Nobel map gets updated is when the visualization is initialized. At this point the selected dataset is unfiltered, containing all the Nobel Prize winners. Subsequently, in response to filters applied by the user (e.g., all the Chemistry winners or those from France), the dataset will change and our map changes to reflect that.

So updating the map involves sending it a dataset of the Nobel Prize–winning countries with their current prize haul, dependent on the user filters applied. To do this, we use an updateMap method:

```
let updateMap = function(countryData) { //...
              }
```

The countryData array has this form:

```
[
  {
    code: "USA",
    key: "United States",
    population: 319259000,
    value: 336 ❶
  },
  // ... 56 more countries
]
```

❶   The number of winners for the US in the currently selected dataset.

We want to convert this array before sending it to our D3 map. The following code does this job, providing an array of country objects with properties geo (the country's GeoJSON geometry), name (the country name), and number (the country's number of Nobel Prize winners):

```
let mapData = countryData
    .filter(d => d.value > 0) ❶
    .map(function(d) {
      return {
        geo: cnameToCountry[d.key], ❷
        name: d.key,
        number: d.value
      }
    });
```

❶   Filters out countries with no winners—we only display winning countries on the map.

❷ Uses the country's key (its name in this case) to retrieve its GeoJSON feature.

We want to display a red circular indicator at the center of our winning countries, indicating the number of prizes won. The circles' areas should be proportional to the number of prizes won (absolute or per capita), which means (by circle area = pi × radius-squared) their radius should be a function of the square root of that prize number. D3 provides a handy `sqrt` scale for just such a need, allowing you to set a domain (min and max prize number in this case) and a range (min and max indicator radius).

Let's see a quick example of the `sqrt` scale in action. In the following code, we set a scale with a domain between 0 and 100 and a zero-based range with a maximum area of 25 (5 × 5). This means calling the scale with 50 (half the range) should give the square root of half the maximum area (12.5):

```
var sc = d3.scaleSqrt().domain([0, 100]).range([0, 5]);
sc(50) // returns 3.5353..., the square root of 12.5
```

To create our indicator radius scale, we create a `sqrt` scale using the maximum and minimum radii specified in *nbviz_core.js* to set its range:

```
var radiusScale = d3.scaleSqrt()
    .range([nbviz.MIN_CENTROID_RADIUS,
    nbviz.MAX_CENTROID_RADIUS]);
```

In order to get the domain to our scales, we use this `mapData` to get the maximum number of winners per country and use that value as the domain's upper value, with 0 for its lower:

```
var maxWinners = d3.max(mapData.map(d => d.number))
// DOMAIN OF VALUE-INDICATOR SCALE
radiusScale.domain([0, maxWinners]);
```

To add our country shapes to the existing map, we bind `mapData` to a selection on the `countries` group of class `country` and implement an update pattern (see "Updating the DOM with Data" on page 421) to first add any country shapes required by the `map Data`. Instead of removing unbound country paths, we use the CSS `opacity` property to make the bound countries visible and the unbound invisible. A two-second transition is used to make these countries fade in and out appropriately. Example 19-6 shows the update pattern.

Example 19-6. Updating the country shapes

```
let countries = svg
    .select('.countries').selectAll('.country')
    .data(mapData, d => d.name)
// Use a data-join to make selected countries visible
// and fade them in over TRANS_DURATION milliseconds
```

```
countries
  .join(
    (enter) => {
      return enter
        .append('path') ❶
              .attr('d', function (d) {
                    return path(d.geo)
        })
        .attr('class', 'country')
        .attr('name', d => d.name)
        .on('mouseenter', function (event, d) { ❷
          d3.select(this).classed('active', true)
        })
        .on('mouseout', function (d) {
          d3.select(this).classed('active', false)
        })
    },
    (update) => update,
    (exit) => { ❸
      return exit
        .classed('visible', false)
        .transition()
        .duration(nbviz.TRANS_DURATION)
        .style('opacity', 0)
    }
  )
  .classed('visible', true)
  .transition() ❹
  .duration(nbviz.TRANS_DURATION)
  .style('opacity', 1)
```

❶   Use the GeoJSON data to create country map shapes using our path object.

❷   UI placeholders, which set the SVG paths to class *active* on mouse-over. Note that we use the function keyword here as opposed to the usual arrow notation shorthand (⇒). This is because we wish to use D3 to access the DOM element (map region) entered by the mouse using the this keyword, which is not available with arrow functions.

❸   A customized exit function that fades out (sets opacity to 0) the country shape over 2000 (TRANS_DURATION) milliseconds.

❹   Any new countries are faded in (opacity 1) over 2000 (TRANS_DURATION) ms.

Note that we add a CSS country class to freshly entered countries, setting their color to a light green. In addition to this, the mouse events are used to class the country active if the cursor is over it, highlighting it with a darker green. Here are the CSS classes:

```
.country{
    fill: rgb(175, 195, 186); /* light green */
}

.country.active{
    fill: rgb(155, 175, 166); /* dark green */
}
```

The update pattern shown in Example 19-6 will smoothly transition from old to new datasets, produced in response to user-applied filters and passed to updateMap. All we need now is to add similarly responsive filled circular indicators, centered on the active countries and reflecting their current value, either an absolute or relative (per capita) measure of their Nobel Prize haul.

Adding Value Indicators

To add our circular value indicators, we want an update pattern that mirrors that used to create our country SVG paths. We want to bind to the mapData dataset and append, update, and remove our indicator circles accordingly. As with the country shapes, we'll adjust the indicators' opacity to add and remove them from the map.

The indicators need to be placed at the center of their respective countries. D3's path generator provides a number of useful utility methods for dealing with GeoJSON geometries. One of them is centroid, which computes the projected centroid for the specified feature:

```
// Given the GeoJSON of country (country.geo)
// calculate x, y coords of center
var center = path.centroid(country.geo);
// center = [x, y]
```

While path.centroid does a pretty good job as a rule, and is very useful for labeling shape, boundaries, and so on, it can produce strange results, particularly with highly concave geometries. Handily, the world country data we stored in "Getting Country Data for the Nobel Dataviz" on page 128 contains the central coordinates of all our Nobel Prize countries.

We'll first write a little method to retrieve those given a mapData object:

```
var getCentroid = function(d) {
    var latlng = nbviz.data.countryData[d.name].latlng; ❶
    return projection([latlng[1], latlng[0]]); ❷
};
```

❶ Get the latitude and longitude of our country's center by name, using the stored world country data.

❷ Use our equirectangular projection to turn these into SVG coordinates.

As shown in Example 19-7, we bind our `mapData` to the selection of all elements of class `centroid` in the `centroids` group we added in Example 19-5. The data is bound via the `name` key.

Example 19-7. Adding prize-haul indicators to the Nobel countries' centroids

```
let updateMap = function(countryData) {
//...
  // BIND MAP DATA WITH NAME KEY
  let centroids = svg
    .select('.centroids').selectAll('.centroid')
    .data(mapData, d => d.name) ❶
  // JOIN DATA TO CIRCLE INDICATORS
  centroids
    .join(
      (enter) => {
        return enter
          .append("circle")
          .attr("class", "centroid")
          .attr("name", (d) => d.name)
          .attr("cx", (d) => getCentroid(d)[0]) ❷
          .attr("cy", (d) => getCentroid(d)[1])
      },
      (update) => update,
      (exit) => exit.style("opacity", 0)
    )
    .classed("active",
      (d) => d.name === nbviz.activeCountry)
    .transition()
    .duration(nbviz.TRANS_DURATION) ❸
    .style("opacity", 1)
    .attr("r", (d) => radiusScale(+d.number))
};
```

❶ Binds the map data to the centroid elements using the `name` key.

❷ Uses the `getCentroid` function to return pixel positions for the geocoordinates of the countries' centers.

❸ This 2000 ms transition fades the circular marker in by increasing its opacity while simultaneously transitioning to its new radius.

Using a bit of CSS, we can make the indicators red and slightly transparent, allowing map details and, where they are densely packed in Europe, other indicators to show through. If the country is selected by the user, using the country filter on the UI bar, it is classed as `active` and given a golden hue. Here's the CSS to do that:

```
.centroid{
    fill: red;
    fill-opacity: 0.3;
    pointer-events: none;  ❶
}

.centroid.active {
    fill: goldenrod;
    fill-opacity: 0.6;
}
```

❶ This allows mouse events to propagate to country shapes below the circles, allowing the user to still click on them.

The active centroid indicators we just added are the last element of our Nobel Prize map. Now let's take a look at the complete article.

Our Completed Map

With the country and indicator update patterns in place, our map should respond to user-driven filtering with a smooth transition. Figure 19-5 shows the result of selecting Nobel Prizes for Economics. Only winning countries remain highlighted and the value indicators are resized, reflecting American dominance of this category.

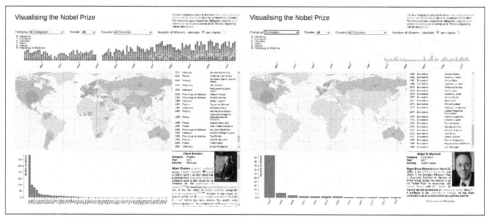

Figure 19-5. (left) Shows the map with the full Nobel dataset; (right) prizes are filtered by category, showing the Economics winners (and the dominance of the US economists)

The map as it stands in not interactive but does show when a user hovers over a particular country with a mouse, by calling the mouseenter and mouseout callback functions and adding or removing an active class. These callbacks could easily be used to add more functionality to the map, such as tooltips or the use of the countries as clickable data filters. Let's now use these to build a simple tooltip, to show the country the mouse is hovering over and some simple prize information.

Building a Simple Tooltip

Tooltips and other interactive widgets are the kind of thing commonly demanded of data visualizers and though they can get quite involved, particularly if they themselves are interactive (e.g., menus that appear on mouse hover), there are some simple recipes that are very handy to know. In this section, I'll show how to build a simple but pretty effective tooltip. Figure 19-6 shows what we're aiming to build.

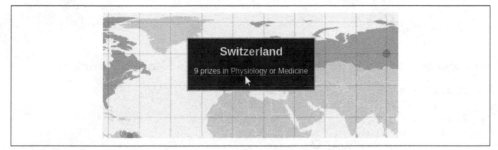

Figure 19-6. A simple tooltip for our Nobel Prize map

Let's remind ourselves of our current `countries` update, where `mouseenter` and `mouseout` event handlers are added during a data-join:

```
// ENTER AND APPEND ANY NEW COUNTRIES
countries.join((enter) => {
  return enter.append('path')
  // ...
    .on('mouseenter', function(d) {
        d3.select(this).classed('active', true);
    })
    .on('mouseout', function(d) {
        d3.select(this).classed('active', false);
    })
  })
  ;
```

In order to add a tooltip to our map, we need to do three things:

1. Create a tooltip box in HTML with placeholders for the information we want to display—in this case, country name and number of wins in the selected prize category.

2. Display this HTML box over the mouse when the user moves it into a country and hide it when they move the mouse out.

3. Update the box when displayed using the data bound to the country underneath the mouse.

We create the HTML for the tooltip by adding a content block to the Nobel-viz map section, with ID map-tooltip, an <h2> header for its title, and a <p> tag for the tooltip's text:

```
<!-- index.html -->
    <!-- ... -->
      <div id="nobel-map">
        <div id="map-tooltip">
          <h2></h2>
          <p></p>
        </div>
      <!-- ... -->
```

We'll also need some CSS for the tooltip's look and feel, added to our *style.css* file:

```
/* css/style.css */
/* MAP TOOLTIP */
#map-tooltip {
    position: absolute;
    pointer-events: none; ❶
    color: #eee;
    font-size: 12px;
    opacity: 0.7; /* a little transparent */
    background: #222;
    border: 2px solid #555;
    border-color: goldenrod;
    padding: 10px;
    left: -999px; ❷
}

#map-tooltip h2 {
    text-align: center;
    padding: 0px;
    margin: 0px;
}
```

❶ Setting pointer-events to none effectively lets you click on things underneath the tooltip.

❷ Initially, the tooltip is hidden far to the (virtual) left of the browser window, using a large negative x index.

With our tooltip's HTML in place and the element hidden to the left of the browser window (left is –9999 pixels), we just need to extend our mousein and mouseout callback functions to display or hide the tooltip. The mousein function, called when the user moves the mouse into a country, does most of the work:

```
// ...
countries.join(
    (enter) => {
    .append('path')
```

```
            .attr('class', 'country')
            .on('mouseenter', function(event) {

                var country = d3.select(this);
                // don't do anything if the country is not visible
                if(!country.classed('visible')){ return; }

                // get the country data object
                var cData = country.datum();
                // if only one prize, use singular 'prize'
                var prize_string = (cData.number === 1)?
                    ' prize in ': ' prizes in ';
                // set the header and text of the tooltip
                tooltip.select('h2').text(cData.name);
                tooltip.select('p').text(cData.number
                    + prize_string + nbviz.activeCategory);
                // set the border color according to selected
                // prize category
                var borderColor =
                  (nbviz.activeCategory === nbviz.ALL_CATS)?
                    'goldenrod':
                    nbviz.categoryFill(nbviz.activeCategory);
                tooltip.style('border-color', borderColor);

                var mouseCoords = d3.pointer(event); ❶
                var w = parseInt(tooltip.style('width')), ❷
                    h = parseInt(tooltip.style('height'));
                tooltip.style('top', (mouseCoords[1] - h) + 'px'); ❸
                tooltip.style('left', (mouseCoords[0] - w/2) + 'px');

                d3.select(this).classed('active', true);
        })
        .on('mouseout', function (d) {
          tooltip.style('left', '-9999px') ❹
          d3.select(this).classed('active', false)
        })
      }, // ...
    )
```

❶ D3's `pointer` method returns the mouse coordinates from the event object (here, relative to the parent map group) in pixels, which we can use to position the tooltip.

❷ We get the computed width and height of the tooltip box, which has been adjusted to accommodate our country title and prize string.

❸ We use the mouse coordinates and the width and height of the tooltip box to position the box centered horizontally and roughly above the mouse cursor (the width and height don't include our 10 pixels of padding around the tooltip's `<div>`).

❹   When the mouse leaves a country, we vanish the tooltip by placing it to the far left of the map.

With the `mouseenter` callback function written, we now only need a `mouseout` to hide the tooltip by placing it far to the left of the browser window:

```
countries.join(
    (enter) => {
    .append('path')
    .attr('class', 'country')
    .on('mouseenter', function(event) {
    // ...
    })
    .on('mouseout', function (d) {
      tooltip.style('left', '-9999px') ❶
      d3.select(this).classed('active', false)
    })
  }, // ...
)
```

❶   When the mouse leaves the country we shift the tooltip far to the left, out of the browser viewport, and remove the `'active'` class from the country, returning it to the default country color.

With the `mouseenter` and `mouseout` functions operating in concert, you should see the tooltip appearing and disappearing where needed, just as shown in Figure 19-6.

Updating the Map

When the map module is imported, it appends a callback function to the callbacks array in the core module. When data is updated in response to user interaction, this callback function is called and the bar chart updated with new country data:

```
nbviz.callbacks.push(() => { ❶
  let data = nbviz.getCountryData()
  updateMap(data)
})
```

❶   This anonymous function is called in the core module when data is updated.

Now that we've built the map component of our Nobel dataviz, let's summarize what we've learned before moving on to show how user input drives the visualization.

Summary

D3 mapping is a rich area, with many varied projections and lots of utility methods to help with manipulating geometries. But building a map follows a fairly standard procedure, as demonstrated in the chapter: you first choose your projection—say, a Mercator or maybe the Albers conic projection (*https://oreil.ly/Nz6Ar*) commonly used for mapping the US. You then use this projection to create a D3 `path` generator, which turns GeoJSON features into SVG paths, creating the map you see. The Geo-JSON will normally be extracted from more efficient TopoJSON data.

This chapter also demonstrated how easy it is with D3 to interactively highlight your map and deal with cursor movements. Taken together, the basic set of skills should allow you to start building your own mapping visualizations.

Now that we've constructed all of our SVG-based graphical elements, let's see how well D3 works with conventional HTML elements by building our winners list and an individual's biography box.

## CHAPTER 20

Visualizing Individual Winners

We want our Nobel Prize visualization (Nobel-viz) to include a list of currently selected winners and a biography box (aka bio-box) to display the details of an individual winner (see Figure 20-1). By clicking on a winner in the list, the user can see his or her details in the bio-box. In this chapter, we'll see how to build the list and bio-box, how to repopulate the list when the user selects new data (with the menu bar filters), and how to make the list clickable.

Winners' list			Bio-box
1923	Physiology or Medicine	Frederick G. Banting	
1923	Chemistry	Friderik Pregl	
1922	Chemistry	Francis William Aston	**Albert Einstein**
1922	Literature	Jacinto Benavente	Category Physics
1922	Peace	Fridtjof Nansen	Year 1921
1922	Physiology or Medicine	Otto Fritz Meyerhof	Country Germany
1922	Physics	Niels Bohr	
1921	Chemistry	Frederick Soddy	**Albert Einstein** (/ˈælbərt ˈaɪnʃtaɪn/;
1921	Peace	Hjalmar Branting	German: [ˈalbɛrt ˈaɪnʃtaɪn] (🔊 listen); 14
1921	Peace	Christian Lous Lange	March 1879 – 18 April 1955) was a
1921	Physics	Albert Einstein	German-born theoretical physicist.
1921	Literature	Anatole France	Einstein's work is also known for its
1920	Physics	Charles Édouard Guillaume	influence on the philosophy of
1920	Literature	Knut Hamsun	science.[4][5] He developed the general theory of relativity,
1920	Chemistry	Walther Nernst	one of the two pillars of modern physics (alongside
1920	Peace	Léon Bourgeois	quantum mechanics).[3][6]:274 Einstein is best known in
1920	Physiology or Medicine	August Krogh	popular culture for his mass–energy equivalence formula E
1919	Peace	Woodrow Wilson	$= mc^2$ (which has been dubbed "the world's most famous
1919	Literature	Carl Spitteler	equation").[7] He received the 1921 Nobel Prize in Physics
1919	Physics	Johannes Stark	for his "services to theoretical physics", in particular his
1919	Physiology or Medicine	Jules Bordet	
1918	Chemistry	Fritz Haber	

Figure 20-1. The chapter's target elements

As this chapter will demonstrate, D3 isn't just for building SVG visualizations. You can bind data to any DOM element and use it to change its attributes and properties or its event-handling callback functions. D3's data joining and event handling (achieved via the on method) play very well with common user interfaces such as the clickable list of this chapter and selection boxes.[1]

Let's deal first with the list of winners and how it is built with the dataset of currently selected winners.

Building the List

We build our list of winners (see Figure 20-1) using an HTML table with Year, Category, and Name columns. The basic skeleton of this list is provided in the Nobel-viz's *index.html* file:

```
<!DOCTYPE html>
<meta charset="utf-8">
<body>
...
    <div id="nobel-list">
      <h2>Selected winners</h2>
      <table>
        <thead>
          <tr>
            <th id='year'>Year</th>
            <th id='category'>Category</th>
            <th id='name'>Name</th>
          </tr>
        </thead>
        <tbody>
        </tbody>
      </table>
    </div>
...
</body>
```

We'll use a little CSS in *style.css* to style this table, adjusting the width of the columns and their font size:

```
/* WINNERS LIST */
#nobel-list { overflow: scroll; overflow-x: hidden; } ❶

#nobel-list table{ font-size: 10px; }
#nobel-list table th#year { width: 30px }
#nobel-list table th#category { width: 120px }
#nobel-list table th#name { width: 120px }
```

---

1 We'll cover selection boxes (as data filters) in Chapter 21.

```
#nobel-list h2 { font-size: 14px; margin: 4px;
text-align: center }
```

 overflow: scroll clips the content of the list (keeping it within our nobel-list container) and adds a scroll bar so we can access all the winners. overflow-x: hidden inhibits the addition of a horizontal scroll bar.

In order to create the list, we will add <tr> row elements (containing a <td> data tag for each column) to the table's <tbody> element for each winner in the current dataset, producing something like this:

```
...
<tbody>
  <tr>
    <td>2014</td>
    <td>Chemistry</td>
    <td>Eric Betzig</td>
  </tr>
  ...
</tbody>
...
```

To create these rows, an updateList method will be called by our central onData Change when the app is initialized and subsequently when the user applies a data filter and the list of winners changes (see "Basic Data Flow" on page 393). The data received by updateList will have the following structure:

```
// data =
[{
  name:"C\u00e9sar Milstein",
  category:"Physiology or Medicine",
  gender:"male",
  country:"Argentina",
  year: 1984
  _id: "5693be6c26a7113f2cc0b3f4"
},
...
]
```

Example 20-1 shows the updateList method. The data received is first sorted by year and then, after any existing rows have been removed, used to build the table rows.

Example 20-1. Building the selected winners list

```
let updateList = function (data) {
  let tableBody, rows, cells
  // Sort the winners' data by year
  data = data.sort(function (a, b) {
    return +b.year - +a.year
  })
```

```
// select table-body from index.html
tableBody = d3.select('#nobel-list tbody')
// create place-holder rows bound to winners' data
rows = tableBody.selectAll('tr').data(data)

rows.join( ❶
  (enter) => {
    // create any new rows required
    return enter.append('tr').on('click', function (event, d) { ❷
      console.log('You clicked a row ' + JSON.stringify(d))
      displayWinner(d)
    })
  },
  (update) => update,
  (exit) => {
    return exit ❸
      .transition()
      .duration(nbviz.TRANS_DURATION)
      .style('opacity', 0)
      .remove()
  }
)

cells = tableBody ❹
  .selectAll('tr')
  .selectAll('td')
  .data(function (d) {
    return [d.year, d.category, d.name]
  })
// Append data cells, then set their text
cells.join('td').text(d => d) ❺
// Display a random winner if data is available
if (data.length) { ❻
  displayWinner(data[Math.floor(Math.random() * data.length)])
}
}
```

❶ A now familiar join pattern, using the bound winners' data to create and update list items.

❷ When the user clicks on a row, this click-handler function will pass the winner data bound to that row to a displayWinner method, which will update the bio-box accordingly.

❸ This custom exit function fades out any excess rows over the transition period of two seconds, reducing their opacity to zero before removing them.

❹ First, we use a winner's data to create an array of data with year, category, and name, which will be used to create the row's <td> data cells...

❺ …we then join this array to the row's data cells (`td`) and use it to set their text.

❻ Each time the data is changed, we select a winner at random from the new dataset and display him or her in the bio-box.

As the user moves the cursor over a row in our winners table, we want to highlight the row and also to change the style of pointer to `cursor` to indicate that the row is clickable. Both of these details are fixed by the following CSS, added to our *style.css* file:

```css
#nobel-list tr:hover{
    cursor: pointer;
    background: lightblue;
}
```

Our `updateList` method calls a `displayWinner` method to build a winner's biography box when a row is clicked or when the data changes (with a random choice). Let's now see how the bio-box is built.

Building the Bio-Box

The bio-box uses a winner's object to fill in the details of a little mini-biography. The bio-box's HTML skeleton is provided in the *index.html* file consisting of content blocks for the biographical elements and a `readmore` footer providing a Wikipedia link to further information on the winner:

```html
<!DOCTYPE html>
<meta charset="utf-8">
<body>
...
    <div id="nobel-winner">
      <div id="picbox"></div>
      <div id='winner-title'></div>
      <div id='infobox'>
        <div class='property'>
          <div class='label'>Category</div>
          <span name='category'></span>
        </div>
        <div class='property'>
          <div class='label'>Year</div>
          <span name='year'></span>
        </div>
        <div class='property'>
          <div class='label'>Country</div>
          <span name='country'></span>
        </div>
      </div>
      <div id='biobox'></div>
      <div id='readmore'>
```

```
        <a href='#'>Read more at Wikipedia</a></div>
    </div>
...
</body>
```

A little CSS in *style.css* sets the positions of the list and bio-box elements, sizes their content blocks, and provides borders and font specifics:

```
/* WINNER INFOBOX */

#nobel-winner {
    font-size: 11px;
    overflow: auto;
    overflow-x: hidden;
    border-top: 4px solid;
}

#nobel-winner #winner-title {
    font-size: 12px;
    text-align: center;
    padding: 2px;
    font-weight: bold;
}

#nobel-winner #infobox .label {
    display: inline-block;
    width: 60px;
    font-weight: bold;
}

#nobel-winner #biobox { font-size: 11px; }
#nobel-winner #biobox p { text-align: justify; }

#nobel-winner #picbox {
    float: right;
    margin-left: 5px;
}
#nobel-winner #picbox img { width:100px; }

#nobel-winner #readmore {
    font-weight: bold;
    text-align: center;
}
```

With our content blocks in place, we need to make a callback to our data API to get the data needed to fill them. Example 20-2 shows the displayWinner method used to build the box.

Example 20-2. Updating a selected winner's biography box

```
let displayWinner = function (wData) {
  // store the winner's bio-box element
  let nw = d3.select('#nobel-winner')

  nw.select('#winner-title').text(wData.name)
  nw.style('border-color', nbviz.categoryFill(wData.category)) ❶

  nw.selectAll('.property span').text(function (d) { ❷
    var property = d3.select(this).attr('name')
    return wData[property]
  })

  nw.select('#biobox').html(wData.mini_bio)
  // Add an image if available, otherwise remove the old one
  if (wData.bio_image) { ❸
    nw.select('#picbox img')
      .attr('src', 'static/images/winners/' + wData.bio_image)
      .style('display', 'inline')
  } else {
    nw.select('#picbox img').style('display', 'none')
  }

  nw.select('#readmore a').attr( ❹
    'href',
    'http://en.wikipedia.org/wiki/' + wData.name
  )
}
```

❶ Our nobel-winner element has a top border (CSS: border-top: 4px solid), which we will color according to the winner's category, using the categoryFill method defined in *nbviz_core.js*.

❷ We select the <span> tags of all the divs with class property. These are of the form <span name=*category*></span>. We use the span's name attribute to retrieve the correct property from our Nobel winner's data and use it to set the tag's text.

❸ Here we set the src (source) attribute on our winner's image if one is available. We use the image tag's display attribute to hide it (setting it to none) if no image is available or show it (the default inline) if one is.

❹ Our winner's name was scraped from Wikipedia and can be used to retrieve their Wikipedia page.

Updating the Winners List

When the details (winners list and bio) module is imported, it appends a callback function to the callbacks array in the core module. When data is updated in response to user interaction, this callback function is called and the list updated with new country data, using Crossfilter's country dimension:

```
nbviz.callbacks.push(() => {  ❶
  let data = nbviz.countryDim.top(Infinity)
  updateList(data)
})
```

❶ This anonymous function is called in the core module when data is updated.

Now that we've seen how we add a bit of personality to our Nobel-viz by allowing users to display a winner's biography, let's summarize this chapter before moving on to see how the menu bar is built.

Summary

In this chapter, we saw how D3 can be used to build conventional HTML constructions, not just SVG graphics. D3 is just as at home building lists, tables, and the like as it is displaying circles or changing the rotation of a line. Wherever there is changing data that needs to be reflected by elements of a web page, D3 is likely able to solve the problem elegantly and efficiently.

With our winners list and biography box covered, we've seen how all the visual elements in our Nobel-viz are built. It only remains to see how the visualization's menu bar is built and how the changes it enables, to both the dataset and the measure of prizes, are reflected by these visual elements.

## CHAPTER 21

The Menu Bar

The previous chapters showed how to build the visual components of our interactive Nobel Prize visualization, the time chart to display all Nobel Prize winners by year, a map to show geographic distributions, a list to display the currently selected winners, and a bar chart to compare absolute and per capita wins by country. In this chapter, we will see how the user interacts with the visualization by using selectors and buttons (see Figure 21-1) to create a filtered dataset that is then reflected by the visual components. For example, selecting Physics in the category-select box filters will display only Physics prize winners in the Nobel Prize visualization (Nobel-viz) elements. The filters in our menu bar are cumulative, so we can, for example, select only those female chemists from France to have won the Nobel Prize.[1]

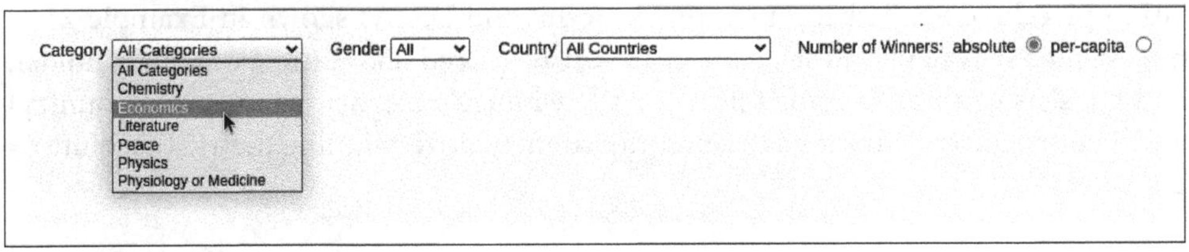

Figure 21-1. This chapter's target menu bar

In the sections ahead, I will show you how to use D3 to build the menu bar and how JavaScript callbacks are used to respond to user-driven changes.

---

1 Remarkably, Marie Curie and her daughter Irène Joliot-Curie hold this distinction.

Creating HTML Elements with D3

Many people think of D3 as a specialized tool for creating SVG visualizations composed of graphical primitives such as lines and circles. Though D3 is great for this (the best there is), it's equally at home creating conventional HTML elements such as tables or selector boxes. For tricky, data-driven HTML complexes like hierarchical menus, D3's nested data-joins are an ideal way to create the DOM elements and the callbacks to deal with user selections.

We saw in Chapter 20 how easy it is to create `table` rows from a selected dataset or fill in the details of a biography box with a winner's data. In this chapter, we'll show how to populate selectors with options based on changing datasets and how to attach callback functions to user interface elements such as selectors and radio boxes.

 If you have stable HTML elements (e.g., a select box whose options are not dependent on changing data), it's best to write them in HTML and then use D3 to attach any callback functions you need to deal with user input. As with CSS styling, you should do as much as possible in vanilla HTML. It keeps the codebase cleaner and is easier to understand by other devs and non-devs. In this chapter, I stretch this rule a bit to demonstrate the creation of HTML elements, but it's pretty much always the way to go.

Building the Menu Bar

As discussed in "The HTML Skeleton" on page 384, our Nobel-viz is built on HTML `<div>` placeholders, fleshed out with JavaScript and D3. As shown in Example 21-1, our menu bar is built on the `nobel-menu` `<div>`, placed above the main chart holder, and consists of three selector filters (by the winners' category, gender, and country) and a couple of radio buttons to select the country prize-winning metric (absolute or per capita).

Example 21-1. The HTML skeleton for the menu bar

```
<!-- ... -->
<body>
<!-- ... -->
  <!-- THE PLACEHOLDERS FOR OUR VISUAL COMPONENTS  -->
    <div id="nbviz">
      <!-- BEGIN MENU BAR -->
      <div id="nobel-menu">
        <div id="cat-select">
          Category
          <select></select>
        </div>
```

```
      <div id="gender-select">
        Gender
        <select>
          <option value="All">All</option>
          <option value="female">Female</option>
          <option value="male">Male</option>
        </select>
      </div>
      <div id="country-select">
        Country
        <select></select>
      </div>
      <div id='metric-radio'>
        Number of Winners: 
        <form>
          <label>absolute
            <input type="radio" name="mode" value="0" checked>
          </label>
          <label>per-capita
            <input type="radio" name="mode" value="1">
          </label>
        </form>
      </div>
    </div>
    <!-- END MENU BAR  -->
  <div id='chart-holder'>
<!-- ... -->
</body>
```

Now we'll add the UI elements in turn, starting with the selector filters.

Building the Category Selector

In order to build the category selector, we're going to need a list of option strings. Let's create that list using the CATEGORIES list defined in *nbviz_core.js*:

```
import nbviz from './nbviz_core.mjs'

let catList = [nbviz.ALL_CATS].concat(nbviz.CATEGORIES) ❶
```

❶ Creates the category selector's list ['All Categories', 'Chemistry', 'Econo mics', …] by concatenating the list ['All Categories'] and the list ['Chemis try', 'Economics', …].

We're now going to use this category list to make the options tags. We'll first use D3 to grab the #cat-select select tag:

```
//...
    let catSelect = d3.select('#cat-select select');
```

With `catSelect` to hand, let's use a standard D3 data-join to turn our `catList` list of categories into HTML option tags:

```
catSelect.selectAll('option')
    .data(catList)
    .join('option')
    .attr('value', d => d)
    .html(d => d);
```

 After data binding, append an `option` for each `catList` member.

 We are setting the `option`'s `value` attribute and text to a category (e.g., `<option value="Peace">Peace</option>`).

The result of the preceding `append` operations is the following `cat-select` DOM element:

```
<div id="cat-select">
  "Category "
  <select>
    <option value="All Categories">All Categories</option>
    <option value="Chemistry">Chemistry</option>
    <option value="Economics">Economics</option>
    <option value="Literature">Literature</option>
    <option value="Peace">Peace</option>
    <option value="Physics">Physics</option>
    <option value="Physiology or Medicine">
    Physiology or Medicine</option>
  </select>
</div>
```

Now that we have our selector, we can use D3's on method to attach an event-handler callback function, triggered when the selector is changed:

```
catSelect.on('change', function(d) {
      let category = d3.select(this).property('value');
      nbviz.filterByCategory(category);
      nbviz.onDataChange();
});
```

 `this` is the select tag, with the `value` property as the selected category option.

 We call the `filterByCategory` method defined in *nbviz_core.js* to filter our dataset for prizes in the category selected.

 `onDataChange` triggers the visual-component update methods that will change to reflect our newly filtered dataset.

Figure 21-2 is a schematic of our select callback. Selecting Physics calls the anonymous callback function attached to our selector's change event. This function initiates the update of the Nobel-viz's visual elements.

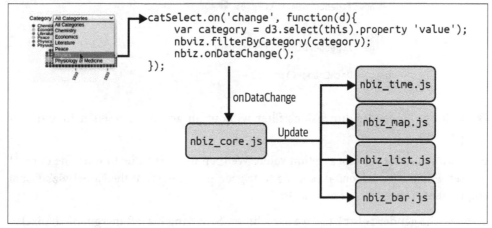

```
catSelect.on('change', function(d){
    var category = d3.select(this).property 'value');
    nbviz.filterByCategory(category);
    nbiz.onDataChange();
});
```

Figure 21-2. The category select callback

Within the category selector's callback, we first call the `filterByCategory` method[2] to select only the Physics winners and the `onDataChange` method to trigger an update of all the visual components. Where applicable, these will reflect the changed data. For example, the map's distribution circular indicators will resize, vanishing in the case of countries with no Nobel Physics winners.

Adding the Gender Selector

We have already added the HTML for our gender selector and its options, in the menu bar's description in *index.html*:

```
<!-- ... -->
    <div id="gender-select">
      Gender
      <select>
        <option value="All">All</option>
        <option value="female">Female</option>
        <option value="male">Male</option>
      </select>
    </div>
<!-- ... -->
```

All we need to do now is select the gender `select` tag and add a callback function to handle user selections. We can easily achieve this using D3's on method:

---

2 Defined in the *nbviz_core.js* script.

```
d3.select('#gender-select select')
    .on('change', function(d) {
        let gender = d3.select(this).property('value');
        if(gender === 'All'){
            nbviz.genderDim.filter(); ❶
        }
        else{
            nbviz.genderDim.filter(gender);
        }
        nbviz.onDataChange();
    });
```

❶ Calling the gender dimension's filter without an argument resets it to allow all genders.

First, we select the selector's option value. We then use this value to filter the current dataset. Finally, we call onDataChange to trigger any changes to the Nobel-viz's visual components caused by the new dataset.

To place the gender select tag, we use a little CSS, giving it a left margin of 20 pixels:

```
#gender-select{margin-left:20px;}
```

Adding the Country Selector

Adding the country selector is a little more involved than adding those of category and gender. The distribution of Nobel Prizes by country has a long tail (see Figure 17-1), with lots of countries having one or two prizes. We could include all of these in our selector, but it would make it rather long and cumbersome. A better way is to add groups for the single- and double-winning countries, keeping the number of select options manageable and adding a little narrative to the chart, namely the distributions of small winners over time, which might conceivably say something about changing trends in the Nobel Prize award allocation.[3]

In order to add our single- and double-country winner groups, we will need the crossfiltered country dimension to get the group sizes by country. This means creating the country selector after our Nobel Prize dataset has loaded. To do this, we put it in an nbviz.initUI method, called in our main *nbviz_main.js* script after the crossfilter dimensions have been created (see "Filtering Data with Crossfilter" on page 400).

The following code creates a selection list. Countries with three or more winners get their own selection slot, below the All Winners selection. Single- and double-country winners are added to their respective lists, which will be used to filter the dataset if

---

3 It does show that among single winners, the Nobel Prize for Peace predominates, followed by Literature.

---

the user selects the Single Winning Countries or Double Winning Countries from the selector's options.

```
export let initMenu = function() {
    let ALL_WINNERS = 'All Winners';
    let SINGLE_WINNERS = 'Single Winning Countries';
    let DOUBLE_WINNERS = 'Double Winning Countries';

    let nats = nbviz.countrySelectGroups = nbviz.countryDim
        .group().all() ❶
        .sort(function(a, b) {
            return b.value - a.value; // descending
        });

    let fewWinners = {1:[], 2:[]}; ❷
    let selectData = [ALL_WINNERS];

    nats.forEach(function(o) {
        if(o.value > 2){ ❸
            selectData.push(o.key);
        }
        else{
            fewWinners[o.value].push(o.key); ❹
        }
    });

    selectData.push(
        DOUBLE_WINNERS,
        SINGLE_WINNERS
    );
    //...
})
```

❶ Sorted group array of form (`{key:"United States", value:336}`, ...) where `value` is the number of winners from that country.

❷ An object with lists to store single and double winners.

❸ Countries with more than two winners get their own slot in the `selectData` list.

❹ Single- and double-winning countries are added to their respective lists based on the group size (value) of 1 or 2.

Now that we have our `selectData` list with corresponding `fewWinners` arrays, we can use it to create the options for our country selector. We first use D3 to grab the country selector's `select` tag and then add the options to it using standard data binding:

```
let countrySelect = d3.select('#country-select select');
```

```
countrySelect
    .selectAll("option")
    .data(selectData)
    .join("option")
    .attr("value", (d) => d)
    .html((d) => d);
```

With our `selectData` options appended, the selector looks like Figure 21-3.

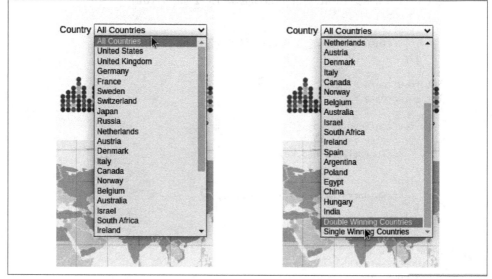

Figure 21-3. Selector for prizes by country

Now all we need is a callback function, triggered when an option is selected, to filter our main dataset by country. The following code shows how it's done. First, we get the select's `value` property (1), a country or one of `ALL_WINNERS`, `DOUBLE_WINNERS`, or `SINGLE_WINNERS`. We then construct a list of countries to send to our national filter method, `nbviz.filterByCountries` (defined in *nbviz_core.js*):

```
countrySelect.on('change', function(d) {

    let countries;
    let country = d3.select(this).property('value');

    if(country === ALL_WINNERS){ ❶
        countries = [];
    }
    else if(country === DOUBLE_WINNERS){
        countries = fewWinners[2];
    }
    else if(country === SINGLE_WINNERS){
        countries = fewWinners[1];
    }
```

```
        else{
            countries = [country];
        }

        nbviz.filterByCountries(countries); ❷
        nbviz.onDataChange(); ❸
    });
```

❶ These conditionals make a `countries` array, depending on the `country` string.
This array is empty, single-valued, or with one of `fewWinners` arrays.

❷ Calls `filterByCountries` to filter our main Nobel-winners dataset using the
array of countries.

❸ Triggers an update to all the Nobel-viz's elements.

The `filterByCountries` function is shown in Example 21-2. An empty `country
Names` argument resets the filter; otherwise, we filter the country dimension `country
Dim` for all those countries in `countryNames` ❶.

Example 21-2. Filter by countries function

```
nbviz.filterByCountries = function(countryNames) {

    if(!countryNames.length){ ❶
        nbviz.countryDim.filter();
    }
    else{
        nbviz.countryDim.filter(function(name) { ❷
            return countryNames.indexOf(name) > -1;
        });
    }

    if(countryNames.length === 1){ ❸
        nbviz.activeCountry = countryNames[0];
    }
    else{
        nbviz.activeCountry = null;
    }
};
```

❶ Resets the filter if the `countryNames` array is empty (the user chose All Countries).

❷ Here, we create a filter function on our `crossfilter` country dimension, which
returns `true` if a country is in the `countryNames` list (containing either a single
country or all single or double winners).

❸ Keeps a record of any single selected country in order—for example, to highlight it in the map and bar chart.

Now that we've built the filter selectors for our category, gender, and country dimensions, all we need to do is add the callback function to deal with changes to the prize-winning metric radio button.

Wiring Up the Metric Radio Button

The metric radio button has already been built in HTML, consisting of a form with `radio` inputs:

```
<div id='metric-radio'>
  Number of Winners:  ❶
  <form>
    <label>absolute
      <input
        type="radio" name="mode" value="0" checked> ❷
    </label>
    <label>per-capita
      <input type="radio" name="mode" value="1">
    </label>
  </form>
</div>
```

❶ ` ` is used to create a nonbreaking space between the form and its label.

❷ Inputs of type `radio` sharing the same name (`mode`, in this case) are grouped together, and activating one deactivates all others. They are differentiated by value (`0` and `1` in this case). Here we use the `checked` attribute to activate value `0` initially.

With the radio button form in place, we need only select all its inputs and add a callback function to deal with any button presses triggering a change:

```
d3.selectAll('#metric-radio input').on('change', function() {
      var val = d3.select(this).property('value');
      nbviz.valuePerCapita = parseInt(val); ❶
      nbviz.onDataChange();
   });
```

❶ Update the value of `valuePerCapita` before calling `onDataChange` and triggering a redraw of the visual elements.

We are storing the current state of the button with our `valuePerCapita` integer. When the user selects a radio box, this value is changed and a redraw with the new metric is triggered with `onDataChange`.

We now have the menu bar elements to our Nobel-viz, allowing users to refine the displayed dataset and drill down to subsets they are most curious about.

Summary

In this chapter, we saw how to add selectors and radio-button elements to our Nobel Prize visualization. There are a number of other user interface HTML tags, such as button groups, groups of checkboxes, time pickers, and plain buttons.[4] But implementing these controllers involves the same patterns as shown in this chapter. A list of data is used to append and insert DOM elements, setting properties where appropriate, and callback functions are bound to any change events. This is a very powerful method that plays very well with such D3 (and JS) idioms as method chaining and anonymous functions. It will quickly become a very natural part of your D3 workflow.

---

4 There are also native sliders in HTML5, where before one relied on jQuery plug-ins.

## CHAPTER 22

Conclusion

Although this book had a guiding narrative—the transformation of some basic Wikipedia HTML pages into a modern, interactive JavaScript web visualization—it is meant to be dipped into as and when required. The different parts are self-contained, allowing for the existence of the dataset in its various stages, and can be used independently. Let's have a short recap of what was covered before moving on to a few ideas for future visualization work.

Recap

This book was divided into five parts. The first part introduced a basic Python and JavaScript dataviz toolkit, while the next four showed how to retrieve raw data, clean it, explore it, and finally transform it into a modern web visualization. This process of refinement and transformation used as its backbone a dataviz challenge: to take a fairly basic Wikipedia Nobel Prize list and transform the dataset contained into something more engaging and informative. Let's summarize the key lessons of each part now.

Part I: Basic Toolkit

Our basic toolkit consisted of:

- A language-learning bridge between Python and JavaScript. This was designed to smooth the transition between the two languages, highlighting their many similarities and setting the scene for the bilingual process of modern dataviz. Python and JavaScript share even more in common, making switching between them that much less stressful.

- Being able to read from and write to the key data formats (e.g., JSON and CSV) and databases (both SQL and NoSQL) with ease is one of Python's great strengths. We saw how easy it is to pass data around in Python, translating formats and changing databases as we go. This fluid movement of data is the main lubricant of any dataviz toolchain.

- We covered the basic web development (webdev) skills needed to start producing modern, interactive, browser-based dataviz. By focusing on the concept of the single-page application (*https://oreil.ly/v0vDP*) rather than building whole websites, we minimize conventional webdev and place the emphasis on programming your visual creations in JavaScript. An introduction to Scalable Vector Graphics (SVG), the chief building block of D3 visualizations, set the scene for the creation of our Nobel Prize visualization in Part V.

Part II: Getting Your Data

In this part of the book, we looked at how to get data from the web using Python, assuming a nice, clean data file hasn't been provided to the data visualizer:

- If you're lucky, a clean file in an easily usable data format (i.e., JSON or CSV) is at an open URL, a simple HTTP request away. Alternatively, there may be a dedicated web API for your dataset, with any luck a RESTful one. As an example, we looked at using the Twitter API (via Python's Tweepy library). We also saw how to use Google spreadsheets, a widely used data-sharing resource in dataviz.

- Things get more involved when the data of interest is present on the web in human-readable form, often in HTML tables, lists, or hierarchical content blocks. In this case, you have to resort to *scraping*, getting the raw HTML content and then using a parser to make its embedded content available. We saw how to use Python's lightweight Beautiful Soup scraping library and the much more featureful and heavyweight Scrapy, the biggest star in the Python scraping firmament.

Part III: Cleaning and Exploring Data with pandas

In this part, we turned the big guns of pandas, Python's powerful programmatic spreadsheet, on the problem of cleaning and then exploring datasets. We first saw how pandas is part of Python's NumPy ecosystem, leveraging the power of very fast, powerful low-level array processing libraries but making them accessible. The focus was on using pandas to clean and then explore our Nobel Prize dataset:

- Most data, even that which comes from official web APIs, is dirty. And making it clean and usable will occupy far more of your time as a data visualizer than you probably anticipated. Taking the Nobel dataset as an example, we progressively cleaned it, searching for dodgy dates, anomalous datatypes, missing fields, and all the common grime that needs cleaning before you can start to explore and then transform your data into a visualization.

- With our clean (as we could make it) Nobel Prize dataset in hand, we saw how easy it is to use pandas and Matplotlib to interactively explore data, easily creating inline charts, slicing the data every which way, and generally getting a feel for it, while looking for those interesting nuggets you want to deliver with visualization.

Part IV: Delivering the Data

In this part, we saw how easy it is to create a minimal data API using Flask, to deliver data both statically and dynamically to the web browser.

First, we saw how to use Flask to serve static files and then how to roll your own basic data API, serving data from a local database. Flask's minimalism allows you to create a very thin data-serving layer between the fruits of your Python data processing and their eventual visualization on the browser. The glory of open source software is that you can often find robust, easy-to-use libraries that solve your problem better than you could. In the second chapter of this part, we saw how easy it is to use best-of-breed Python (Flask) libraries to craft a robust, flexible RESTful API, ready to server your data online. We also covered the easy online deployment of this data server using Heroku, a favorite of Pythonistas.

Part V: Visualizing Your Data with D3 and Plotly

In the first chapter of this part, we saw how to take the fruits of your pandas-driven exploration, in the form of charts or maps, and put them on the web, where they belong. Matplotlib can produce publication-standard static charts, while Plotly brings user controls and dynamic charts to the table. We saw how to take a Plotly chart directly from a Jupyter notebook and put it in a web page.

I think it's fair to say that taking on D3 was the most ambitious part of this book, but I was determined to demonstrate the construction of a multielement visualization, such as the kind you may well end up being employed to make. One of the joys of D3 is the huge number of examples (*https://oreil.ly/nYKx8*) that can easily be found online, but most of them demonstrate a single technique and there are few showing how to orchestrate multiple visual elements. In these D3 chapters, we saw how to synchronize the update of a timeline (featuring all the Nobel Prizes), a map, a bar chart, and a list as the user filtered the Nobel Prize dataset or changed the prize-winning metric (absolute or per capita).

Mastery of the core themes demonstrated in these chapters should allow you to let loose your imagination and learn by doing. I'd recommend choosing some data close to your heart and designing a D3 creation around it.

Future Progress

As mentioned, the Python and JavaScript data-processing and visualization ecosystems are incredibly active right now and are building from a very solid base.

While the business of acquiring and cleaning datasets learned in Part II and Chapter 9 improves incrementally, getting a lot easier as your craft skills (e.g., your pandas fu) improve, Python is throwing out new and powerful data-processing tools with abandon. There's a fairly comprehensive list (*https://oreil.ly/ODNE1*) at the Python wiki. Here are a few ideas you might want to use to create some visualizations.

Visualizing Social Media Networks

The advent of social media has provided a huge amount of interesting data, often available from a web API or eminently scrapeable. There are also curated collections of social media data such as Stanford's Large Network Dataset Collection (*https://oreil.ly/2E02E*) or the UCIrvine collection (*https://oreil.ly/x09oi*). These datasets can provide an easy testing ground for adventures in network visualization, an increasingly popular area.

The two most popular Python libraries for network analysis are graph-tool (*https://graph-tool.skewed.de*) and NetworkX (*https://networkx.org*). While graph-tool is more heavily optimized, NetworkX is arguably more user-friendly. Both libraries produce graphs in the common GraphML (*http://graphml.graphdrawing.org*) and GML (*https://oreil.ly/18AUU*) formats. D3 cannot read GML files directly, but it's easy enough to convert them to a JSON format it can read. You'll find a nice example of that in this blog post (*https://oreil.ly/thuBE*), with accompanying code on GitHub (*https://oreil.ly/3IHVR*). Note that in D3 version 4, the forceSimulation API changed. You can find a gentle introduction to the new API, which uses a `forceSimulation` object to keep track of things, on Pluralsight (*https://oreil.ly/DZxAz*).

Machine-Learning Visualizations

Machine learning is more than a little in vogue at the moment, and Python offers a fantastic set of tools to allow you to start analyzing and mining your data with a huge range of algorithms, from the supervised to unsupervised, from basic regression algorithms (such as linear or logistic regression) to more esoteric, cutting-edge stuff like the family of ensemble algorithms such as random forest. See this nice tour (*https://oreil.ly/IR8LZ*) of the different flavors of algorithm.

Premier among Python's machine-learning stable is scikit-learn (*https://oreil.ly/gjAKs*), which is part of the NumPy ecosystem, also building on SciPy and Matplotlib. scikit-learn provides an amazing resource for efficient data mining and data analysis. Algorithms that only a few years back would have taken days or weeks to craft are available with a single import, well designed, easy to use, and able to get useful results in a few lines of code.

Tools like scikit-learn enable you to discover deep correlations in your data, if they exist. There's a nice demonstration (*https://oreil.ly/Q0GVd*) at R2D3 that both introduces some machine-learning techniques and uses D3 to visualize the process and results. It's a great example of the creative freedom that mastery of D3 provides and the way in which good web dataviz is pushing the boundaries, making novel visualizations that engage in a way that hasn't been possible before—and, of course, are available to everybody.

There's a great collection (*https://oreil.ly/wZ1bJ*) of IPython (Jupyter) notebooks for statistics, machine learning, and data science at the IPython GitHub repo. Many of these demonstrate visualization techniques that can be adapted and extended in your own works.

Final Thoughts

The suggestions in the previous section just scratch the surface of where you might take your new Python and JavaScript dataviz skills. Hopefully this book has provided a solid bedrock on which to build your web dataviz efforts for the many jobs now opening up in the field or just to scratch a personal itch. The ability to harness Python's immensely powerful data wrangling and general-purpose abilities to JavaScript's (D3 being prominent here) increasingly powerful and mature visualization libraries represents the richest dataviz stack I know. Skills in this area are already very bankable, but the pace of change and scale of interest is increasing at a rapid rate. I hope you find this exciting and emergent field as fulfilling as I do.

D3's enter/exit Pattern

As shown in "Updating the DOM with Data" on page 421, D3 now has a more user-friendly join method to replace the old implementation of data-joining using patterns based around the enter, exit, and remove methods. The join method is a great addition to D3, but there are thousands of examples online using the old data-joining patterns. In order to use/convert these it helps to know a little bit more about what's going on under the hood when D3 joins data.

In order to demonstrate D3's data joining, let's look under the hood when D3 joins data. Let's start with our bar-less chart, with SVG canvas and chart group in place:

```
...
    <div id="nobel-bar">
      <svg width="600" height="400">
        <g class="chart" transform="translate(40, 20)"></g>
      </svg>
    </div>
...
```

In order to join data with D3, we first need some data in the right form. Generally that will be an array of objects, like our bar chart's nobelData:

```
var nobelData = [
    {key:'United States', value:336},
    {key:'United Kingdom', value:98},
    {key:'Germany', value:79},
    ...
]
```

A D3 data-join is made in two stages. First, we add the data to be joined using the data method then we perform the join using the join method.

To add our Nobel data to a group of bars, we do the following. First, we select a container for our bars, in this case our SVG group of class chart.

Then we define the container, in this case a CSS selector of class bar:

```
var svg = d3.select('#nobel-bar .chart');

var bars = svg.selectAll('.bar')
               .data(nobelData);
```

We now come to a slightly counterintuitive aspect of D3's data method. Our first select returned the chart group in our nobel-bar SVG canvas, but the second selectAll returned all elements with class bars, of which there are none. If there are no bars, what exactly are we binding the data to? The answer is that behind the scenes, D3 is keeping the books and that the bars object returned by data knows which DOM elements have been bound to the nobelData and, just as crucially, which haven't. We'll now see how to make use of this fact using the fundamental enter method.

The enter Method

D3's enter method (*https://oreil.ly/veBF9*) (and its sibling, exit) is both the basis for D3's superb power and expressiveness and also the root of much confusion. Although, as mentioned, the newish join method simplifies things, it's worth coming to grips with enter if you really want your D3 skills to grow. Let's introduce it now, with a very simple and slow demonstration.

We'll start with a canonically simple little demonstration, adding a bar rectangle for each member of our Nobel Prize data. We'll use the first six Nobel Prize–winning countries as our bound data:

```
var nobelData = [
    {key:'United States', value:200},
    {key:'United Kingdom', value:80},
    {key:'France', value:47},
    {key:'Switzerland', value:23},
    {key:'Japan', value:21},
    {key:'Austria', value:12}
];
```

With our dataset in hand, let's first use D3 to grab the chart group, saving it to an svg variable. We'll use that to make a selection of all elements of class bar (none at the moment):

```
var svg = d3.select('#nobel-bar .chart');

var bars = svg.selectAll('.bar')
    .data(nobelData);
```

Now although the bars selection is empty, behind the scenes D3 has kept a record of the data we've just bound to it. At this point, we can use that fact and the enter method to create a few bars with our data. Calling enter on our bars selection returns a subselection of all the data (nobelData, in this case) that was not bound to a bar. Since there were no bars in the original selection (our chart being empty), all the data is unbound, so enter returns an enter election (essentially placeholder nodes for all the unbound data) of size six:

```
bars = bars.enter(); # returns six placeholder nodes
```

We can use the placeholder nodes in bars to create some DOM elements—in our case, a few bars. We won't bother with trying to put them the right way up (the y-axis being down from the top of the screen by convention), but we will use the data values and indices to set the position and height of the bars:

```
bars.append('rect')
    .classed('bar', true)
    .attr('width', 10)
    .attr('height', function(d){return d.value;}) ❶
    .attr('x', function(d, i) { return i * 12; });
```

❶ If you provide a callback function to D3's setter methods (attr, style, etc.), then the first and second arguments provided are the value of the individual data object (e.g., d == {key: 'United States', value: 200}) and its index (i).

Using the callback functions to set height and the x position (allowing a padding of 2 px) of the bars and calling append on our six node selection produces Figure A-1.

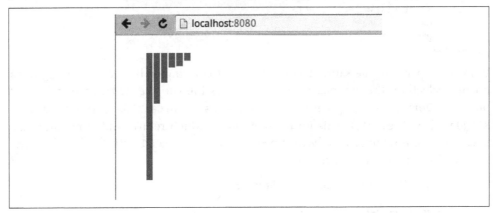

Figure A-1. Producing some bars with D3's enter method

I'd encourage you generally to use Chrome's (or equivalent) Elements tab to investigate the HTML your D3 is producing. Investigating our mini–bar chart with Elements shows Figure A-2.

Figure A-2. Using the Elements tab to see the HTML generated by enter *and* append

So we've seen what happens when we call enter on an empty selection. But what happens when we already have a few bars, which we would have in an interactive chart with a user-driven, changing dataset?

Let's add a couple of bar class rectangles to our starting HTML:

```
<div id="nobel-bar">
  <svg width="600" height="400">
    <g class="chart" transform="translate(40, 20)">
      <rect class='bar'></rect>
      <rect class='bar'></rect>
    </g>
  </svg>
</div>
```

If we now perform the same data binding and entering as before, on calling data on our selection, the two placeholder rectangles bind to the first two members of our nobelData array (i.e., [{key: 'United States', value: 200}, {key: 'United Kingdom', value:80}]). This means that enter, which returns only unbound data placeholders, now returns only four placeholders, associated with the last four elements of the nobelData array:

```
var svg = d3.select('#nobel-bar .chart');

var bars = svg.selectAll('.bar')
    .data(nobelData);

bars = bars.enter(); # return four placeholder nodes
```

If we now call append on the entered bars, as before, we get the result shown in Figure A-3, showing the last four bars (note that they preserve their index i, used to set their x positions) rendered.

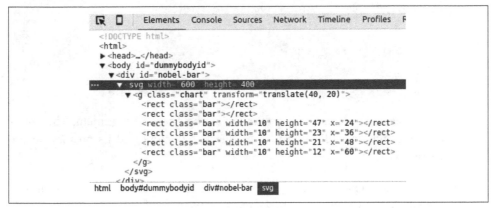

Figure A-3. Calling enter *and* append *with existing bars*

Figure A-4 shows the HTML generated for the last four bars. As we'll see, the data from the first two elements is now bound to the two dummy nodes we added to the initial bar group. We just haven't used it yet to adjust those rectangles' attributes. Updating old bars with new data is the one of the key elements of the update pattern we'll see shortly.

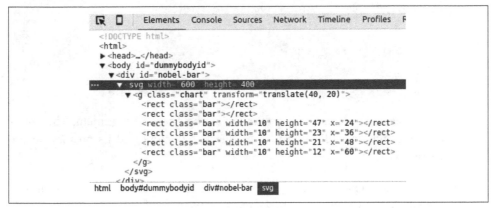

Figure A-4. Using the Elements tab to see the HTML generated by enter *and* append *on a partial selection*

To emphasize, coming to grips with enter and exit (and remove) is vital to healthy progress with D3. Play around a bit, inspect the HTML you're producing, enter a bit of data, and generally get a bit messy, learning the ins and outs. Let's have a little look at accessing the bound data before moving on to the D3's nexus, the update pattern.

Accessing the Bound Data

A good way to see what's happening to the DOM is to use your browser's HTML inspector and console to track D3's changes. In Figure A-1, we use Chrome's console to look at the rect element representing the first bar in Figure A-3, before data has been bound and after the nobelData has been bound to the bars using the data method. As you can see, D3 has added a __data__ object to the rect element with which to store its bound data—in this case, the first member of our nobelData list.

The __data__ object is used by D3's internal bookkeeping and, fundamentally, the data in it is made available to functions supplied to update methods such as attr.

Let's look at a little example of using the data in an element's __data__ object to set its name attribute. The name attribute can be useful for making specific D3 selections. For example, if the user selects a particular country, we can now use D3 to get all its named components and adjust their style if needed. We'll use the bar with bound data in Figure A-5 and set the name using the key property of its bound data:

```
let bar = d3.select('#nobel-bar .bar');

bar.attr('name', function(d, i){ ❶

    let sane_key = d.key.replace(/ /g, '_'); ❷

    console.log('__data__ is: ' + JSON.stringify(d)
    + ', index is ' + i)

    return 'bar__' + sane_key; ❸
    });
// console out:
// __data__ is: {"key":"United States","value":336}, index is 0
```

❶ All D3 setter methods can take a function as their second argument. This function receives the data (d) bound to the selected element and its position in the data array (i).

❷ We use a regular expression (regex) to replace all spaces in the key with underscores (e.g., United States → United_States).

❸ This will set the bar's name attribute to 'bar__United_States'.

All the setter methods listed in Figure 17-3 (attr, style, text, etc.) can take a function as a second argument, which will receive data bound to the element and the element's array index. The return of this function is used to set the value of the property. As we'll see, interactive visualizations' changes to the visualized dataset will be reflected when we bind the new data and then use these functional setters to adapt attributes, styles, and properties accordingly.

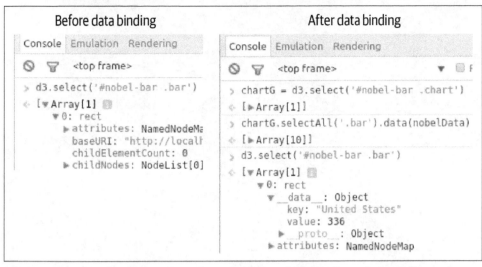

Figure A-5. Using the Chrome console to show the addition of a __data__ object after data binding using D3's data method

Index

numbers, differences in Python and JavaScript, 26

numeric type (NumPy arrays), 184
  64-bit integer type, 185
  changing with astype method, 185
  dtype (default type), 186

NumPy, 26, 183
  about, 183
  arrays, 184-190
    arithmetic on, 184
    basic operations with, 188-190
    creating, 186
    creating array functions, 190
    indexing and slicing, 187
    number of dimensions, shape, and numeric type, 184
    reshaping a one-dimensional array, 184
  merging and importing with pyplot, 244
  pandas and, 194
  polyfit function, 262
  random module, 228
  use of arrays for homogeneous, numerical number crunching, 195

O

object type, 275

object-oriented Matplotlib
  figures and, 250
  pyplot and, 243

ObjectIds (MongoDB), 73

objects, 28
  iterating over key-value pairs in JavaScript, 31
  simple JavaScript object, 35

objects object (TopoJSON), 455

OECD (Organisation for Economic Cooperation and Development) web API, 126

on method (D3), 478, 488

onDataChange method (JavaScript), 398, 444, 479, 488

ones method (NumPy), 186

opacity property (CSS), 466

opacity property (SVG), 107, 115

OpenGL visualizations, 89

openpyxl module (Python), 202

option tags (HTML), 488

OrderedDict type (Python), 41, 70

ordinal scales, 419, 438, 444

OS X, installing MongoDB, 8

P

packages, building in Python, 17

padding method (D3 scales), 419

pagination, data returns from RESTful API, 332-335

PairGrids, 270-272

pandas, xiv, 128
  cleaning and exploring data with, xv, 498
  cleaning data with, 211-241
    adding born_in column to Nobel winners dataset, 236
    clean_data function, 235
    dates and times, 232-235
    finding duplicates, 223-225
    finding mixed types, 220
    indices and pandas data selection, 216-220
    inspecting data in a DataFrame, 213-216
    loading dirty data into a DataFrame, 213
    missing fields, 230-232
    removing duplicates, 226-229
    removing rows, 222
    sorting data, 225
  exploring data with, 273-304
    age and life expectancy of Nobel Prize winners, 295-302
    cleaned Nobel Prize dataset, 273
    diaspora of Nobel Prize winners, 302
    gender disparities in Nobel Prize winner dataset, 277-284
    national trends in Novel Prize winners, 284-294
    plotting with pandas, 276
    starting to explore, 274-276
    stories to investigate in Nobel Prize dataset, 274
  introduction to, 193-210
    benefits of pandas for dataviz, 193
    categorizing data and measurements, 194
    combining Series into DataFrames, 207-210
    creating and saving DataFrames, 199-207
    DataFrames, 195-198
  use with Matplotlib, 244
  using with gspread data, 132

Panel (pandas), to_excel method, 204

panes (multiple) in text editors, 83

About the Author

Kyran Dale is a journeyman programmer, ex–research scientist, recreational hacker, independent researcher, occasional entrepreneur, cross-country runner, and improving jazz pianist. During 15-odd years as a research scientist, he hacked a lot of code, learned a lot of libraries, and settled on some favorite tools. These days he finds Python, JavaScript, and a little C++ go a long way to solving most problems out there. He specializes in fast prototyping and feasibility studies with an algorithmic bent but is happy to just build cool things.

Colophon

The animals on the cover of *Data Visualization with Python and JavaScript* are the blue-banded bee (*Amegilla cingulata*), the orchid bee (of the *Euglossini* tribe), and the blue carpenter bee (*Xylocopa caerulea*). Bees are crucial to agriculture, as they pollinate crops and other flowering plants while they collect pollen and nectar.

The blue-banded bee is native to Australia, in habitats including woodlands, heath, and urban areas. As its name suggests, its distinctive physical feature is the iridescent blue bands on its abdomen: males have five, while females have four. These bees practice what is known as "buzz pollination," meaning they use vibration to shake pollen loose. This species can vibrate a flower at an astonishing 350 times per second. Many plants, including tomatoes, are pollinated most efficiently in this manner.

The orchid bee is a colorful insect found in the rainforests of Central and South America. They have shiny metallic coloration in vivid shades of green, blue, gold, purple, and red. Their long tongues are almost twice the length of their body. Male orchid bees have specialized legs with small hollows that collect and store fragrant compounds, which are then released at a later time (perhaps in a mating display). Several orchid species hide their pollen in a particular spot marked with a scent the male orchid bee is attracted to, thus relying solely on this species for pollination.

The blue carpenter bee is a large insect (on average, 0.91 inches long) covered in light blue hair. It is widely distributed in Southeast Asia, India, and China. They are so named because nearly all species nest within dead wood, bamboo, or timbers of manmade structures. They bore holes by vibrating their bodies and scraping their mandibles against the wood (however, carpenter bees feed on nectar; the wood they bore through is discarded). They are solitary and so do not form large colonies, but it is possible for several individuals to build nests in the same area.

The cover illustration is by Karen Montgomery, based on an antique line engraving from *Insects Abroad*. The cover fonts are Gilroy Semibold and Guardian Sans. The text font is Adobe Minion Pro; the heading font is Adobe Myriad Condensed; and the code font is Dalton Maag's Ubuntu Mono.

O'REILLY®

Learn from experts.
Become one yourself.

Books | Live online courses
Instant Answers | Virtual events
Videos | Interactive learning

Get started at oreilly.com.

9 781098 111878